Data and Democracy at

Data and Democracy at Work

Advanced Information Technologies, Labor Law,
and the New Working Class

Brishen Rogers

The MIT Press
Cambridge, Massachusetts
London, England

© 2023 Massachusetts Institute of Technology

This work is subject to a Creative Commons CC-BY-ND-NC license.
Subject to such license, all rights are reserved.

(cc) BY-NC-ND

The MIT Press would like to thank the anonymous peer reviewers who provided comments on drafts of this book. The generous work of academic experts is essential for establishing the authority and quality of our publications. We acknowledge with gratitude the contributions of these otherwise uncredited readers.

This book was set in Stone Serif and Stone Sans by Westchester Publishing Services. Printed and bound in the United States of America.

Library of Congress Cataloging-in-Publication Data

Names: Rogers, Brishen, author.
Title: Data and democracy at work : advanced information technologies, labor law, and the new working class / Brishen Rogers.
Description: Cambridge, Massachusetts : The MIT Press, [2023] | Includes bibliographical references and index.
Identifiers: LCCN 2022015330 (print) | LCCN 2022015331 (ebook) |
 ISBN 9780262545136 (paperback) | ISBN 9780262373364 (epub) |
 ISBN 9780262373357 (pdf)
Subjects: LCSH: Labor laws and legislation—United States. | Employees—Effect of technological innovations on—United States.
Classification: LCC KF3319 .R64 2023 (print) | LCC KF3319 (ebook) |
 DDC 344.7301—dc23/eng/20220831
LC record available at https://lccn.loc.gov/2022015330
LC ebook record available at https://lccn.loc.gov/2022015331

10 9 8 7 6 5 4 3 2

For Fernanda, Simone, and Giovanni

Contents

Acknowledgments ix

    Introduction 1
1 Technology, the Service Transition, and the New Working Class 13
2 The Legal Construction of Workplace Neoliberalism 35
3 Inductive Knowledge and Digital Taylorism 57
4 Workplace Privacy and Associational Power 81
5 Data, Fissuring, and Consolidation 105
6 Data and Economic Democracy 131
    Afterword: Law and the Technological Mundane 157

Notes 161
Selected Bibliography 239
Index 267

Acknowledgments

I have been working on the research that informed this book for over five years now. Several of the chapters draw on previously published work, as indicated in the notes and bibliography. I am very grateful to have had the opportunity to present at many law schools and related venues. Those include presentations to the Bristol University Centre for Law and Work, the Work on Demand project at Glasgow University, the Oxford Reading Group on AI at Work, the Yale Private Law Theory Colloquium, the University of Texas Colloquium on Human Rights and Global Inequality, the University of Indiana Law School's Center for Law, Society & Culture, and as the Douglas Cunningham Memorial Lecture in Labour Law at Queens University Law School, in Kingston Ontario, Canada. I also presented some of this work to faculty workshops at Washington University in St. Louis, Georgetown University Law Center, and the Cornell University School of Industrial and Labor Relations. In addition, I am thankful to have presented some of that work at conferences including the LPE Blog Workshop on the Political Economy of Technology at Yale Law School, the Hebrew University/Friedrich Ebert Stiftung Workshop on Social Media and Worker Organizing, the St. Louis University Symposium on Law, Technology, and the Organization of Work, and the Fordham Law School Conference on the Sharing Economy, as well as conferences sponsored by the Labor Law Group, the Labor Law Research Network, and the Association of American Law Schools.

I was also thankful to reach interdisciplinary audiences at various conferences. Those include events sponsored by the Andrea Mitchell Center for the Study of Democracy at the University of Pennsylvania, the Law and Public Affairs (LAPA) Program at Princeton University, the Association of Promotion of Political Economy and the Law (APPEAL), the Rutgers-Renmin Center for Global Work and Employment, the Society for the Advancement of Socio-Economics (SASE), and the Labor and Employment Relations Association (LERA). Several other organizations and think tanks also hosted presentations, including the Federal Reserve Bank of Philadelphia, the Economic Policy Institute, the Ford Foundation, the Washington Center for Equitable Growth, and the Korean Development Agency.

Academic research takes place within communities, and many colleagues graciously helped me work through these ideas, providing specific comments on drafts of this book and earlier works. Those include Einat Albin, Ifeoma Ajunwa, Kate Andrias, Kate Bahn, Richard Bales, Yochai Benkler, Matthew Bodie, Alan Bogg, Ricardo Buendia, Brian Callaci, Anupam Chander, Deborah Chasman, Joshua Cohen, Julie Cohen, Guy Davidov, Manoj Dias-Abey, Matthew Dimick, Ruth Dukes, Jeffrey Dunoff, Cynthia Estlund, Matthew Finkin, Michael Fischl, Catherine Fisk, William Forbath, Charlotte Garden, David Hoffman, Jason Jackson, Amy Kapczynski, Tammy Katsabian, Pauline Kim, Karl Klare, Karen Levy, Wilma Liebman, Rakeen Mabud, Daniel Markovits, Salil Mehra, Lawrence Mischel, Guy Mundlak, Paul Ohm, Sanjukta Paul, Frank Pasquale, Jeremias Prassl, Sabeel Rahman, Valerio De Stefano, Katherine Stone, Kathleen Thelen, Dorian Warren, and Noah Zatz. Many apologies for anyone I have missed.

I am also extremely grateful to Emily Taber at MIT Press for taking on this project and guiding me through it. She was unfailingly kind and helpful through the entire process despite many delays on my part. I would also like to thank several anonymous reviewers for MIT Press, whose comments on both my original book proposal and my first complete draft were invaluable. Kendra Bozarth, Audra Wolfe, and Betsy Kuhn provided superb editorial assistance, as did, Marcy Ross at MIT Press and Susan McClung and Helen Wheeler at Westchester Publishing Services. Justin Moyer provided outstanding research assistance. Most of this work was undertaken while I was on the faculty at Temple University, and I would like to thank JoAnne Epps, Greg Mandel, Rachel Rebouche, and others at Temple for their unflagging support. I completed the book while on the faculty of the Georgetown University Law Center, and I would like to thank Dean William Treanor and Research Dean Lilian Faulhaber for their support. The Roosevelt Institute also provided financial assistance for a time and published both a working

Acknowledgments

paper on the political economy of workplace technology, and a report on labor law reform that I cowrote with Kate Andrias.

Finally, I owe the greatest debt to my wife, Fernanda Nicola, who helped me refine these ideas over the years, pressed me to finish the project, and at great personal sacrifice took over all parental responsibilities for long periods—including during COVID—so I could finish this manuscript. This book is dedicated to her and our two children, Simone and Giovanni.

Introduction

COVID and the Technological Class Divide

COVID-19 upended the American economy—but not its class, gender, and racial hierarchies. While the coronavirus did not discriminate based on income or race, exposure, complications, and death skewed heavily along those lines. A major factor in individuals' total risk was whether they could work remotely, which revealed a longstanding technological class divide. Under social distancing mandates, professionals retreated to their homes or second homes, using new videoconferencing platforms to keep working—designing products, analyzing data, writing legal briefs, coordinating strategies, and so on. This was especially trying for parents who had to care for children as they did their own jobs, and the burdens of childcare fell disproportionately on women. Yet professionals had it comparatively easy. Their relative comforts depended on armies of low-wage workers in a vast service economy, who had to perform their jobs in person. Those workers, who are disproportionately nonwhite, had a very different relationship with technology. Rather than using it to create goods and services or to manage enterprises, those workers were often managed *by* technology, receiving orders and even official discipline through apps, tablets, and the like.

Many canonical images from the pandemic juxtaposed US companies' stunning technological sophistication with their workers' vulnerability. Amazon warehouse staff—who work alongside armies of robots and whose every task is assigned and monitored by artificially intelligent devices—became infected early on because the company did not maintain physical distancing or provide masks in the workplace. Workers at grocery stores and many restaurants faced similar risks of infection even as they were monitored by point-of-sale devices that tracked how long they took to perform certain tasks. The potential scope of the app-based gig economy also came into focus as delivery platforms like Instacart and DoorDash scaled up to meet consumer demand. Their workers needed to enter businesses and homes and interact directly with customers, leaving them at a high risk of infection, and were supervised, demoted, and even fired via smartphone apps.

The pandemic therefore highlighted and exacerbated long-simmering grievances in the US's economy and society. Many workers simply reached their breaking point and began to protest against dangers and mistreatment. Early in the pandemic, health-care workers who used cutting-edge medical technologies called out their employers' failure to provide them with adequate safety equipment. Many others followed suit, walking out of warehouses, meatpacking and poultry plants, fast food restaurants, and other businesses, to the point that some believe that COVID sparked a bona fide strike wave.[1] As pandemic restrictions began to ease in 2021, many companies struggled to staff back up, especially in the hospitality industry. Some longtime restaurant and hotel workers told reporters that they were unwilling to tolerate such risks again, or they were exhausted after years of physically grueling service work. COVID was the final straw. Then, 2022 saw a major upsurge in worker organizing, including successful unionization drives at numerous Starbucks locations, and at an Amazon warehouse on Staten Island where key worker grievances included lax safety protocols and automated productivity monitoring.[2]

A decade from now, scholars may view the coronavirus pandemic as the end of an era in the American political economy. That era began in the late 1970s and was defined both by astonishing technological progress and by exponential growth in precarious service jobs. This book argues that those trends—in technological development and in the degradation of work—were completely intertwined, in the sense that companies increasingly used new technologies to limit workers' power.[3] It further argues that our labor laws—that is, the entire complex of US laws constituting and governing work—enabled companies to use technology in that manner.[4] Over the same period, companies established broad rights to gather data on workers and their performance, to exclude others from accessing that data, and to use that data to preempt worker organizing. Put more formally, companies have used their *legal* and *technological powers* to suppress workers' *associational power*, driving down wages and eroding working conditions.[5] These long-running developments yielded many of the problems that exploded into the public eye under COVID: low wages, meager benefits, lean staffing, unpredictable schedules, lack of basic safety protocols, and misclassification of employees as independent contractors.

This book also argues that there is a deeper causal logic at work: these technological and legal changes were driven by capital's demands for high returns in today's large service sectors. Companies in those sectors often require armies of workers without rare or specialized skills, and they are often plagued by slower productivity growth than their industrial peers. Those companies have maintained profitability in part by using new technologies to limit workers' power. These trends are global, but this book focuses on the United States, where they are especially pronounced. Finally, this book argues that a more fair and sustainable future of work is possible, but achieving it will require ambitious reforms to democratize the governance of workplaces, workplace data, and the economy.

On that note, as I finalize this book in mid-2022, there is great excitement in labor circles due to the recent victories at Amazon and Starbucks. Those developments may signal the beginnings of a broader ideological and political-economic shift, in which capital loses some influence and legitimacy, and in which workers are able to build substantial associational power and even a cohesive class identity, and perhaps to push for transformative changes to our labor laws. Alternatively, those victories may not have much long-term impact because of entrenched employer resistance or other, more contingent factors. Regardless of how those and other campaigns play out, I hope that the developments discussed in this book help readers and scholars make sense of them in two ways. First, the technological, legal, and political-economic transformations of the last few decades helped to generate the grueling and often alienating working conditions that led many workers to organize in 2022. Second, Amazon, Starbucks, and other companies may aggressively resist further organizing efforts through the legal and technological means that this book discusses.

The rest of this introduction outlines the book's narrative in more detail, situates it within the literature, and then summarizes the arguments that will be made in subsequent chapters.

Data-Driven Technology, Inductive Knowledge, and Class Power

While this book focuses on recent developments, conflicts over workplace technology and information are not new. For well over a century, workers and companies have fought over the generation and control of workplace information, since both parties recognize that access to information shapes the labor process and the parties' correlative powers. For example, to unionize or take collective action, workers typically must be able to meet, to discuss common concerns, and to plan together without management's knowledge or involvement. In that sense, to build associational power, workers need some privacy, meaning some control over informational flows.[6] Conversely, companies have long sought to generate, capture, and quantify information about workers and work processes and to use that information to suppress worker mobilization. They can do so directly, by retaliating against worker or union leaders, or indirectly, by designing production systems and processes in ways that deter worker organizing.[7]

In recent decades, however, companies' ability to use data to reshape production and class relations has been supercharged by developments in law and in data processing. Regarding the law, companies have pushed on multiple fronts to achieve greater freedom of action vis-à-vis workers and the state. They enjoyed such authority prior to the Great Depression but lost it after the New Deal once workers unionized in large numbers. Companies pressed hard for such freedoms beginning in the 1970s, responding to various economic pressures, including industrial overcapacity.[8] As courts and legislatures responded, our labor laws were gradually transformed. Today, those laws treat employment as fundamentally contractual, largely disregarding the background inequalities that affect workers' and companies' bargaining power, and treat the enterprise more like the employer's sovereign property. As argued later in this book, this consolidation of legal power reflects broader trends in the evolution of law over the same period—the era of neoliberalism—when vast swaths of our society were reorganized around idealized visions of market ordering.[9]

That long-running shift in labor law both facilitated and responded to the maturation of networked information technologies, as well as to broad changes in the class structure. As industrial production declined, service industries became dominant, and many of the nation's largest employers came to be in fields like retail, food service, logistics, and hospitality. Those companies face different sorts of pressures than their industrial forebears.

They need to hire and manage huge armies of service workers in thousands of small worksites rather than in a few huge factories. They also need to oversee immensely complex global and national supply networks. Finally, because it is harder to increase productivity in services than in manufacturing, service-sector companies have very strong incentives to limit labor costs. Successful companies have often used novel surveillance technologies for all those purposes.

Those technologies differ from past means of worker surveillance in several respects, each of which is reflected in their design as well as their use.[10] For example, data-driven surveillance can operate over a vast distance, enabling cheaper oversight of massive numbers of workers or huge and far-flung supplier networks from corporate headquarters. Those technologies also operate asymmetrically, enabling companies to monitor workers but preventing them from monitoring management in return. Most important, nascent forms of artificial intelligence (AI) operate very differently from human cognition. They analyze very large data pools to discern patterns and draw statistical inferences in ways that humans never could. This leads to a new way of "seeing" or knowing the world that is *inductive* in character and genuinely different from other forms of productive knowledge. As the sociologist Gary Marx explained in a related context, such techniques enable judgments based not just on the unique individual being surveilled, but on that individual "in relation to statistical averages and aggregate categories."[11] Contemporary AI systems nevertheless have an Achilles heel: they have no sense of the social and real-world contexts for their analyses.[12] Those contexts are inescapable in the workplace, and they limit companies' ability to automate today's jobs. For the foreseeable future, then, the greater share of workplace AI will likely be dedicated to extending, deepening, and transforming managerial control over workers.

In the United States, the results of these intertwined shifts in law, technology, and class relations are all around us. For example, acting entirely within their rights, companies may closely monitor workers, demand an ever-faster pace of work, and terminate those who complain without giving any reason.[13] They may use AI to reshape schedules, physical spaces, and workflow in ways that prevent workers from even speaking with one another, making it more difficult for them to take collective action. Companies may shunt workers outside their corporate boundaries, denying them basic legal protections and rendering many forms of worker collective action illegal, even as they closely supervise those workers' performance.[14] What's more, companies can take these steps even as they exploit their control over valuable information to build a dominant position within their sectors, giving them structural power over workers, competitors, and even lawmakers. This intensification of surveillance and management is not always intended to erode workers' associational power—but it often has that effect. Workers are fragmented from one another physically, socially, and legally, even as they are subject to similar forms of centralized control.

Companies can also use new surveillance devices and inductive learning technologies to suppress workers' organizing efforts actively, directly, and aggressively.[15] For example, companies can monitor internal employee message boards using natural language recognition algorithms, spotting keywords that might indicate that a unionization drive is afoot and then retaliating against the ringleaders. Such retaliation is often illegal—and yet companies may be able to launder personnel decisions through new algorithms that obscure their intent from workers and regulators, making enforcement much more difficult.[16] There are many reported examples of such efforts today. For example, Amazon in 2020 posted (and then rapidly deleted) a job announcement for "intelligence analysts" who would take such efforts to scale, utilizing worksite data analytics and public data sources to detect "labor organizing threats" against the company.[17] Companies may also be able to use new recruiting algorithms to aggregate data on applicants' employment history with data on their social media posts or consumer behavior, and then screen out workers who are likely to challenge management's authority.

All of this culminates in today's labor politics, in which knowledge and control are centralized, surveillance is constant, and line-level workers have little autonomy and no voice on the job. Companies' power then extends, fractal-like, from the individual workstation, to the worksite, to the supply and distribution chain, and to the broader political economy. Workers must compete with one another for jobs, for desired shifts, or to stay in their employer's good graces, and therefore face substantial market discipline. As a result, service workers are increasingly a class in a structural sense, occupying similar positions in the division of labor and enduring similar inequities, even if they do not always understand themselves to be a class. Their lack of collective power drives down wages and working conditions, enabling companies to remain profitable and capture the lion's share of productivity gains. The enormous power disparities in today's labor market may even

Introduction

have skewed the development of AI itself, encouraging investment in technologies to control and discipline workers. In that sense, new technologies and their associated class politics are central to the political economy of contemporary capitalism.

There are silver linings here. The fact that recent changes in technology and class relations were facilitated and shaped by law—a human creation ultimately subject to democratic revision—suggests that reforms to workplace and data governance could encourage a far better future of work. Such an outcome will require political mobilization, but there are promising signs there as well.[18] For one thing, service workers are the paradigmatic so-called essential workers of the COVID era—the ones who make sure that we are all fed, clothed, housed, transported, and cared for. They have enormous latent power, which they have recently begun to exert, as noted previously. Service workers also have a natural community of shared interest with many consumers, including a younger generation unwilling to tolerate an unfair and unsafe future. Together, those groups could push for a more just, equitable, and sustainable political economy.

In this book, several chapters that discuss technical developments and their effects on workers also suggest reforms to address discrete harms. The final chapter then proposes a far more ambitious reallocation of workplace rights and powers. Those proposed reforms draw inspiration from the radical democratic tradition of thought and action, which insists that all major spheres of social action—politics, the economy, and civil society—should be constituted and governed in a democratic fashion.[19] In labor law specifically, those reforms aim to make workers' associational power a legitimate modality of governance once again. Law today encourages employer dominance in many ways—but law can also encourage a different political economy and a different class politics, with a broader and richer sphere of human freedom.

Situating This Book in the Literature

The book sits at the intersection of three bodies of scholarship that illuminate the role of laws and other institutions in shaping contemporary work relationships and longer-term processes of capitalist development.

The first body of literature considers the role of law in political-economic orders and governance. That was a major theme of early-twentieth-century legal realism, which illuminated how legal rules and processes established the terrain on which economic and political action occurred.[20] Labor law scholars have often drawn on legal realism to explore how law constitutes and shapes class relations. For example, a number labor law scholars have argued that the New Deal labor regime, by continuing to protect various pre-New Deal employer prerogatives, failed to deliver on the promise of workplace and industrial democracy.[21] Others have sought to understand the myriad ways in which labor laws shape workers' capacities for collective action, and how that collective action can become an autonomous source of legal or quasi-legal authority.[22] Still others have elaborated on the relationship among class and other axes of social subordination, including race, gender, and citizenship.[23]

Another important body of post-realist scholarship is now clustered around the Law and Political Economy (LPE) project and movement.[24] That literature is diverse, cutting across subject fields and methodologies, but much of it has extended and updated the realist project of understanding the legal constitution of the political economy.[25] Some LPE scholars have focused specifically on the relationship between law and capitalist development outside the labor context, and the book draws extensively from their work.[26] Others working in and around LPE have argued that the data revolution is altering workplace privacy practices and compliance with antidiscrimination mandates.[27] With important exceptions, however, scholars have said less about the role of new information technologies in *class politics* specifically, or about those technologies' relationship to changes in labor law.[28]

The second body of literature considers the relationship between technology and institutions, including but not limited to the law. This is another immense topic, and the book can't hope to do justice to all the debates among technology scholars, but several are worth noting. One branch of science and technology studies has illuminated how political and social institutions can shape technological development and deployment, and how technologies in turn can shape political and social institutions.[29] Another rich vein of scholarship focuses on how new information technologies facilitate network- or platform-based forms of social organization with distinctive logics and tensions, including tendencies toward monopoly.[30] Legal scholars, for their part, have long argued that rights to develop or deploy technology are a crucial source of social and economic power, and that the design of technologies themselves can regulate and shape social behavior.[31] As inductive learning technologies have been deployed at scale in the private sector, various legal scholars have traced how they are legally constituted, how companies are using them to reshape relationships with consumers and others in ways that threaten individual privacy, and how they are altering state and administrative processes.[32] As noted earlier, this book draws insights from those bodies of work and applies them to the recent evolution of workplace technology and class relations.

The third body of literature focuses on the political economy of work and technology more generally, but it often says less about law and legal processes. This is a theme in various classics of political economy, including work by Adam Smith, Karl Marx, Joseph Schumpeter, and more recently Immanuel Wallerstein.[33] One body of contemporary research—in fields including comparative political economy and welfare state studies—illuminates the relationship among workers' associational power, other institutions, and patterns of development across capitalist economies.[34] Another line of research—in heterodox economics, economic sociology, and labor history—focuses more specifically on how workplace technology structures class relations.[35] A core insight that cuts across much of that scholarship is that companies may choose technologies that are less productive or efficient than reasonable alternatives, where doing so helps them contain workers' power and thus capture a higher share of profits.[36] While classic works in this tradition were written prior to the emergence of networked information technologies, in recent years sociologists and other social scientists have studied how processes of algorithmic management are proliferating across the economy and exacerbating economic and other inequalities.[37]

While these literatures diverge in many respects, they all focus on the constitutive role of social institutions in capitalism, whether historically, within nations today, or in comparative cross-national perspective. The book draws from each body of scholarship to develop its own theory of the law and political economy of workplace technology. Its overall argument then pushes forward two now-classic insights from these literatures, which are in tension with one another. The first, common to legal realism and its descendants, is that law is a human creation and can be revised to advance the broader social good. While processes of social change cannot be driven entirely by legal change, legal reforms and processes are central to social orders in modern democratic societies. Moreover, unlike social norms and forms of traditional authority, laws can be contested, questioned, and altered pursuant to intentional deliberative and political processes. The second insight, which is central to radical political economy and heterodox economics, is that capitalism, as an economic and social order, has a deeper logic that is not reducible to the views and aspirations of its denizens and that pervasively shapes the legal order. For example, capitalism encourages intense competition through much of the economy, leading to perpetual changes in technology and to new work structures that erode existing social protections. What's more, capital's structural power even in democratic societies may limit the potential scope of democratically motivated efforts to decommodify labor and social goods.

In other words, the book stands *both* with those who insist that capitalism tends to erode or swamp all opposing normative orders *and* with those who note that, by acting together, nonelites have frequently limited the power of capital and democratized social and economic life through legal reforms. As shorthand, the book refers to this dynamic as the tension between capitalism and democracy, recognizing that both terms are immensely complex and contested. My hope is that embracing this tension will enable a sober, clear analysis of the crises facing us today, while also generating space to envision a future of work and workplace technology that is far more egalitarian and sustainable than the present.

Summary of Chapters

The book has six chapters, in addition to this introduction and a brief afterword. Chapters 1 and 2 are the book's theoretical core, chapters 3–5 provide empirical detail, and chapter 6 considers possible policy responses. Chapter 1 outlines the book's theory of the relationship among workplace technology, labor law, and capitalist development, and sketches the transition from the postwar political-economic order to the contemporary regime of accumulation. Chapter 2 discusses the transformation of labor law in recent decades as companies and investors responded to the challenges of the service transition by pushing for greater operational freedom vis-a-vis workers and the state. It also sketches parallel changes in intellectual property, trade secrets, and other doctrines that helped turn informational goods into profit centers.

The next three chapters discuss how companies are using their legal powers over data and technology to reshape work. Chapter 3 shows how companies are using data-driven technologies to automate some tasks and to alter the skills required for others, as part of an overall trend toward what the book calls "digital Taylorism."[38] That chapter also summarizes the promise and limits of contemporary AI and robotics and suggests that automation is unlikely to displace world-historic numbers of low-wage workers in the foreseeable future. Chapter 4 addresses the relationship between employee privacy and associational power. It first shows how companies can use data aggregation techniques to discern many workers' skills, aptitudes, and off-duty conduct. It then shows how companies may use that data to screen out prospective employees who are likely to challenge managerial authority, to determine whether their current workers are seeking to unionize, and to combat unionization efforts. Chapter 5 discusses how companies are using new technologies to alter the scope of their enterprises. As it shows, many major companies today purchase labor without hiring workers as employees and therefore avoid labor law duties, even as they build massive enterprises that enjoy substantial market power. As a result, power in many low-wage sectors today is highly concentrated in a few corporate headquarters, but legal responsibility for working conditions is diffuse.

The final chapter, chapter 6, discusses how policymakers could respond to these transformations of work. It suggests that policymakers should aim to extend democratic norms and practices deep into the spheres of production and distribution, and sketches two far-reaching sets of reforms that would advance that goal. The first set would guarantee workers the right to participate in workplace and economic governance through new forms of collective representation. The second set would reshape the governance of workplace data by banning various forms of workplace surveillance, giving workers a voice in the deployment of other data-driven technologies, and turning still other novel technologies into public goods. Together with new investments in care, social reproduction, and a green transition, these policies could help build a much more sustainable economy.

1 Technology, the Service Transition, and the New Working Class

Introduction

Over the last several decades relatively well-paid and unionized employment in manufacturing plummeted in the US, while low-wage, precarious, non-union employment in service industries surged.[1] Parallel economic transformations occurred across wealthy economies during the same period, but inequality has grown more in the US than in many of its peer nations.[2] The US has also been at the forefront of technological development over that time, helping to drive the mainstreaming of enterprise computers and personal computers in the 1980s, the growth of the internet in the 1990s and 2000s, the proliferation of mobile devices and other data-gathering sensors in the 2010s, and recent developments in robotics and artificial intelligence (AI).

The US' leadership in both technological innovation and precarious work is not a coincidence. As discussed in the introduction, this book argues that US employers have increasingly used new technologies as tools of class domination, suppressing workers' efforts to unionize or build other forms of associational power, and therefore keeping a lid on wages. This book further argues that employers' technological choices are intertwined with our labor laws and other institutions, so that institutions shape technological choices over time and vice versa. In other words, labor laws can encourage or limit employers' use of technology as a modality of domination, and the balance of political-economic power between workers and companies can shape the development of labor law. Still more ambitiously, this book suggests that the coevolution of technology and institutions over time reflects a deeper tension between capitalist imperatives and democratic aspirations.

Each of these arguments breaks with mainstream analyses of workplace technological development.

This chapter summarizes and defends the book's assumptions and underlying theory. Section 1.1 sketches neoclassical theories that view technological change and labor standards as being driven by apolitical forces of supply and demand, as well as contrasting theories of political economy that understand production regimes and labor standards as being more socially embedded. Drawing from those latter theories, as well as critical legal scholarship, section 1.2 proposes a model of the political economy of work and technological change in capitalist democracies. In that model, companies and workers advance their interests by deploying *power resources* across the class divide, including legal entitlements, control of data and technology, and capacities for collective action. Section 1.3 clarifies the role of class in this model and its relationship to other axes of subordination, including race and gender. Next, section 1.4 elaborates the role of technology in this model, explaining how companies can use technology both to enhance productivity and to augment their power over workers. Finally, section 1.5 traces the coevolution of technology and class relations in the long-running shift to a service economy as employers put pressure on and eventually displaced our post–World War II ("postwar") model of industrial relations.

1.1 Institutions, Technologies, and Labor Standards: Existing Models

This book's analysis of the relationship among institutions, technologies, and labor standards differs substantially from mainstream treatments of those questions. Before elaborating, it may help to define the terms "institutions" and "technologies." As used in this discussion, "institutions" indicates the laws, norms, and accepted patterns of behavior that undergird political, economic, and social life.[3] Institutions serve multiple, sometimes conflicting purposes within capitalist societies. For example, they facilitate market ordering and therefore capital accumulation, while also protecting less-powerful interests against certain forms of exploitation. Institutions, therefore, both reflect and shape social power relations. The term "technology" indicates "congealed practical knowledge embedded in material culture."[4] Technologies make it easier to do some things and harder to do others, as captured by the notion of technological "affordances," or the uses that technologies enable in particular contexts.[5] Telescopes extend our ability to see over distances and boats make seas passable, changing activities such as warfare and agriculture. Like institutions, technologies can be tools of domination, as some individuals and groups in society develop or utilize technologies to reinforce their power over other groups. Technologies and institutions, therefore, are both important means of shaping and maintaining social order. The two are distinct, though, since technologies are material while institutions are social.[6]

Leading theories about the relationship among institutions, technological change, and labor standards build on neoclassical models of the labor market. Those models, in turn, assume that no party has significant power over another, and understand wages as being set by market forces of supply and demand for particular skills.[7] This leads many scholars to presume that workplace technological change is productivity-enhancing—that is, it enables workers to produce more without increased effort—on the grounds that firms in competitive markets that do not maximize productivity will lose market share.[8] The influential model of skill-biased technological change, for example, explains stagnant wages for most workers in recent decades as an effect of technological changes like industrial automation, which reduced demand for midskilled workers, alongside changes like computerization, which increased demand for highly educated workers.[9] Technology in that model is therefore an "exogenous and politically neutral force," which develops in response to engineering advances and market imperatives.[10]

Institutional shifts like deunionization may contribute to inequality in this view, but those shifts are themselves largely driven by technological developments rather than political forces.[11] Indeed, such analyses tend to be skeptical that classic worker-protective laws are effective, sustainable, and/or desirable. Instead, they tend to posit a trade-off between equity and efficiency and hold that unionization and wage regulations will lead to declining overall output.[12] This approach generates a clear labor policy toolkit: states should focus on "upskilling" the workforce by investing in education,[13] should ensure fluid and nondiscriminatory labor markets, and should use the tax system to transfer resources from rich to poor where necessary.[14] But states should not generally empower workers through collective bargaining laws or minimum wage laws.

A different account of the role of power and institutions in economic ordering emerges from studies in economic sociology and comparative political economy. As a substantial body of research in those fields has shown, prosperous economies simply have not converged on a single set of labor market or social institutions over the last forty years, despite being subject to many of the same pressures of technological change, deindustrialization, and globalization. Instead, wage inequality and precarious work have grown the most in so-called liberal market economies and welfare states (such as the US and the UK), less significantly in continental Europe (especially in nations that have active industrial policies), and even less in social democratic Scandinavia.[15] There is even evidence that companies' technological preferences differ across nations, with employers in liberal nations more likely to favor "radical innovation" that develops entirely new goods or production processes, while their counterparts in more coordinated economies favor incremental changes to existing processes or goods.[16] Moreover, workers' ability to build and maintain associational power and to make alliances with other groups appears to be a major causal factor behind those observed differences.[17] That finding suggests different policy prescriptions than those emerging from neoclassical analyses. Namely, rather than addressing distributional concerns only through the tax-and-transfer system, which may be impossible in any event since wealth begats political might,[18] it may be most effective to address them by bolstering labor's power vis-à-vis capital. Chapter 6 considers how to do so in today's political economy.

As noted in the introduction, there are natural affinities and methodological overlaps between those branches of institutionalist social science and legal realism and its descendants, which include recent scholarship in "Law & Political Economy" or "LPE." Essentially, both focus on how institutions can shape political-economic processes and outcomes. Legal scholarship nevertheless focuses on law, while institutionalist social science treats law as one among other institutions. From a legal realist perspective, the law shapes the distribution of resources and power in numerous respects. In the workplace context, for example, labor laws grant workers substantive rights, against their employers, to goods like safety, equal opportunity, and decent wages. But the law also shapes production and distribution in more subtle ways that nonlawyers may not appreciate, such as by establishing and enforcing background entitlements of contract, property, and tort, and by creating legal constructs like the joint stock corporation, which can hold property and hire employees.[19] To take one example, as legal realists and their descendants have long emphasized, the enforcement of contracts between parties with disparate property holdings will tend to exacerbate economic inequalities. In such cases, the party with greater resources—typically the employer in the labor context—can typically hold out for a better deal, while the party with fewer resources may need to work in order to eat and so will be more motivated to settle quickly. Yet in various historical periods the law has presumed that such bargains were freely chosen and that the existing distribution of property is itself fair or natural.[20] In that sense, law may both shape and legitimate particular distributive outcomes, sometimes in ways that escape popular scrutiny.

1.2 Power Resources, Labor Practices, and Capitalist Development

Those latter bodies of literature suggest an alternative model of the relationship among institutions, technologies, and labor standards, which this section elaborates upon.[21] The sociological concept of *power resources* is central to this model.[22] Power resources are "the attributes (capacities or means) of actors (individuals or collectivities) that enable them to reward or to punish other actors."[23] For the purposes of this book's analysis, the most important power resources are legal entitlements within enterprises (including the rights of investors), control over technology, and capacities for collective action, or "associational power."[24] The latter two power resources—control over technology and associational power—are shaped by law but not reducible to law. For this book's purposes, the key groups are workers, companies, and investors, and subgroups within each group. To simplify the analysis, however, the book will often refer to "workers" (or "labor") and "companies," and will usually refer to their conflicts as "class conflicts."[25] When investors' and companies' interests align, the book will refer to that unity as "capital."

Companies, workers, and their allies deploy power resources across the class divide constantly in a dynamic, iterative, path-dependent process. They do so at all levels of the economy, from the individual employment contract, to the organization of work within enterprises, to battles in courts and legislatures over the basic legal structure of production. Collective action is usually workers' most important power resource, although skilled workers have some control over workplace technology, and today workers have an array of statutory protections against exploitation. Companies' most important power resources are their legal control of the enterprise and workplace technology, but they too utilize collective action. The firm itself is a form of collective action, since it aggregates investments and gives the resulting legal entity various legal powers over workers.[26] Companies also act collectively through trade associations and employer associations.[27] These battles lead to political settlements that define the terms on which labor can be purchased and sold. Those settlements are typically instantiated in law and in practice, including industrial relations systems, and then underlie facially consensual processes of economic governance. Supply and demand, therefore, help determine wages, but they are best understood not as discrete curves but as broad bands, within which the distribution of power matters greatly.[28] Neoclassical economics can treat the market as a sphere of individual freedom only by abstracting away from these overtly political battles and studying the bargains reached in their aftermath or shadow.

As discussed later in this section, workers are far from powerless in these processes—and yet capital has substantial structural advantages that persist over time. One reason is that workers depend on companies and investors for jobs, and states depend on them for taxes. That dependence limits workers' and states' capacity to oppose capital's interests.[29] Another reason is that while both workers and companies deploy power resources to seek advantages within existing production regimes, companies also deploy power resources for a very different purpose: to reshape or displace existing production methods and political settlements. (Labor does this as well—but less often and usually less successfully given its structural dependence on capital). Indeed, constant technological and social innovations are foundational to capitalism itself, as many of its classical theorists observed.[30] The reason is that capitalism encourages both unending accumulation and incessant competition, and competition tends to reduce profits over time. As a result, companies constantly seek out technological innovations that can give them first-mover advantages or exclusive legal rights, which translate into monopolies over scarce resources and above-average profits—or what Immanuel Wallerstein called "high-voltage" profits.[31] Such innovations, together with aggressive expansion strategies, can also give companies substantial market power, further bolstering profits. Companies also seek to extend market processes into social spheres governed by nonmarket logics, or to upend existing laws and institutions that limit market discipline, again to ensure continued high profits and accumulation.[32] This overall process is then "full of frictions, contradictions, and dysfunctions . . . but still patterned according to an identifiable logic of expansion and accumulation."[33]

Indeed, companies often seek to alter technologies and institutions at the same time, as the case of Uber illustrates. In addition to developing a proprietary app to link drivers and passengers without human intermediation, the company reshaped a heavily regulated labor market by putting drivers on the street who did not have taxi licenses, in cars that were not outfitted or registered as taxis.[34] By doing so, Uber forced drivers to compete with one another, pushing down wages. In other words, the company sought to protect its core innovations from market competition, even as it subjected workers to market discipline.[35] While Uber is not clearly profitable, many leading service-sector companies have followed similar strategies in recent decades, as chapters 3–5 show.

Workers and others nevertheless resist such efforts constantly by organizing, taking wages out of competition, and pressing for statutory protections.[36] In other words, they deploy *associational power* to counteract capital's *legal* and *technological powers*. Indeed, without some limits on capital's power and capacity to reshape social relations, the system itself may stumble: workers may eventually be unable to feed themselves or their children, consumer markets may fail, the trust that is a crucial precondition for human cooperation may erode, and the natural environment may be destroyed.[37] This interplay between forces of commodification and decommodification highlights a deeper tension between capitalism and democracy. Namely, labor regulations and welfare programs embed capitalist work and social relations within "non-capitalist social orders"[38] involving norms of solidarity—and yet capital's relentless pressure for accumulation always threatens to break out of those institutions, which "both contain and sustain" capitalism as a system.[39]

Now, to suggest that the tension between democracy and capitalist imperatives influences or structures political-economic developments does not imply any *necessary* trajectory of historical or technological change. The argument here is instead that our political economy is shaped by ongoing battles in which capital has deep structural advantages, but where capital can never wholly dominate other groups or suppress other values. With that caveat in mind, one can then see this process playing out over successive business cycles. So-called competitive capitalism gave way to Gilded Age consolidation, where high profits were in steel, railroads, and industry; and then to the New Deal and postwar settlement, where high profits were still found in heavy industry; and finally to contemporary neoliberalism, as discussed in detail later in this chapter. Today, the high-voltage profits are in sectors like pharmaceuticals, biotech, finance, and business services, while the low-voltage profits are in service-intensive sectors like retail, food service, hospitality, and care and social reproduction (including elder care, childcare, long-term care, and education). Law also coevolved with political-economic developments over that long period. As other legal scholars have suggested, there are conceptual harmonies between laissez-faire economics and the "classical legal thought" of the late nineteenth and early twentieth centuries, between postwar managed capitalism and legal realism's understanding of law as a means to social ends,[40] and between the contemporary resurgence of market ordering and the importation of neoliberal ideas into legal theory.[41] The role of law in both the postwar order and the contemporary political economy is discussed in more detail in chapter 2.

Two nuances of this model are worth highlighting before moving on. First, to say that the ongoing marketization of life generates a conflict between capitalism and democracy is not to valorize majority rule per se, but rather to highlight the deep-seated tension between capital's demands for ongoing accumulation and workers' and others' demands for basic material security. As discussed in section 1.3, workers are not a monolithic group, and decommodification efforts have often excluded non-white, nonmale workers. Workers in particular sectors or occupations nevertheless have common interests that cut across racial and gender categories, and their demands for protection of those interests are appropriately understood as democratic, in the sense that they are opposed to the interest of a privileged minority of investors and managers.

Second, class conflicts are not always zero-sum games. In many cases, companies and workers have allied with one another in particular industrial sectors to advance common goals.[42] In other cases, working-class organization has benefited companies by reducing interfirm competition or by giving companies a partner with whom they can collaborate to unlock productivity gains. The sociologist Erik Olin Wright sought to capture this idea with a model of "positive class compromise," under which increases in workers' associational power "adversely affect capitalist-class interests until such power crosses some intermediate threshold beyond which further increases in working-class power are potentially beneficial to capitalists' interests."[43] That being said, Wright's model may be more relevant to industrial than service economies given the possibility of compounding productivity growth in industry, as discussed in section 1.5. Moreover, as discussed in subsequent chapters, companies today may be able to use new technologies to better understand what groups of workers want and to find workers with necessary skills at low cost, replicating two functions performed by unions in the past, but without empowering workers in the process.

1.3 Deeper into Class and Associational Power

The political settlements sketched above instantiate the distribution of resources and power along lines of *class* as well as race, gender, and other axes of subordination. Class itself is a deeply contested concept that has generated many theories over the years. But as the historian Ellen Meiksins Wood argued, "There are really only two ways of thinking theoretically about class: either as a structural *location* or as a social *relation*."[44] The former approach involves sorting individuals into objective groupings based on indicia of stratification, such as income, educational attainment, or position within the division of labor, but does not posit that classes necessarily have opposed interests. The latter approach, which today is strongly associated with the work of Erik Olin Wright, understands class relations as rooted in control over productive resources and as antagonistic due to *exploitation*, or the process through which one class appropriates the fruits of another class's labor.[45] Companies' efforts to suppress wages among line-level workers so that investors, top managers, or both can capture a greater share of profits are a straightforward example of antagonistic class relations of this sort. Just as capitalism is ever-evolving, this tradition views class relations as being in constant flux due to technological, political, and social change.[46]

Class in this sense plays little role in mainstream theorizing about work. As noted previously, neoclassical models of the labor market assume power relations away, and therefore also assume that antagonistic class relations simply do not exist. Class also plays a circumscribed role in many "information society" theories that seek to explain how the maturation of information technologies has altered capitalist economies. For example, Daniel Bell's foundational and still-influential 1973 book *The Coming of Post-Industrial Society* foresaw many of the key conflicts and tensions of postindustrial economies, but it also suggested that class conflicts would simply become less important as production workers became more and more technically skilled.[47] Some subsequent information society theories have drawn on Bell's work and methodology and have echoed Bell in viewing class conflicts as being less important in today's economy. Manuel Castells, for example, has argued that "production-based, social classes, as constituted, and enacted in the Industrial Age, cease to exist" in today's economy.[48] This statement is difficult to parse—in other writings Castells has suggested that work today entails persistent conflicts and inequalities—but it can be read to suggest that class conflicts are no longer important.[49] Similarly, Shoshana Zuboff's influential recent work on "surveillance capitalism"—which explores the tech giants' business model in relationship to consumers—says little about workplace and economic power relations, as several reviewers have noted.[50]

While it is true that industrial-era class conflicts no longer predominate, a major theme in this book is that class conflicts have not disappeared in the past few decades. Rather, they have evolved and even became more acute in some respects. A distinguishing characteristic of the workers in today's service sector is that they have much less associational power than their industrial forebears. This is so for various reasons, but a major one is that companies across the service economy have adopted business models that depend on suppressing workers' associational power, as discussed in later chapters.

In addition to Wright's and Wood's theories, two other bodies of thought help elucidate the role of institutions and technology in shaping class relations. The first is associated with the historian E. P. Thompson and others who have emphasized that class formation involves political contests carried out in both the economic and symbolic registers.[51] A simple example from the union-organizing context illustrates this point. Employers in the US tend to resist unionization bitterly and frequently terminate union activists.[52] Doing so is illegal, but employees typically get the intended message that organizing is futile or dangerous.[53] As a result, it is often *irrational* for workers to try to unionize in the US, since the benefits of unionization are uncertain and will arrive only in the long term, while the costs of joining a union are often immediate and severe. Workers can overcome employer resistance and their own fears, however, "by defining a *collective identity*" in which "being a member is a value in itself [and] each member is legitimately required to practice solidarity."[54] The foundation of that identity is workers' common experience—that is, a similar occupation or craft, colocation in a large and dangerous factory,

Technology, the Service Transition, and the New Working Class

religious or ethnic ties, and other factors. Deeper bonds of solidarity are then forged among workers through the process of organizing and challenging managerial authority, as chapter 4 discusses in more detail.[55] But as also discussed in chapter 4 and elsewhere, companies can make it harder for workers to build solidarity by surveilling them more intensively, monitoring their communications, and arranging production to limit workers' interpersonal contact.

Another body of class theory, developed by the sociologist Aage B. Sørensen, helps explain the *ends* of contemporary class politics. Sørensen argued that class relations are geared toward creating economic rents, generally by protecting resources against competition.[56] A rent-based class analysis, Sørensen argued, may explain how capitalist production generates antagonistic and exploitative class relations without relying on the problematic labor theory of value.[57] Profitable companies are those who create maximal product market rents or quasi-rents, often aided by robust intellectual property (IP) rights, even as they endeavor "to produce a labor market conforming to the assumption of neoclassical economics," where workers compete for jobs, wages, and assignments.[58] Workers, meanwhile, seek to avoid market discipline by developing specialized skills or by organizing and therefore cartelizing the supply of labor.[59] As the Uber example in section 1.2 illustrated, and as subsequent chapters argue, today's large, low-wage employers utilize both strategies: they protect their own innovations against competition even as they subject workers to intense market discipline.[60] Through those twin processes, they ensure that investors and managers—not line-level workers—capture the lion's share of profits.

Now, to emphasize a point noted earlier, this book does not assert that class is the most important form of social division. After all, workers are not now and have never been a monolithic group. Indeed, as scholars within the Black Radical tradition have emphasized, it is simply impossible to understand class formation outside of processes of racial differentiation and subordination.[61] Similarly, as numerous feminist scholars have argued, it is impossible to understand class politics in the paid labor market without accounting for unpaid labor in the home, which is disproportionately performed by women,[62] as well as the tendency for women to be shunted into low-paid service jobs.[63] Such asymmetries were written into New Deal and postwar labor law, which excluded agricultural and domestic workers,[64] failed to guarantee equal opportunity on the basis of race or gender until 1964,[65] and failed to recognize unpaid care work within homes as labor. Capitalism in the New Deal and postwar eras was therefore socially embedded both in norms of working-class solidarity that mitigated market discipline within the industrial core and in norms of patriarchy and white supremacy that defined who was inside and outside the relatively privileged working class.[66] In that sense, to say that workers' class-based demands for social protections are "democratic" glosses over this exclusion of most workers from the political-economic "demos."

At the same time, just as class relations cannot be understood outside the context of race, race-based subordination cannot be fully understood outside the context of class. As the historians Destin Jenkins and Justin Leroy have recently argued, racial differentiation has been central to capitalist development, in part because "the violent dispossessions inherent to capital accumulation operate by leveraging, intensifying, and creating racial distinctions."[67] In the US, that process was acutely visible during slavery and Jim Crow. But it has continued through to the present, where non-white individuals remain especially vulnerable to wealth expropriation (e.g., through housing foreclosure).[68] Furthermore, Jenkins and Leroy argue, race-based differentiation helps to legitimate capitalism itself by "naturalizing the inequalities produced by capitalism."[69] In this light, the longstanding exclusion of Black and other non-white workers from full social citizenship was not motivated simply by animus or racism. It also reflected many elites' material interest, in both the North and South, in maintaining a large pool of subordinate labor.

Race, gender, and class are also intertwined in the sense that opposition to labor commodification can cut along race and gender lines, as collective action often grows out of common experiences of racial and gendered oppression. The Black Freedom movement in the 1960s pushed for landmark civil rights legislation, including Title VII, in part to ensure a path out of poverty for Black workers. Similarly, a movement among healthcare workers linked to the Black Freedom movement led state legislatures to extend collective bargaining rights to public-sector workers in the 1960s and 1970s, eventually spurring Congress to extend rights under the National Labor Relations Act (NLRA) to most private hospital workers.[70] Many of the most vibrant workers' rights movements in recent years have evolved among, and have been led by, women and Black, Indigenous, and people of color (BIPOC) individuals. These include health-care and public-sector organizing, the Justice for Janitors campaign, which fights for the rights of janitors across the US and Canada, the Fight for $15, a movement of low-wage workers in fast food and elsewhere who have been pushing for a $15 minimum wage and unionization, and the successful effort to organize Amazon's Staten Island Warehouse.[71] While public debates around progressive policies often pit concerns of race, class, and gender against one another, in reality the three overlap quite substantially in today's economy. In that respect, and as chapter 6 argues, ensuring a more democratic political economy would advance equity along all three lines.

1.4 Technology as a Power Resource, Past and Present

As noted previously, this book agrees with mainstream accounts that workplace technological change often enhances labor productivity—but it breaks with mainstream thinking by emphasizing that workplace technology is also an important tool of class power. Technological innovation can enhance labor productivity in various ways. For example, companies often use machinery and algorithms to perform work previously performed by humans. They also improve existing machinery and algorithms to make them faster, more accurate, or more energy efficient. And they can alter workplace processes without changing machinery, for example by changing the layout of machinery in a factory so that goods travel a shorter distance between workstations. In many occupations and sectors, companies have incentives to upskill their workforce when integrating new technologies. Such efforts are common, for example, in advanced manufacturing and health care.[72] Companies may be more likely to offer such training where they have reached the sort of "positive class compromise" discussed earlier, which facilitates trust and long-term joint commitments between workers and companies.[73]

While many (or even most) workplace innovations enhance productivity, companies also adopt technologies to augment their power over workers and capture a greater share of profits.[74] Power-augmenting technology takes two basic forms. First, companies can use technology to deskill or "homogenize" work, enabling it to be performed by individuals without the need for extensive training.[75] Homogenization strategies were central to the transformation from craft-based to industrial production and to the emergence of Taylorist/Fordist modes of production, as discussed later in this section. Second, companies can monitor work more closely, projecting a credible threat that underperforming workers will be identified and terminated.[76] In that sense, surveillance is a political intervention by companies designed to maintain their unilateral control over workplace processes and the pace of work.[77]

There are various well-known historical examples of employers using technologies as tools of class power. The simplest cases involve changes in productive machinery that lead to a greater capital share of profits but static or even declining labor productivity. The technology scholar Langdon Winner gives as an example the decision by the nineteenth-century industrialist Cyrus McCormick to install pneumatic molding machines that were more expensive and less precise than the state of the art. In other words, those machines were inefficient, but after adopting them, McCormick was able to prevent unionization of his plant by firing the skilled craft workers who had previously performed the task. After several years, McCormick got rid of the machines, "but by that time they had served their purpose—the destruction of the union."[78]

A likely more common case involves technologies that enhance both productivity and employer power. For example, sociologists and economists have frequently noted the blurred line between productivity enhancement and power augmentation in the transformation from cottage industry to factory production in textiles. Industrialists created factories not just to gather productive machinery in one place, but also to monopolize productive knowledge and instill a modern form of labor discipline, in which workers show up on a regular schedule and can be closely monitored.[79]

The later transition to heavy industrial production was again based on interlocking changes in productive technology and workplace surveillance. Frederick Winslow Taylor's system of "scientific management" was specifically designed to centralize management's control over production, wresting it away from craft workers and their unions, which controlled apprenticeship programs, chose technologies, and established output rates and wages as the "law" for their crafts.[80] As Taylor put it, scientific management was "directly antagonistic to the old idea that each workman can best regulate his own way of doing the work."[81] He instructed industrial engineers to closely observe and measure workers' actions, and then break production into "discrete, rationalized, low-skill tasks" that could be performed by workers with little specialized training.[82] Craft workers were well aware of the engineers' motives and would often resist such monitoring, or even refuse to work at all if supervisors were present.[83]

Today's companies continue this tradition, using information and communications technologies both to enhance productivity and to augment their power over workers. In that respect, the politics of workplace technology today carries forward many of the class conflicts of the industrial era. One through line, which runs all the way back to early industrialization, is that companies can use technologies to render work processes and workers' interactions more legible to a central authority, and therefore more susceptible to centralized control.[84] The telegraph, the telephone, and the fax machine all enabled the integration of enterprises across vast distances, generating economies of scale but also enabling closer supervision of workers. Today, companies use information and communications technologies for similar purposes, but modern tools of surveillance are vastly more powerful than their forebears. As chapters 3–5 explore, companies today frequently aspire to surveillance that is constant (always operating), universal (reaching all aspects of work and production, and even workers' lives outside of work), and controlled centrally rather than being embodied in individual supervisors.[85] Surveillance today is also asymmetric: companies are able to monitor workers with or without their knowledge, and to prevent workers from monitoring management. It also appears that companies are increasingly using technological design choices to govern work where feasible, since workers may then be unable to contest those actions.[86] If it is impossible to use Uber's app without accepting location tracking, for example, then drivers and consumers must either consent or lose access.[87]

Modern data-driven technologies differ from what came before in another respect as well. As noted in the introduction, contemporary forms of AI often work by discerning patterns in very large data pools, leading to a genuinely new form of knowledge that is *inductive* in character. Through new techniques of surveillance and data analysis, companies can place workers in statistical groupings based on aspects of their behavior on and off the job that are revealed in massive data sets. In the consumer context, companies are utilizing those insights to shape consumer choices at scale through behavioral nudges, targeted advertisements, curated social media feeds, and platform structures that reward ongoing iterative engagement.[88]

In the labor context, nudges and behavioral modification occur, but they may be less necessary since companies already enjoy hierarchical authority over workers and can simply order them to perform certain tasks—or even to refrain from doing certain things outside of work. Those efforts are discussed in chapters 3–5.

1.5 Explaining Change Over Time: From the Postwar Order to Neoliberalism

The model sketched in this chapter seeks to illuminate patterns of exchange and technological deployment at particular moments, as well as changes to political settlements over time. Political settlements come under pressure for many reasons, including technological developments, changes in geopolitics, and changes in the relative power of groups across class and other lines.[89] One such transition occurred in the late 1970s and early 1980s, when our postwar model of industrial relations was displaced by what the book calls "workplace neoliberalism."[90] This final section of this chapter traces the technological and class-relational aspects of that shift, and chapter 2 discusses the role of law in that shift.

Crisis and reconstruction The postwar industrial relations regime in the US, which became known as "industrial pluralism," emerged out of the political and economic crises of the late nineteenth and early twentieth centuries.[91] During those years, the US experienced wave upon wave of labor violence as companies and states suppressed worker movements. Congress eventually asserted the power to regulate the national economy during the New Deal, passing landmark worker protection legislation, including the NLRA in 1935, which became a centerpiece of the postwar order.[92] The NLRA declared a national policy of "encouraging the practice and procedure of collective bargaining and . . . protecting the exercise by workers of full freedom of association."[93] Workers then unionized in massive numbers, especially in heavy industry, and over time they secured wage gains that tracked productivity, as well as generous health and other benefits. The merits and limits of the postwar regime and of postwar labor law are discussed in more detail in chapter 2.

The postwar regime was relatively stable not only because it protected workers, but also because it helped to solve problems that companies and the state could not solve on their own.[94] For example, collective bargaining substantially reduced the labor violence that plagued the US prior to the New Deal.[95] Moreover, where industries were unionized across the board, collective bargaining tended to set relatively uniform wages, which helped the more productive firms thrive.[96] As a result, wealthy economies enjoyed a virtuous cycle of full employment, price stability, economic growth, and economic equality. Unions also enabled workers to raise concerns about conditions and tensions on the shop floor or to identify inefficient workplace processes, contributing to overall productivity.[97] The postwar political-economic order combined these labor market institutions with Keynesian economic planning, which boosted aggregate demand, and with the hegemonic position of the US over much of the Global South, which ensured cheap access to raw materials and large export markets.[98] Similar structures were built across wealthy nations at the time, which appears to be a major reason that this was the only period of sustained shared prosperity (within those nations) in the history of capitalism.[99]

Yet even in this remembered heyday of more coordinated and egalitarian American capitalism, class fissures and antagonisms were ever present.[100] One reason was that unions were effectively unable to organize new industries after Congress ratcheted back their powers and enabled states to pass "right to work" laws in 1947's Taft-Hartley Act.[101] As discussed in chapters 2 and 4, another was that the National Labor Relations Board (NLRB) and the courts gave employers various powers to resist unionization beginning early in the New Deal era, which they exercised through the postwar era. Yet another was that the New Deal order democratized the economy in a limited fashion, failing to protect many of the nation's most vulnerable workers. Those elements of the postwar regime helped prevent the emergence of a robust and multiracial labor movement.[102] Unions were then caught flat-footed by shifts in the geopolitical environment in the 1970s as oil shocks, competition in global manufacturing, and stagflation generated a crisis of profitability.[103]

Companies and investors then pressed for and achieved a new political settlement, now widely known as "neoliberalism," which enabled them to generate sustained profits once again.[104] Financial interests, for example, advocated for the repeal of New Deal–era restrictions on banking activities,[105] while manufacturers pressed governments to open up new markets to trade and pressed for union concessions in their domestic operations. The results include the legal architecture of globalization that is now familiar:

liberalized trade in goods and services, protections for cross-border movements of capital, and strong, harmonized IP rules. Together with industrialization in many Global South nations, this generated a massive shift in global income: elites across the world and peasants and middle classes in the Global South saw enormous gains, lifting hundreds of millions out of grinding poverty, but the Global North's middle and working classes saw their income stagnate or even fall.[106]

The service transition These institutional shifts occurred alongside the shift to a service economy across wealthy nations. In the US, that transition actually began early in the postwar era, as industrial machinery became more efficient and new computer systems developed during the war were implemented in factories.[107] As a result, the core industrial working class was itself eroding throughout the postwar era, with manufacturing jobs declining as a percentage of total employment beginning in the mid-1950s.[108] Meanwhile, as the demand for industrial workers was declining, the demand for service workers was growing.[109] This trend also began early in the postwar era, as prosperity and the US's global leadership in manufacturing increased demand for business services such as advertising, accounting, and law—which in turn generated demand for low-end services catering to urban professionals and the middle class, including restaurants, hotels, and retailers.[110] The entry of women into the paid workforce in large numbers further bolstered demand for services once performed in the home.[111]

In the US, the inflection point came in the early 1980s, as successive waves of deindustrialization eviscerated many communities across the country.[112] Companies' technological choices played a substantial causal role here. Automation became cheaper and easier due to factory robotics, though robotics were also largely limited to the industrial context.[113] Outsourcing was facilitated by nascent, networked information technologies that improved over time, enabling companies to keep in close contact with (or surveil) suppliers and workers in far-flung, global production networks.[114] The social ills of deindustrialization, such as addiction and mental health—and the ongoing needs of a retired or displaced industrial workforce—then generated increased demand for health care in many cities. Over time, cost pressures and interest group politics encouraged a model of health-care provision that depended on a highly exploited workforce.[115]

The service transition also altered the economics of work and social protections, generating new pressures on employers, collective bargaining regimes, and welfare states.[116] The reason is that service-dominated economies cannot easily replicate the virtuous postwar cycle of higher wages, higher productivity, and economic growth because it is more difficult to generate compounding productivity gains in services. This has become known as the "cost disease," after the economist William Baumol's theory that the relative price of services increases over time as productivity growth reduces the cost of manufactured goods.[117] Baumol's original example was a string quartet: the productivity of string quartets has not increased at all in centuries, yet performers are paid much more today than they were in Beethoven's Vienna. The in-person services that dominate today's economy are often susceptible to the cost disease, either because the good produced is a worker's labor (in the case of performing arts or home-based health care) or because workers are performing tasks that are difficult to mechanize (e.g., a waiter delivering meals to customers, a retail worker stocking shelves or helping a customer, or a gig worker delivering a package).

While the cost disease affects all major economies today, its effects are mediated through policy and institutions. Those institutions have pushed costs and risks onto workers to a greater extent in the US than in most other wealthy nations. As Kathleen Thelen has put it, the US' response to the service transition involved "a neoliberal offensive in which class cleavages predominate[d]."[118] During the acute phase of deindustrialization, for example, industrial workers were basically left to fend for themselves. Congress's major targeted response, the 1988 Worker Adjustment and Retraining Notification (WARN) Act, does not require worker retraining or even severance pay. Rather, it simply requires in many cases that companies give notice to workers before mass layoffs.[119] To this day, the US has few structured job training programs, relying instead on educational institutions—which are often for-profit enterprises—to train workers in specific skills and to grant occupational certifications. Other countries responded differently. In Denmark, for instance, the state's "active labor market policies" aim to retrain and rehire workers as quickly as possible.[120] Germany pivoted to high value-added manufacturing, which enabled its companies to maintain profitability despite high wages and robust systems of worker representation, including industry-level bargaining, works councils, and seats on companies' supervisory boards.[121] Service workers in Germany, however, are exposed to substantial market discipline, much like their American counterparts.[122]

In any event, the distinctly liberal approach to welfare, worker training, and industrial policy in the US has left us with a high proportion of low-wage and precarious work. In reality, we have a new working class—one that is employed in services rather than industry, that is disproportionately non-white and female, and that is barely unionized.[123] The outlines of that new working class are apparent in data on employment levels and wages. Before COVID-19, there were around 13 million manufacturing workers, with a median wage of around $22 per hour.[124] They still represented a substantial proportion of the workforce. However, prior to COVID, there were nearly as many workers in food service alone—11 million, including almost 4.5 million in fast food. There were also nearly 10 million retail workers, over 4 million hand laborers (including warehouse workers), 2.5 million janitors, and almost 2 million in hotels and hospitality. Over the same era, demographic and other trends also generated greater demand for health care, which has overtaken manufacturing as the largest sector in many cities.[125] To be clear, there are still many skilled craft workers in the US, as well as midskilled workers in the health-care and technology fields. But the growth of employment in low-wage services remains one of the most important economic and political developments of the last few decades.

Compared to their industrial forebears, service-sector companies face distinct challenges. Most important, low productivity growth in services incentivizes those companies to suppress wages, arguably to a greater extent than industrial firms. Many service-sector companies also have smaller workplaces or more dispersed workforces, operate on different schedules day by day and over the course of business cycles, and require a greater proportion of workers to interact with customers. That requires a new sort of worker, one who is able to work outside of ordinary business hours and has good social skills. As discussed in subsequent chapters, companies increasingly turned to data-driven technologies to address these challenges. In particular, they used those technologies to curate a different sort of workforce and to prevent those workers from building associational power. Given the transformations in labor law addressed in the next chapter and workers' generally declining associational power over time, companies were able to take those steps with minimal resistance. As a result, by the mid-2010s, nearly half of all workers in the US—65 million individuals—made less than $15 per hour. That included a majority of Black workers and nearly 60 percent of Latino/a workers.[126]

Conclusion

This book's theory of workplace technology breaks with mainstream and dominant theories in two respects. First, while mainstream accounts tend to assume that no party has power over others in our economy, this book assumes, with heterodox economists and others, that power relations—especially of class, race, gender, and nationality—suffuse and structure the economy at every level. Second, while mainstream accounts tend to assume that companies use technologies simply to enhance productivity, this book argues that companies also frequently use technologies to augment their power over workers. The next chapter rounds out the book's theory by discussing how law has both facilitated and been shaped by these developments.

2 The Legal Construction of Workplace Neoliberalism

Introduction

The transformations in our political economy over the last several decades have left their mark on the law.[1] Or more precisely, our labor laws and our political economy *coevolved* during that time, as the postwar political settlement gave way to a new regime that many have characterized as neoliberal. Since the passage of the National Labor Relations Act (NLRA or "the Act"), our labor law has embraced *both* democratic commitments to worker self-organization *and* employers' traditional common-law prerogatives to organize production as they wish. But the relative import of those values has shifted over time. In the postwar era, democratic commitments were somewhat more prominent, and labor law theory even imagined employment—at least for relatively privileged industrial workers—as a social relationship jointly constituted by the working class and employers. Through the period of neoliberalism, the democratic strands of our labor law receded, and the common-law strands rose to dominance. Various forces discussed in chapter 1 helped to drive that evolution, including deindustrialization and the service transition, the rise of advanced information technologies, the globalization of much economic activity, and a concerted effort by capital to reassert control over the spheres of production and distribution.

Legally, that effort played out in litigation and lawmaking processes as companies sought greater freedom of action vis-à-vis workers and the state: greater freedom to hire and fire workers at will, to avoid unionization and to erode unions' power, to reshape production as they wish, and to gather and utilize data in their operations with few restrictions. Those freedoms enabled greater profitability and a greater return on invested capital, especially in service sectors with low productivity growth. Those changes also cohered over time into a new legal conception of employment as an individual contract between putative equals rather than a social relationship. Today our labor law no longer understands workers as a group with obvious shared interests best advanced through collective action, nor does it assume that workers deserve protection simply because of their subordinate position in the division of labor. In that sense, our labor law helped to create the new working class, even as it denies that a working *class* still exists. The book calls this new labor law regime "workplace neoliberalism," and links it to broader trends in governance over the same period.

In this chapter, section 2.1 outlines the shift from postwar industrial pluralism to contemporary workplace neoliberalism and places that story in the context of broader legal transformations over the same period. Sections 2.2 and 2.3 then discuss the doctrinal shifts in detail. Section 2.2 explains how workplace governance was reshaped around the logic of individual contract. Section 2.3 traces the relationship of labor law to workplace technology over the same period and discusses companies' more recent efforts to gather and enclose workplace and worker data. These legal developments helped constitute the contemporary accumulation regime discussed in chapter 1, and which is explored in detail in chapters 3–5.

A note before proceeding: the law is immensely complex, and its content can be difficult to determine even for experienced attorneys. Cases and bodies of doctrine are often in tension with one another, or may even contradict one another. Because this book is intended to be accessible to laypeople as well as legal scholars, the discussion of law in this chapter and subsequent chapters remains at a fairly high level. The main text aims to trace general trends in the law, and to demonstrate their relationship to technological and political-economic factors. To make that possible, various nuances of legal doctrine will appear in the endnotes. I hope the breadth of coverage enabled by that strategy will compensate for any loss of precision.

2.1 From Industrial Pluralism to Workplace Neoliberalism

Prior to the New Deal, our labor law was essentially a branch of the common law, or the judge-made law—including the fields of contract, tort, property, and domestic relations—that the US inherited from England. During that era, companies enjoyed near-plenary rights to hire and fire at will, state courts often enjoined worker protest under civil conspiracy laws,[2] and the Supreme Court struck down various legislative regulations of employment on the grounds that they unconstitutionally infringed freedom of contract.[3] It took a crisis of capitalism and state legitimacy during the Great Depression to displace that system. As noted in chapter 1, the centerpiece of the new order was the NLRA, which altered employers' common law contract and property rights by prohibiting retaliation against workers for union organizing and related activities. In litigation over the constitutionality of the NLRA and other worker statutes, the Supreme Court shifted its approach to questions of constitutional political economy and ratified broad federal regulatory authority.[4] Those cases helped set the stage for the postwar labor relations regime.

Yet in *National Labor Relations Board v. Jones & Laughlin Steel*, the very case in which the Supreme Court upheld the NLRA, the Court also signaled that the Act did not fully displace the earlier common law's emphasis on freedom of contract and employer property rights. As the Court explained, the Act forbade employers from retaliating against workers for unionizing and required them to bargain in good faith with their employees' unions, but it did not "compel agreements between employers and employees." Nor did it "interfere with the normal exercise of the right of the employer to select its employees or to discharge them," so long as the employer did not do so in retaliation for protected activity.[5] The emerging regime therefore envisioned a system of collective private ordering, in which the state would not generally scrutinize managerial decisions, and in which employers retained many unilateral powers. Indeed, *Jones & Laughlin*'s reasoning reflected a fundamental tension of our collective bargaining law: that it protects both workers' rights to pursue industrial democracy *and* continued employer prerogatives in the workplace, as reflected in the earlier common law whose legitimacy was based on tradition rather than democratic ideals.[6]

After the war, our collective bargaining law consolidated around the ideology of "industrial pluralism," which sought to resolve this tension between the state's promotion of collective bargaining and the older common law.[7] As the legal scholar Katherine Stone put it in a canonical article, "Industrial pluralism is the view that collective bargaining is self-government by management and labor." Through collective bargaining, the parties "engage in debate and compromise, and together legislate the rules under which the workplace will be governed."[8] Importantly, the organs of state—especially courts and administrative agencies—were expected to refrain from interfering in that process to the greatest extent possible.[9] Somewhat paradoxically, while the New Deal led to a much larger administrative state and to the progressive extension of federal regulations into more and more spheres of the economy and private life, industrial pluralism entailed a *retreat* from intimate state involvement in labor relations. The role of the state—here, the NLRB and the courts—was not to govern employment directly, but rather to establish the legal entitlements necessary for autonomous private lawmaking.[10]

Under industrial pluralism, then, workers' organizations obtained some lawmaking power, or at least their values and practices became legitimate sources of workplace authority.[11] Collective bargaining agreements accordingly had a status more fundamental than individual contracting, being instead akin to legislation, or even a constitution for workplace governance.[12] Similar notions of collective bargaining as a form of autonomous collective ordering informed European labor law systems at the time.[13] US courts then embraced collective bargaining and governance not just because they would make workplaces more fair, but also because they would induce employee loyalty. In the latter respect, industrial pluralism was heavily indebted to the "human relations" school of industrial sociology, which held that workers who could share their concerns and feelings about work were more likely to be productive and reliable.[14] Labor law theorists at the time argued that grievance arbitration could serve that function in unionized workplaces,[15] and the Supreme Court suggested in a leading case that "the processing of even frivolous claims" through arbitration "may have therapeutic values" in the workplace.[16]

Yet due to the persistence of employers' common law entitlements, industrial pluralism delivered a rather thin form of workplace and economic democracy.[17] Through the postwar era, employers often sought to erode unions' power through strategies such as outsourcing, staffing cuts, and crude threats against union supporters.[18] Indeed, various labor law scholars have argued that the industrial pluralist vision of labor and management standing on equal footing was far more ideological than real—reflecting the political valence of human resources theory—and served mainly to legitimate workplace domination and broader political-economic inequalities.[19]

Over time, and especially after the 1970s crisis of the postwar order, the common law side of this equation grew steadily in importance, and today it outweighs (or even dominates) the democratic side. Today's labor law thus enacts a different model of the relationship among workers, companies, and the state, one that gives workers still fewer protections and reflects broader trends in governance over the same period that others have termed "neoliberal."[20] "Neoliberalism" itself is a controversial notion, but at root it describes a set of theories that came to prominence in the 1980s holding that the state should be reorganized to reflect putative market imperatives.[21] As various scholars have argued, while neoliberalism has strong laissez-faire overtones, it is distinct from classical liberalism. The major difference is that classical liberalism viewed "market ordering under the common law" as "part of nature rather than a legal construct,"[22] while neoliberalism supports the affirmative use of law and political power to "restructure areas of law and social life along market lines."[23] The market is at once the outcome of conscious legal and social projects and an ideal-typical model for social and political relations.

In operation, neoliberalism entailed a simultaneous rollback of legal regimes that empower labor and citizens and a rollout of legal regimes that empower companies and capital more generally.[24] Under the influence of neoliberalism, many fields of law that concern the market were "re-oriented around versions of economic 'efficiency,'" crowding out concerns of distributive fairness and democratic legitimacy.[25] These legal changes therefore helped to "encase" the powers and privileges of dominant economic actors against challenge by workers, citizens, and even state actors.[26] For example, within antitrust, corporate litigants and allied scholars reframed merger analysis and related questions around a consumer welfare standard, displacing an older view that antitrust should also limit market power per se. That shift encouraged greater market concentration and corporate power in recent decades, as discussed in chapter 5.[27] Within corporate law, financial interests and various scholars pressed for shareholder wealth maximization as a predominant goal, arguing that investors needed legal tools to limit managers' propensity to enrich themselves.[28] That approach often disregarded the needs of workers, communities, and other corporate stakeholders. Scholars and litigants also consolidated the field of intellectual property (IP) out of disparate doctrines in patent, trademark, and copyright law and reoriented it toward the normative goal of creating incentives for innovation and production.[29] In a related shift, debates regarding the social good were often reframed around idealized notions of consumer freedom, to the point that entire swaths of social life—including educational policies, rights of association, and even voting—were often discussed in terms of individual consumption preferences.[30]

In public law fields, meanwhile, courts insulated various structural inequalities from legal challenge under the Fourteenth Amendment, limiting the extent to which constitutional law could even take account of economic matters.[31] For example, the Supreme Court refused to recognize impoverished individuals as a suspect class in the context of education funding or housing policy.[32] The division of tax revenue between cities and suburbs, zoning decisions that lead to racial segregation, and many other sets of social policies were therefore left to the will of local majorities and placed beyond constitutional scrutiny. In a later set of developments, welfare benefits were ratcheted back and linked to work eligibility, so workers had to get a greater share of essential resources from labor markets.[33] Restricting nonworkers' access to social insurance and welfare effectively imposed greater market discipline on workers, especially female workers and Black workers and other workers of color.

Labor law sits at the intersection of public and private law, and accordingly it has been influenced by both sets of developments. Law and economics scholars argued from the beginning that fundamental worker protections, including collective bargaining and wage/hour laws, in fact interfere with market ordering, competition, and/or individual choices, and therefore reduce aggregate welfare.[34] For a time, this approach to the design of labor market institutions influenced self-identified liberal legal academics, who often suggested that labor markets should be organized to optimize employment levels and looked skeptically at minimum wage and related regulations.[35] Within collective bargaining doctrine, the influence of neoliberalism was most apparent in shifts toward viewing union membership as a matter of individual choice and union organizing as a collective purchase of services.[36] However, neoliberalism was never as powerful among labor law *scholars*, due in part to their tradition of drawing from old institutional economics and political economics.

Meanwhile, employment discrimination doctrine evolved in ways that reflect the general trends in public law noted just above.[37] Starting in the 1970s, and continuing to today, courts increasingly viewed discrimination as a matter of individual animus rather than a structural feature of the labor market.[38] Doctrine now largely endeavors to provide a sort of pure procedural justice: employers must treat workers equally based on their aptitudes, remaining blind to protected traits. But in the absence of policies that correct for background inequalities that correlate with those traits—including poverty and housing and educational inequality for racial minorities, and disproportionate care burdens for women—employment discrimination doctrine has only a limited capacity to ensure real equal opportunity. Moreover, as the legal scholar Ahmed White has argued, our lack of industrial policy made it nearly impossible to ensure racial equity in industrial employment after Title VII. Nascent deindustrialization occurred at the same time as efforts to desegregate industrial workplaces, but Title VII protected incumbent workers' seniority, which meant that Black workers never had equal access to manufacturing jobs.[39] Later, as the state retreated from addressing structural injustices, the racial wage gap expanded and progress in remedying patterns of workplace discrimination stalled.[40] Neoliberalism and the service transition therefore left us with more pronounced and mutually reinforcing race and class divisions, and with fewer public tools to address those inequalities.

2.2 Foundational Shifts in Labor Law

As discussed in section 2.1, workplace neoliberalism realigned authority among workers, companies, and the state. Rather than basic terms of employment being set by collective bargaining, they were set by individual negotiations against a backdrop of statutory protections. Past labor law scholars have explored the differences between this "individual rights" regime and the industrial pluralist regime of the postwar era.[41] The discussions in this section and section 2.3 draw on that work, while situating this transition in the broader shift to neoliberalism.[42] This section shows how companies subjected workers to greater market discipline by eroding unions' strength and coverage and, where possible, eliminating employment relationships entirely. Section 2.3 shows how companies expanded and encased their property rights, including their rights in workplace technology and data. These two legal shifts were closely linked, both conceptually and operationally. Where an employer enjoys broad powers to set employment terms by fiat, and to hire and fire workers at will, that employer is also well positioned to reshape production as it likes, including through technological means (since workers who object can be fired).

Deunionization and the individualization of employment relationships The first foundational legal shift under workplace neoliberalism involved the long-running decline of private-sector unionization and collective bargaining.[43] As noted in sections 1.5 and 2.1, companies never stopped resisting union power, even in the postwar heyday of collective bargaining. In their ongoing legal battles with unions and workers, companies pressed their own interpretations of the NLRA and its limits, frequently emphasizing their residual common law rights. Over decades, those efforts led to broad shifts in labor law. But the seeds of the transformation lay in core aspects of labor law as it emerged in the New Deal.

For example, as noted in chapter 1, the New Deal labor regime instantiated the racial and gendered political economy of the 1930s, and therefore excluded many workers from protection. That labor law regime also sharply limited workers' rights to strike, which made it harder for workers to sustain their associational power in the postwar era and to rebuild it after the crisis of the 1970s. To paraphrase a common-sense understanding shared by US labor lawyers, strikes are legal in this country unless and until they are effective. Early in the NLRA's history, companies argued—and the Board, the courts, or both agreed—that various strikes were "unprotected" in labor law parlance, meaning that employers could lawfully discipline or even fire employees for engaging in them. Those include slow-down strikes, sit-down strikes, and intermittent strikes, all of which were quite effective weapons in labor's arsenal.[44] Companies may also "permanently replace" workers who are striking to achieve an economic goal, which in many cases is tantamount to being fired.[45] While employers have had that right since 1939, they exercised it more often and more aggressively beginning in the 1980s.[46] The 1947 Taft-Hartley Act also prohibited unions from engaging in most "secondary boycotts," or strikes and pickets through which workers put pressure on a company other than their immediate employer.[47] Exploiting that restriction, firms such as McDonald's have sought to immunize themselves against labor unrest by organizing their operations through a franchising model, since our labor law often treats franchisors and franchisees as independent enterprises.[48] Line-level McDonald's workers then have few if any rights vis-a-vis McDonald's corporate, which substantially limits their power. This issue is discussed in more detail in chapter 5. Finally, companies established broad rights to campaign against unionization soon after the war, as discussed in more detail in chapter 4.[49]

Another longstanding problem that has become especially acute lately is that our labor law favors localized or enterprise-level bargaining. This is reflected in several foundational rules. The NLRA itself provides that the "unit appropriate for the purposes of collective bargaining shall be the employer unit, craft unit, plant unit, or subdivision thereof," which has discouraged multiemployer bargaining structures.[50] That emphasis is consistent with our labor law's rules of majority rule and exclusive representation. Workers usually have no rights to bargain collectively under our law unless and until they unionize with a majority vote in an NLRB-supervised election, or until an employer voluntarily recognizes a union that has majority support.[51] A resulting collective bargaining agreement will then apply to all workers in the bargaining unit but only to them, not to other workers in the industry. Similarly, even if workers have organized at a majority (or all) of a company's existing locations, the company retains the background right to operate new locations or new lines of business on a nonunion basis.[52]

These doctrines, together with employers' rights to resist organizing, have made it nearly impossible for workers to build unions at many major employers today, as discussed in more detail in chapter 4. Each of these doctrines also contrasts with rules and practices in European systems where postwar class settlements were more stable. In many such systems, collective bargaining is centralized rather than fragmented,[53] and workers enjoy some collective representation as a matter of right though institutions other than unions.[54] Cross-national evidence shows a strong correlation among bargaining centralization, wage equality, and the generosity of welfare states.[55] Chapter 6 discusses the possibility of building more centralized bargaining structures in the US today.

For now, the key point is that companies have exercised their various rights and powers to reorder work relations around individual rather than collective agreements. The change can be visualized by placing employment contracting practices on a continuum running from highly centralized on the left to highly individualized on the right. The left pole of that continuum would be occupied by some European peak bargaining systems, in which unions and companies set standards at the national level. Moving to the right, the next grouping would involve coordinated bargaining between unions and multiple companies in the same sector. In our own history, the "pattern bargaining" strategy of the United Auto Workers (UAW) is perhaps the canonical example. For decades, the union has negotiated an agreement with one of the Big Three automakers—General Motors (GM), Ford, and Chrysler—and then pushed the other two to match terms.[56] The

UAW and other unions built such arrangements in the postwar period, despite the legal impediments to doing so, by building substantial political-economic power at key moments. But due both to institutional drift and companies' ongoing resistance, collective bargaining in the US over time has become increasingly localized, as well as increasingly rare. The current unionized sector, therefore, sits a step or two to the right of pattern bargaining. Workers there have union protections but often bargain only at the workplace or enterprise level.

The right side of this continuum reflects reality for most workers today. Nonunionized workers in the US have no rights of collective representation at all; instead, they bargain individually with their employers. The vast majority of private-sector workers today are not unionized, including low-wage workers in manufacturing, retail, health care, logistics, and food services. Finally, the right pole of the continuum is occupied by individual workers who do not even have a legal employment relationship with the company or companies for whom they work. As discussed later in this section, that group includes many gig economy workers, workers for franchised fast-food companies and hotels, janitors, and temporary workers. The overall trend in the US over the last few decades has therefore been progressive individualization of employment: decentralization of bargaining, deunionization, and then elimination of the employment relation itself. As we move from left to right on this continuum, workers have less and less power to take wages out of competition, or even to restrict the labor supply, and are therefore subject to greater and greater market discipline.

To be clear, this individualization of employment has coincided with a substantial expansion of statutory workplace protections. In the 1960s and 1970s, for example, Congress passed several pieces of landmark legislation to protect individual workers' rights, including Title VII of the Civil Rights Act of 1964, the Occupational Safety and Health Act of 1970 (OSHA), and the Employee Retirement Income Security Act of 1974.[57] Later on, Congress and state legislatures passed numerous privacy protections starting in the 1980s,[58] and Congress extended employment discrimination protections to individuals with disabilities in 1990.[59] Many states and localities have also raised their minimum wages recently.[60] Those statutes and others provide essential protections against many forms of workplace mistreatment and subordination. However, effectuating such rights is a perpetual challenge for less privileged workers. Unions had once ensured that employers complied with such laws through collective action as well as litigation. In unions' absence, such protections can be chronically underenforced.[61] Moreover, the workers at the right pole of the continuum are frequently ineligible even for those meager protections, since they are not legally classified as employees. In that sense, the collapse of unions and the individualization of employment contracting have stripped workers of many basic legal entitlements.

The contractualization of employment   A second major development of the last few decades has been the reshaping of employment contracts around notions of liberty and consent reminiscent of the pre–New Deal era. This trend carries forward industrial pluralism's focus on private ordering. However, under workplace neoliberalism, the contracting parties on the employee side are individual workers rather than workers' organizations. Workers' consent to particular terms and conditions of employment then renders those terms and conditions legally binding, even if workers had little real bargaining power. Workplace neoliberalism therefore discards the idea that workers need associational power to actually advance their interests, as well as the notion that employers' workplace authority is most legitimate when based on collective bargaining processes.

The influence of this view of contract on employment law is most apparent in the resurgent importance of the employment-at-will doctrine. Under that rule, an employer "may dismiss their employees . . . for good cause, for no cause, or even for cause morally wrong . . ." as long as doing so is not otherwise unlawful.[62] In practice, unless there is evidence of other wrongdoing, such as fraud or a statutory violation, the employment-at-will rule deters courts from second-guessing companies' decisions to terminate workers.[63] Under the rule an employee may also quit employment at any time and for any reason, with or without giving notice. There is nothing new about the at-will rule, which became dominant in the late nineteenth century[64] and was foundational to labor law prior to the New Deal. As the Supreme Court wrote in a canonical 1908 case, *Adair v. United States*, "the right of the employee to quit the service of the employer, for whatever reason, is the same as the right of the employer, for whatever reason, to dispense with the services of such employee. . . . In all such particulars, the employer and the employee have equality of right."[65] Practically, however, employment at will was less important under industrial pluralism since collective bargaining agreements typically provided that employees could be terminated only for "good cause," such as poor performance, violation of work rules, or absenteeism. Nonunion employers often adopted similar policies during the same period to avoid unionization.

In the 1980s, various state courts chipped away at the at-will rule. The cases arose in the broader political-economic context of deindustrialization and union decline, which left workers increasingly vulnerable. Terminated workers then claimed that their employers' promises of job security were contractually binding, and won a number of landmark cases.[66] Around the same time, state courts carved out another exception to employment at will that forbade employers from terminating workers for activities that implicate major public policies, such as a worker's performance of jury duty.[67] Yet except for Montana, no state reversed the at-will default.[68] What's more, the logic of contract and consent in such cases was easily deployed to *limit* workers' rights over time. Early cases reasoned in part that promises of employment security were binding because employees had the right to quit, and therefore their continued work bound the employer to its promise.[69] In some subsequent cases, companies argued—and courts agreed—that employees' continued work could constitute acceptance of revised employer policies that *eliminated* job security provisions.[70]

The logic of *Adair* itself has even made a comeback. In *Epic Systems Corporation v. Lewis*, a 2018 case considering the enforceability of agreements to arbitrate employment-related disputes, Supreme Court Justice Neil Gorsuch stated the question presented as follows: "Should employees and employers be allowed to agree that any disputes between them will be resolved through one-on-one arbitration?"[71] The issue, in this framing, is not whether an employer may require the employee, as a condition of employment, to sign such an agreement, taking into account the clear imbalance of bargaining power, nor the fact that arbitration may undermine enforcement of statutory employment rights. Rather, it is whether the employee should have the power to contract for such a term—as if the *employee* had demanded it.[72] Illustrating the importance of and malleability of such notions of consent, some other courts have held that employers can bind their employees to a duty to arbitrate workplace disputes by presenting an agreement one day and telling workers that they are bound by it unless they quit.[73]

The contractualization of employment is also apparent elsewhere in our collective bargaining laws. For example, in this era jurisprudence around collective bargaining and worker organizing efforts came to emphasize workers' preferences, often viewing their decision on whether to join a union or to organize as being similar to their decisions to purchase a good or service.[74] In his opinion in the 1992 *Lechmere, Inc., v. NLRB* case, holding that a company may exclude non-employee union organizers from a mall parking lot that is open to the public in almost all circumstances, Justice Clarence Thomas reasoned that the union had alternative means of getting in touch with workers, including advertising in local newspapers or putting up signs on public property abutting the lot. In that view, the organizing effort was like a marketing operation rather than an agonistic social process that has real value in a democracy.[75]

A similar emphasis on employee choice has informed the Supreme Court's recent jurisprudence around union dues and agency fees. In 2018's *Janus v. AFSCME*, the Court held that public employee unions cannot require represented workers to defray costs of representation. As in *Epic Systems*, the Court in *Janus* framed the issue around employee choice, stating that "[u]nder Illinois law, public employees are forced to subsidize a union, even if they choose not to join and strongly object to the positions the union takes in collective bargaining and related activities."[76] The logic is flawed because a majority of workers had *chosen* to negotiate an agency fee, and workers who objected had the right to seek another job. Indeed, the concept of employee choice in *Janus* is in serious tension with the concept in *Epic Systems*: in *Janus*, the Court disregarded the workers' past choices and present capacity to leave their jobs, while in *Epic Systems*, the Court viewed the fact that workers did not quit as indicating their assent.[77] Operationally, the cases nevertheless push in the same direction: they reorient employment around a vision of individualized contract and away from enabling "collective action as a means of checking employer power."[78]

The decline of employment The third foundational aspect of workplace neoliberalism is that in recent decades companies have increasingly been able to avoid labor law obligations entirely.[79] They have done so by exploiting the fact that our labor laws only grant protections to individuals who are legally classified as employees, and only give those employees rights against entities that are legally classified as their employers. Workers who are classified as independent contractors are not covered by those laws, and those who work for temporary labor agencies, subcontractors, or franchisees usually have rights only against their immediate employers—not against user firms or franchisors that contract with their employers, even if those other firms have more power to set their wages and working conditions. Chapter

5 discusses these issues in detail, but a brief summary here will be helpful in understanding what follows.

Independent contracting and subcontracting are not new. In fact, they were well established liability-blocking strategies in the early twentieth century.[80] As a result, the issue concerning which workers were covered by the key New Deal statutes—the NLRA, Fair Labor Standards Act (FLSA), and Social Security Act (SSA)—was litigated soon after those statutes' passage. In each case, the Supreme Court held that workers who provided some of their own tools and/or worked without much direct supervision—newspaper vendors in the case of the NLRA, a gang of specialized slaughterhouse workers under the FLSA, and coal loaders under the SSA—were employees rather than independent contractors. In so doing, the Court interpreted the statutory language purposively and broadly to protect vulnerable workers, and to encourage companies to directly employ workers who were essential to their enterprises.[81] In other words, by defining employment broadly, Congress and the Court at the time sought to encourage companies to internalize the costs of their operations and to deter subcontracting and other strategies that undermined the overall statutory schemes.

That expansive definition of employment was short-lived. Following employer pressure, Congress responded in Taft-Hartley by specifying that independent contractors were *not* covered under collective bargaining laws.[82] As a result, the NLRA and most other worker protective statutes today use the legal definition of "employment" from the common law of agency, which asks whether the putative employer controls the worker's performance.[83] That test was developed to determine whether a worker or the company he or she works for is responsible when a tort by the worker injures a third party, and it may have worked reasonably well for that purpose. But that test does not reflect the statutory purpose of employment regulations, which is to protect workers against social harms such as low wages, unsafe working conditions, and discrimination.[84] Thus, it is arguably too narrow per se. Moreover, that statutory definition is often too narrow in operation. This is in part because many work relationships do not fall neatly into classic categories of employment or independent contracting, and in part because the doctrine is confusing and highly malleable. Many courts and agencies use a multifactor test with ten or more factors to determine employment status, but the precise factors emphasized can vary from case to case and court to court.[85] This both leads to uncertainty and raises the costs of proving a violation, since workers seeking to prove that they are employees must develop an extensive factual record. The legal analysis of user firms' duties toward employees of subcontractors and franchisees is similar and is discussed in chapter 5.

Over the period of neoliberalism, companies have increasingly pressed on those ambiguities, avoiding labor law duties by classifying workers as independent contractors or by using subcontracting and franchising arrangements. These strategies have collectively come to be known as the "fissuring" of employment since they each place a legal gap between workers and the companies that utilize their work, much like the fissures that break through boulders over time.[86] Fissuring is devastating to workers' associational power. It places workers outside of a company's legal boundaries, making it difficult for them to make moral or legal claims on the company. Indeed, the Taft-Hartley ban on secondary boycotts made it *illegal* in most cases for unions to picket or strike companies other than the immediate employer.[87] Fissuring is also a *consequence* of unions' declining power, in the sense that well-organized workers could at times block fissuring efforts, even if they had few or no *legal* rights to do so.[88] As a result, for decades companies have had incentives to organize work relationships or new lines of business in ways that avoid employment duties entirely.[89] New surveillance technologies have also made fissuring more attractive to companies by enabling them to closely monitor far-flung networks of workers and suppliers. As chapter 5 shows, these various factors have led many of today's leading companies to employ far fewer workers than their postwar predecessors.

2.3 Encasement of Workplace Information

Over this same period, companies claimed broader and deeper property and property-like rights in workplace technology, in workplace data, and even in their employees' knowledge and know-how. These developments paralleled shifts in other areas of doctrine—including IP and trade secrets—that helped facilitate the tech giants' explosive growth and the extension of data-driven technologies across the economy.

Labor law and workplace technology As discussed in chapter 1, the growth of heavy industry and the factory system involved intense conflicts between craft workers and companies over the control of workplace technology and the labor process. Companies won that battle for the most part, but after the

New Deal, insurgent industrial unions sought to put the issue back into contention. For example, soon after World War II, the UAW struck GM for nearly four months, demanding both higher wages and a freeze in consumer prices.[90] This was part of UAW President Walter Reuther's agenda to give workers a greater voice in production planning and economic management generally. GM resisted furiously, and the UAW lost. Two years later, Congress passed Taft-Hartley, restricting unions' capacity to organize and strike in myriad ways. After that point, unions tended to focus on winning a share of productivity gains rather than a voice in production strategies themselves.

As a matter of practice, that settlement was formalized in the so-called Treaty of Detroit, the landmark 1950 UAW-GM contract in which GM "regained control over one of the crucial management functions ... long-range scheduling of production, model changes, and tool and plant investment," in exchange for guaranteed wage growth over time and generous private benefits.[91] The Supreme Court later ratified the settlement, in a sense. In a famous 1964 concurrence, Justice Potter Stewart wrote that employers have no duty to bargain over issues of company strategy and related matters at the "core of entrepreneurial control," including the decision "to invest in labor-saving machinery."[92] The full Court mostly adopted Stewart's reasoning in 1981, amid the Reagan-era deindustrialization wave, holding that employers have a duty to bargain over decisions to adopt technologies that would displace workers only "if the benefit, for labor-management relations and the collective-bargaining process, outweighs the burden placed on the conduct of the business."[93] That standard counts the employer's interests on both sides of the balance, which may explain why there is little case law addressing the duty to bargain over labor-displacing innovations.[94]

Unionized workers nevertheless retained important legal rights and extralegal sources of power around workplace technology. Legally, employers must bargain over the *effects* of technological changes that displace workers.[95] In practice, that mostly means that the employer must meet and confer with the workers' union in good faith.[96] But well-organized unions can often achieve *some* voice in technological change through extralegal means.[97] Employers that wish to avoid shop-floor unrest (regardless of its legality) then have incentives to engage with unionized workers before rendering jobs redundant through technology, or even before adopting new machinery that required retraining. As unions lost ground within firms and the broader political economy, however, workers were less able to protect themselves through such means.

A different set of rules apply to technological changes that enhance employers' surveillance capacities or that alter disciplinary practices. In the unionized context, since employers have a duty to bargain over wages, hours, benefits, and disciplinary policies, they must bargain with unions *before* adopting such technologies.[98] Even in a nonunion workplace, workers may be protected against employer discipline if they protest a new technology that would lead to a faster pace of work.[99] In one recent case, an NLRB administrative law judge held that a nonunion teacher could not be disciplined over her complaints about a higher workload resulting from the school district's request that teachers use a new technological platform.[100] Such cases are nevertheless rare, again due to the general decline of unions and workers' associational power. As a result, for most workers, the key protections against harms resulting from workplace surveillance arise under workplace privacy laws.

Employee privacy The broad and general expansion of employers' powers over enterprises and workers discussed previously has also influenced the development of workplace privacy laws. There have been two developments in this area that at first glance push in opposite directions. Courts and legislatures have established various privacy protections that apply in discrete circumstances, at the same time that they have tolerated (or even facilitated) significant increases in employer surveillance and searches. This subsection gives a brief overview of privacy as a concept and of those developments. Chapter 4 discusses these issues in more detail.

"Privacy" is a deeply complex and contested idea, in part because privacy law is called on to protect numerous distinct interests, and in part because a wide array of statutes and common law doctrines affect privacy.[101] As other scholars have argued, the social or normative value of privacy cannot be understood simply in terms of individual liberty or control, or in terms of one's ability to keep information secret or inaccessible from another person or entity. Rather, "privacy law" here denotes a variety of rule complexes that govern information flows and protect interests in individual dignity and autonomy, as well as some forms of collective autonomy.[102] As chapter 4 will discuss, privacy protections in that sense are essential for workers to build associational power. Reflecting that need, our labor law tries to carve out space for workers to speak with one another about common workplace concerns, and to meet and plan collective action, without their employers' knowledge. As chapter 4 also indicates, novel information technologies have nearly eviscerated those protections by vastly expanding companies' surveillance capacities.

The most important generally applicable workplace privacy protection is the tort of intrusion upon seclusion,[103] under which employers may be liable to workers for searches that harm their dignity or lead to humiliation.[104] Courts have held employers liable under that tort when they placed video cameras in a changing room, for example, or searched an employee's home or hotel room.[105] That tort has only a limited impact on contemporary data practices, however, for a few reasons. It was designed to address invasions of individuals' living quarters or persons, so courts have held that private-sector employers may often search employees' desks, personal effects, or even their automobiles without individualized suspicion of wrongdoing.[106] The bar for recovery is also high: to win, a plaintiff must show that the invasion at issue was "highly offensive to a reasonable person."[107] Moreover, the *reasonableness* of an intrusion is determined in part by reference to common practice. As a result, when many companies adopt new surveillance techniques in significant numbers and require workers to accept them or quit, that wide-scale adoption itself can limit those companies' possible liability.[108]

As employers have implemented new monitoring devices across the economy, the law has mostly ratified their actions. For example, in a public-sector case, where employee privacy rights are somewhat broader, a federal court held that a public employer could utilize video surveillance in public areas of the workplace, reasoning that workers in that context had no reasonable expectation of privacy.[109] As a result of these doctrines, and of the general expansion of employer property rights discussed earlier, there are in reality few legal restrictions on employers' rights to monitor employees while they are performing work tasks. It is worth reiterating that, practically speaking, employers did not always have that power: in the early industrial era, workers often acted collectively to prevent such surveillance, as discussed in chapter 1.

In the workplace context, privacy also indicates a very different set of interests in employee *autonomy*, or the freedom to engage in personal, political, and expressive conduct.[110] A key dividing line here is between the workplace and other areas. While employers have now established their rights to surveil workers in the workplace in many circumstances, their monitoring of

The Legal Construction of Workplace Neoliberalism 53

workers' off-duty conduct is in flux. Only a few states have adopted legislation or constitutional provisions protecting workers against discipline for off-duty activities,[111] and a number of state courts have held that employers may terminate workers for off-duty political or personal conduct, with or without a good reason, under the employment-at-will doctrine.[112] There is also quantitative evidence that employers frequently press employees to take political action supporting their favored candidates or issues.[113] Companies' ability to track employees' off-duty conduct, as well as to use the data gleaned from that tracking to reshape labor practices, has been substantially augmented by new technologies, as discussed in chapter 4.

Companies' surveillance and data-gathering powers are mitigated somewhat by legislative prohibitions on specific acts that have triggered public concern.[114] One wave of legislation developed around drug testing in the 1980s, and subsequent waves covered health and genetic information,[115] biometric information,[116] and, more recently, privacy in electronic communications.[117] Those laws provide important protections but still permit companies to surveil workers right up to the line of prohibition. California recently passed the California Consumer Privacy Act (CCPA), the first omnibus data privacy regulation in the US.[118] However, like most other privacy regulations in the US, the CCPA does not treat privacy as a fundamental right; rather, it presumes that companies may collect and use data as they wish unless those actions are prohibited by specific legal rules.[119] That approach contrasts with the dominant approach in Europe. The European General Data Protection Regulation (GDPR), for example, treats data protection as a fundamental right and prohibits data collection and processing unless the gathering and processing are legally justified.[120]

Moreover, many privacy statutes in the US effectively or explicitly exempt employers from coverage. The Federal Stored Communications Act, for example, prevents employers from accessing workers' personal email accounts in most cases,[121] but it does not apply to employer-provided email accounts.[122] In other cases, workplace privacy statutes permit employer monitoring or privacy invasions, so long as workers consent. This is the approach that various states have taken to employer monitoring of telephone or electronic communications.[123] Employers often have little problem obtaining such consent, however, from at-will employees. The result, as detailed in chapters 3–5, is extensive and expanding worker surveillance, especially in low-wage sectors.

Enclosure of employee knowledge and know-how Finally, employers have increasingly claimed property-like rights in employee knowledge and know-how. Those efforts parallel other developments under neoliberalism through which companies have used IP doctrines and contracts to affect "the propertization (or enclosure) of intangible resources."[124] This process also has been going on for decades, with the trend over time clearly toward expansion of IP protections.[125] For example, the Supreme Court and Congress have classified more and more goods as proper subject matter for patents (with some important exceptions, such as for data), and have progressively extended the temporal length of protections under copyright laws, while also creating new property rights in subsidiary works.[126] As corporate-held IP is developed by employees in most cases, this entire process involves companies' extracting and legally encasing their workers' knowledge. Indeed, as Catherine Fisk has shown, IP doctrine itself was transformed in the late nineteenth and early twentieth centuries—the era of Taylorism, as discussed in chapter 1—to grant employers legal title in their employees' writings and inventions.[127]

The standard justification for those rule complexes has also shifted over time: whereas in earlier eras legal actors tended to emphasize "the public benefits to be gained from underwriting progress in science and learning," today they more often emphasize "incentives to production."[128] That again reflects the influence of neoliberal ideas about the role of law in creating and sustaining market orders. Similarly, legal actors have increasingly argued that the benefits of "innovation" justify various forms of regulatory avoidance or forbearance with regard to networked information technologies.[129] This contrasts with the more precautionary approach in food and drug regulation, under which agencies balance the potential benefits of innovation against the risks of unsafe drugs or food additives, and again reflects broader trends under neoliberalism toward a focus on market ordering.

Data occupies an ambiguous or even contradictory space in IP law and some other bodies of law. On the one hand, lawmakers have consistently held that data itself cannot be owned under IP law.[130] For example, while the act of compiling a database can lead to a copyright in the database,[131] the Copyright Act specifies that the data itself cannot be the subject of a copyright. Similarly, algorithms themselves cannot be patented under Supreme Court doctrine because they are abstract ideas or mathematical formulas rather than devices.[132] On the other hand, consumer-facing companies have enclosed user data through a variety of methods. They often deploy contract doctrine and user agreements to claim and maintain exclusive property-like rights over data, including the rights to sell or process that data in the future with few restrictions.[133] Companies have also enclosed data through expanded trade secrets protections, in a development that cuts across the consumer and employment fields. Current doctrine in most states, and under the federal Defend Trade Secrets Act, enables a company to claim property-like protections for information that has value due to its secrecy, and that the company has taken reasonable steps to keep confidential.[134] Employers have even claimed trade secrets protection in data flows generated from hiring practices.[135] Moreover, once a company asserts that certain information is a trade secret, courts will typically not compel its disclosure without a fight that public interest litigants may be unable to wage.[136]

Companies have frequently justified those efforts to the public, meanwhile, by casting user data as what Julie Cohen calls a "bio-political public domain"—that is, a pool of resources that are just there for the taking, much like the public domain in IP law.[137] This helps explain the common refrain in public-facing discussions of big data and tech that data is "the new oil"—both a natural substance and the most important economic resource of the day.[138] The analogy is misleading, as data is a human creation through and through, but it helps to justify and legitimate data collection and collation efforts.

In the workplace, meanwhile, companies have expanded the legal tools at their disposal to claim property-like rights in workers' knowledge and know-how. For example, companies may require employees who develop firm-specific knowledge to agree not to work for a competitor for some period of time after leaving their current jobs.[139] Historically, courts strongly disfavored such noncompete agreements because they may prevent workers from leaving an undesirable employment relationship, and could therefore undermine one of the key rationales for employment at will. The modern trend, reflecting courts' deference to the terms of employment contracts, has been to hold employees to the terms of noncompetes so long as they are reasonable in terms of duration, covered work, and geographic scope.[140] In some cases, courts have even held that employees were bound to a covenant because they continued to work after their employer presented it to them.[141] In states where covenants are not enforceable, employers have at times achieved similar goals through nonsolicitation and nondealing clauses in employment contracts, which prohibit past employees from soliciting or doing business with clients of the company.[142] The net effect of such efforts is that companies are claiming extensive rights over workers' knowledge or "cognitive property."[143] As we'll see in subsequent chapters, at times companies can even reverse-engineer that knowledge through advanced forms of data analytics, and then lease it back to workers.[144]

Conclusion: Workplace Legality and Employer Power

Under industrial pluralism, employment was jointly constituted by unions and management, at least in theory. Now employment is constituted largely by contract, and companies have broader property rights in the workplace and in workplace technology and data. To be sure, companies' authority over workers is far from absolute. But institutions and norms of workplace democracy have clearly diminished in power and importance. To return to an argument developed in chapter 1, this new legal regime did not emerge in a political-economic vacuum, nor did it emerge randomly. Rather, it came about as companies pressed for a new operating environment amid the crisis of the postwar order and the secular economic shifts of deindustrialization and the service transition. Through those efforts companies established greater freedom of action vis-à-vis workers and the state: freedoms to hire and fire at will, to establish and enforce workplace rules without workers' involvement, to establish lines of production that deny workers basic employment protections, to gather data on workplace processes and workers themselves, and to develop new tools from that data that become their property.

Contemporary labor law thus helped birth today's working class, all while denying that a working *class* still exists. The notion that workers are not just objects of state protection, but also part of a collective agent that deserves lawmaking authority, has been largely lost. So has a sense that workers deserve protection simply by virtue of their position in the division of labor. It is surely no accident that these shifts occurred at the very historical moment when the working class became less white and less male. Along with other legal changes and the maturation of networked information technologies, these shifts in our labor law helped to establish a new accumulation regime, in which high-voltage profits are in high-end services and high tech, but employment is concentrated in lower-end services. As the next three chapters explore, under that accumulation regime major service sector employers have increasingly used data-driven technologies to suppress workers' associational power.

3   Inductive Knowledge and Digital Taylorism

Introduction

Amazon's semiautomated warehouses are modern marvels, demonstrating both the emerging capacities and the limits of robotics and artificial intelligence (AI). In classic warehouses, goods are kept on rows of shelves, and workers roam among those shelves on foot or in a vehicle to grab goods and prepare them for shipping. For a time, Amazon sought to develop warehouse robots to directly replace such human workers, but that turned out to be impossible due to the limits of robotic hands and of humanoid robots generally.[1] So the company redesigned its warehouses and labor practices around robots' actual capabilities. Amazon worked with Kiva, a robotics firm that it later purchased, to develop robots that carry shelves to two groups of workers. One set, known as "stowers," place goods in numerically coded bins on those shelves. Amazon then uses video cameras trained on stowers' workstations, together with image recognition algorithms, to document where particular goods were placed. Kiva robots then move the shelves back to storage until needed. When an order arrives, a robot will bring the shelf to one of the second set of workers, known as "pickers," who locate ordered items on shelves, grab them, and put them into plastic bins.[2]

The Kiva robots' movement of shelves is uncanny, and even beautiful in a way. The robots and shelves are physically separated from workers by reinforced chain-link fence. This is necessary to minimize dangers, since the robots have limited abilities to sense their environment. They move quickly and constantly, guided by barcodes on the floor, often driving right toward one another and then pivoting at the last moment and moving ninety degrees in another direction. Their movements are directed and optimized by suites of algorithms that ascertain where each robot is and where it needs to go, with the overarching goal of minimizing the time to fill orders.[3] As a result, a sort of alien intelligence is immanent here. The robots function as a team or network, but each is executing instructions sent to it from a coordination node and does not consider what other robots are doing. In that sense, the robots fulfill a task once performed by humans, but in a completely new manner, and while moving and relating to each other in ways that humans never would. As this chapter explains in detail, the Kiva robots exemplify how a great deal of automation occurs today. Today's robots are rarely anthropomorphic and do not perform tasks in the same way that humans previously did. Meanwhile, their installation often leads to increased consumer demand (and therefore labor demand), and therefore does not threaten massive worker displacement.

Yet there is a dark side to this story: many human workers in such warehouses are little more than production inputs, and their work lives are anything but sublime. A picker's entire job involves grabbing goods off of shelves as quickly as possible and placing them in bins for further processing. Each individual picker works in a phone booth-sized area, where they may be unable to make eye contact with others and where they are constantly monitored by video cameras and image-recognition algorithms.[4] A large digital stopwatch in front of each picker shows how long she or he is taking to perform each task, enforcing time discipline down to the second. Once a picker has filled a bin with goods, it is sent via a network of automated conveyor belts to a third group of workers known as "packers." They spend just fifteen seconds on each order, sealing boxes with tape that is automatically dispensed at the right length and affixing a barcode to the package. The boxes then move to a sorting station, where another machine scans that barcode, determines which shipping method or company to use based on its destination and other data, and sorts the packages accordingly. Many packages are later delivered by contractors whose workers are subject to similarly pervasive surveillance and time discipline.[5]

While warehouse jobs pay relatively well—Amazon raised starting wages to $15 in 2018 following public pressure and nascent worker organizing efforts, and to $18 in 2021[6]—they are physically and mentally very demanding. As a *New York Times* reporter observed, "Unlike pickers in manual warehouses," who walk among shelves to find goods, "the pickers [at a semiautomated warehouse] have almost no relief from plucking goods off shelves, other than their breaks."[7] Since each job is exceptionally repetitive and involves virtually no teamwork, workers can be trained quickly to act as stowers, pickers, or packers. Before COVID, due to spikes and valleys in order volume, Amazon hired and trained more workers than it needed at any given time and developed a scheduling system to blast out requests for workers to take or give up shifts at all hours of the day. While many workers have a regular schedule, they also monitor shift requests so they can put in extra hours or get time off.[8] Vending machines just off the warehouse floor supply ear protection, gloves, and the Advil that many workers take regularly to alleviate inflammation from repetitive stress on joints or acute injuries from lifting heavier items. When workers do not perform rapidly enough, or they take a bathroom break without preclearance, algorithmic monitoring systems may report as much to managers, sometimes even recommending termination.[9] As noted in this book's introduction, those sorts of practices were among the issues that motivated Amazon workers in Staten Island to unionize.

Amazon's efforts to seamlessly integrate robotics, AI, pervasive surveillance, and deskilled human labor exemplify an overall sociotechnical system that this book calls "digital Taylorism."[10] The reference is to early-twentieth century Taylorism, a system of scientific management that established managerial control over the labor process. Like its forebear, digital Taylorism involves intertwined processes of automation and intensified surveillance. Where possible, companies use algorithms and robots to perform tasks once performed by line-level workers—though typically not in the anthropomorphic manner envisioned by Hollywood writers. Rather, companies aim to break jobs "into discrete, rationalized, low-skill tasks," some of which are automated and others that can be performed by workers with little specialized training.[11] Then, regardless of which sorts of tasks workers are performing, companies use new data-processing mechanisms to assign tasks, to schedule and to oversee workers, and to discipline them. Following emerging usage, the book calls that latter set of practices "algorithmic management."[12]

As the discussion in this chapter also shows, these processes fuel one another: through intensive surveillance and algorithmic management, companies can often extract, formalize, and encase employees' knowledge and know-how, sometimes even claiming intellectual property (IP) rights in that expertise. These new capabilities in turn reinforce patterns toward market concentration by leading firms, including in low-wage sectors, which chapter 5 discusses in more detail. Like its forebear, then, digital Taylorism aspires to create and enforce a division of labor in which managerial authority is centralized, while line-level workers are hired to perform tasks that require uniquely human skills such as fine motor control and situational judgment. Also like its forebear, digital Taylorism makes it much harder for workers to organize and therefore helps keep labor costs down. Indeed, that is part of its attraction to companies.

Yet digital Taylorism differs from its namesake in important respects, which this chapter also discusses. With new surveillance and data-processing devices, companies are able to oversee workers' performance in vastly more detail than before. Even when thousands of workers labor side by side, they stand at the end of surveillance spokes that extend out from a corporate nerve center. Companies are also using data-processing tools in substantively new ways, which this chapter also explores. In particular, AI today frequently operates by drawing inferences from very large data sets, spotting patterns that humans never could. This leads to what the chapter calls "inductive" knowledge, which is different in kind both from the highly formal productive knowledge sought by classical Taylorism and from the tacit or embodied knowledge that characterized craft production. These distinctions among inductive, formal, and tacit knowledge illustrate both the promise and limits of contemporary automation efforts—and how companies are using technology to reshape class relations.

This chapter says less about law than the others, in part because companies' authority to take such steps is so well established today that it no longer gets litigated. Labor law, as it evolved under neoliberalism, nevertheless operates constantly in the background. The recent expansion of employers' property rights has given them near-plenary legal authority to install monitoring devices and reshape workplace practices around them. The contractualization of employment has made it easier to terminate workers for protesting those efforts or otherwise challenging managerial authority. A helpful way to think about the role of labor law here is that it establishes a set of *background* entitlements that are so powerful that companies can often use them to erode *foreground* obligations. Digital Taylorism, therefore, puts pressure on workers' statutory labor rights, especially under wage and hour laws and collective bargaining laws.[13] The following two chapters build on this account and discuss legal issues in more detail, in part because the legal issues they address—discrimination protections, privacy rights outside the workplace, workers' rights of association, and the legal definition of employment—are more in flux.

Section 3.1 discusses the three forms of knowledge in production and how each one is a subject of class-based politics. Section 3.2 then summarizes the promise and limits of contemporary automation efforts. Section 3.3 addresses algorithmic management, showing how major companies today combine it with task automation as interlocking and complementary strategies.

3.1 The Rise of Inductive Knowledge

As discussed in chapter 1, companies can use new workplace technologies for two quite different ends: to enhance labor productivity (i.e., to enable workers to generate more output per unit of input) and to augment their power over workers and therefore limit labor costs. As also noted in chapter 1, control over workplace information has long been an important form of workplace power and a subject of pitched battles between workers and companies. For some time now, new information and communications technologies have been deepening and sharpening companies' capacity to keep tabs on what happens in the workplace and its contemporary equivalents, like the delivery driver's vehicle or the client's or the worker's home. More recently, those technologies have begun to generate new ways of seeking and knowing the world, which companies are integrating at scale into management processes. This section discusses the three forms of knowledge involved in production planning and execution today—formal, tacit, and inductive—and how companies and workers deploy or protect each to advance their interests.

Formal versus tacit knowledge Classical Taylorism and its limits were defined by the separation of conception and action. This reflected an important distinction between two sorts of knowledge, both of which have always been important to modern production. The first is what this book calls "formal" knowledge. It is highly abstract and ordered, ideally susceptible to expression in mathematical equations or detailed engineering specifications. Formal knowledge can be described and transmitted with great specificity. But it also envisions the world of production and society from the top down. The second form is "tacit" knowledge. This is perhaps best captured by Michael Polanyi's observation that "[w]e know more than we can tell."[14]

Our tacit knowledge of how the world operates and how we operate within it enables us to perform many physical day-to-day tasks—walking, cracking an egg, and so on—that we could not possibly explain or codify. This is also the realm of social norms and customs, body language, and the way that a slight change in tone of voice can signal a great deal. The sort of "situation sense" developed over time by craft workers and experts involves a combination of formal and tacit knowledge. When an experienced lawyer confronts a new legal problem and has a rough sense of how it will play out, or when a doctor examines a patient and has an intuition about what is wrong, the lawyer and doctor are drawing on both forms of knowledge.

The relationship between formal and tacit knowledge poses fascinating philosophical and scientific questions, which are directly relevant to issues of automation and the future of work. For example, in some understandings of cognition, higher-level reasoning faculties—formal knowledge— are actually dependent on and inseparable from our embodied existence in the world.[15] The tension between those forms of knowledge also helps to illustrate some challenges of classic Taylorism and automation. In essence, machines have long been very good at doing the same thing again and again in the same way. In that sense, factory machinery basically encodes formal knowledge. Humans, meanwhile, are very good at exercising situational and social judgment, performing fine motor actions, and adapting tools to new circumstances, all of which require tacit knowledge.[16] Historically, Taylorism sought to formalize some of workers' tacit knowledge so that managers could exert control over production. But there were always limits to that process, which reflected the limits of formal knowledge itself. James C. Scott, for example, argues that many social disasters of the nineteenth and twentieth centuries resulted from rulers' "high modernism," or their extreme faith in the ability of technical rationality to reorder human affairs.[17] Collective farms, tree plantations, massive modernist public housing projects, and many other efforts failed spectacularly, Scott argues, due to their disregard of citizens' social intelligence and embedded tacit knowledge. One of Scott's go-to examples is the "work-to-rule" strike, in which workers follow engineers' or managers' commands to the letter rather than using all the workarounds and flexible judgments that characterize actual social processes—and thereby bring a factory or office to a standstill.[18]

Inductive knowledge   Today, there is a third emergent form of knowledge—referred to here as "inductive" knowledge—which has developed iteratively and become more important as new data-gathering and processing devices have proliferated across the lifeworld.[19] Those include cellular phones, internet-connected computers, and all manner of digital devices, including video cameras, payment processing systems, and networked appliances. Many or most of those devices generate data about users' activities and whereabouts, which is then collected and analyzed by tech companies of all stripes. As other scholars have illustrated, companies across the consumer space have sought to claim property-like rights in such data, to analyze and utilize that data to discern customers' preferences and behavior, and then over time to *shape* customer demand and other facets of social behavior.[20] For example, companies have often sought not just to gather and hold extensive user data, but also to aggregate it with data from other sources and then to draw various inferences about individuals even when the underlying data sets are spotty or anonymized.[21] An entire industry of data brokers has arisen to gather, clean up, and process such data,[22] and to sort consumers into statistically based categories like "Affluent Baby Boomer" or "Rural Everlasting," in order to market to them.[23] Chapter 4 discusses data-aggregation efforts in more detail, insofar as they intersect with contested questions of employee privacy, equal opportunity, and worker self-organization.

A related form of data analytics builds on data aggregation and statistical analysis, essentially taking it to scale and generating new ways of seeing and knowing the world. It is best reflected in the subfield of AI known as "machine learning," which differs substantially from earlier efforts to develop AI. For some time, computer scientists sought to develop AI through encoded formal knowledge, developing rules that would guide algorithms through performing certain tasks. That approach worked for tasks such as playing chess but then stalled, due in part to the enormous complexity of many fields of human endeavor.[24] For example, efforts to develop translation programs by encoding grammatical rules in a formal "if-then" format ultimately failed. Human language is too complicated, too nuanced, too situationally specific to be captured that way. As a result, researchers were constantly plugging holes in their algorithms through ad hoc patches, while struggling to obtain accurate outcomes.[25]

Machine learning works differently: it draws advanced statistical inferences from large data sets.[26] While the technique is not entirely new, several papers in the early 2010s demonstrated how machine learning could be used for purposes of image recognition in ways that had seemed impossible in the past.[27] A relatively simple machine learning algorithm can be "trained" to determine whether a particular picture is of a dog or a cat.[28] Programmers would train it by uploading thousands of pictures of dogs and cats, appropriately labeled as such—the so-called training data—into the machine. The machine would then develop statistical correlations between the pixels in images labeled "dog" or "cat" and the outcomes "dog" and "cat," and programmers would adjust the various algorithms' inferences until the overall system could recognize dogs and cats accurately. When the data sets are large enough, the results can be remarkably precise, and the applications are extensive. Banks and other financial institutions use machine learning to process loan applications and to assist in fraud prevention by spotting irregular activity.[29] Machine learning can help determine whether particular moles are cancerous and help interpret radiological scans.[30] Google has also used machine learning in its search responses and to develop language translation programs that are remarkably good.[31]

But while machine learning often replicates the *outcomes* of human judgments fairly well, it does not replicate our reasoning processes. Instead, its underlying logic can be idiosyncratic, even baffling. Google's development of a suite of algorithms to play the game Go helps to illustrate this point. Unlike chess, which has many rules, Go has very few—it simply involves placing white and black tiles on a surface. The number of possible moves over time is several orders of magnitude larger than chess, however, which made it impossible to hard-code a machine to play the game. For related reasons, there are defined national and regional styles of play, analogous to dialects, since individuals have typically learned how to play in particular communities. So Google enabled a machine called DeepMind to train itself to play Go after being given some basic parameters.[32] During one match, DeepMind made several moves that no human player would have made because they went against all conventional wisdom and did not match any known style of play. At times, these moves cost the machine in the short term but paid off in the end.[33] One observer said that watching the match was like watching "an alien civilisation inventing its own mathematics."[34] Amazon's warehouse robots evince a similar uncanny logic.

Machine learning and related techniques are therefore "inductive and atheoretical."[35] They reveal patterns in large data sets that humans could never see, and then they classify individuals or items within those data sets into either predefined or discovered groups.[36] In the hiring context—discussed in the next chapter—such techniques may provide clues to an applicant's "future health, future productivity, or likely tenure with an employer."[37] As scholars have noted in other contexts, a major use case of such technologies involves discerning whether individuals who share some observable characteristic (x) will also tend to share some unobservable characteristic (y). As Salome Viljoen has put it, "a basic purpose of data production as a commercial enterprise is to relate people to one another based on relevant shared population features."[38] In part for that reason, as also discussed in the next chapter, it is difficult to fully grasp the harms of such practices through individualized conceptions of privacy—the harms are more social by their nature, since they lead to individuals losing opportunities on the basis of membership in statistical categories.[39]

There are many use cases for inductive learning technologies in the workplace and labor markets, as discussed later in this chapter. But only rarely can they replace human workers—or even do tasks performed by human workers—on a one-to-one basis. Rather, companies tend to utilize formal and inductive knowledge in combination and to rely on human workers to supply tacit knowledge. Reflecting historical practice, moreover, companies use formal and inductive knowledge both to enhance productivity and to augment their power over workers. As a result, ultra-advanced technologies coexist with low-wage, demobilized labor across large segments of today's economy.

3.2 Automation and Its Limits

In the late 2010s, these developments in AI generated widespread fear—bordering on panic—that a looming automation wave would lead to massive unemployment or even economic collapse. Tech leaders didn't hesitate to stoke those fears by describing their products as near-magical. To take one of many examples, Sundar Pichai, the chief executive officer of Alphabet (parent company of Google) said in 2020 that AI is "more profound than fire or electricity."[40] Many major magazines ran cover stories on the supposed automation threat, with titles like "Welcoming Our New Robot

Overlords" and "Learning to Love Our Robot Co-workers."[41] A widely discussed study by two Oxford researchers predicted that "about 47% of total US employment" is at high risk of automation.[42] Labor leaders and leading labor law professors asked whether and how we need to adapt to a world with much less work.[43] Some viewed automation as a mortal threat to workers and even society, while others viewed it as our best hope for liberation from toil.[44]

Such fears are not new. In the wake of industrialization and the growth of modern factories, which had already led to a sharp decline in agricultural employment due to tractors and other implements, John Maynard Keynes famously speculated that his grandchildren would be able to work a fifteen-hour week.[45] In the 1960s, companies' incorporation of computers and other advanced information technologies into their operations—then known as the "cybernation revolution"—led again to widespread fear of a looming automation wave.[46] In those past moments of sociotechnical change, however, work did not disappear, for two interrelated reasons. First, companies passed some productivity gains on to consumers through lower prices, which bolstered consumer demand, and therefore demand for workers to produce, distribute, and sell those goods. Second, companies developed new goods and services—leisure goods, safer and more efficient appliances and automobiles, and health-care products and services—to sell to workers and consumers whose lives had become more comfortable as a result of this technological progress. Workers who wanted to be able to purchase such goods were then willing—or required—to put in the long hours necessary to afford them. Taking the long view, productivity growth, together with the expansion and deepening of global markets, led over time to shifts in the composition of the labor market: first from agriculture to manufacturing, and then from manufacturing to services.

Many wondered, however, whether this time was different. After all, the tech sector *had* revolutionized various other parts of the economy in the preceding decade. Napster and other file-sharing services, and then YouTube, iTunes, and Netflix, transformed music and video distribution. The development of smartphones completely changed photography and the market for cameras and film. Facebook and Google altered the economics of news media by aggregating stories and capturing online ad revenue. The explosive growth of Uber and Lyft then suggested that tech companies were poised to alter economic sectors that involved heavy investment in *physical*

Inductive Knowledge and Digital Taylorism

technology. This narrative may also have taken root because journalists had seen their career prospects erode due to Facebook and Google's influence, and therefore may have been inclined to believe tech companies' promises to revolutionize physical work. Some companies also stoked automation fears for self-interested reasons. When fast food workers began demanding $15 an hour, industry groups argued that if companies were required to raise wages, they would implement kiosk-based ordering more quickly.[47]

Granted, from the standpoint of Silicon Valley, perhaps it was reasonable to think that machine learning would only grow ever more powerful. Those at the center of contemporary data-gathering and -processing networks were able to "see" across much greater distances, and in much greater detail, over the course of the 2010s. As more and more facets of social behavior became legible, why wouldn't the nerve structures of the digital economy evolve into something like intelligence? And if so, then wouldn't they continue to evolve? Such thinking led to various predictions of a looming "technological singularity," the point at which AI would be able to replicate all aspects of human intelligence and then improve at an exponential rate.[48] A prominent computer scientist argued that such a machine would be "the last thing we'll ever have to invent because, once we let it loose, it will go on to invent everything else that can be invented."[49] The rate of progress in all sorts of technologies would speed up, breaking through many of the engineering challenges that bedevil robotics today, and integrate advanced intelligence into those robotics. In some versions of the story, AI would then go rogue, seeking to dominate human society or even the galaxy, or become psychotic and seek to turn all known matter into paper clips or some such.[50]

This is science fiction—it is literally the plot of the *Terminator* and *Matrix* franchises. And in reality, such a revolution in AI would likely be necessary to displace today's service workforce.

The limits of machine learning and robotics The notion that inductive knowledge could generate a world without work suffered from several basic errors. For one thing, there was no hard evidence that automation was a major threat.[51] Nobody could ever point to an army of robots standing ready to displace huge numbers of workers, especially in services, and consumers' day-to-day experiences of physical technology are often underwhelming. As the economist Martha Gimbel has said, "Any time anyone tries to claim robots are coming to take our jobs I ask them how well their printer works and that usually ends the conversation."[52] What's more, if companies were installing robotics and related technologies in large numbers, that effect would surely be visible in the data on productivity growth over time, since workers as a whole would be generating more output per hour. But productivity growth has recently been as slow as at any time since World War II,[53] and productivity growth in the manufacturing sector—where task automation has historically been easiest—has been especially tepid.[54] Meanwhile, an automation wave would lead to significant increases in unemployment, but prior to COVID-19, joblessness was relatively low in the US.[55]

Predictions of a looming automation wave also disregarded the costs of robotics and other mobile physical devices like vehicles. Bluntly, they are not cheap. The price for Amazon's Kiva system is not publicly available, but a distribution center consultant estimated the cost for a typical warehouse of 50–100 robots as being between $2 million and $4 million, and a large warehouse of 500–1000 robots as being from $15 million to $20 million. As the consultant wrote, "these are some serious figures as far as distribution center capital investments are concerned."[56] Just as important, the unit economics of robotics are dramatically different from the unit economics of algorithms. App-based tech companies have grown rapidly in part because the marginal cost of producing new versions of an app or software is effectively zero. That is why file-sharing and related technologies posed such a devastating threat to the music and entertainment industries: once music and movies can be digitized, they can be shared essentially at will, and for free, which made it impossible for artists and legacy companies to profit from those products. Robotics and other semiautonomous machines, in contrast, involve physical technology. While mass production of robots would drive down costs, those costs will never approach zero due to the simple costs of materials such as metals and plastics, as well as of intermediate physical inputs like batteries and light detection and ranging (LIDAR) or other sensing systems. Now, labor isn't cheap either, and when labor shortages or worker organization drives up labor costs, companies will have greater incentives to economize through task automation. As a result, the impetus to automate is not going away. The point is rather that progress in physical automation presents economic challenges that are very different from progress in the gig economy, file sharing, online search, social

Inductive Knowledge and Digital Taylorism

networking, and other activities in which the marginal costs of adding new units or users can approach zero.

Predictions of a looming automation wave also significantly overstated the capacities of inductive learning, simply assuming that it could substitute for tacit and formal knowledge across many spheres of human behavior and action. For better or worse, it seems increasingly clear that machine learning is not a path to imminent artificial general intelligence, and therefore not to an army of robots who would displace line-level workers.[57] The basic problem is that machine learning relies on drawing statistical inferences from massive but also discrete data sets, often in laboratory conditions.[58] Programmers and commentators often reported progress in AI with reference to particular benchmarks—for example, in image recognition or language translation—without considering whether performance on those benchmarks, in laboratory conditions, actually measured progress toward creating generalizable analytical systems.[59]

When machines or programs move into the physical and human world, however, all sorts of new and unpredictable challenges emerge that cannot be solved through statistical analysis because—almost by definition—those challenges did not appear in the training data. For example, such systems have difficulty making contextual judgments about human and social affairs since they have no innate sense about the world.[60] Minor changes in a system's input layer, therefore, can lead it to fail, sometimes catastrophically.[61] A recent language program and model by OpenAI has made progress on issues such as these, and yet it still delivers strange and absurd results at times and clearly has no awareness of the social or real-world contexts for its conversations.[62] In 2020 a programmer showed that while it was impressively accurate in answering straightforward questions, it was stumped by questions that humans would recognize as absurd, such as "How many eyes does a blade of grass have?" The program's answer: "A blade of grass has one eye."[63]

These underlying problems have stymied progress in many fields, including autonomous vehicles. After Uber grew spectacularly, companies rushed into the space, with Google, Tesla, and General Motors (GM) all promising fully autonomous cars by 2019.[64] The implications for workers would be obvious: a prominent labor reporter predicted that self-driving cars could displace five million professional drivers, including truckers, cab drivers, and other delivery drivers.[65] The first company to develop and patent fully autonomous vehicles—or the critical technology for them—would also capture massive product market rents. But for several years now, companies in the sector have been trying to lower expectations.[66] The problem is that the real world constantly presents novel situations that do not map onto the algorithms' training data. Drivers need to react to sudden changes in weather, intoxicated people running into the road, or items flying off of other cars. In those circumstances, machine learning algorithms get stumped or respond in erratic ways. That sort of event helped cause one of Uber's self-driving cars to hit and kill a pedestrian in 2018, as the image-recognition devices misidentified the pedestrian and therefore did not respond in time.[67] Similarly, former Tesla employees have accused that company of repeatedly overstating its vehicles' autonomous capabilities, and the National Highway Traffic Safety Administration has investigated the company on related grounds.[68]

In other contexts, engineers can mitigate that problem by engineering social and physical environments so that machines have to process only a limited amount of information. In the industrial and warehouse settings, for example, engineers often place production robots in cages to isolate them from humans since they are heavy and very powerful and have difficulty sensing that people are around, and therefore can injure humans quite easily.[69] Those robots are then programmed to perform particular tasks, which involves formal rather than inductive knowledge. That approach isn't plausible for vehicles, however, since it would require redesigning our entire system of roads so that pedestrians cannot access them. Alternatively, engineers could program an autonomous vehicle to stop every time it is stumped by an object in the distance, but in that case, passengers will get impatient or carsick, and other drivers will get irritated.[70] What seems more likely going forward is that the technologies that have already been developed will be deployed in environments where environmental control is easier. Autonomous long-haul trucking seems plausible, therefore, but human drivers would still need to take the trucks off highways to their final destinations within cities or suburbs.

Those challenges compound for other sorts of robots. Promotional videos by the robotics company Boston Dynamics show humanoid and dog-like robots walking unattended, dancing, and even performing backflips.[71] But the company has admitted that they are either remotely controlled by humans or programmed in minute detail—encoding formal knowledge.[72]

Inductive Knowledge and Digital Taylorism

Even industrial automation is far more difficult than many appreciate.[73] There are basic technical limitations in the design and strength of robotic arms and hands, which lead to a trade-off between strength and safety: robotic arms that are strong enough to perform many industrial and other tasks need to be heavy, which both increases energy costs and makes it challenging to deploy them alongside humans. Similarly, Apple ended up abandoning many automation efforts after investing heavily in a secret lab in California that brought together top robotics researchers in an effort to solve production challenges.[74] Those researchers learned, for example, that it is exceptionally difficult to design a robot to insert a small screw into an iPhone chassis, given the fine motor skills and vision required for the task.[75] The Kiva example that opened this chapter gives a much clearer picture of how mobile robots are being integrated into production: they are used to perform single tasks in controlled environments that are organized around their capabilities, and they are not anthropomorphic.

Implications for service workers These technical and financial limitations suggest that the majority of automation going forward will likely be slow and iterative, especially among service-sector workers. Consider the tasks performed by delivery drivers for a company such as FedEx or Amazon Flex. Those individuals need to drive, of course. Then, once arriving at a destination, they need to park, exit their vehicles, find the packages that they are planning to deliver, and walk up to a building, often across an uneven sidewalk. Once there, they need to determine whether packages can be left safely in a particular area, or whether a particular person is responsible and capable enough to take a package—for example, not a minor, an intruder, or an individual with dementia. Similarly, baristas don't just make a cappuccino, but also answer questions from customers, modify the drink based on a customer's random requests, and hand it to the customer. Supermarket clerks don't just put boxes on shelves—a task that is still remarkably difficult for robots—but also make strategic decisions about where to store excess inventory, spot hazards, and defuse conflicts among customers if necessary.[76] Nursing home aides and home-care workers don't just dispense medication—they also move patients through irregular physical spaces and determine whether a patient's grunts signify pain versus frustration. It is impossible to automate such jobs without anthropomorphic and extremely intelligent robots, and those robots are far in the future.

In each of these cases, companies continue to automate particular tasks, of course. The FedEx driver may receive navigation instructions from an app and track packages using a barcode scanner that sends information straight to the company's servers. In a prior era, the driver would have navigated without electronic assistance and filled out paperwork to track deliveries. Both developments also enhance productivity and are in some respects desirable for workers. They also enable closer surveillance, as discussed in section 3.3. On the consumer-facing side, cafes are integrating tablet- or app-based ordering systems, which also enable more extensive worker surveillance. The list goes on, but the point should be clear enough: automation is affecting work, but through many small iterative changes rather than the sudden displacement of whole categories of workers. How these trends will play out is fundamentally unknowable, especially given the massive disruptions of COVID. By the time this book is published, engineers and computer scientists will surely have made progress on some of the challenges noted here. Conversely, by that time, other companies may have decided to cut their losses and cease trying to automate particular tasks.

As a result, lawmakers have quite a bit of space to ensure decent work in the near future, and even to shape the course of automation processes themselves. Other scholars have begun to consider how to steer workplace automation in directions that complement rather than undermine human creativity and autonomy.[77] Chapter 6 discusses and builds on those efforts and argues that worker-protective reforms are a necessary component of such efforts. By raising labor costs, such protections can actually *encourage* automation, and thus a degree of worker displacement. And yet under the right institutional conditions, including robust mechanisms for worker voice and power, companies have incentives to collaborate with workers to unlock productivity gains.

Here, some comparative evidence may help illustrate the point. As alluded to in chapter 1, German manufacturers responded to technical change and globalization in the 1980s by focusing on high-wage, high-skill, high-value-added strategies.[78] Today, there is some evidence that German companies are more likely to use "co-bots," or robots that work alongside and complement factory workers, while their counterparts in the US typically seek to replace workers entirely.[79] In 2020, moreover, several economists documented that German companies subject to a stricter form of codetermination—the German system of worker representation, including on corporate supervisory

Inductive Knowledge and Digital Taylorism

boards—had higher capital intensity than companies subject to forms of codetermination that gave workers less power. This suggests that worker voice and power can encourage companies to pursue higher-productivity strategies.[80] An important goal for labor market and industrial policy in the US going forward is to generate similar virtuous cycles of productivity and wage growth, including in service sectors when possible.

3.3 Algorithmic Management

Given the limits of robotics and machine learning discussed thus far, companies today cannot avoid labor politics entirely. But the second component of digital Taylorism—algorithmic management—is giving companies powerful new means of reducing labor costs, even while employing massive numbers of workers. The overview of Amazon's labor practices in the introduction to this chapter illustrates. The company uses robots and algorithms to perform tasks that can be engineered in precise detail through a combination of formal and inductive logic, such as moving shelves of goods, directing pickers to grab particular goods, sorting packages, and affixing mailing labels to them. Amazon then hires workers to perform tasks requiring tacit knowledge and fine motor skills, such as stowing irregularly shaped goods on shelves and grabbing them back off those shelves. The company also deploys new surveillance devices and data-processing algorithms to surveil and manage those workers at scale. That system also involves task automation, but many of the tasks involved are cognitive rather than physical, and were once carried out by managers. Line-level workers, then, are cogs in an enormously sophisticated machine whose operations are obscured from them.

Algorithmic management practices are already well established among large companies in the low-wage labor market[81] and seem very likely to become more important going forward. On the demand side, because it is difficult to generate breakthrough productivity gains in service occupations, and because so many sectors in the US are dominated by a low-wage, low-productivity model, companies frequently maintain profitability by squeezing ever-greater effort from workers. Algorithmic management techniques can help them to do so. On the supply side, algorithmic management devices and technologies are substantially cheaper than physical automation devices. Algorithmic management requires new physical sensors, including cameras, infrared and barcode scanners, listening devices, and the like. But those devices themselves do not need to move around or apply physical force to the environment, which makes deploying them cheaper and operationally simpler than deploying new robotics. Such efforts are also clearly cheaper than human-powered surveillance and management in many cases.[82]

Companies can use algorithmic management both to concentrate valuable information in fewer hands[83] and to intensify work efforts.[84] The discussion in the next subsection first surveys developments here and then assesses their effects on class relations. It focuses on production activities and relations between managers (or algorithms) and individual workers. The next chapter takes up hiring processes, discrimination, and workers' organizing, which raise distinct legal issues. As noted in the introduction of this chapter, this section doesn't say much about law because companies have broad authority to take these steps.

Algorithmic management—an overview Algorithmic management is now well established in at least three subfields of management practices: assigning tasks to workers, scheduling workers for shifts, and setting the pace of work. The most prominent examples of algorithmic tasking involve the gig economy.[85] Uber claims to match consumers and drivers more quickly and reliably than street-hail systems, drawing on data gleaned from drivers' and consumers' cell phones. There is evidence that it enhanced productivity through that method, at least for a time and in some jurisdictions.[86] But Uber has also exploited its control of tasking algorithms to erode drivers' capacity to earn a decent living.[87] As the company moved into cities (often illegally), it led customers to expect not just reliability but also quick availability, so it could build market share rapidly. Uber did so by flooding the market with drivers[88] and then tightly controlling their access to information. Early on, at least, when the app sent a ride request to a driver, the driver had only fifteen seconds to accept it—and had to do so without knowing the destination or fare. Drivers who refused too many requests, or who canceled rides after accepting them, risked deactivation. Uber also uses various behavioral "nudges" to keep drivers on the road, for example by selectively sending ride requests to drivers who seem likely to log off.[89] Similarly, on weekends when it expects a high volume of ride requests, Uber sometimes sets up incentive structures where drivers can receive bonuses if they carry out a certain number of rides and accept a certain percentage of requests.

Inductive Knowledge and Digital Taylorism 75

But drivers have alleged that the company may use its panoptic knowledge about the market to prevent most drivers from reaching the bonus stage by cutting off ride requests once they get close to that point, or by sending them "phantom" ride requests that they are unable to accept.[90] In these and other ways, Uber enforces market discipline on workers, requiring them to compete—tacitly or actively—to remain on the platform and to get the best opportunities. Similar tasking strategies are used across the low-wage gig economy, among companies like Lyft, Instacart, Doordash, and Amazon. In a telling example of how precarious workers have become dependent on these companies and their tasking algorithms, in September 2020, it was reported that Amazon delivery drivers had taken to hanging smartphones from trees near distribution centers and Whole Foods stores, and then syncing their own phones to those. In that way, they hoped to get early notification of potential gigs since the company's algorithms would send pings to whichever delivery drivers were physically closest to the job site.[91]

Another transformation in management has occurred around scheduling practices, where many large companies now use algorithms to assign workers to shifts. Those algorithms claim to predict demand based on past sales, as well as factors such as weather reports, and then schedule workers accordingly in an effort to ensure that work sites are neither overstaffed nor understaffed.[92] This may involve inductive learning to determine which external and internal factors are likely to affect demand the most. Indeed, the use of such algorithms is not necessarily a negative development from the worker's perspective. If workers can specify times that they would ideally like to work, and an algorithm can figure out how to optimize the schedule for a manager, a company can reduce managerial costs and help ensure worker satisfaction.[93]

Companies have frequently used algorithmic scheduling, however, to reduce workers' time on the clock to an absolute minimum. Fast food workers have complained that their shifts are canceled at the last minute or that they are sent home in the middle of shifts without notice.[94] In other cases, companies use algorithms and apps to make schedule alterations on an on-demand basis. Amazon's scheduling practices were noted earlier in this chapter; some Amazon workers suspect that their willingness to accept shift changes on a moment's notice is factored into the company's decision of whether to offer them desirable shifts, overtime, or both.[95] Other companies have scheduled workers for shifts that make it impossible for them to fulfill caregiving responsibilities, or even to sleep. The issue came to public attention with Starbucks' practice of "clopening," where workers had to close the store one night and then open it the next morning, making it nearly impossible for them to sleep.[96] In the wake of media attention, Starbucks promised more reasonable and predictable schedules going forward.[97]

For the most part, these new scheduling practices do not even trigger scrutiny under federal working time regulations. The federal Fair Labor Standards Act (FLSA) does not actually guarantee steady hours or minimum or maximum hours.[98] All it requires regarding hours is that employers pay time-and-a-half for all hours worked over a statutory norm, which has long been forty hours per week. Worker advocates have pressed states and localities to legislate on the issue recently. The state of Oregon, as well as a number of cities including New York and San Francisco, have passed "fair workweek" laws, which require companies to provide workers more notice of schedules; some also require companies to guarantee a certain number of hours off between shifts.[99] Algorithmic scheduling practices may also facilitate "wage theft," or the failure to pay workers all they are owed under wage and hour laws. Three legal scholars who reviewed common timekeeping software programs that are often used in conjunction with algorithmic scheduling found that their default settings would often undercount hours, and that the programs enabled employers to edit down hours worked, which is a crude and obvious FLSA violation.[100]

Finally, companies are using algorithmic monitoring—and their legal powers to terminate workers at will—to require workers to perform at a rapid pace. This is again not a new development.[101] In the 1970s, as supermarkets began to introduce barcode scanners at cashier stations, the sociologist Harry Braverman warned that the technology could be used to track employee performance.[102] Since then, those systems have become far more powerful and sophisticated. The sociologist Karen Levy has documented how long-haul trucking companies use telematics-based monitoring to push their drivers to work all the hours permitted under federal law, substantially reducing the autonomy that was once a point of pride among truckers.[103] At one company, such speedups correlated with a significant increase in workplace injuries.[104] Home-care workers are increasingly required to use "electronic visit verification" apps that invade their clients' privacy, and which may lead workers to underreport their hours of work, in turn leading to

Inductive Knowledge and Digital Taylorism 77

lost wages.[105] Even white-collar workers now face such monitoring. Under COVID, many companies have ramped up surveillance of remote workers, using laptop cameras and facial recognition to discern, minute by minute, whether professionals were focused on assignments.[106]

Amazon has deployed similar technologies within its warehouses to determine how quickly workers are performing tasks and to push them to work faster.[107] Documents disclosed as part of a labor dispute between Amazon and a worker who alleged that he had been fired in retaliation for union organizing efforts showed that various aspects of that oversight had been automated.[108] "Amazon's system tracks the rates of each individual associate's productivity," one document said, "and automatically generates any warnings or terminations regarding quality or productivity without input from supervisors."[109] Around 300 workers in that warehouse, representing over 10 percent of the warehouse's staff, had been terminated via that process, for productivity reasons alone, in a twelve-month period.[110] Other companies are trying to observe human workers' movements very closely using networks of sensors, radar, and machine learning.[111] Still others are developing wearable devices to track workers' movements through the workplace.[112]

Effects of algorithmic management Algorithmic management seems to be maturing more rapidly than robotics, and when this book is published, various new affordances will likely be in use. Nevertheless, the field is sufficiently well developed that some of its aggregate effects on workers seem clear.

The first is that algorithmic management will often put downward pressure on wages. With near-perfect information about individual workers' performance and the capacity to run experiments in wage setting across large-scale enterprises, companies should be able to determine exactly how much they need to pay particular workers to keep them around. Put differently, these technologies are eliminating some informational asymmetries that give workers some bargaining power even if they are not in unions. As labor economists in an earlier technological era argued, when it is not easy to observe workers' output or effort levels, companies may pay above-market wages to induce employee loyalty, and therefore sound performance.[113] That could occur if individuals worked in teams, for example, or if workers had used collective action to block employer surveillance efforts. The converse also appeared true at the time: where companies can cheaply detect underperforming workers, they have less incentive to pay above-market wages.[114] In such cases, workers were subject to significant external market discipline. As should be clear from the discussion in this chapter, companies today often use data-driven workplace surveillance to detect underperforming workers. Peer-reviewed research on new tracking efforts and wages is rare, but one study of the platform Freelancer.com found that the introduction of a monitoring system that tracked keystrokes and other actions led to a substantial increase in bids, including from inexperienced workers, and lower prices for labor.[115] The authors reasoned that the monitoring system reduced the value of established workers' reputations and mitigated the risks that companies faced when hiring workers without a history on the platform.

Second, algorithmic management can erode or suppress workers' associational power. After all, workers' best means of protecting themselves against very low wages or an unsustainable pace of work in the past has been to organize.[116] But workers who are constantly supervised and physically separated from one another have little time to meet and make common cause. Chapter 4 says more about this, discussing the organizing process in detail. Similarly, workers who have multiple jobs with irregular schedules may be too exhausted to even think about planning collective action. Meanwhile, the homogenization of work tasks under digital Taylorism makes it easier for companies to plug workers into and out of jobs fairly easily, reducing companies' training costs and their incentives to invest in their workforce and making it still more difficult for workers to organize. Labor markets then resemble their neoclassical models, with workers not much different from classic commodities.

Meanwhile, the use of algorithmic management and other surveillance efforts are enabling companies to replicate and capture some of workers' tacit knowledge. This is a third aggregate effect of algorithmic management. It was also a central function of classical Taylorism, but digital technologies have extended the process into new spheres. For example, Uber has integrated global positioning system (GPS)–powered navigation into the driver side of its app, and the company may be able to improve it continuously using data from past rides.[117] But taxi drivers' specialized knowledge of how to navigate a crowded city historically gave them some labor market power. In London, cab drivers even need to pass a test showing that they know the names and locations of all streets in the area so that they can get to any

Inductive Knowledge and Digital Taylorism

location without a map.[118] In essence, Uber has captured or replicated some of taxi drivers' classical knowledge and craft skills, claimed property rights in them via IP doctrines and trade secrets, and leased that IP back to drivers. Through those efforts, the company can put downward pressure on wages since the new technology enables almost anyone with a vehicle to do the job. Similar efforts may be underway in customer service call centers as companies implement natural language-recognition and processing algorithms, and in fast food as franchisors discern facts about local management strategies or labor practices that aren't visible from the shop-floor level.

There is a final cross-cutting issue here: past a certain point, companies' efforts to reduce labor costs by squeezing workers may become self-defeating. As the industrial relations scholar Zeynep Ton has shown, retailers can get caught in a "vicious cycle" of low wages and low productivity. Overworked cashiers end up misscanning items, for example, and stock clerks end up placing excess goods in random locations because their stores are constantly short-staffed.[119] That appears to be especially common in the US for institutional and path-dependent reasons discussed previously: through the era of neoliberalism, US companies have been especially focused on labor discipline strategies. Comparative scholarship on industrial relations in retail and other service sectors such as call centers suggests that many European firms take a more collaborative approach to labor relations, with more upskilling and broader worker discretion.[120] That reflects, in part, workers' greater capacity in Europe to foreclose the zero-sum and discipline-intensive managerial practices common in the US, due to European nations' more robust collective bargaining systems and privacy protections.

Unfortunately, companies can find it quite challenging to break out of Ton's vicious cycle, especially where their competitors are mostly using the same managerial techniques. A similar dynamic appeared among delivery companies in the US after COVID. In 2021, FedEx was significantly underperforming UPS in terms of on-time package delivery and profit margins, due largely to labor shortages. As discussed in chapter 5, FedEx uses independent contractors rather than employees and keeps wages low, while UPS employs drivers directly, is unionized, and pays drivers more than its rivals. Those factors helped UPS thrive during the post-COVID labor shortage and suggest that FedEx may be unable to push as many costs onto drivers going forward.[121]

Conclusion: Institutions and Digital Taylorism

Digital Taylorism reflects a clear underlying logic: companies are using their legal and operational powers over data to automate some tasks, reorganize production accordingly, and supervise workers much more intensely. By doing so, companies can both enhance productivity and ensure that workers cannot capture a significant share of profits. As should also be clear, this process is facilitated and shaped at every stage by law. Whether and when companies can monitor workers, what they can do with the data they have gathered, and who "owns" any new products they develop using that data all involve legal questions. Through digital Taylorism, companies are using their control over technology to reconfigure workplaces and jobs, and then to monitor and manage workers in new ways, often through means that erode or suppress workers' associational power.

In that sense, companies' power over technology gives them the capacity to override workers' legal rights and to encase their own powers against workers' challenges. Those efforts have helped bring into being today's working class, which as chapter 1 discussed is heavily concentrated in service sectors. At the same time, the fact that alternative models of labor relations have persisted in other nations suggests that a different politics of workplace technology is possible. Chapter 6 returns to this question, asking how labor law reforms could contribute to such a transformative agenda.

4 Workplace Privacy and Associational Power

Introduction

Soon after the Ford Motor Company implemented the moving assembly line in 1913, it confronted a problem of labor supply and discipline. Workers were quitting in huge numbers due to the rigors and stresses of the job, which required them to perform physically grueling and repetitive tasks, for long periods, without losing focus, in loud, hot, and dirty conditions. This was also an era of worker uprisings and labor violence, including the landmark 1912 Bread and Roses strike among textile workers in Lawrence, Massachusetts, and the 1914 Ludlow Massacre, where Colorado National Guard troops and private security forces killed more than twenty in an encampment of striking mine workers. In this heated political context, Ford sought to create an industrial workforce out of workers who had often been raised as peasants or sharecroppers, as well as to avoid labor militancy. As is well known, one of Ford's strategies to do so involved hiking wages to $5 a day.

In a development that is less well known today, Ford also created a so-called Sociological Department to screen and groom workers.[1] As the Henry Ford Museum of American Innovation now recounts, the department "established a system of rules and codes of behavior for Ford employees that they had to meet, in order to qualify for the $5 day pay rate."[2] Its staff did not just monitor workers while in the factory; they also made "unannounced visits to employees' homes" to check on their cleanliness and whether their children were attending school, and it "monitored bank records to verify that employees made regular deposits."[3] Through those efforts, the company's agents also kept an eye out for "labor disturbers," including communists and socialists. Ford also deployed detectives to conduct independent investigations and tasked foremen with closely monitoring workers' shop-floor conversations. A union organizer who worked at a Ford plant in 1925 wrote that workers there were "not disposed to unionize" due to the Sociological Department's efforts, and Ford workers did not do so until 1941.[4] This sort of crude intervention in workers' off-the-job lives declined during and after the New Deal, especially as unions gained power.

Yet modern data-driven technologies are giving companies new means of shaping a pliant workforce that may be just as powerful as those used by Ford. Consider what a potential worker—call her Julia—may have to go through to get a job at a large company in retail, food service, logistics, or hospitality today. Julia may have to take an online test that asks her how she would respond to an underperforming colleague and makes clear that the company wants workers who will not question management. Before hiring her, the company may review Julia's public social media posts and turn her down if she has been a vocal supporter of political causes that the company or its managers oppose. If Julia is hired, the company may closely monitor her conversations with colleagues over email and other platforms, and by doing so may determine that they are seeking to unionize. If Julia and her coworkers go on strike, the company will surely prevent them from using its website or apps to appeal to the public. In an earlier era, Julia and her coworkers could have used those platforms' offline equivalents (like the sidewalk) to enlist support from customers.

In other words, companies today can use new technologies to curate, surveil, and discipline their workforces in a manner reminiscent of Ford's actions before the New Deal. These efforts raise legal issues that are more complex than those raised by automation and digital Taylorism. As chapters 2 and 3 noted, employers' rights to monitor employees as they are working in the workplace are now basically unquestioned. In contrast, the matters treated in this chapter often fall into more of a gray area, sometimes under the law and sometimes under privacy norms. A well-developed line of scholarship has warned that these developments are eroding traditional consumer and worker privacy rights and reinforcing inequalities on the basis of race, gender, national origin, and disability. This chapter draws from those studies to better understand how companies may use such technologies to prevent worker organizing. In each case, employers can exploit new information flows to learn aspects of workers' activities (or even personalities) that the workers could previously keep secret. In this sense, algorithmic hiring and monitoring practices are a modern Sociological Department—one engineered to operate in the background of social life, often without employees even noticing, but with effects that may be just as profound.

Section 4.1 summarizes how new means of data aggregation and analysis are affecting employee privacy and equal employment opportunity. Section 4.2 discusses union-organizing strategies today and their complex relationship to workplace privacy and new technologies. Section 4.3 addresses how companies can use new technologies of surveillance, data aggregation, and inductive learning to resist and suppress workers' organizing efforts.

4.1 Data Aggregation, Privacy, and Equal Opportunity

Employers' uses of data to restructure hiring and human relations processes have built on consumer-facing companies' earlier efforts to reshape consumer markets and behavior through data analytics. As privacy scholars have shown, consumer-facing firms' efforts were facilitated by our "notice and choice" model of consumer privacy.[5] In that model, data harvesting and use is legitimate so long as companies disclose what they are going to do with the data and the data subjects choose to go along.[6] A major problem with that paradigm, as scholars have argued, is that individuals' "choices" in this context are highly constrained, both epistemologically and practically. Very few consumers read or could understand complex privacy notices, and even fewer can realistically monitor companies' revisions to privacy policies.[7] As Daniel Solove has put it, "Consent legitimizes nearly any form of collection, use, and disclosure of personal data."[8]

What's more, companies have learned that by aggregating data from multiple sources—web browsing histories and purchases, social media postings, geographical locations, magazine subscriptions, and so on—they can infer "*additional* information about the data subjects beyond what is directly observed."[9] The notice-and-choice paradigm has facilitated those efforts by encouraging many companies to vacuum up and hold as much data as possible, and to sell or share it with one another. Banks and automobile insurance companies have used data aggregation and analysis to determine individuals' credit risks, for example, and the Transportation Security Agency has used similar processes to develop no-fly lists.[10] Companies' use of modern data analytics in such processes can render the underlying decisional processes opaque even to programmers—in Frank Pasquale's memorable phrase, the processes themselves are a "black box,"[11] raising major concerns about due process and self-governance.

Such efforts also threaten to eviscerate traditional understandings of consumer privacy—and by extension worker privacy—in a manner illustrated by the philosopher and privacy scholar Helen Nissenbaum, who has analogized data-aggregation efforts to a "food chain." Starting at the bottom of the chain and moving up, the steps in modern data analytics include tracking and monitoring that generate data, often with individuals' explicit consent; aggregating and analyzing that data to draw inferences; and finally, using the analyzed data to make a business decision.[12] Information flows upward through hierarchical steps, as companies apply more complex processing techniques to the data, and draw ever-finer inferences about data subjects. The chain is therefore a "hierarchy in which data of a higher order is a function of data of a lower order."[13] As a result, data that a consumer has willingly provided by using a credit card or joining a company's rewards program can help determine their access to goods across various domains. As is depressingly predictable, vulnerability to harms due to data aggregation skews along class and race lines both inside and outside the workplace, with less-skilled workers and people of color subject to more intensive and intrusive forms of surveillance than white and wealthier individuals.[14]

A well-known case arising at Target illustrates how such techniques can erode individual privacy. The company inferred that some customers were pregnant based on their purchases and sent them pregnancy-related advertisements.[15] Target moved "up" the food chain, in Nissenbaum's terms, from limited data about a consumer's behavior to a critically important inference about their health status. Many people reacted with horror to the story, reflecting the tension between existing normative understandings of consumer privacy and the capacities of modern inductive learning technologies. The norms are straightforward and reflected in health law and antidiscrimination law: information about toiletries and vitamins is different in kind from information about pregnancy, given the profound importance of pregnancy to individuals' well-being. As Nissenbaum argues, "instead of privacy norms about toiletries and vitamins attaching to pregnancy, those applying to pregnancy should travel *down* to toiletries and vitamins."[16] Yet efforts such as Target's are typically permissible under existing law.

Learning from such efforts in the consumer space, employers have increasingly incorporated data analytics in their hiring processes in recent years. Large companies often do so internally, while others may turn to labor market intermediaries such as hiring and screening platforms that operate at sufficient scale to make inductive learning possible.[17] By one estimate, around 90 percent of employers used online recruiting strategies by 2020.[18] To understand the landscape of algorithmic hiring, it may help to start at the bottom of the data food chain and move up. Some hiring programs just gather basic data from applicants to discern their qualifications and availability. For example, one Toronto-based start-up has helped large retailers with hiring by screening résumés, gathering information from applicants regarding their shift availability and skills via chatbot, and recommending qualified candidates.[19] Chatbots themselves can be quite helpful for this purpose since they can ask specific questions—Can you work evenings? Do you have a car? Do you have retail experience?—that generate yes or no answers. In a sense, all that has happened is that text-based factual and job-related information once disclosed on paper or in a job interview is now being provided online. Companies may nevertheless find these programs very helpful for hiring large numbers of less-skilled workers.

Moving one or two steps up the chain, various companies have sought to apply inductive learning to hiring practices.[20] The theory is that data analytics may identify aspects of applicants' experience or aptitudes that correlate with success in particular positions but which have not traditionally been taken into account. This is superficially plausible where there is a large supply of data about current workers, their backgrounds, and their performance, as well as a large supply of data about applicants. At that point, companies can use machine learning and related technologies to draw statistical inferences from the first data set (on current workers) and apply those inferences to sort the second data set (on applicants). There are some well-known success stories involving this technique. Deloitte, for example, reports that a client in the financial services industry learned that experience in sales and a lack of typographical errors on a résumé were better predictors of success in sales than which college the applicant attended.[21] That use case exemplifies the potential upside of people analytics: it can *reduce* bias and inequality by identifying objective criteria that are "correlated with business or employment success" and using that data to make decisions in ways that "replace subjective decisionmaking by managers."[22]

But those processes can also exacerbate inequalities on the basis of race, gender, immigration status, and disability.[23] As a number of scholars have argued, it is absurd on some level to ask artificial intelligence (AI) to be nonracist or nonsexist since AI is always trained by humans, using human-generated data, and therefore it will reflect social and economic divisions on the basis of ascriptive identities.[24] For example, companies may seek to hire workers who they expect will stick around for a while so they can recoup their training costs. In developing hiring algorithms, companies might seek to discern which aspects of applicants' backgrounds correlate with longer tenures. But if a key variable is how far applicants live from the worksite—since that determines their commuting times—such an algorithm may exclude African American or Latinx workers at a disproportionate rate depending on patterns of housing segregation.[25] Such a screening could also exacerbate the disadvantages faced by poor applicants who lack reliable transportation. Since training costs may be greater for managers, that sort of algorithm will also disproportionately sort white applicants into managerial roles. For similar reasons, machine-learning tools may correlate success in more technical positions with being a man when the existing workforce skews male.[26] Algorithmic wage-setting also seems to have generated a gender pay gap among Uber drivers because the algorithms rewarded drivers for driving more quickly, and men tended to drive faster than women.[27]

A similar set of issues arises when companies try to use algorithms to discern whether workers have the personality traits required for success. This is plausible, since the "big five" personality traits—openness to experience, conscientiousness, extraversion, agreeableness, and emotional stability—do have a documented relationship to job performance in some cases, and companies have used personality tests in hiring processes for decades.[28] Some online hiring platforms today purport to have automated such assessments. For example, the prominent platform HireVue records interviewees answering a series of questions via an AI-powered videoconferencing interface. HireVue's chief "industrial-organizational psychologist" told the *Washington Post* in 2019 that its thirty-minute assessments "can yield up to 500,000 data points" from applicants' facial expressions, word choices, and tone of voice, "all of which become ingredients" in the applicant's "employability" score.[29] The company claims to use that data to discern the applicant's "willingness to learn," "conscientiousness & responsibility" and "personal stability,"[30] traits that overlap with the "big five" personality traits.

But there are reasons to doubt such claims. For one thing, it is simply not possible to discern individuals' emotions from facial expressions, as researchers in affective computing take pains to emphasize.[31] A recent metastudy of the issue by academic psychologists, for example, noted that "how people communicate anger, disgust, fear, happiness, sadness, and surprise varies substantially across cultures, situations, and even across people within a single situation."[32] This raises the question of exactly what HireVue's algorithm *does* measure. The company has been secretive about its specific technologies and clientele, citing trade secrets and the inscrutability of some machine learning processes.[33] A relatively benign explanation is that the algorithms test for certain outward *behaviors*—as opposed to personality traits—that service-sector employers value, such as speaking clearly and making good eye contact. Attempting to quantify interpersonal behaviors, however, can bring substantial bias into the process. If a company's workforce is almost entirely white, male, native-born, and Ivy League–educated, a hiring algorithm may "learn" that an ideal employee has linguistic, social, and other traits that correlate with those statuses.[34] In the case of HireVue and other platforms, some AI researchers have suggested that the system could end up "penalizing nonnative speakers, visibly nervous interviewees or anyone else who doesn't fit the model for look and speech."[35]

Analyzing verbal skills gets quickly into territory where facially legitimate job qualifications can conflict with patterns of racial, ethnic, national, and regional difference. Under our employment discrimination laws, an employer cannot deny employment to an applicant because they have a "Black" or "foreign" accent—but it can deny employment because that employee lacks the verbal skills to communicate effectively with customers or coworkers. The line between the two can be fuzzy.[36] Such tests may also reinforce biases against individuals with disabilities. The Americans with Disabilities Act restricts companies' ability to use personality tests to detect mental health disorders like depression, anxiety, or schizophrenia.[37] To the extent that algorithms pick up on behaviors that correlate with those disorders, companies may end up excluding individuals on forbidden grounds.

While these are serious concerns, they are now widely recognized, and both researchers and some companies are trying to address them.[38] Some algorithmic hiring companies already seek to detect bias at multiple stages of their screening processes, and may "downweight or remove" variables that correlate with race, gender, or another protected class.[39] In 2021 the federal Equal Employment Opportunity Commission also began an initiative to better understand the issue, which may lead to rulemaking or new enforcement strategies.[40] Notably, while our employment discrimination laws do not take economic class specifically into account,[41] mitigating algorithmic bias would help mitigate class disparities. In many cases, companies are using algorithmic strategies to sort some workers into managerial or supervisory positions, and others into menial jobs. If an algorithm determines that the optimal manager has traits similar to white, college-educated employees, then individuals without those traits will be more often pushed into lower-paying, less prestigious positions. In that sense, just as existing forms of AI reflect existing racist and sexist practices, they also reflect assumptions about class: who is employable at all, who should be a relatively menial worker, and who should be a manager.

4.2 Informational Flows and Worker Organizing

New tools of workplace surveillance and data aggregation also shape and affect workers' capacity to organize and take concerted action. In that sense, those tools implicate both labor laws and privacy laws, which have traditionally been understood to protect quite different goods. Labor law is a means of managing class relations and is closely connected to issues of economic distribution, while privacy law protects a more varied and overarching set of individual and collective interests. Extending outward in concentric circles from the individual or data subject, those include rights of autonomy and individual expression, then dignity or freedom from humiliation, and then the ability to enter and maintain healthy intimate and professional relationships. None of those is necessarily connected to class politics—and yet a final privacy interest is. As various privacy scholars have observed, privacy protections can also foster the sorts of speech and nonintimate associations essential to strong communities and democracy more generally,[42] a category that includes working-class organizations like unions.

The relationship between privacy and associational power, therefore, cannot be captured by a privacy theory based on secrecy. It is better captured by theories that understand privacy as being about rules regarding information flows, and that account for how those information flows shape the dynamic relationship among individual and group concerns and identities.[43] Workers can best communicate with one another and organize in tailored versions of what one privacy scholar has called "safe social spaces," or "environments of information exchange in which disclosure norms are counterbalanced by norms of trust backed endogenously by design and exogenously by law."[44] In particular, workers need spaces where they can deliberate and plan safely with one another while limiting companies' ability to learn about their efforts. Current doctrine, as discussed in this chapter, assuredly does not create those safe spaces in the workplace, and those few spaces that do exist risk being closed to workers via employer surveillance. The discussion below focuses on how our labor laws give companies and managers broad authority to shape and control informational flows in the workplace.

Before doing so, it will help to review some basic aspects of worker organizing and the law. As discussed in chapter 1, unionization campaigns and tactics in the US are designed almost entirely to avoid or overcome managerial opposition. The major reason is that US employers have strongly opposed unionization, especially in comparison to their counterparts in other wealthy nations. That opposition is partly ideological and partly an economic response to our model of enterprise bargaining, which can place unionized firms at a competitive disadvantage.[45] Employers often terminate union supporters, which can permanently arrest a drive's momentum.[46] While that is clearly unlawful, it can take years before the National Labor Relations Board (NLRB) reaches a final judgment and orders the typical remedy, which is reinstatement and back pay.[47] In the meantime, under longstanding Supreme Court precedent, unlawfully terminated workers are required to mitigate their damages by finding another job.[48] Such delays are potent anti-union tools since rational workers will often choose not to take lawful concerted action rather than risk unlawful termination.

Then, even if workers demonstrate overwhelming and indisputable support for a union, companies may exploit legal procedures to delay an election for months, or even years.[49] If workers then *do* vote to unionize, companies have a duty to bargain in good faith, but the NLRB has no power to order them to accept particular terms. That creates further incentives to delay real bargaining in hopes that the union will lose support. Finally, as noted in chapter 2, workers have limited rights to strike under US law. Labor law scholars, therefore, have argued for decades now that the NLRB's union certification regime no longer adequately protects workers' rights to organize, and in fact facilitates management's efforts—both lawful and unlawful—to delay and resist unionization.[50] In recent decades unions have often responded to this regime's weaknesses by attempting to sidestep it: demanding that an employer voluntarily recognize their union and begin bargaining rather than insisting on a drawn-out election and certification process.[51] (In April 2022, the NLRB's General Counsel urged the Board to return to a legal standard under which an employer must recognize a union based the union's showing of majority support, unless the employer can establish that it has a good faith doubt about the union's claims. The case was pending as this book went to press.)[52]

Given this hostile environment, successful organizing campaigns need to define, shape, or extend a solidaristic collective identity among workers. The reason is that workers who share such an identity—and who can take collective action to protect one another—will be in a better position to prevail despite management's near-certain opposition. That collective identity can be rooted in various axes of common experience: being colocated in a large factory or worksite and subject to the same set of managerial policies, sharing craft or occupational skills, or being part of a social group that may overlap with class position, such as race, gender, and nationality. In nearly all cases, however, that identity is *constructed* (or at least bolstered) by workers' concerted action during the organizing process.[53]

Workers who are leading organizing drives will therefore meet with coworkers to identify common concerns, and then press them—often through emotional appeals—to fight for better treatment. Unions often encourage workers to scale up those efforts in an iterative fashion over the course of a campaign. They might first take small steps in private, like signing a petition or union authorization cards, and then more public actions, like wearing union buttons, and ultimately a significant action, such as striking. Unions may also push workers to resolve disputes with management through concerted action during the drive so that folkways of solidarity and mutual support develop. Organizers sometimes call this "acting like a union," meaning exerting collective power well before certification.[54] The sociologist Rick Fantasia's account of the internal dynamics of a wildcat strike is illustrative. He found that many workers were initially noncommittal and decided to walk off the job only after emotional appeals by strike leaders. After the strike succeeded, however, many workers within the shop felt a new sense of empowerment. Fantasia argues that the strike created "a locus of oppositional sentiment . . . which remained solidly rooted in the day-to-day culture of the department" and led to a second successful strike a few months later.[55]

Given the importance of interworker communications and trust, the rules governing workplace information flows shape workers' and employers' correlative powers through this process. In the initial stages of an organizing drive, workers may need to keep their discussions and plans secret from employers so that they may identify common concerns and chart a course of action before the employer learns of their campaign. At the same time, workers' identities cannot remain secret from one another since they need to be able to trust each other. In other words, such communications need to be nonanonymous in relationship to other workers, but anonymous in relationship to employers. In the later stages of an effort, workers will have stepped out publicly with demands, and their deliberations are no longer entirely secret. At that point, workers have autonomy interests that overlap with privacy concerns, the most important of these being the ability to speak and act publicly without suffering retaliation.

Yet existing law gives companies broad control over workplace information flows. For example, companies can lawfully exclude non-employee organizers from most parts of their premises, including many publicly accessible areas, which makes it much harder for workers to learn about and exercise their collective bargaining rights.[56] Once workers begin organizing, companies may call on consultants and law firms that specialize in advising companies how to resist organizing.[57] A common management tactic is to require workers to attend "captive audience" meetings, at which managers argue against unionization, but from which unions are excluded and in which workers may be prohibited from asking questions.[58] Through those meetings and other tactics, companies try to send the message that unionization is either irresponsible, futile, or unnecessary.[59] For example, management may suggest that the union itself is a third party in relationship to workers, and may allude to union "bosses" or the possibility of corruption. (Organizers with the Amazon Labor Union [ALU], which unionized the Staten Island warehouse, were less vulnerable to that argument because they were all either current or former workers at the warehouse, and because the ALU was not affiliated with a national union).[60] Or a company may suddenly present itself as open to workers' concerns, so workers do not need a collective representative.[61] Or managers may predict that unionization will lead to worksite closures, job cuts, or both.[62] The key is that management tries to maintain and telegraph its unilateral control over information and the workplace generally.

Meanwhile, our labor law allows management to prohibit workers from using internal communications tools for organizing in many cases. This creates yet another skew in technology and class politics: networked information technologies are powerful tools of corporate integration and control, but not (yet) powerful tools of worker mobilization. The Supreme Court's 1945 decision in *Republic Aviation Corp. v. National Labor Relations Board* is an important backdrop. There, the Court held that an employer could not prevent employees from soliciting union support from other employees during nonworking time on the employer's property unless the employer could show that "special circumstances made the rule necessary in order to maintain production or discipline."[63] This infringement of the employer's property rights was justified, the Court reasoned, because the workplace is the "place uniquely appropriate and almost solely available to them" for organizing purposes.[64]

Despite the strength of that precedent, employers have established fairly broad powers to prohibit organizing activity on some of the modern technological equivalents of the locker room, the break room, and the plant entrance. The most prominent line of cases involved employees' use of their employers' email systems for organizing purposes during nonworking hours. There, the NLRB first held in 2007 that employers could legitimately ban workers from doing so, reversed course in 2014 (under the administration of Barack Obama), and then reversed course again in 2019 (under the administration of Donald Trump).[65] (Such shifts in doctrine are not uncommon at the NLRB when the presidency changes parties, and some of the Trump-era cases discussed in this chapter may be overturned before this book is published). The Trump-era case, *Caesar's Entertainment*, treated the issue as a straightforward question of employers' property rights: "an employer's communication systems, including its email system, are its property," the Board majority reasoned. "Accordingly, employers have a property right to control the use of those systems."[66] By extension, employers may also prevent workers from using other communications tools such as intranets, chat platforms, and Slack pages for organizing purposes unless those are the "only reasonable means for employees to communicate with one another."[67] In a sense, these cases reverse the presumption in *Republic Aviation* that the employer must cede some sovereignty over its property, reflecting the general shift in labor law from industrial pluralism to workplace neoliberalism.

Another line of cases considered whether employers may ban employees from using cameras or other recording devices in the workplace. Several Obama-era cases held that employers could not enforce blanket bans on recording since that could stymie employee organizing.[68] In one, *Whole Foods Market*, the Board majority held that such efforts would be protected where they involved, for example, "recording images of protected picketing, documenting unsafe workplace equipment or hazardous working conditions, documenting and publicizing discussions about terms and conditions of employment," or documenting an employer's inconsistent application of work rules.[69] The Trump NLRB changed course, however, in the 2017 *Boeing* case. There, the NLRB articulated a new approach to employer work rules cases that was significantly more employer-friendly than in *Whole Foods*, and held that Boeing's own ban on camera-enabled devices was justified. The Board did not rely on the common law property rights rationale of *Caesar's*, but rather on Boeing's stated interests in protecting classified data related to national security, trade secrets, and employee privacy.[70]

The analysis is somewhat different when workers use a communications platform that the employer does not control. The Obama NLRB extended protection to workers' speech and organizing efforts on social media, essentially holding that workers cannot be disciplined for otherwise lawful discussions about workplace issues on Facebook, Twitter, and other online forums.[71] While the law basically translates from the offline to the online context here, the fact that speech occurred on social media may alter some practical dynamics of litigation. Public social media posts provide clear evidence of what workers said and when they said it, which makes it far easier to prove that they were taking or planning collective action and that the employer knew about it. At the same time, where such posts are public, they are legible to management—especially given modern data-driven surveillance techniques. In contrast, in the absence of audio surveillance, an in-person conversation may remain strictly between the workers who spoke and never come to an employer's attention. As a result, social media posts may invite employer retaliation more readily than offline conversations.[72]

To the extent that workers' communications on social media are protected, however, it can be a powerful organizing tool. For example, users' ability to embed audio or video in social media posts has been central to mobilizations against police violence. Worker organizers have done this as well. In Israel, for example, organizers have used WhatsApp to send audio and video messages to workers who speak the same language but do not necessarily read or write it.[73] Similarly, in a landmark 2018 teachers' strike in West Virginia, teachers organized and mobilized via Facebook pages, streamed their strike votes on "Facebook Live," and rejected an initial settlement offer following Facebook deliberations.[74] More recently, the Amazon Labor Union built support by posting campaign videos on TikTok, including some that showed organizers being arrested.[75] In such cases, social media can bolster and amplify workers' in-person organizing efforts.

Social media also enables genuinely new sorts of organizing among people who are not physically colocated and who do not know one another offline.[76] The internet has long brought to light latent but widespread grievances, or even latent ideologies, as individuals find communities of similar-thinking people online.[77] Some of those conversations take place on public forums such as Twitter or message boards. But given the obvious risk of employer surveillance in those contexts, the more fruitful efforts have often involved speech in nonpublic spaces. For example, Walmart workers who had few or no allies at their own stores have met up online through a platform set up by OUR Walmart, a union-affiliated organization, where they found that they had similar experiences and concerns. As one worker put it in an interview with a sociologist, "You're used to dealing with your individual store and then when you see it is nationwide and you're talking to other people—it kinda blows your mind away."[78] Fight for $15, a movement of low-wage workers in fast food and elsewhere who have been pushing for a $15 minimum wage and unionization, has used similar tactics to organize far-flung fast food workers who do not share a common worksite.[79]

Workers can also use new technologies for *external* organizing, which involves broadcasting public messages regarding campaigns and enlisting public support. Here, new technologies have dramatically reduced certain communications costs for workers and unions, just as they have for businesses and civil society organizations.[80] For example, Fight for $15 has used social media to enlist allies to turn out for rallies and to press elected officials to pass stronger minimum-wage laws.[81] The Chicago teachers had a robust social media presence during their 2019 strike, in which teachers developed and posted videos of picket lines, often with teachers or supporters singing or performing dance routines or skits that garnered substantial

Workplace Privacy and Associational Power

public attention. In both cases, the public support wasn't based simply on the workers' demands, but on the fact that unions were pushing more explicitly moral messages about worker power, neoliberalism, and the public good.[82] While most people who engage with those messages will only do so online, others will move into offline action, and in the process, their ties to the movement and one another may become much stronger.[83]

Due in part to the email and work rule case precedents, however, workers do *not* have a right that could be quite powerful today: the right to use their employer's website, app, or other technological platform to communicate with the public. There simply is no digital equivalent to the in-person picket line or leafletting effort on or near the employer's physical property. As a result, when consumers order goods online from a department store or grocer, workers who are on strike against that very retailer have no rights to use that website or app to inform the consumer of the labor dispute. In an earlier era, workers could leaflet consumers as they were entering stores. In fact, workers can be required to advance *companies'* political agenda through technological design choices, even when doing so is directly against the workers' interests. In one recent example, Uber and Lyft bombarded drivers and passengers with messages to support a California ballot initiative, Proposition 22, that reduced drivers' employment rights. There are even allegations that the companies required workers to express support for the initiative before logging in.[84]

Due to such restrictions, it is impossible to know at this point how effectively workers could use new communications technologies for organizing. On the one hand, none of the online organizing efforts discussed in this section—at Walmart, among fast food workers, and at Uber—have actually led to unionization. (West Virginia and Chicago teachers were already unionized at the time, and ALU's campaign involved nearly a year of constant in-person organizing.) On the other hand, that is unsurprising given the difficulties that workers have with organizing in general, and the fact that companies can simply deny workers access to many workplace communications platforms. This brings us back to the lopsided legal regime that workers confront. Without the ability to translate nascent associational power into formal bargaining rights, workers' gains through online organizing typically will be fleeting. Workers can mobilize around major shared grievances at certain moments, but they have a much harder time building organizations and institutions that can protect them on an ongoing basis.

4.3 Data-Driven Surveillance and Union Avoidance

Meanwhile, even as workers struggle to use new platforms to organize, companies can utilize new technologies to spot and suppress organizing efforts or to help ensure that organizing drives never begin in the first place. Such efforts build on a long tradition of workplace surveillance geared toward stopping unionization, which reach back before Ford's Sociological Department. In some cases, employer efforts remain rather crude: listening to workers' conversations, watching what they are doing, and harassing or terminating potential union activists. But data-driven technologies are augmenting companies' powers dramatically. Those efforts play out at the initial screening and hiring stages, as well as during workers' day-to-day activities once hired.

Hiring and union avoidance Employers have long sought to preempt workers from ever seriously considering unionization. As the legal scholar Mark Barenberg has put it, companies today often "weave a lawful 'anti-union campaign' into the organizational warp and woof of the enterprise."[85] Novel information technologies are in many ways enhancing their powers to do so by reducing the costs of information gathering and transmission, and enabling companies to sidestep legal protections for workers' rights to organize. For example, under the National Labor Relations Act (NLRA), it is illegal for employers to discriminate in hiring on the basis of workers' past union activities or opinions about unionization.[86] The NLRB has also held that employers can poll workers regarding their union sympathies only in very limited circumstances because such polling can chill collective action and enable an employer to retaliate against activists.[87]

But there is significant evidence that the personality tests and other preemployment screenings discussed in this chapter can be used to deter unionization.[88] To be clear, there is not much evidence that individuals' personality traits correlate with their propensity to support unionization.[89] Rather, there is evidence that preemployment screenings can be used to discern workers' beliefs about labor relations and to discourage pro-union workers from taking jobs. Indeed, union avoidance consultants often advertise their ability to elicit such information from workers so that companies can avoid hiring them.[90] In her book *Nickel and Dimed*, Barbara Ehrenreich recounts interviewing for one job where she was given a personality test that asked whether she thought "management and employees will always be in conflict because they have totally different sets of goals."[91] An employer could clearly use that information to screen out individuals inclined to question management's authority. Such tests can also be designed to communicate that workers have little or no voice in the firm. At another point, Ehrenreich took a test that asked how strongly she agreed with the proposition that "rules have to be followed to the letter at all times," and she was marked down for agreeing "strongly" rather than "totally" with the statement.[92]

Some overseas automakers have used similar tactics when staffing for plants in the US. Gregory Saltzman, an industrial relations economist, participated in and studied one such plant's hiring process. As part of the screening, Saltzman wrote, applicants were required to watch a video where an employee asked for time off to take her daughter to the doctor, and the supervisor studied her attendance record before deciding whether she could take the time. Human resources (HR) staff then asked applicants a series of questions about the video, and applicants scored highly if they agreed that the worker's ability to take the time should depend in part on her attendance record. Saltzman argued that this process put applicants "on notice that they could expect long hours, no advance notice of overtime, and limited willingness of the employer to accommodate family needs."[93] His paper also matched hiring and tenure records with a survey that he performed of applicants regarding their union sympathies, finding that pro-union workers were "much more likely to withdraw their applications or quit shortly after being hired."[94]

Novel technologies could augment employers' capacities to thwart unionization during the hiring process. To be clear, the activities discussed next are extrapolations from established past and existing practices. I am not arguing that they are already in widespread use, but rather that they are technologically plausible and would be valuable to some companies. One option would be to use online screenings to deliver the same sort of message that Ehrenreich and Saltzman discuss. For example, many McDonald's franchisees use a centralized candidate screening system that makes some algorithmic assessments of workers before a manager ever reviews their applications.[95] A subtle or overt anti-union message could be woven into that process. For example, something like the video-screening portions of the automobile plant interview process studied by Saltzman could easily be performed online. Over time, the data gleaned from such screenings also could be used to hone the company's messages about their own operations, as well as their insights about particular candidates.

Another possibility is more dystopian. By aggregating data from multiple sources, companies may be able to predict which sorts of applicants are likely to challenge management. For example, a worker who in the past has filed an NLRB charge may be more likely to resist managerial authority. An algorithm that is intentionally designed to screen out such workers would likely be unlawfully discriminatory under the NLRA. However, as noted in chapter 2, employers in many states are permitted to discriminate among workers on the basis of their nonwork-related political and social activities *outside* the workplace.[96] Those activities might be a good proxy for attitudes toward managerial authority, and they might be discerned through analysis of social media posts and consumer spending. Moreover, because algorithmic hiring often takes place under a cloud of secrecy, workers and regulators may struggle to even access the underlying algorithms and discern any discriminatory intent or effect.

What's more, companies' abilities to spot workers' out-of-work activities are also far more powerful today than in the past. Data brokers may already possess clean and usable profiles on applicants that indicate their probable political beliefs. Meanwhile, as facial recognition software continues to develop, it may enable companies to determine quickly and cheaply whether particular individuals attended particular protests. Even if applicants did not post pictures of themselves on social media, their images may well have been posted by other attendees. Some protesters in Hong Kong and the US have already taken to covering their faces or carrying umbrellas in order to avoid facial recognition software, though they have been more worried about state than private repression.[97] Finally, the fact that hiring platforms themselves are becoming important labor market intermediaries could perpetuate such blacklisting. Hiring platforms may use data gathered about an individual from one company's application when that individual applies at another company later. In that case, Company A's rejection of that person could lead Companies B through X to reject them without even knowing why. Or if Company A uses a borderline or illegal screening mechanism, other companies may unknowingly rely on that mechanism down the line.

Workplace Privacy and Associational Power

Again, it is not clear whether such tools are already in use. In fact, an empirical study published in 2021 found that employers did *not* take workers' past union activities into account in hiring, even when workers reveal those activities on their résumés. But the authors suggested that in today's economy, "union weakness itself" may have mitigated employers' incentives to screen out union supporters.[98] That research was also carried out before the post-COVID upsurge in worker activism, and if worker mobilization becomes a significant political-economic force again, the sorts of tools surveyed here could be potent. That would be the case even if the tools themselves were imperfect, delivering only a partial picture of workers' political beliefs and actions. After all, union avoidance often occurs at the margins. The whole point is to reduce the percentage of workers who are inclined to unionize not to zero, but to a level where organizing efforts cannot get off the ground. Statistical inferences from large data sets may be very helpful in that context.

Surveillance and union avoidance Meanwhile, there is substantial evidence that companies are already trying to use novel information technologies to detect and suppress nascent organizing efforts among their workers. In the workplace, much surveillance is actually open and obvious to workers, albeit not advertised as surveillance. As the labor historian Nelson Lichtenstein put it in a book on Walmart's transformation of retail, "The 'employee attitude survey' has long been a staple of the nonunion workplace. Sears perfected the system in the 1950s when it employed skilled social scientists to identify patterns of discontent and the employees who were most disloyal" before that sentiment led to a unionization drive.[99] Today, companies of all sorts utilize surveys and other means—including inductive techniques that run on masses of data about interworker communications—to detect signs of discontent. In an earlier era, this may have required reading memoranda or physically listening in on conversations, but today it can involve electronic monitoring and may be much less expensive.

For example, the tech giants appear to be developing anti-union tools that are both fairly crude and quite powerful. During the recent period of employee unrest at Google, employees often used enterprise software to set up meetings and to discuss workplace concerns. In late 2019, several worker activists discovered that Google had developed a tool that automatically notified management when workers created a "calendar event with more than 10 rooms or 100 participants." Worker activists interpreted that as an attempt to determine when workers were meeting to discuss workplace concerns.[100] Google employees later learned that one of the HR officials who had driven the development of that tool had been meeting over the preceding months with a union avoidance consultant.[101] Amazon, similarly, has admitted that it closely monitors internal message boards, including boards that have been developed by workers from communities of color and other groups typically underrepresented in Silicon Valley, to detect union organizing.[102] Finally, in an internal presentation in June 2020 regarding "Facebook Workspace," a chat and collaboration platform meant to compete with Slack, Facebook executives noted that administrators could remove posts on certain topics and prevent such posts from trending. Among the terms that moderators suggested companies might want to block was "unionize."[103]

Other companies are aggregating data from both inside and outside their workplaces in an ongoing effort to remain union-free. For example, in 2020, journalists found that several companies, including Whole Foods and Amazon, had developed "heat maps" that sought to determine unionization risk "via a calculation that relied on employee survey data, timing of the last pay raise, and dozens of other factors."[104] As noted in this book's introduction, in 2020 Amazon posted a job announcement for "intelligence analysts" who could utilize data analytics and other tools to detect, among other things, "labor organizing threats."[105] Presumably such tools will continue to develop and become more powerful over time. For example, where companies have already deployed listening devices, keystroke monitors, and similar technologies across their worksites, those devices could likely be turned to this purpose, observing when workers use certain keywords—not just "union" but "meeting" and "protest" and "act together"—and then alerting management that workers may be planning concerted action.

Under existing doctrine, some such efforts are unlawful, others are lawful, and still others borderline. In an early case, the Supreme Court had no difficulty holding that an employer's use of "industrial spies and undercover operatives" to review a union's literature and activities and to follow several organizers outside of work violated the NLRA.[106] At the same time, employers have extensive rights to monitor the workplace, and even conversations within the workplace, under current law. Balancing those considerations, the NLRB has held that an employer's intentional observation of workers' concerted action becomes unlawful once it "goes beyond casual and becomes unduly intrusive."[107] Such efforts are most likely to run afoul of the law when they are either targeted at specific union supporters or suspected supporters—in which case they may constitute discrimination on the basis of union support—or where they are intensified in response to union activity, in which case they constitute interference with that activity.[108] Facebook's monitoring of online conversations to detect and block words like "unionize" would very likely constitute unlawful surveillance.

That said, under Trump-era doctrine, companies have another option: they could ban union speech on their internal platforms so long as they also prohibit all other political and associational speech on those platforms. In that case, the company would be acting within its rights to limit the use of those platforms for nonwork activities. Facebook did just that following some worker unrest.[109] Another option, which is again increasingly practical, is simply to weave intensive surveillance into the "warp and woof" of the enterprise. Under existing doctrine, employers are permitted to engage in pervasive surveillance of the workplace for productivity or security purposes, even if in doing so they also thwart some worker organizing.[110] This is because, like much other privacy doctrine, NLRB doctrine here takes existing monitoring and surveillance activities as a baseline, and tends only to police or forbid surveillance efforts that are unusual for that worksite.[111] Plus, detecting the surveillance itself is necessary before workers can bring a charge to the NLRB, and in most cases workers are not permitted access to their employer's algorithms.[112] As data-driven surveillance becomes easier and cheaper over time, companies may therefore have incentives to implement the most extensive surveillance possible, potentially avoiding the scrutiny that would result if they ramp up surveillance when a unionization drive has begun. Chapter 6 will return to this issue, arguing that the only way to effectively protect workers in this context may be to prevent a great deal of workplace data-gathering in the first place.

Conclusion

The introduction to section 4.2 noted the overlap between workplace privacy and workplace organizing rights. The discussion that followed also suggests a conceptual overlap between some branches of critical privacy theory and critical labor law theory. Both are focused on the relationship among information flows, individual self-understandings and actions, and the social context within which we all operate. With protections for and against particular informational flows, workers can talk to coworkers about their concerns and plan collective action without worrying that their employers will find out or take action against them. This process does not enact preferences, but rather *shapes and creates* preferences—and even a class identity. Workers' ability to take such action rests upon a foundation of interpersonal communication and trust, and on strong protections against employer interference or domination. Theories of privacy that understand it as protecting individuals' right to keep certain information secret simply do not capture the complexity or the normative implications of informational flows in this context. Among other things, existing rules and practices around workplace information enable employers to suppress workers' organizing efforts, and therefore to minimize labor costs.

Addressing these issues will require reforms on many fronts, including substantial reforms to the governance of workplace data and technology. Chapter 6 will discuss those possibilities in more detail. But workers' abilities to build associational power within their workplaces or companies would necessarily remain foundational to any project to change the political economy of work and technology. Workers need to be able to discuss common concerns and the merits of collective action, up to and including unionizing quickly and easily—often without their employers' knowledge, and certainly without their employers' resistance. Given the broad consensus around such matters, labor-affiliated members of Congress have frequently introduced legislation to remedy these shortcomings of existing law. The most recent, the Protecting the Right to Organize Act (PRO Act), would also bolster the NLRB's power to deter and remedy unfair labor practices, streamline the certification process, and expand workers' rights to strike.[113] This would enable significantly more worker mobilization and working-class power.

Yet it would not fully address technological threats to workers' associational power. So long as companies can access extensive data on worker speech and performance in the workplace, they will be able to use it to detect and then thwart organizing. Moreover, so long as employers or hiring platforms can aggregate data from multiple sources including employee screenings and supervision, they may be able to use it to curate a workforce that is less inclined to unionize or protest. One way of protecting workers in this context may be to borrow a strategy from the consumer privacy field and prevent the gathering or distribution of that sort of data in the first place—in effect, intervening at a lower stage of the data food chain.[114] Another would be to subject data-gathering and usage processes to democratic control at multiple levels. This reflects a point made by the legal scholar Salomé Viljoen, that the harms of data-gathering and aggregation today are irreducible to an individual worker's or citizen's interests. The very fact that inductive learning operates at population-wide levels and draws inferences about individuals from limited data suggests that appropriate policy responses must be social rather than individual in nature.[115] That could include devolving some governance rights over workplace data to workers themselves as part of a broader strategy to democratize workplace governance. Chapter 6 elaborates such an agenda.

5 Data, Fissuring, and Consolidation

Introduction

In the early 1940s, vendors who sold papers on the streets of Los Angeles sought to unionize under the recently passed National Labor Relations Act (NLRA or "the Act"), which raised the legal question of whether they were employees with rights under the Act or independent businesspeople with no such rights. That dispute generated a landmark 1944 Supreme Court case, *National Labor Relations Board v. Hearst Publications*.[1] Almost seventy-five years later, ride-share drivers sued Uber and Lyft for unpaid wages and other work-related expenses, posing the same legal question under California law and again generating important judicial opinions.[2] The facts of the cases were remarkably similar. Both involved business models in which workers perform tasks alone, scattered over a wide geographical territory, without the sort of in-person supervision that is standard in factories or offices. The cases nevertheless differed in one major respect: the newspaper vendors were never subject to electronic monitoring, which did not exist at the time. Uber and Lyft, in contrast, are among the most technologically advanced companies on the planet, whose entire business model depends on pervasive surveillance of their drivers and passengers.

Through the litigation process, the newspapers and the gig-economy companies argued that they simply provided workers with opportunities to sell goods and services, and as a result, the workers were more like businesspeople than employees. The companies in *Hearst* pointed out that they did not pay the vendors a salary or track their sales; instead, they sold them newspapers each day, which the vendors would in turn sell to customers.[3] The companies also noted that the vendors sold items other than the newspapers at issue, including newspapers by other publishers; they could "hire assistants and relief men"; and they could sell their "spots," the sites where they sold papers, to other vendors.[4] Uber and Lyft, for their part, argued that their applications simply matched drivers with passengers so they could ply their trade, and the drivers had the right to accept or decline ride requests. The drivers then provided their own vehicles, worked when and where they chose, were paid based on individual rides rather than on a salary basis, and had minimal contact with supervisors.[5]

The courts were not wholly convinced by such arguments. In *Hearst*, the Supreme Court held that the vendors were employees.[6] The Court noted that the companies effectively controlled wages by determining how many papers each vendor would receive, gave them "explicit instructions" regarding hours of work and sales strategies, and had terminated vendors for failing to follow such directions.[7] This made the vendors an "integral part of the publishers' distribution system."[8] The Court in *Hearst* also established a new (but short-lived) legal test for employment, which is discussed further in section 5.1 of this chapter. In the Uber and Lyft cases, meanwhile, the judges held that neither company could establish that their drivers were independent contractors, and therefore that the issue had to be resolved by a jury. (The cases later settled before trial.) In support of that holding, the judge in the Uber case noted that the "contracts seem to allow Uber to fire its drivers for any reason and at any time," that drivers needed to accept a high number of rides or be deactivated, and that Uber had set many standards around drivers' dress, music choice, and car cleanliness.[9]

More important, the judge in Uber's case reasoned that the company's technological capacities gave it substantial control over the drivers. Uber had argued that since its managers had little or no contact with drivers, it was unlike FedEx in an important precedent case, where FedEx supervisors would ride along with drivers four times a year.[10] But as the judge observed, Uber drivers were in fact subject to near-constant surveillance by customers since drivers who fell below a particular rating could be deactivated. What's more, the judge reasoned, "Uber's application data can . . . be used to constantly monitor certain aspects of a driver's behavior . . . arguably [giving] Uber a tremendous amount of control over the manner and means of its drivers' performance."[11] While the judge did not clarify which "application data" he was referring to, the opinion had earlier discussed Uber's monitoring of drivers' acceptance rates, which would be visible to the company in real time.[12] Remarkably, the opinion then quoted Michel Foucault's observation in *Discipline and Punish* that a "state of conscious and permanent visibility . . . assures the automatic functioning of power."[13] Subsequent disclosures have shown that Uber uses its app to monitor drivers' speed and to require them to follow algorithmically generated driving routes.[14]

Uber, Lyft, and other gig-economy companies exemplify a business model that has become common in recent years, which this chapter discusses. In that model, companies are using new data-driven technologies for two interrelated purposes. First, companies are purchasing labor without hiring workers as legal employees, even as they surveil and manage those workers as closely as traditional employees. The phenomenon of purchasing labor without hiring workers—which, again, dates back to well before *Hearst*—has become more widespread in recent decades, and has become known as the "fissuring" of employment.[15] As noted in chapter 2 of this book, the analogy is to the cracks or fissures that open in boulders, much as companies have opened up legal gaps between themselves and their labor forces. Second, companies are exploiting advanced information technologies to build substantial market power. For example, Uber, Lyft, Amazon, and many other companies operate as *platforms* through which parties exchange goods and services. Successful platforms often grow rapidly and come to dominate their sectors. In other cases—including in retail, fast food, and hospitality—companies have gained market power by purchasing rivals, and/or by developing technologically advanced logistics systems for their enormous global production and distribution networks. As discussed later in this chapter, the growth of platform firms and the consolidation of other service sectors overlap with broader trends toward market concentration in recent decades that were enabled by our antitrust laws.

In a sense, these developments are in tension with one another. Fissuring leads to smaller payrolls and disaggregated production as line-level workers are shunted outside a company's legal boundaries. In contrast, platform firms tend to be very large, generating and exploiting concentrated knowledge regarding production and distribution. But both developments undermine workers' associational power. Fissuring forces workers and outside suppliers to compete with one another, driving down wages and enabling lead firms and their investors to capture a greater share of profits. Consolidation can undermine workers' power in several ways. It can leave them with fewer exit options from their current employment, enable companies to dominate political decision-making, and make unionization extremely difficult. In that sense, fissuring and consolidation reflect the same underlying politics of work and technology: Both force less-skilled workers to compete with one another while protecting companies' core innovations against competition.

Section 5.1 discusses fissuring. It first outlines some basic facts about fissuring and its incidence, discusses how our labor laws encourage fissuring, and finally suggests some potential policy responses. Section 5.2 then addresses the growth of platform firms. It first summarizes more general trends toward industrial consolidation and the legal backdrop to those developments, then discusses platform firms and their effects on work, and finally suggests that policymakers consider leveraging platform and other companies' surveillance capacities to protect workers' rights.

5.1 Data-Driven Fissuring

As noted in chapter 2, Congress and other legislatures have passed a wide array of labor laws over the last century to promote social goods such as economic equality, workplace safety, workplace democracy, and equal opportunity. While those laws are central to the modern regulatory state and social contract, the scope of those laws is limited in two important respects. First, nearly all of our labor laws define *some but not all* work relationships as employment, and then give employees *but not non-employees* certain legal rights. The most important group of non-employees today are independent contractors, or individuals who are operating their own businesses. A classic example of an independent contractor is a plumber who has their own company and is hired by a business or homeowner to repair a faucet. Second, with important exceptions, our labor laws regulate only the immediate employer/employee relationship, as legally defined. Employees therefore have rights against their employers—but *only* against their employers, not against companies who have business relationships with those employers. If worker A is legally employed by company B—which is a supplier, subcontractor, or franchisee of company C—then worker A usually has no labor law rights against company C.[16]

Complying with labor laws can be costly. When a company hires workers as employees, it must pay minimum wages and overtime, must respect those workers' rights to unionize, must ensure its managers do not engage in illicit discrimination, must pay premiums for unemployment insurance and workers' compensation, and must withhold payroll taxes.[17] In contrast, when a company hires workers as independent contractors or through a subcontractor, it only needs to pay a fee for services provided. Employers may also promise their legal employees some due process prior to discipline or termination, which restricts their capacity to terminate workers and to reorganize operations at will. Purchasing labor from nonemployees, therefore, can both save money and give companies more freedom to manage their workforces.

Given these costs, companies have long sought to fissure away workers and avoid legal employment relationships. But they have done so more and more in recent decades, especially in the wake of the service transition and the decline of unions. An important "push" factor has been pressure from investors to maximize returns by shedding tasks and operations that are not profit centers.[18] An important "pull" factor has been new technologies of legibility, which have made it easier to ensure quality and sound performance even among nonemployees.[19] Those trends have developed to the point that fissuring has put pressure on our entire system of labor regulation—and will almost certainly continue to do so in the absence of legal reforms.

The political economy of fissuring There are three key fissuring strategies today. The first involves classifying (or misclassifying) individual workers as independent contractors rather than employees.[20] This is common in the gig economy and among taxi companies, delivery firms including FedEx, and elsewhere in the logistics sector.[21] Such workers may in reality have little or none of the independence enjoyed by a classic independent contractor—few specialized skills, no ability to negotiate with the companies that use their labor, and no capacity to sell their services to a competing company. Yet those workers may struggle to prove that they are employees under the law, as discussed later in this section. A second fissuring strategy is subcontracting, in which user firms hire labor through a temporary agency or a third-party contractor.[22] Unlike independent contractors, subcontracted workers usually have a legal employer—the agency or subcontractor—but the user firm may have more power to set wages and working conditions. Subcontracting is especially common in building services, agriculture, logistics, hotels, and warehouses.[23] The third strategy is franchising, where core firms, especially in fast food and retail, license their trademarks and product lines to independent businesses, who in turn employ line-level workers.[24] There again, the franchisor may be the party with the most economic power, and may exert substantial control over franchisees' operations and business decisions—but it may have no duties toward the franchisees' workers.

A neoclassical economic model suggests that workers' wages should track their skills or productivity, and therefore that fissuring should not generally save money. But this is not how things work out in practice. Workers classified as independent contractors are not eligible for basic labor protections, which can drive down their pay. Similarly, a large study of franchisees found substantially lower rates of compliance with wage/hour laws in franchise locations that were independently owned compared to those owned by the franchisor.[25] Other studies have found that subcontracted janitors and security guards can make 15 percent less than in-house workers doing the same jobs, and that workers at outsourced call centers tend to make less than call center workers employed by the companies they're serving.[26]

The lower pay earned by fissured workers makes sense under a model of labor standards that takes power disparities seriously. Fissuring helps to ensure that reliable profit centers—such as proprietary technologies, product design and management functions, and aspects of production that require rare skills—are held within one legal entity, while workers who perform less profitable functions are excluded from that entity.[27] In that context, fissuring can reduce or suppress workers' associational power—and therefore labor costs—in two ways. First, fissured workers may struggle to place moral demands on a user firm for decent treatment.[28] For example, where fissuring leads to workers being outside a company's physical plant or having little to no contact with that company's staff, they will have a harder time getting to know the company's other employees or managers. Second, as discussed in more detail in the next subsection, fissuring functions as a liability shield, even when workers may have sound arguments that they meet the legal definition of employment.

Why a company would *ever* accept the costs that go along with employment regulations if they can be avoided through fissuring? There are several reasons. The workers involved may have skills that are sufficiently rare that the company needs to pay well to recruit and retain them, and the company can remain profitable while following all legal obligations. Conversely, workers with few particularized skills, who are basically just selling their labor power, will be disproportionately fissured away. The company may also need to be able to schedule workers for regular shifts, supervise them closely, and require them to work as part of a team. That helps explain, for example, why McDonald's franchisees classify their workers as employees rather than independent contractors, while many gig-economy companies have resisted having their workers classified as employees—though in the former case, McDonald's corporate has pushed labor costs down to the franchisees. That being said, digital Taylorism is eroding the need for teamwork in many cases. As discussed in chapter 3, Amazon has designed warehouses so that workers labor alone and can be trained quickly, which should facilitate hiring warehouse workers as temps or through labor agencies. Finally, the law surrounding employment status may simply make it impossible for companies to avoid having any responsibilities for their workers. In such cases, however, labor law duties impose costs but few benefits on companies, which has encouraged companies to continually test the law's boundaries, as discussed in the next subsection.

Fissuring and the law Fissuring's liability-blocking effects are almost entirely a function of how our laws define employment. This issue has bedeviled courts, agencies, and legislatures since well before *Hearst*.[29] As the Supreme Court observed in that case, "few problems in the law" have led to as many inconsistent results as "cases arising in the borderland between what is clearly an employer-employee relationship and what is clearly one of independent entrepreneurial dealing."[30] Chapter 2 gave a brief overview of the law in this area, but a more detailed summary is now appropriate.

Prior to the New Deal, the question of whether a worker was a legal employee arose most often where a worker caused a physical injury to a third party, such as in a traffic or construction accident. The injured parties often sued in tort—the law governing liability for accidental and intentional physical injuries—and argued that the worker was acting on behalf of the company that had hired them, and therefore that the company was financially responsible. In addressing such questions, the courts developed a multifactor test to distinguish between employees and independent contractors. That test centered on whether the hiring party had the right to control the performance of the work at issue—and to this day, it is often known as the "control test"—but it also looked at related factors, such as whether the worker was in a "distinct occupation or business," the worker's skill level, the length of the relationship, and the method of payment.[31] In

Hearst itself, the companies argued that the NLRA incorporated this definition of employment.[32] As discussed later in this subsection, the Supreme Court ended up applying a different test in *Hearst*, but Congress overruled that opinion, and a version of the "control test" has governed the question of employment under the NLRA for decades now.

There are several problems with utilizing the control test to determine who has rights under worker-protective statutes. First, that test does not necessarily generate predictable results even in tort cases due to the wide variety of work relationships in our economy, the malleability of various factors, and the challenges that courts face when trying to weigh competing factors against one another. As the Court observed in *Hearst*, the test's focus on the right to control delivered more "simplicity of formulation than of application."[33] Second, while the right to control bore a straightforward relationship to the issue in tort cases—which party was best able to prevent the harm—that policy goal is not obviously relevant in the employment context. In a case like *Hearst*, the control test would direct attention to whether vendors posed a physical risk to customers or other third parties. But the NLRA itself is focused on a very different issue: altering economic power relations between workers and companies. As another scholar has put it, the difficulty of accounting for economic power under the control test "invite[s] employers to structure their relationships with employees in whatever manner best evades liability."[34] Third, the very complexity of the control test creates barriers to justice. Lower-wage workers may struggle to find counsel to take on such cases, given the low damages at stake and the high cost of developing a factual record around numerous disparate factors. Delays in litigation also structurally favor employers in such cases by generating pressure on workers to settle claims.

Those problems pre-dated *Hearst*, and led the Court there to hold that employment should be defined "broadly, in doubtful situations" through reference to "underlying economic facts" rather than common law technicalities.[35] In the case at hand, it reasoned, the vendors were vulnerable and lacked economic power in their individual negotiations, so they were employees under the NLRA.[36] In a sense, then, the *Hearst* court treated the legal definition of employment as a test for class position, even if it did not use the term "working class."[37] Similarly, in an early case arising under the Fair Labor Standards Act (FLSA), *Rutherford Food Corp. v. McComb*, the Supreme Court held that a slaughterhouse legally employed a group of workers who had been hired and supervised by an independent foreman to debone carcasses. The Court reasoned that the workers were employees of the slaughterhouse, notwithstanding the common law, because they were working on the company's premises and providing a service that was integral to the company's overall operations.[38] By defining employment broadly and purposively, Congress and the Court sought not just to protect individual workers in those cases, but also to deter similar practices going forward, since their widespread use undermined the statutory goals of workplace democracy and income equality.

The Court's purposive test for employment was short-lived under the NLRA. Congress responded to *Hearst* by specifying in 1947's Taft-Hartley Act that the NLRA did not cover independent contractors,[39] and the Supreme Court later interpreted that provision to require that the common law control test governed under the NLRA.[40] Subsequent cases established that the control test applies under most federal worker-protective statutes.[41] The definition of employment under the FLSA is somewhat broader, incorporating multiple, sometimes conflicting factors but focusing on the "economic realities" of the parties' relationship.[42] State wage-and-hour laws have also defined employment somewhat more broadly. For example, although the test under California law that applied to Uber and Lyft drew from the common law,[43] the court in the Lyft case observed that that test should be "liberally construed" to protect vulnerable workers.[44]

Regardless of the specific test, however, courts and agencies in recent years have often focused on a putative employer's contractually specified rights rather than on indicia of economic power.[45] This is especially true in the NLRA context, reflecting the general trend toward contractualism and formalism in recent decades. The discussion that follows will focus on that statute because, of all employment regulations, it does the most to shape workers' associational power. In a 2009 case arising under the NLRA, the US Court of Appeals for the District of Columbia Circuit (D.C. Circuit) reasoned that "evidence of unequal bargaining power" between a company and a putative independent contractor does not give rise to an inference of an employment relationship.[46] Neither, the court continued, does evidence showing "the economic controls which many corporations are able to exercise over independent contractors."[47] That case also held that the National Labor Relations Board (NLRB) should focus, in such cases, on whether a putative independent contractor enjoyed "the opportunities and risks inherent in entrepreneurialism."[48] On its face, a focus on entrepreneurialism seems to give courts and the NLRB a helpful lens through which to interpret the multiple, often-conflicting factors at issue, by posing the question of whether individuals are more like wage workers or more like businesspeople. But that approach can have a perverse effect: when companies shift risks or costs to workers via a contractual agreement, those workers' very vulnerability to manipulation and exploitation can make courts and agencies *less* likely to view them as individuals in need of protection.[49]

Meanwhile, regardless of the merits of "entrepreneurialism" as a focal point, the NLRB has interpreted it in ways that disregard economic and social realities. Entrepreneurship typically involves the development of new business models and methods, and especially of new technologies that give a company a competitive advantage.[50] Yet in a recent case, the NLRB found that drivers for the airport transportation service SuperShuttle were independent contractors, even though they were required to use SuperShuttle's proprietary technology to receive all assignments.[51] Similarly, the NLRB under President Donald Trump adopted a new rule for joint employment—a doctrine under which two companies can share employment duties toward particular workers—which also disregarded economic power. Joint employment can arise both in horizontal relationships between firms that share employees, and in vertical relations between user firms and subcontractors, or franchisors and franchisees. Under the Trump-era test, a putative joint employer had to actually exercise "substantial direct and immediate control,"[52] not just reserve the *right* to exercise control, as the common law control test has traditionally required. That standard further specified that one entity does not jointly set wages for another's workers even if the two enter into a cost-plus contract—again, disregarding the economic realities of the relationship.[53]

In still other cases, the NLRB and courts have drawn bright-line rules between business entities that disregard power relations between or among them. For example, the NLRB has held that a company does not necessarily violate the NLRA by terminating a subcontractor because its employees have unionized,[54] a ruling that creates powerful disincentives for such workers to organize.[55] Similarly, the NLRB has held that subcontracted workers have limited rights to picket user firms, on the ground that the user firms are separate entities from the workers' employers.[56] This sort of logic can generate borderline-absurd results in the franchising context. There, franchisees and franchisors may be treated as separate businesses for the purposes of

Data, Fissuring, and Consolidation 115

labor laws, so franchisors avoid duties to workers—even as they are treated as a single entity for the purposes of antitrust laws, enabling franchisors to exert substantial control over franchisees' activities.[57]

The effect of such strategies is that the real parties in interest have few or no duties toward the workers whose labor they purchase through intermediaries. A company relentlessly focused on cost-saving, then, may use judgment-proof contractors or franchisees—or require contractors and suppliers to compete on price until it is not possible to profit without violating labor laws—safe in the knowledge that the costs of labor law violations are unlikely to be passed on to them.[58]

Examples of data-driven fissuring Again, while fissuring has been a longstanding feature of the employment landscape, new technologies of legibility have made it much easier for companies to monitor and exert power over suppliers, contractors, and individual workers. In the industrial context, those technologies have enabled companies to formalize what had previously been tacit knowledge and then outsource it. As a study sponsored by the US Census Bureau put it, "the act of collecting data [on manufacturing processes] serves to codify information, which makes it more explicit and less tacit." This involves a move "from 'art' to 'science', whereby managerial efforts focus on greater standardization, mechanization, and instrumentation of the process."[59] Using such techniques, companies can break production into discrete tasks, farm some of them out to suppliers, and use advanced technologies to monitor those suppliers' performance.[60]

Such close oversight of contractual partners marks a significant change from the past. The "putting-out" system in textile manufacturing, where early capitalists gave materials to individuals for weaving in their homes, often led to low quality and a slow pace of work.[61] More recently, firms that outsourced labor often did so under the table, using an intermediary but not engaging in active supervision. The newspaper-vendor relationship is *Hearst* is one example. Similarly, in what became known as the "sweating system" in garment production in the early twentieth century, companies hired contractors who would in turn hire subcontractors, or even let out work to individual sewers in their houses, to keep labor costs to an absolute minimum. Companies could ensure discipline through product specifications, piece rates, and ex post inspections, but they had little or no real-time information about work performance.[62] Today, in contrast, firms can use advanced information technologies to gain some of the benefits of employment—close supervision and coordination of work to ensure high quality—without the legal obligations that come with it.

Walmart is a paradigm case here in the service context. Over the course of the 1980s and 1990s, as networked information technologies matured, Walmart used them to grow into a retailing behemoth.[63] The company's "retail link" system, for example, uses data on store-level inventory, sometimes gathered through point-of-sale systems, to optimize its sourcing and distribution systems.[64] Decisions about store inventories are made in the corporate office in Bentonville, Arkansas, rather than locally, and the company delivers cereal, paper towels, and other basic goods before local managers are even aware that they are running low.[65] While Walmart directly employs the workers in its stores, its economic footprint extends around the globe to incorporate a vast network of suppliers—and Walmart has used both its leverage as a major purchaser and its extensive data on market trends and supply networks to exert power over those suppliers.[66] For example, it may push suppliers to keep prices to an absolute minimum, even as it dictates specific terms to them, such as requesting that they alter package sizes and shapes to make shipping and shelf stocking easier.[67] Recent economic studies have strongly suggested that these efforts drive down wages among Walmart suppliers,[68] even as Walmart bears no legal duties toward those workers.

Like Walmart before it, Amazon's labor footprint extends well beyond its own corporate boundaries. As discussed in section 5.2 later in this chapter, Amazon also uses data on consumer demand and past purchases to determine sales prices, which gives it power over suppliers similar to that enjoyed by Walmart. Meanwhile, Amazon has outsourced delivery both to independent contractors for Amazon Flex, and to various outside companies it terms "Delivery Service Partners" (DSPs). As one article explained, Amazon's contracts require DSPs to "provide Amazon physical access to their premises and all sorts of data the retailer wants, such as geo-locations, speed and movement of drivers—information the company says it has the power to use however it wants."[69] Such monitoring efforts can give Amazon the best of both worlds: the powers traditionally associated with employment without the duties and costs.

Similar trends are apparent in fast food. Here Starbucks is an outlier: rather than using a franchising model, it directly owns and operates most of its locations in the US. That has likely made it easier for Starbucks workers to organize, because they do not have to establish that Starbucks is their employer. In contrast, McDonald's is not a single legal enterprise, but an amalgamation of tens of thousands formally distinct entities. At the center is McDonald's corporate. At the edges are the McDonald's locations that the company itself runs, along with the many McDonald's franchises that are independently owned and operated as separate corporations.[70] The franchise business model pushes many start-up costs and risks onto individual franchise owners. Yet McDonald's has standardized how work is performed across franchisees by training managers and other staff,[71] and it has set specifications for the performance of specific tasks, sometimes down to the second.[72]

Unions and regulators have also argued that point-of-sale and payroll management systems are integrated between franchisees and McDonald's corporate. For example, during the Barack Obama administration, the NLRB's then–general counsel Richard Griffin filed an amicus brief in a case where the Board was reconsidering its joint employer doctrine. While that case arose out of a recycling facility, it had obvious relevance for McDonald's and other franchise businesses. Part of the brief summarized the evidence on franchisors' use of technology to manage their relationships with franchisees as follows:

> Some franchisors even keep track of data on sales, inventory, and labor costs; calculate the labor needs of the franchisees; set and police employee work schedules; track franchisee wage reviews; track how long it takes for employees to fill customer orders, accept employment applications through the franchisor's system; and screen applicants through that system. Thus, current technological advances have permitted franchisors to exert significant control over franchisees, e.g., through scheduling and labor management programs that go beyond the protection of the franchisor's product or brand.[73]

Many major hotel chains also use a franchise model, in which the brand leases operating rights to independent businesses that own particular properties. Indeed, by 2011, Marriott "owned and managed only 1 of the 356 properties operating under one of its brands."[74] At the same time, Marriott has integrated systems for reservations and supply chain management to serve its global network of hotels. As a recent article put it, the company has a single platform for both sourcing and accounts payable, which "ensures data that can be analysed and be transparent, enabling Marriott to better determine where commodities are needed, in real-time."[75] In that sense, Marriott is also acting as a platform toward its franchisees. Hotel franchisees may then utilize contractors to ensure "clean rooms, cheery front desk staff, or prompt curbside service."[76] Cleaning staff and front desk staff, therefore, can be two or more contractual degrees removed from the company with real power over their working conditions.

There are many other examples, especially in the low-wage economy.[77] In an illustration of how automation, algorithmic management, and fissuring are interrelated, medical transcriptionists at the University of Pittsburgh Medical Center learned during a unionization drive that their jobs were being outsourced, since the task of transcribing records could be performed anywhere, on an on-demand basis.[78] The maturation of natural language recognition technologies is creating similar opportunities among customer service companies and contractors. As customers increasingly experience, companies are using natural language processing via chat windows or verbal interfaces to answer some questions previously answered by workers. Human workers may be brought in to address more complex questions. But if it is not economically beneficial for those workers to be colocated, the company using their services will find it easier to classify them as independent contractors, or to subcontract their work. Gig-economy companies and others have also been developing temporary-services apps for other sorts of jobs, including hotel cleaners, janitors, dishwashers, cooks, and warehouse workers.[79] At some companies and locations, those sorts of jobs require teamwork and a stable workforce with company-specific knowledge, making them somewhat less amenable to fissuring. But in many other cases, workers can be plugged in and out of companies relatively quickly with little training. As a result, the law is all that prevents companies from fissuring away work in many enterprises today.

Potential policy responses to fissuring Addressing fissuring under existing law is quite difficult since existing law positively encourages the practice. Notably, the US is becoming an outlier on this issue, at least at the federal level. During the Trump administration companies pushed for and obtained broader legal rights to fissure away workers under the NLRA, including gig economy workers,[80] even as courts in various other nations and some US states had held that Uber and Lyft drivers were employees for some purposes.[81] In late 2021, the European Commission also issued a set of proposals to improve working conditions on labor platforms, which would require member-states to establish more worker-friendly tests for employment on digital platforms. Notably, under the directive, workers on platforms would be presumed to be employees so long as the platform met two of the following five criteria of control: setting pay, setting specific work rules, surveilling the performance of work, restricting workers' ability to choose working hours or reject assignments, and restricting workers' outside opportunities.[82]

Legislatures in the US have sought to respond to fissuring as well. A common proposal to address independent contractor misclassification would replace the "control" and/or "economic reality" tests that now predominate with the so-called ABC test for employment. Under the ABC test, individuals hired to perform work for pay are presumed to be employees, and the employer can rebut that presumption only by showing that (A) it does not exert control over its workers, (B) the work performed is outside the usual scope of the employer's business, and (C) the worker is engaged in an independent trade, occupation, or business. California has now adopted that test for its state labor code, though gig-economy companies obtained an exemption in 2020 via a ballot measure known as Proposition 22.[83] That test has also appeared in some versions of the PRO Act, an omnibus labor law reform proposal at the federal level.[84] In addition to such reforms or as an alternative, Congress could specify that certain individual workers classified as independent contractors still have the right to organize and bargain collectively, as well as the right to a minimum wage and overtime pay.[85]

Companies surely would resist such moves, of course. Through 2021, the gig-economy companies pressed for exemptions from employment duties in various states.[86] And even when companies lose legislative or court battles, they may be able to leverage new technologies to avoid liability. For example, when Uber and Lyft were faced with the possibility of ramped-up enforcement in California, they floated the idea of reorganizing: instead of their current independent contractor model, they would utilize a franchisee or subcontractor model.[87] There is precedent for that move. After losing a set of wage and hour lawsuits, FedEx required its drivers in some states to set up corporations and to hire staff, to help ensure that they would be treated as contractors in the future.[88] Using electronically signed contracts and user agreements, Uber and Lyft could do the same thing today with *no* physical reorganization of their or their drivers' operations at all. Companies' capacity to rearrange operations so easily—especially when layered atop their broad legal powers to set up their enterprises using fissured labor in the first place—suggests that legislatures may need to think more aggressively about how to allocate employment duties.

One option here would be to statutorily define work relationships in certain sectors as legal employment for the purposes of particular statutes. Legislatures could declare, for example, that gig-economy and logistics companies employ their drivers or could adopt a version of the European Commission's proposed factor-based analysis. Legislatures could take a similar approach to joint employment, declaring for example that fast food and hotel franchisors jointly employ their franchisees' workers, that general contractors on construction sites jointly employ their subcontractors' workers, and that janitors in large commercial office buildings are jointly employed by the companies who own or manage the properties. California has taken steps in that direction.[89] Such legislation could also instruct enforcement agencies to identify other sectors or types of relationships where employment or joint employment will be presumed. Another option would be for legislatures to instruct enforcement agencies to develop economic models that capture power differences between companies that can be expected to reduce wages for workers at contractors or vendors.[90] When Amazon and Walmart more or less dictate prices to suppliers, or hotel brands dictate prices to cleaning contractors, that fact could be taken into account in determining those companies' responsibilities.[91] Chapter 6 explores a related idea—namely, that legislatures should take companies' surveillance capacities into account when assigning legal responsibility for working conditions, on the theory that such surveillance is an exercise of class power. Finally, reforms to make it easier for workers to unionize would also help address fissuring, because unionized workers could protest fissuring efforts, take wages out of competition across sectors, or both.[92] That idea is also explored in chapter 6.

5.2 Inductive Knowledge, Consolidation, and Platforms

A notable fact about many of the companies discussed in this book is that they are quite large, enjoying substantial shares of their respective product markets, despite the fact that they have fissured away many workers. Uber is again a helpful example. Before it arrived in many cities, the taxi sector was characterized by intense competition among many small companies and independent operations. Today, Uber and Lyft are by far the largest players.[93] These developments reflect a broader and longer-running trend: various industrial sectors have become more concentrated at the national level in recent decades, with a smaller number of companies controlling a greater share of the market.[94] Companies have often pursued market dominance for a simple reason: it can generate outsized profits since companies that face less competition can "create a relatively wide margin between the costs of production and the sales price."[95] These developments have also generated widespread academic and political concern and have led scholars to rejuvenate an earlier tradition of antitrust thinking that was suspicious of concentrated corporate power given its tendency to thwart innovation and to give leading firms excessive political-economic power.[96] This section first addresses the causal factors behind consolidation and explores how consolidation may affect workers. It then discusses the rise of platform firms like Uber, Lyft, and Amazon and the additional challenges they pose for workers.

Market consolidation Trends toward consolidation have been driven by numerous factors, including both legal and technological developments. Legally, a key factor was the reshaping of antitrust law in the 1980s around a consumer welfare standard, under which a company's size alone typically will not trigger antitrust scrutiny unless the company also increases consumer prices.[97] Regulators then took a more permissive attitude toward mergers and megafirms, which enabled more industrial consolidation over time. Regarding technology, several forces were especially important. In the tech sector, firms like Google and Facebook established first-mover advantages in search and social networking that compounded over time, fueled in part by those companies' exclusive control over user data. Like other companies that traffic in information goods, Google and Facebook also could scale up very quickly since they did not require the investments in machinery, storefronts, or other physical capital that are required of manufacturers, for example.[98] But the trend was not limited to pure technology companies. Walmart, fast food companies, and hotels scaled up in part by leveraging supply-chain management technologies. More recently, Amazon's explosive growth helped to consolidate online retail.[99] Hospital and long-term-care markets have also become more concentrated, due in large part to mergers.[100]

In analyzing these trends, a number of leading economists and legal scholars have argued that growing market concentration is harming workers.[101] Now, in assessing those arguments, it is important not to assume that workers and employers had equal power in a prior era, or that market share is the only important form of employer power. As discussed in chapter 1, power imbalances are a structural feature of most labor markets and labor relations regardless of employer concentration. At the most basic level, the firm itself aggregates capital so that investors can bargain collectively with individual workers who may face a stark choice between working and destitution, so that employment contracts are entered on an uneven playing field.

Market concentration therefore does not create power imbalances, but it can exacerbate them. Most starkly, where a single employer dominates a particular labor market, it will enjoy *monopsony power*, here meaning the power to set prices for the purchase of labor. Since that company's employees will have few outside options, they will not be able to threaten to leave in order to get their employer to increase their wages.[102] The classic case is a company town, in which there is literally one employer, but recent empirical studies have suggested that monopsony and wage suppression are also common outside that context. One study found that hospital mergers that led to substantial increases in market concentration reduced wage growth among workers with health care-specific skills.[103] After the mergers, those workers presumably enjoyed less competition for their services. Concentration can also augment employers' power by facilitating coordination among employers to suppress worker mobility. McDonald's and various other fast food chains, for example, included provisions in their franchise agreements for years that prohibited franchisees from poaching staff from corporate-owned restaurants. The companies agreed to rescind those provisions in 2018, under pressure from the Washington State attorney general.[104] Finally, unionization may be nearly impossible at very large companies today, due to the enormous expense that a union would have to assume to organize those companies' workers. As discussed in chapters 2 and 4, such a union would need to organize site by site and then merge the organized sites into larger bargaining units—all against well-funded and technologically sophisticated employer resistance.

The empirical evidence on the relationship between firm size and working conditions is nevertheless complicated. For one thing, while wages have stagnated alongside greater market concentration in recent decades, other institutional shifts clearly played a role in wage stagnation, including deunionization, fissuring, and the various labor discipline strategies discussed in prior chapters. Indeed, unions may be able to mitigate some of the negative effects of consolidation: one recent empirical study found that mergers in health care had less of a negative effect on wages when workers were unionized.[105] Moreover, employees of larger firms have historically earned *higher* wages than workers at smaller firms in the same industry.[106] That may be because larger firms can extract monopoly rents from consumers, or because those firms enjoy economies of scale or greater productivity due to their investments in technology. Or it might be because workers and the public think that larger and more profitable firms should share the wealth by paying higher wages.[107] The large-firm wage premium does seem to have declined in recent years, however, perhaps due to a combination of deunionization and the service transition.[108] In any event, the complex relationship between monopsony and working conditions suggests that policy responses should include not just new antitrust strategies, but also reforms that bolster workers' own countervailing power. Some such strategies are discussed below and in chapter 6. But first, it is necessary to discuss the growth of platform firms in the low-wage service economy.

The rise of platforms In addition to the factors discussed previously, consolidation has been driven by the greater availability of data on consumer and worker behavior, and by new means of utilizing that data. As noted in chapters 3 and 4, data analytics work best at scale, where companies can profit from the sorts of statistical judgments they generate. That is one reason why leading companies both in and beyond the tech sector have gathered and exploited ever-greater quantities of data on production, distribution, and consumer behavior.[109] As discussed in chapter 2, their capacities to do so have been shaped and facilitated by law, including the expansion of intellectual property (IP) rights and courts' acquiescence in companies' use of trade secrets and contract doctrines to claim property-like entitlements in data. As just noted, these developments also encourage consolidation because companies that are best able to exploit data can leverage first-mover advantages into market dominance.

Many companies have done this through a particular business model: the "platform" firm, in which a company sits between and establishes the basic terms of commerce for customers and sellers of goods and services.[110] Facebook and Google are the preeminent examples. While their labor footprints are not that large,[111] many large, low-wage employers have adopted elements of the model. Uber, Lyft, DoorDash, Instacart, and other gig economy companies are all platforms that match consumers and workers for short-term tasks. Amazon, similarly, utilizes data on customer demand, supplier behavior, and supply chains to operate a two-sided platform for the sale and delivery of goods. It has been dominant in online retail for some time now, and is gaining market share in grocery delivery.[112] Some large retailers, franchised hotel chains, and fast food companies have also used elements of the model. McDonald's both licenses operating rights to franchisees and acts in some sense as a platform intermediary between them and suppliers by purchasing agricultural commodities like potatoes, pork, and beef and distributing them to stores. As discussed in chapter 4, employee recruitment is also increasingly carried out through online platforms. Those companies occupy a truly enviable position: they can obtain market share rapidly due to the low marginal costs of adding job listings and accepting applications, and they may also be able to gather and maintain data on particular candidates and clients over time.

In the labor context, platforms generate profits by establishing a choke point through which a huge volume of transactions must pass. Their control over exchange then gives them the power to charge a fee on those transactions. If Uber and Lyft someday generate sustainable profits, it will be because they have done this and effectively "taxed" most rides in major cities. Similarly, Amazon essentially taxes transactions on its platform, all while using its own market power to undercut or compete with vendors.[113] While the technologies here are novel, the strategy of establishing a choke point and taxing transactions is not new. Immanuel Wallerstein argues that it has been the favored strategy of mafias in many cases, because it enables the accumulation of capital in otherwise highly competitive markets where innovations are scarce.[114] That helps explain why the model has been especially successful in local delivery, taxis, and online retail.

Indeed, platforms may be profitable *only* if they have a degree of monopoly power, some of which is in fact baked into the platform model. Successful platforms often rely on network effects, where the addition of users actually increases the welfare of existing users rather than diminishing it, which generates "tendencies toward monopoly."[115] Uber's model again helps illustrate this point: in order to ensure that customers do not have to wait long for a car, the company needs to have many drivers on the street; and to keep those drivers on the street, it needs to have robust consumer demand—or to lead drivers to believe that there is robust demand.[116]

Similarly, social media platforms depend on a large user base that stays engaged, so they often promote content that is viral, polarizing, or both.[117] Those network effects, together with first-mover advantages and platforms' control over data, can generate monopoly power, along both horizontal and vertical dimensions. Horizontally, users become dependent on the platform and cease to utilize competitors' services, while vertically, buyers and sellers on such platforms are subject to the platform's terms and conditions.[118]

That has various negative consequences. Some platform firms (especially Google, Facebook, and Amazon) have near-monopoly power over essential resources, including search technologies and media and communications tools. Indeed, the technology giants today enjoy a sort of power that in the past was enjoyed only by sovereigns: the power to exclude citizens from essential resources and certain standard privileges and immunities of citizenship. Social media companies' exclusion of users for violating terms of service is one example.[119] Amazon enjoys a similar power over vendors on its platform. As argued in the prior section, gig-economy workers are vulnerable due to to their platforms' power to change their policies or deactivate workers without cause, and franchisees and their workers are vulnerable due to franchisors' power to set performance standards. Meanwhile, platforms' control over data and technology gives them some capacities to avoid regulations. If regulators can neither access companies' data (due to trade secrets and constitutional protections) nor understand those companies' algorithms (due to their complexity), it may be nearly impossible to ensure that the companies are abiding by the law.[120]

Indeed, by consolidating data and inductive knowledge about economic behavior, platforms may be generating a historic shift in collective economic behavior. As a mode of business operation, they sit somewhere between market ordering and planning. In a sense, they are trying to solve what Hayek called the "knowledge problem" that plagued earlier generations of planned economies: no sovereign or entity could ever gather or grasp the widely diffuse knowledge that consumers bring to markets, and planners could not allocate goods effectively as a result. As Hayek put it, "The knowledge of the circumstances of which we must make use never exists in concentrated or integrated form but solely as the dispersed bits of incomplete and frequently contradictory knowledge which all the separate individuals possess."[121] Markets, Hayek argued, brought together all consumers and reflected their preferences, generating price signals that captured those preferences in the aggregate. Today, through their privileged access to and control over user data, platforms aspire to capture and exploit the signals that customers and sellers are sending. They aspire to become the sort of sovereign that Hayek thought was impossible: one with panoptic knowledge about market behavior and the power to steer it.[122] In other words, platforms are *constructing* new modes of and sites for competition and cooperation, but always in ways that serve their interests and augment their power.

Legibility and conditions of possibility At the same time, the increased legibility of work today—which has helped to drive fissuring, consolidation, and the growth of platforms—could create some opportunities to ensure better work in the future. As Rebecca Johnson and Tanina Rostain have argued in a related context, big data and related tools can "shin[e] a spotlight on inequality and subject[] powerful institutions to enhanced oversight."[123] This may be occurring in the labor context, where in some sectors data-driven surveillance has encouraged greater formalization of work relationships. For example, prior to Uber's and Lyft's emergence, the taxi sector in many cities was highly fragmented and informal.[124] Individuals or companies would purchase medallions that gave them a license to operate and lease out the operating rights to another party, who would in turn lease out a cab to an individual. That system put workers several contractual degrees away from the investors who ultimately profited from their labor, which made enforcement of basic labor standards challenging. The industry's lack of technological sophistication made enforcement still more difficult.[125] It is easy to forget that taxis operated on cash in many cities until quite recently.

The growth of Uber and Lyft greatly harmed incumbent drivers, especially those who owned their own cabs, but the companies also made drivers proximate to a very large and well-capitalized firm with extensive governance capacity.[126] That fact doesn't necessarily help drivers much at this point—but it could. Those companies have data on drivers' wages and performance that were not readily available to taxi companies or regulators in the past, which could be leveraged to ensure compliance with basic labor standards. Similar transformations have occurred elsewhere in the gig economy.[127] DoorDash and Instacart, for example, have quickly built power in their sectors of restaurant delivery and grocery delivery, respectively, where in the past, delivery services were informal and delivery workers were often paid well below minimum wage.[128]

Regulators could require such companies to use their surveillance capabilities to ensure decent labor standards. This is not an entirely novel proposal: past labor and employment scholars have argued that large firms should have the duty to use their own internal governance processes—which they often develop to ensure high-quality goods or services—to enforce statutory mandates.[129] In fact, companies already must do this to some extent in the sexual harassment context, and the Supreme Court has suggested that large firms may need to have more detailed and sophisticated reporting practices than smaller firms, given their greater governance capacities.[130] (Whether such antiharassment policies work as currently designed is another question entirely.)[131] Large firms are also often better positioned than small ones to ensure equal employment opportunity, because they employ large numbers of workers. Compare a local restaurant sector with many small players to a sector dominated by a couple of large chains. In the former case, rooting out discriminatory hiring patterns (e.g., women as hosts and servers, men as bartenders, whites in front, Black and Latino workers in back) may require regulators to police many firms' behavior. In the latter case, the large chains can take on much of that burden, tracking applicant flow data, establishing effective affirmative action programs, and setting policies within the organization.

The same strategies could be applied to economic rights. For instance, virtually all companies are required to comply with wage and hour laws, but large companies often keep these records automatically, while in the informal economy such records are often on paper (if they even exist). Where a platform enters an informal labor market, it also generates and tracks data about that sector's workers into timekeeping and payment software. Similarly, some freelancer platforms automatically measure workers' hours and take screen grabs that document their work as they perform it, allowing remote clients to monitor their progress. While such a system raises privacy issues, some platforms have instituted the practice as part of a precommitment mechanism: workers who agree to such monitoring are guaranteed fast payment, from the platform if not the client.[132] The data gleaned through those efforts could be used to ensure legal compliance as well. Some large platform firms would also be natural collective bargaining partners if they were defined as their workers' employers. A bargaining unit of Uber drivers could substantially raise standards in the sector, and such drivers make up a natural "community of interest," as required under US labor law, since they perform virtually identical work.[133] Indeed, where unions would need to establish a multiemployer bargaining unit to bargain with taxi companies in many cities, that is not the case for Uber since the company itself has direct relationships with its drivers. To reiterate, data-driven consolidation has had largely negative effects on workers so far. The point of the examples in this subsection is just that consolidation also creates some possibilities for more effective regulation in the future.

Conclusion

Of all the developments discussed over the last three chapters, fissuring, consolidation, and the growth of platforms may reflect the closest connection among law, new technological affordances, and class relations. Relatively narrow definitions of employment have long incentivized fissuring, while changes in antitrust policy and information law have encouraged consolidation. The maturation of data-driven technologies has aggravated both tendencies. As a result, today's largest low-wage employers are truly massive and often focus their core operations around their own IP and trade secrets, which tend to be highly profitable since they are protected against external competition. Market dominance can also generate high profits, and in some sectors, companies' market dominance through platforms and their control over productive data reinforce one another in a cyclical fashion. Meanwhile, companies are using their operational and legal control over data to reconfigure labor practices in ways that force workers to compete with one another, keeping wages down and ensuring that investors and managers capture a greater share of profits.

Responding to fissuring and consolidation will likely require an antimonopoly strategy and a worker power strategy that can operate hand-in-hand. In the franchise context, companies that are treated as one entity for antitrust purposes could be treated as one entity for labor law purposes. Amazon could be restricted from competing with other vendors on its platform and also could be held to some duties toward workers within its sphere of influence. Merger review could take more explicit account of a proposed merger's potential effects on workers as well as consumers.

Some platforms with monopoly power, like gig-economy companies, could potentially be broken into regional or even local operators and required to use their data to ensure compliance. Or, now that the capacities of market-mediating algorithms have been proven, policymakers could encourage their diffusion into smaller companies, at least for the purposes of ensuring legal compliance. Chapter 6 takes up related questions in detail, asking how data-driven technologies can be repurposed to enhance rather than undermine workplace democracy.

6 Data and Economic Democracy

This book has argued that companies are using networked information technologies as tools of class power. Companies are deploying those technologies to displace workers through automation, to reduce the skills required for various tasks, to physically separate workers from one another, to surveil workers more and more intensely, to prevent or suppress organizing, and even to deny workers their basic legal rights. As a result, less-skilled workers are subject to ever-greater market discipline, even as rent-generating innovations and control over data are concentrated in fewer and fewer hands. This book has also argued that such developments reflect deeper structural forces, the most important of which are investors' demands for sustained profits despite lagging productivity growth in many service sectors. Our labor laws have coevolved with and facilitated these efforts, now treating employment much like any other contract, and giving employers near-plenary authority over the workplace and associated data. These trends may even have skewed the development of artificial intelligence (AI), as companies favored devices that would bolster their power over workers.

And yet the future of work and technology is by no means certain. Laws shape companies' decisions and workers' capacities of resistance at nearly every level, and workers and citizens can demand reforms to ensure greater equality and sustainability, more fair uses of technology, and even different paths of development. This final chapter outlines a set of law reforms to do just that. While the agenda sketched here is complex, its overarching vision is clear: it seeks to encourage *economic democracy*, or a political-economic system in which workers and citizens have genuine rights to participate in major decisions that affect their lives.

Before elaborating such reforms, it may help to sketch how they could change work for the better. Chapter 4 discussed the job search of Julia, a hypothetical worker today or in the near future. Suppose that Julia was hired as an Amazon warehouse worker, and that Congress passed a new set of labor laws in early 2024. Under these new laws, nonunion workers would vote on whether to unionize each year—perhaps right around Labor Day—and if they did unionize, the resulting union would have exclusive bargaining rights at their workplace. Julia and her coworkers voted to unionize the first time they had a chance. At the moment, their union only represents Julia and her coworkers at that particular warehouse. But Julia and her coworkers are considering whether to affiliate their union with a national union, or with other local warehouse unions. To help decide, and to refine their own bargaining strategy, Julia's union is holding a teleconference with other unions at Amazon warehouses and elsewhere.

The first agenda item is a proposal from Amazon's management to track workers' movements through the warehouse using facial recognition devices. The company wants to implement that system at several warehouses in the region, but under the new labor laws it needs workers' sign-off. Julia and her coworkers need to decide whether to reject the proposal, accept it, or agree to it only in exchange for something. After discussion, the various unions determined that the system would deliver few benefits to workers while enabling the company to press for a faster pace of work. They decided to coordinate their bargaining strategies, agreeing to the system only in exchange for higher wages and different scheduling practices.

After that, another warehouse union briefed attendees on a novel strategy to combat wage theft, or nonpayment of all wages owed. That union had bargained for access to Amazon's payroll data and its data on workers' arrival and departure times. The union then analyzed that data to spot instances where workers had been underpaid and pressed Amazon to make them whole. As part of its efforts, that union took advantage of a provision of the new labor laws that allows unions to access employers' public-facing websites and apps for discrete periods each year to communicate with customers. The union told visitors to Amazon's website about the alleged wage theft and provided a link to contact Amazon about the issue. Over 10,000 customers had done so, which moved Amazon to begin settlement talks.

The next briefing came from a union that represents delivery drivers at Amazon. Those drivers had previously been treated as independent contractors, but they were clearly employees under the new laws due to Amazon's surveillance of their work. They had unionized, but in negotiations

Amazon was refusing to budge on surveillance, pay, or schedules. Frustrated, the drivers had begun considering whether to build a delivery cooperative. That approach would let them work with companies other than Amazon, choose their own hours, and select (or refuse) monitoring technologies. A new state agency dedicated to helping workers form cooperatives was giving them technical and financial assistance, as were other new worker cooperatives among taxi drivers, home health aides, and childcare providers.

Finally, the warehouse unions heard from fast food workers who had merged their locals into one bargaining unit across the New York metro area. Since those locals represented 55 percent of regional fast food workers, they were entitled under the new law to negotiate jointly with all major fast food employers for a contract that would become legally binding across the region. The fast food workers were planning their bargaining strategy, including preparations for a strike. While many of the workers were formally employed by franchisors, under the new labor laws they could also take concerted action against fast food brands.

The new labor laws are reshaping work in many ways. Julia and her coworkers obtained bargaining rights without a massive fight, and they are now more likely to share in Amazon's productivity gains. They have a voice in Amazon's technological decisions, and can use some of the company's technologies to advance their own goals. Through their local organizations, they can develop a common understanding of the challenges they face, as well as networks of trust and solidarity within the workplace and across workplaces. By joining with other workers in the same industry, they can also ramp up their power and set regional standards. While this may seem like science fiction, each of these rights has an analogue in existing labor laws in the US or elsewhere. Establishing this new system in the US would nevertheless require substantial reforms, and perhaps even a new political settlement to displace neoliberalism.

The overarching principle behind these reforms is *economic democracy*. Where neoliberalism tended to encase capital's privileges against democratic challenge, these reforms would devolve substantial governance authority to workers.[1] Economic democracy would also differ from industrial pluralism, because it would aim to include all vulnerable workers, ratchet back companies' ability to resist unionization, and give unions a much greater voice in workplace technology. But economic democracy would not entail state socialism, in which productive assets were owned and controlled by the state and workers and citizens had little real input into the conditions of their lives. As a vision of political-economic governance, it draws from Erik Olin Wright's proposals to subject both the state and companies to "social power," or "power rooted in the capacity to mobilize people for cooperative, voluntary collective actions of various sorts in civil society."[2] As an agenda for labor relations reform, it overlaps with Ruth Dukes and Wolfgang Streeck's recent proposals that labor laws should enable workers to generate shared solidaristic beliefs and translate them into law.[3]

There are many arguments for economic democracy, but the most straightforward is that workers' collective power is the best check on companies' power. In fact, it may be the only sustainable check in the workplace and labor market. Workers are the parties best-positioned to protect themselves against abuse or exploitation, through institutions like unions as well as ground-level practices of solidarity. Legislators can pass minimum wage laws and workplace safety standards, of course. But agencies can be captured by companies, and when workers are demobilized, companies can often evade legal obligations by subcontracting work, implementing new surveillance devices, or terminating worker activists. Effective vindication of statutory rights thus often requires countervailing power. In that respect, these reforms do not envision "democracy" as cool deliberation insulated from collective pressure. Democracy is instead a more agonistic process, including sometimes-heated battles over resources and ideology—the sorts of battles that are typically necessary for subordinate groups to obtain equal standing.

Section 6.1 outlines reforms to encourage unionization and collective action, section 6.2 sketches a new regime of workplace data and technology governance, and section 6.3 discusses complementary reforms to welfare state policy and industrial policy. Throughout, the discussion proceeds on the heroic assumption that these reforms will become politically feasible sometime soon. The conclusion, presented in section 6.4, takes up that question and suggests that there is some reason for hope.

6.1 Economic Democracy and Associational Power

As chapter 2 noted, scholars and advocates have studied and debated our labor law's strengths and weaknesses for decades, and they have developed various law reform proposals to rejuvenate worker organizing and collective bargaining. One set of long-standing proposals would restore workers' rights to organize at the worksite or company level, while a more recent set would encourage workers to build power at scale and bargain at the sectoral level. In important respects, these proposals treat the working class as a class once again, bestowing some legal rights on workers simply by virtue of their position within the division of labor. The discussion that follows draws on such proposals and extends them at times, but it does not rehash them in detail. Instead, it focuses on how they would respond to the transformations sketched in chapters 3–5.

Localized bargaining The failures of the existing National Labor Relations Act (NLRA) regime to deliver on its own promises have been clear for some time. As a robust line of scholarship has shown, and as discussed in prior chapters, fissuring enables companies to deny rights to many workers, our union certification process gives employers far too many tools to delay and resist unionization, and the NLRA regime sharply limits workers' rights to strike.[4] Revising those doctrines would certainly help facilitate unionization and would be an essential first step toward rebuilding workers' associational power.[5]

But even with a more favorable regime for organizing at the local level, workers may struggle to build real power at scale in today's large service sectors. Leading companies in fast food, logistics, retail, and hospitality have organized their business models around a demobilized workforce, and they tolerate substantial turnover each year—or at least they did before COVID. Workers in such circumstances are less likely to organize than workers with deep roots at a company since they have fewer connections to their coworkers. Moreover, since those workers are fairly easy to replace, employers have more latitude to retaliate against them for organizing. The geography of service work also matters. Gig-economy workers may struggle to meet and organize since they are not colocated, and fast food workers are typically employed in small shops, separate from one another. Union victories at Amazon and Starbucks in 2022 suggest that grassroots, worker-driven campaigns can overcome those hurdles at times—but it is not yet clear whether those victories are the first signs of a broad and sustained worker uprising that can build and sustain power at scale.

Moreover, even if Congress revised the NLRA to make unionization easier, companies could still use data-driven technologies to resist organizing efforts. For example, if Congress revised the NLRA to require union certification on the basis of authorization cards or rapid elections, employers could ratchet up prehire screenings and workplace surveillance to deter unionization campaigns. As chapter 4 argued, such efforts are illegal if undertaken with an anti-union motive, but distinguishing legitimate from illegitimate screenings can be quite difficult, and surveillance itself can be hard to detect. Meanwhile, digital Taylorism gives companies tools to sidestep union threats, such as keeping workers physically separated but closely supervised, and other digital tools facilitate the rapid displacement of incumbent firms. Given our default rule of individual contracting and our lack of "extension" laws that apply the terms of leading union contracts to all competing companies, such displacement almost invariably results in nonunionized workplaces.

Due to the many challenges of organizing today, scholars and some unions have recently advocated more *fundamental* labor law reforms, or reforms to alter core elements of our labor relations regime. For example, some have advocated *guaranteeing* workers a collective voice, cutting out the organizing stage entirely.[6] That could involve weakening or reversing the default rule of individualized employment contracting.[7] Others have proposed that Congress require union elections annually or biannually in all covered but non-unionized workplaces, so that workers have a regular chance to vote on whether to have a union.[8] Ideally under such a system the annual election would cease once workers choose to unionize, though unionized workers would retain the right to petition the NLRB to decertify their union at certain times and with appropriate safeguards to prevent employer domination. Alternately, Congress might mandate forms of workplace codetermination but not collective bargaining, the key difference being whether workers have the right to strike.[9] For example, Congress could declare that key employer policies—around scheduling or around workplace data and privacy—would be legally binding only if developed in consultation with employees. Workers could then refuse to accept a schedule that the employer set unilaterally, for example, without risking discipline. Such collective consultation is unlawful in nonunionized workplaces in the US today due to a provision of the NLRA that promotes unions' independence from management, and any such proposal would need to be carefully designed to prevent cooptation.[10]

New technologies bolster the case for such reforms. When the sociotechnical environment of workplaces is designed to prevent workers from organizing or even meeting, default representation or annual elections would make it far easier for workers to build power. Rather than enduring a long and painful organizing campaign that may lead to nothing, workers under such a system would have collective representation, or the option to choose such representation, as a right. Even without the broad rights to bargain over data practices discussed in section 6.2, this could enable workers to resist the harms of digital Taylorism. Through new collective bodies, workers could push employers to set reasonable schedules, pay reasonable wages, and share productivity gains. Data-driven technologies also make it easier to launch and manage such a system. For example, if elections were held annually or biannually, Congress could mandate that companies compile data on their populations of workers and their schedules and provide that data in an appropriate form to unions or groups of workers during annual campaigns. Default representation would also make it far easier for workers to build power *at scale*. Organizing one Walmart or McDonald's or Amazon warehouse is already an enormous challenge—organizing thousands of them at once is nearly impossible. Reversing the default would not eliminate that problem, but it would give workers footholds from which they could scale up.

Multiemployer and sectoral bargaining A complementary set of recent proposals would address such problems of scale by encouraging bargaining at the multiemployer or industry level, such as bargaining among all fast food workers and all fast food employers.[11] Such "sectoral bargaining" or "social bargaining" is common in Europe, and US unions have built such bargaining structures when possible in the past.[12] Social bargaining has various benefits, especially when coupled with robust local bargaining structures. The most important involve wage equality. As alluded to in chapter 2, there is extensive evidence, cutting across nations and time periods, that localized bargaining correlates with greater wage inequality, and more centralized bargaining correlates with higher wages for low-skill workers and greater income equality overall.[13] One reason for that pattern is that social bargaining takes wages out of competition, so unions are not constantly fighting to protect their gains. Another is that social bargaining is often a tripartite process where the state—under pressure from unions—may push employers for wage concessions where possible.[14] More centralized bargaining structures also seem to encourage unions to represent working-class interests more generally rather than defending their existing members' sometimes-parochial interests.[15]

Social bargaining would also help workers respond to recent technological changes. For example, it could discourage or at least mitigate the harms of fissuring. If social bargaining processes could establish and enforce minimum standards for subcontracted workers like janitors, security guards, or other maintenance workers, principal firms would have less power to force contractors to compete with one another and reduce wages. Social bargaining could also leverage recent market consolidation for workers' benefit. As discussed in chapter 5, many of today's megafirms built market share quite rapidly by using new technologies to build production networks or to optimize supply chains. Now a handful of major players dominate some sectors, which would make it logistically easier—if politically more difficult—to establish tripartite bargaining structures and to extend the terms of agreements across sectors. Social bargaining around privacy and data practices could also limit digital Taylorism and perhaps encourage technological diffusion in some sectors. This possibility is discussed in section 6.2. Finally, unions and regulators could use data-driven technologies to enforce social bargaining agreements. Lead firms could be required to share data on their suppliers' compliance, and regulators could use data on supply-chain relationships to define sectors and employment relationships for purposes of bargaining. Those possibilities are also discussed in section 6.2.

Implementing full-fledged sectoral bargaining from scratch is basically impossible since unions are social organizations as well as legal entities, and workers need to construct them on the ground. But Congress could facilitate social bargaining in various ways. For example, the FLSA, as originally passed, created a system of tripartite "industry committees" empowered to set wages at the sectoral level and designed to complement enterprise-based collective bargaining,[16] but the provision was eliminated in 1949.[17] Congress could revise the FLSA to create a new industry committee system, perhaps targeting today's largest low-wage sectors.[18] Alternatively, Congress could make it much easier for unions to build multiemployer bargaining structures, or grant unions sectoral bargaining rights in stages based upon their support among the workforce, or both.[19] To ensure that such bargaining structures are not captured by companies, it is essential that workers retain real rights to strike, to take other concerted action, and to choose their own representatives without employer interference.[20]

Congress could further bolster worker power at scale through other administrative levers. In some European nations, unions design and administer benefits that are jointly funded by the government, which gives them a means of reaching and engaging workers.[21] Congress could encourage those sorts of arrangements at the federal or state level. Congress could also weave workers into policymaking processes, which again is common in nations where workers have better sustained their associational power. It is perhaps best illustrated by European "social dialogue," in which some states and the European Union devolve some policymaking authority to "social partners" (i.e., unions and employer organizations).[22] At the European level social dialogue processes have recently addressed the COVID response and workplace safety, while a longer-term dialogue has addressed minimum wages.[23] In Germany, meanwhile, the state drove a strategic initiative known as "Industrie 4.0" to discern the best uses of emerging information technologies.[24] In the US, workers have standing representation on certain advisory bodies to administrative agencies (e.g., around workplace safety, pensions, and trade policy).[25] But our labor law is largely sealed off from welfare, social insurance, and industrial policy, limiting unions' ability to decommodify work.

The proposals sketched here have a common core: they would reallocate decision-making rights in ways that bolster workers' associational power. Actual practices on the ground would emerge over time amid negotiation and contestation, and the ultimate shape of workers' bargains with capital would depend on their abilities to organize, mobilize, present a compelling message, and build public support. The law nevertheless shapes unions' and workers' abilities to do so in profound ways, and these reforms certainly would help to rebalance workplace and economic power.

6.2 Democratizing Workplace Data Governance

Alongside such reforms to workplace bargaining structures, lawmakers could subject workplace data to more democratic control and oversight. There are several compelling reasons to do so. Devolving governance authority over workplace data to workers can fill some of the regulatory gaps in this field since lawmakers are often slow to respond to emerging technologies.[26] More important, individual legal entitlements such as new personal privacy rights may be insufficient to address the characteristic harms of inductive learning technologies. As discussed in prior chapters, such technologies often draw statistical inferences from very large data sets, which companies use to categorize people at a population-wide level. In the labor context, a major effect of such technologies is to render workers visible to a central authority, and therefore amenable to management or discipline—in other words, such technologies enable companies to view and manage workers as a class.

This section proposes a set of reforms to data practices that would help alter such class relations. They fall into three categories: some would ban data collection and usage in particular instances, others would subject data practices to bargaining, and still others would place data sources or technologies under public or social control. Stated as a slogan, this would involve *abolishing, bargaining,* and *socializing* data, data practices, and workplace technology.[27] While these reforms would entail substantial changes to workers' and companies' rights, the strategies themselves are not new: existing labor law already utilizes all three strategies to govern data and technology to some extent. As with the discussion in the prior section, the discussion that follows proceeds at a fairly high level, in part because the terrain is developing and changing so rapidly.

Dedigitization—or data abolition A first set of proposals borrows from social movements' demands to dedigitize various spheres of social life. As Ben Tarnoff has put it, some technologies—such as predictive policing and police-controlled facial recognition—mainly exist to enact "relationships of domination," and dismantling those technologies can create space to develop new and more democratic social relations.[28] The goal here is simply to end the gathering and use of certain types of data. Activists in many cities have thus sought to reduce video and other surveillance of communities of color, welfare recipients, and political activists. For instance, the Movement for Black Lives has taken up that issue, calling for the elimination of "gang databases and related information sharing," as well as surveillance, data-gathering, and algorithmic rankings of individuals seeking public benefits and health care.[29] Those demands overlap with demands for intelligence and law enforcement agencies to stop accumulating data on citizens and travelers and to provide notice and due process to anyone on "no-fly" lists or similar databases that limit access to basic privileges of citizenship.[30]

The notion that certain technologies should be simply abolished runs directly counter to much technology policy and ideology in the US. Unlike in the case of drug regulation, for example, companies face no requirements that they preclear novel information technologies before deploying them in consumer markets or workplaces.[31] Practically, companies have incentives to deploy them quickly and at scale, in hopes that they will become "socially locked," shaping consumers' and citizens' practices and expectations and generating barriers to regulation.[32] As discussed in chapters 2 and 4, whether a practice is seen to violate privacy laws frequently depends on whether a complainant had a "reasonable expectation of privacy" in the activity in question.[33] Yet common usage is a major factor in determining whether such an expectation existed, so well-established practices are often insulated from legal scrutiny. Our notice-and-consent model of data privacy regulation, as discussed in chapter 4, also encourages quick deployment of new tech. Few if any consumers (or workers) have the capacity to review and understand companies' data-gathering and -usage policies; as a result, data-intensive companies have every incentive to use "broad consent provisions systematically as a way of circumventing" any such limitations.[34] As also discussed in chapter 4, companies can do all sorts of end runs around even those restrictions, discerning additional and undisclosed information about individuals.

And yet dedigitization has been a fairly common regulatory modality in the employment context, where legislators have often banned certain forms of information and data gathering. An early wave of privacy legislation in the 1980s, for example, regulated employers' use of drug tests.[35] At the federal level, Congress passed the Genetic Information Nondiscrimination Act in 2008, banning employers and health insurance companies from gathering or using human deoxyribonucleic acid (DNA) or ribonucleic acid (RNA) in decisions around employment and health insurance coverage, even though there was not much evidence that companies were using genetic material in that way.[36] State legislatures in many states have also prohibited employers from requiring employees and applicants to provide their social media passwords.[37]

The case for preemptive abolition of some surveillance and data gathering is especially strong today, given the one-sided arms race between employers' technological capacities and workers' associational power. To identify technologies that are candidates for abolition, it may help to consider privacy protections in concentric circles around a data subject, as discussed in chapter 4. Each individual needs a core of dignity rights in the workplace, which are today protected by the tort of intrusion upon seclusion and various statutory protections, such as restrictions on drug testing—which, as noted previously, themselves involve abolition. Moving outward from there, workers need a core of individual autonomy rights, including protections against employer access to social media through legislation like the state laws just mentioned, as well as protections against employer access to private email accounts, as is currently provided by the Stored Communications Act.[38] Then workers need collective autonomy rights, such as protections against employer surveillance of or interference in union organizing efforts.

In each case, we have existing regulations that could be expanded and strengthened to prevent particular forms of data gathering. And yet there may be diminishing returns to such a strategy: As chapter 4 discussed, companies can at times end-run privacy regulations by aggregating data from multiple sources to discern key facts about workers, individually or collectively. Policymakers may therefore need to consider broader prohibitions on data gathering, including bans on some forms of workplace surveillance that are today long established and uncontroversial, such as the monitoring of workers on the shop floor as they perform work tasks. As discussed in several of the chapters of this book, companies have had the right to surveil the performance of work for generations, despite—or because of—the fact that such surveillance is an important means of class power. Through such surveillance, companies can force a faster pace of work and replicate some of workers' tacit knowledge. Given the significant class-based harms that are emerging from the combination of pervasive surveillance and inductive learning, it may be time to consider ratcheting back employers' surveillance rights even in that context.

Indeed, advocates have begun discussing approaches to workplace data that involve a degree of abolition. Researchers at the University of California Berkeley Labor Center, for example, developed a set of recommendations around workers' technology rights following broad consultation with scholars, unions, and others. Their report proposed a ban on worksite facial recognition or the use of algorithms to try to discern workers' emotions, as well as restrictions on employers' collection of worker data that is not "necessary and essential for workers to do their jobs."[39] That same report proposed that employers should use electronic surveillance only where "strictly necessary to enable core business tasks, to protect the safety of workers, or when needed to comply with legal obligations," and that companies be forbidden from using algorithms to make employment decisions around hiring, firing, and discipline without the involvement of a human supervisor.[40]

Abolition may be the most effective way—or the only way—to protect workers against certain data-driven harms. Framed in terms of Helen Nissenbaum's "data food chain,"[41] when companies cannot collect much data at all and can neither transfer it to others nor aggregate it with other data pools to infer novel facts about workers, they will be much less able to develop end runs around statutory worker protections, or to undermine workers' organizing efforts. While cutting off the supply of workplace data would presumably carry some costs in terms of lost innovation, those may be counterbalanced by the benefits of greater worker autonomy, as well as reductions in private domination. Such policies could be rendered still more effective by requiring what we might call "compliance by design," a variant of "privacy by design."[42] For example, natural-language-processing software that is used to monitor workers' chats on employer platforms could be designed to be incapable of spotting terms that are often associated with workers' collective action. Or it could be required to enable private worker chats that would not be visible to the employer. Such redesigns of technology could help ensure that a minimum amount of data is collected and that such data is used only in appropriate ways.

Bargaining rights around technology A second set of reforms would require or facilitate bargaining or consultation around workplace technology. Those would work in tandem with the new protections for worker association discussed in section 6.1, as well as with the socialization and abolition efforts just discussed. Prohibiting off-duty monitoring and facial recognition, for example, would help facilitate interworker deliberation.

Yet bargaining approaches may be preferable to bans and mandates in certain cases. For example, bargaining might be preferable to bans where companies have a colorable argument that the technology at issue will enhance productivity. Indeed, perhaps bargaining should be the default approach, given the state's epistemic limits. Technological progress often requires extensive trial-and-error, and the ultimate shape of technologies only beomes clear over time as they are deployed in social and economic contexts and in turn affect social and economic relations.[43] An outright ban on new workplace monitoring devices could therefore thwart some beneficial innovations, such as efforts to optimize delivery routes. Conversely, requiring bargaining could encourage companies to design or use technologies in ways that do not harm workers, without necessarily foreclosing innovation. Moreover, giving workers the capacity to block or delay technological changes that will erode their associational power should incentivize employers to adopt productivity-enhancing rather than power-augmenting technologies.

Perhaps most fundamentally, bargaining can enhance individual and collective self-governance.[44] The utility of bargaining as a regulatory modality in the workplace reflects an important difference between privacy and technology in the workplace versus the consumer context: while workers face significant collective action problems, they remain less severe than the collective action problems faced by consumers, an enormously diffuse group with less of a tradition of organized representation. Indeed, there are many examples of workers organizing to protest certain uses of technology in the past. Moreover, since workplace technologies embed power relations, bargaining mandates may be necessary for workers to participate meaningfully in setting the rules that structure their lives. This is abundantly true with respect to novel information technologies, which often operate in ways that are inscrutable to line-level workers. Workers today are not just governed by their employers' choices of technology—they are also governed in arbitrary and unforeseeable ways by those technological choices.

The key reforms are straightforward to articulate, although their exact operations would need to be worked out in practice. As discussed in chapter 2, our collective bargaining laws require companies to bargain with unionized workers over technological changes that will alter disciplinary policies, but they also give companies broad powers to implement technologies that will displace workers.[45] Nonunionized workers, meanwhile, have no rights to bargain or consult around workplace technology at all. Congress could alter those rules by making workplace technology a mandatory subject of bargaining in the unionized sector, such that an employer's refusal to bargain is an unfair labor practice.[46] In conjunction with the reforms discussed in this chapter to make it far easier for workers to organize, such reforms would give workers substantial capacity to resist power-augmenting uses of technology. Alternatively, or in conjunction with the reforms sketched in section 6.1, Congress could guarantee all covered workers consultative rights around technological changes regardless of their unionization status.[47] Many German workers have such rights through bodies known as "works councils," which have rights to consult with management over technological and other issues at the workplace level, but do not have rights to strike.[48]

In fact, unions have demanded a voice in workplace technology in several recent strikes. A major issue behind the 2018 West Virginia teachers' strike was the state's effort to establish a new health-care plan that would give teachers premium rebates if they wore Fitbit-type devices that tracked health metrics.[49] The teachers were upset both by the invasion of privacy and by the school district's continuing efforts to push health-care costs onto them. Similarly, when Marriott hotel workers went on strike in 2018, they demanded a voice in how the company used technology to manage them. Cleaners had complained about the company's development of a new app that assigned them to clean rooms, and desk staff had concerns about the company's development of check-in and related apps.[50] The eventual contract gave their union the right to be consulted early about the development and adoption of new technologies.[51]

These examples suggest that bargaining and consultative rights—a form of institutionalized associational power—would enable workers to protect themselves against many harms associated with digital Taylorism, fissuring, and new methods of surveillance. Workers' optimal bargaining strategy when an employer seeks to implement a new technology would vary based on the circumstances. Following standard practice in industrial relations, bargaining mandates in this context could include information-sharing mandates, so that companies would have to disclose proposed and current uses of algorithmic techniques and the like. Depending on the technology at issue, unions might work with the employer to make the innovation as productive as possible, accept the innovation as is but press to ensure that productivity gains are shared via higher wages, or simply refuse to cooperate in the employer's plan to deploy the technology. For example, Amazon warehouse workers might welcome the integration of new robotic systems, and fast food workers might welcome tablet-based ordering systems. But if given the power to bargain over the issue, they could ensure that the company shares the productivity gains with them through higher wages or a more reasonable pace of work. Indeed, in optimal conditions, where labor and management have some common trust (which often develops in collective bargaining), and where workers are protected against sudden job losses, workers may want to *facilitate* forms of task automation that displace boring or dangerous tasks.[52] What's more, bargaining efforts would have a feedback effect on employers' strategies over time. As workers build the associational power necessary to block power-augmenting technologies, employers will have incentives to collaborate with them while developing new technologies, and to favor productivity-enhancing innovations.

The case for bargaining rights is even stronger with regard to algorithmic management. After all, in many cases, employers implement new forms of worker supervision and discipline *in order to* augment their power over workers. Workers with real bargaining rights over such issues, therefore, may require companies to codetermine the inputs to algorithmic management techniques, as well as performance standards. Ride-sharing drivers might permit company-provided global positioning system (GPS) guidance, for example, only if they are free to deviate from a proposed route or have means of communicating that the guidance is somehow flawed. Bargaining in this context may also lead companies to engage workers around technological deployment to unlock productivity gains. For example, hotel cleaners in the Marriott strike argued that the company's app that assigned them to particular rooms when guests checked out disregarded various facts about particular hotels—such as the location of supply closets—and therefore wasn't as efficient as advertised.[53] Engaging the cleaners during the app design could have mitigated that problem since the best way to travel through a particular hotel is the sort of localized knowledge that is difficult for companies to grasp centrally or via inductive learning.

Sectoral or social bargaining could also help to reshape the politics of workplace technology. For example, retail and food-service workers with social bargaining rights might aim to set scheduling policies at the sectoral level, given the prevalence of algorithmic scheduling in both sectors and its negative effects on workers. That may mitigate retailers' and food-service companies' incentives to reduce labor time to an absolute minimum. Indeed, companies themselves may prefer sectoral standard-setting once workers build sufficient associational power, so that enterprise-level bargaining around data practices does not place them at a competitive disadvantage. At the federal administrative level, worker organizations could be woven into the oversight of new technologies, perhaps including new administrative preapproval processes for workplace algorithmic governance methods. In the US context, there are models for such efforts in the literature on participatory budgeting and neighborhood governance, which could be adapted to matters of workplace technology policy.[54]

Socialization approaches A final set of reforms would give workers, the public, or both greater control over data and related technologies: socializing them in the sense of treating them like a public resource. Because contemporary AI has been developed within private companies and public

Data and Economic Democracy

security agencies, there aren't many real-world examples of democratic data governance today—and yet there is nothing new about socialization approaches. An example that predates modern inductive technologies comes from certain welfare states, which have long utilized population-level data to ensure adequate health, housing, and other social outcomes.[55] Data trusts are a promising emergent example. Those are "structure[s] whereby data is placed under the control of a board of trustees with a responsibility to look after the interests of beneficiaries."[56] Those could be used to gather and hold particular kinds of data—such as health data useful for medical research or data on companies' workforce practices—subject to strict privacy controls.[57] In 2022 the European Commission also proposed a Digital Services Act, which would require digital platforms to make data available to independent researchers who can use it to discern, for example, how those platforms are affecting citizens' privacy or limiting the spread of illegal materials.[58]

Another analog comes from scholarship on the platform economy, where K. Sabeel Rahman has argued that platforms such as Amazon, social media companies, and broadband companies "provide a core, infrastructural service upon which other firms, individuals, and social groups depend."[59] They have become essential means of accessing other resources, including employment, government services, important consumer goods, communications with friends and family, and news media. In some cases, Rahman argues, the public might best be served by converting the provider to a public utility.[60] As with data trusts, this would involve building institutions that enjoy some property rights in data but that are not privately controlled.

There are many possible socialization approaches in the workplace. Those could build on the proposals noted here, as well as those given in chapter 5 to leverage companies' new surveillance capacities to ensure compliance. As a first step, regulators could require companies to share much more of the data they gather on workers and work processes for regulatory purposes. This is hardly a novel proposal: Disclosure of workforce data is already required of many companies in order to ensure compliance with certain laws, including antidiscrimination laws.[61] With such data, regulators could develop algorithmic means of spotting basic labor law violations, such as wage and hour noncompliance or patterns of hiring discrimination. Regulators could also use that data to map companies' power over workers. For example, given the prevalence of fissured employment today and the fact that companies often monitor fissured employees quite closely, legislatures could rewrite statutory definitions of employment to take data-driven monitoring into account. In the case of Uber or McDonald's, for example, evidence that the companies monitor how work is performed or help to screen or schedule workers could be presumptive evidence of employment status.

Regulators could also use data on supply-chain governance to help develop social bargaining processes. The key innovation here would be to use those technologies, and the underlying data gathered by companies that use them, to group workers together *across* companies based on their common interests. For example, regulators and unions could benefit by having an accurate list of all active fast food workers in particular regions, their typical schedules, their pay, and the companies (whether franchisors or franchisees) that control their work. In other cases, such a mapping would be helpful in discerning how companies' supply and distribution networks overlap and interpenetrate one another. That is common in logistics and for the myriad firms that supply, for example, hotels and restaurants with food, uniforms, and linens. Such a mapping could be used to design sectoral bargaining units.

Second, public agencies could develop new technological platforms for worker organizing and deliberation, ideally in conjunction with worker organizations. As discussed previously, workers today frequently seek to organize in part via social media and employer communications platforms, but their capacity to do so is limited by the fact that companies can spot such efforts and retaliate. If a system of default or guaranteed collective representation (as discussed in section 6.1) were established, it would be worth considering whether the National Labor Relations Board (NLRB) or another agency could develop online or app-based platforms for worker deliberation and organizing that management cannot access. For example, in a system of default or guaranteed representation, all companies could be required to give the NLRB contact information for all their workers annually, as is now required once the Board has ordered a union election.[62] The agency could then use that information to give workers access to the platform for nominations, campaigning, and elections, and perhaps to give unions some means of contacting workers on those platforms—all with design-based safeguards to deter or prevent employers from accessing the platform. Those would never be foolproof, and companies would get *some* access through illicit means. But such a platform could still facilitate the sorts of worker deliberation and organizing that are already occurring through some social media platforms—albeit with more significant privacy protections for workers.

Similarly, Congress or the NLRB could expand workers' rights to access their employers' proprietary technologies and data sources to bolster organizing efforts. Gig-economy workers, for example, have at times turned off their apps en masse to protest companies' policies.[63] Those protests could be more effective and potent if the workers and organizers could use the apps themselves to contact and mobilize coworkers.[64] Many service workers today—in the gig economy, fast food, retail, logistics, and hospitality—would likewise benefit from being able to communicate directly with customers about their concerns via their companies' apps or websites. As noted in chapter 4, this would be a digital analog of the picket line, where in the past workers would directly speak to or otherwise communicate with potential customers outside a struck business. Now that so many transactions take place in online spaces, workers may need such rights to effectively reach consumers and build power.[65]

Third and finally, regulators could do much more to encourage worker-owned cooperatives, which could then have control rights over data and workplace technologies. Cooperatives may be especially promising in sectors where innovation proceeds more slowly, where there is less need for physical capital, and where there is demand for high numbers of workers. There are quite a few low-wage sectors with those characteristics, including home cleaning, home care and childcare, and taxi-type services. Workers and unions have already formed numerous cooperatives in those sectors,[66] many of which operate via online platforms.[67] The role of the state here would be to help cooperatives in areas where they have struggled historically. For example, it can be difficult for them to obtain financing as compared to for-profit businesses, which banks and lenders understand better.[68] Moreover, cooperative businesses are run on the basis of democratic member control,[69] which can make it difficult to compete with larger companies whose operations are geared toward the accumulation of capital. The growth of online platforms can mitigate some of those concerns by making it easier both for workers to join cooperatives and for consumers to purchase cooperatively provided services. This will not happen at scale, however, without substantial support from government agencies. Local, state, and federal governments can encourage cooperatives by preferring them in procurement and by assisting with financing on favorable terms.[70] Such support can help insulate cooperatives against price competition from for-profit enterprises, as well as escalating pressure from investors for high returns.[71] In sectors like home care, where there are huge numbers of workers paid directly or indirectly through public health programs, states could either encourage worker cooperatives or a hybrid of cooperative and public employment.

As with the dedigitizing and bargaining strategies discussed in this chapter, many of the details around socialization need to be worked out in practice. Moreover, any large-scale data-gathering and -sharing efforts managed by the public and civil society organizations would need to be developed with appropriate safeguards to prevent data breaches, not to mention the coercion of workers by state authorities. But the core idea is clear enough: data should often be treated as public or social property, not as companies' private property.

6.3 Complementary Reforms: Algorithmic Accountability, Universal Benefits, and Industrial Policy

While the reforms sketched thus far are essential, they would ideally be coupled with other reforms to ensure workplace equality and basic material security, as well as to move us toward a green economy. This section briefly discusses a few of the most important of these. Such ideas have been widely mooted in recent years as part of debates regarding the so-called future of work, so this discussion will be brief. It focuses both on their merits and on how they would relate to or complement reforms to rejuvenate collective bargaining and to democratize data governance.

A first set of proposals aims to ensure "algorithmic accountability" in hiring, promotion, and management processes; some of those proposals were discussed in chapter 4.[72] The basic idea is that individuals who lose opportunities due to algorithmic analyses should have due process rights, such as notice of the data that was gathered and analyzed about them, as well as an opportunity to correct any false data and to challenge the underlying decision. Such reforms are absolutely warranted, and in 2021 the federal Equal Employment Opportunity Commission announced a broad effort to study the effect of AI on employment.[73] But these reforms are not my focus here, for reasons noted in chapter 4: even if algorithms were to measure workers' or citizens' skills or aptitudes accurately, that may do little to address labor market inequalities since individuals' skills are in part a function of their background opportunities.[74] Real equal employment opportunity requires not just procedural justice that takes as a given the existing division of labor and the existing class structure, but also a more thorough reshaping of the labor market and political economy. That would include policies to address racial disparities in education, housing, criminal justice, and other fields; affirmative steps to empower women workers, including but not limited to socialized childcare and eldercare; and the sorts of labor law reforms sketched in section 5.2.

Recent technological changes have also led to a resurgence of interest in an unconditional or universal basic income (UBI). The idea is simple: all those who are eligible would receive monthly grants from the state that would be sufficient to meet their basic needs, regardless of whether they work.[75] UBI has garnered attention from a wide array of commentators, and not all arguments for the policy are remotely convincing. Some on the political right, including Charles Murray, see it as a means of eliminating other welfare or social insurance programs.[76] Others see it as a means of heading off a populist revolt. For example, one Silicon Valley UBI advocate has enthused that the policy would allow entrepreneurs to get "as rich as they f***ing want" since workers and the unemployed would at least not starve.[77] Such arguments can be set to the side since they do not take economic equality seriously.[78] Many others have suggested that UBI will become necessary due to automation.[79] Those arguments can be discounted, since as argued in chapter 3, the automation threat has been significantly overstated.

The more compelling arguments for a UBI see it as one of a number of tools to advance economic and political equality in the wake of the service transition. As has been clear for decades now, a core redistributive institution of the postwar era—collective bargaining in industrial production—depended on compounding productivity gains in manufacturing, which are simply harder to come by in the services industry. As a result, today we cannot rely solely on collective bargaining or statutory wage regulations to ensure income equality, much less a minimum standard of living for all. A UBI would certainly help fill that gap. As important, it would delink welfare from work, enabling all recipients to enjoy a "socially acceptable standard of living independently of market participation."[80] That would represent a major shift in our welfare policy, which historically has been borderline punitive, pushing recipients into work, doing little to decommodify goods like health care and childcare, and giving social services agencies broad authority to police recipients' family lives.[81] A UBI (or cognate policies) could also do a tremendous amount to help those tens of millions of adults who cannot work full time due to disability or caregiving responsibilities. Such burdens cut on racial and gendered lines, and a UBI would encourage greater equality on those lines. Perhaps most important, a UBI would empower workers to quit or strike more easily, which would put upward pressure on wages and working conditions.[82] In late 2021, something like this may have occurred in the labor market, as many workers refused to accept jobs at or near their former wages. While the root causes are not yet clear, generous COVID-era unemployment benefits may have raised workers' expectations and given them an economic cushion and more bargaining power.

That being said, it may be more effective to ensure a minimum standard of living through policy mechanisms other than a UBI. For example, policymakers could decommodify many in-kind goods that are often unavailable at reasonable prices in the US, including decent health care, childcare, housing, transportation, food, education, and job training. Those efforts could be coupled with unconditional cash assistance, especially to families with children, perhaps in the form of a permanent child tax credit similar to the one included in the 2021 American Rescue Plan. Such a suite of reforms may also be more politically plausible than a pure UBI because they would build on established programs at the federal and state levels. By socialising care work—especially health care and childcare—such reforms would also improve care jobs by walling them off from demands for profitability, which tends to suppress wage growth.[83] While this approach requires high levels of taxation, citizens may be willing to tolerate those taxes in exchange for high-quality services.[84]

It is also unclear whether a stand-alone UBI or cognate reforms would significantly bolster workers' ability to organize. The reason is that workers' associational power is shaped not just by their material resources but also by our labor laws, which discourage or forbid many sorts of collective action, as discussed in several prior chapters. Meanwhile, passing and defending a generous and universal welfare state will likely require enormous mobilization along class lines. Wealthy individuals would foot much of the bill via higher taxes and lower profits, and they would be expected to resist both the passage and the implementation of such programs. This all strongly suggests that an organized and mobilized working and middle class may be necessary to secure ambitious new welfare and social insurance programs—and that would-be reformers should prioritize fomenting workplace and economic democracy as well as establishing new social benefits.[85]

A final set of proposed reforms would encourage a shift in national industrial policy, especially as part of a green transition.[86] Various economists and others have suggested that policymakers should promote the development and diffusion of highly efficient technologies across our economy, and should encourage the development of technologies that will complement rather than displacing workers.[87] Such proposals overlap with calls for a "Green New Deal" that would include massive public investment in green technology and carbon reductions.[88] There are many sound arguments for these efforts. Reallocating workers toward the care and social reproduction areas is desirable for climate-related reasons since those jobs are not nearly as carbon-intensive as low-wage jobs in luxury hotels and restaurants, the gig economy, and other delivery services.[89] Creating more jobs in manufacturing can also help mitigate the cost disease. Affecting such a substantial shift in our economy would require action in many policy domains, including intellectual property (IP), tax, public finance, and even professional ethics. I'll set those to the side for now so I may emphasize that reforms to rebuild workers' associational power would complement these efforts. On a day-to-day basis, organized workers can foreclose the low road of low-skilled, low-wage, low-innovation production. That can encourage companies to focus more on productivity-enhancing investments and can ensure that workers share in such productivity gains, which would make it easier to achieve broadly shared prosperity.[90]

6.4 Conclusion

This is a very ambitious agenda, and whether it is feasible in the near term is far from clear. The most obvious impediment is that neoliberalism has both bolstered and entrenched capital's power, creating many barriers to these sorts of reforms. As a result, there is no obvious agent or agents with the capacity to advance this sort of program today. Actual existing labor unions are in many cases fighting for their survival, and many unions are firmly opposed to sectoral bargaining. Any reforms to private-sector collective bargaining rights would also need to pass through Congress rather than the states, which makes such reform more difficult given the antidemocratic nature of the Senate.

But a number of trends in our politics may be cause for optimism. Workers and the general public are increasingly concerned about the power of the tech sector and invasions of privacy, which may generate constituencies for some of the abolition and socialization approaches discussed in this chapter. Meanwhile, workers have been striking or protesting in much larger numbers recently, as noted in several chapters. The trend seems to have begun with the 2018 teacher strikes; continued through COVID in the form of many small protests, often by nonunionized workers; and then ballooned in 2021 with a bona fide strike wave among unionized workers,[91] and a wave of new organizing at companies including Amazon and Starbucks. In other words, decades of neoliberal policy may be sparking a real countermovement, and real class-based mobilization. If so, workers may soon be in a position to push for broad labor law reforms. One strategy would be to prioritize reforms that enable workers to build substantial power in the short term, setting the stage for more ambitious reforms down the line.[92]

In those efforts, workers may also find the public more supportive of their efforts than they had been before 2018. Many of the post-2018 teacher's strikes garnered broad support from parents, in part due to teachers' unions making demands—such as for smaller class sizes, social workers in schools, and even rent control in Chicago—that would benefit parents and their children too.[93] More generally, the broader public seems attuned to the miserable working conditions endured by today's working class in the wake of COVID, and unenthusiastic about returning to unrewarding jobs with long hours. Middle-class families are also increasingly frustrated by the difficulty of finding decent and affordable childcare and health care, and younger generations are particularly concerned about climate change. Those groups could be allies in the fight to modernize our welfare state and to encourage a transformative green industrial policy. All such efforts would also be more plausible with the passage of reforms to enhance democracy in our political process, including voting rights reforms.

What's more, the goals behind such reforms have broad appeal. Most of us would like to earn more and work less, to enjoy respect and dignity in our dealings with management, and to count on privacy both at work and in our personal lives. All those goods are far too rare today. The aspiration of this set of reforms is not just to make work more humane, nor even to change the balance of power in our political economy. The aspiration is also to change work relations at a more molecular level—to make contemporary capitalism as democratic as possible. Rather than being subject to arbitrary and sudden discipline, and rather than laboring in isolation from one another, workers would build norms and practices of solidarity, which would in turn inform the law. Workplace surveillance practices would come more into line with common-sense privacy norms, and relentless downward pressure on wages would ease. Workers would have a real voice in the workplace and beyond it. The road to this better future of work will be long, difficult, and uncertain. But the alternative is quite clear, and far less desirable.

Afterword: Law and the Technological Mundane

This book has argued that companies often use new data-driven technologies as a power resource—or even a tool of class domination—and that our labor laws allow them to do so. Chapters 1 and 2 outlined the book's overall theory, which sought to account for the decline of the postwar political settlement and accumulation regime, the growth of the service economy, the maturation of networked information technologies, and the evolution of labor law under neoliberalism. The next three chapters then illustrated how companies are using both law and technology to reconfigure work and production, often in ways that subject workers to greater market discipline. Chapter 3 argued that companies are using technology to automate some tasks, to reduce the skills required to perform other tasks, and to surveil and manage workers more closely. Chapter 4 showed how companies may use their control over workplace data, as well as data on workers themselves, to prevent and resist unionization. Chapter 5 then traced how companies have increasingly denied basic legal protections to their workers, even as they built monopolistic businesses. All these strategies reinforced trends toward income inequality and a lopsided political economy. Finally, chapter 6 proposed reforms to rebuild workers' associational power and to democratize workplace data.

As several chapters have emphasized, neither technology, nor law, nor class relations are ever static, and their futures are far from clear. Workplace artificial intelligence (AI) may be in its infancy today, in which case this book's argument may serve more as a theory to guide future research than as a definitive account of any sort. Alternatively, the COVID-19 era may generate profound political-economic changes, in which case this book may do more to document pre-COVID practices than to envision what comes next.

There are signs that point in both directions. On the one hand, workplace technological change did not cease during the pandemic, as companies rolled out new surveillance techniques for their newly dispersed workforces, and the app-based gig economy and exchange platforms like Amazon only grew. On the other hand, as noted in the introduction and at the end of chapter 6, workers began to rise up in substantial numbers to protest stagnant wages and dangerous working conditions. Today's rising generations may also simply refuse to work as hard as their predecessors for as little pay; demand far more dignity, autonomy, and collective voice on the job; and resist being managed by technology. If nothing else, the pandemic has shown that we all long for authentic human connections, which screens and apps simply cannot deliver, and which modern workplaces are often designed to foreclose.

I'll close with an observation on how these political-economic trends connect to our culture and experiences. There is a telling disconnect between how we often think and talk about technology, both in our culture and in our everyday lives, and how we actually experience technology day to day. We often imagine technology as sublime.[1] Movie plots turn on breakthrough inventions that generate grand existential conflicts, for example, and for much of the 2010s, the media breathlessly reported on each new advance in robotics and AI, stoking widespread automation fears. And as chapter 3 suggested, there is indeed something sublime about automated warehouses, natural-language translation, and even app-based labor intermediation. Those and other cutting-edge innovations are fascinating and terrifying in equal measure. Taking the long view, technology has also given humans godlike powers over the natural world and its many dangers—and has helped bring about the climate crisis. So perhaps some technological animism is unavoidable. If technology has a spirit and a logic of its own, we no longer bear responsibility for its social and environmental harms.

Yet in our day-to-day lives, we rarely experience technology as sublime. As consumers, we adapt quickly to new devices, incorporating them into our routines without much thought and becoming frustrated when they fail to live up to their promises. Just in the last decade or so, that has happened with smartphones, social media, online music platforms, and now the gig economy. Those products might bring a sense of wonder when initially encountered, but they quickly recede into the mundane background of life. As workers, meanwhile, many or most of us have to conform our acts and behaviors to what a technology demands—driving a certain way, talking a certain way, being always recorded and monitored, following a clock. As we do so, the scope of our freedom narrows. The authority relations embedded in workplace technologies then become mundane in a different sense: they seem fixed and unchangeable, a permanent aspect of our social and economic firmament. And yet we never fully adapt to technological demands—nor do we see those demands as fully legitimate—because we are social beings who need community, respect, and space for creativity and self-expression.

This book has sought to ratify that latter set of instincts. As it has argued, workplace technologies and their effects on our society and polity are all well within our control. We are primed to view them as autonomous because democracy has been expelled from the economy. That doesn't mean that the future is knowable, or that any deliberative body could plan out technological developments in detail. This book's forward-looking argument is both more modest and more radical. It is that a more democratic future of work and workplace technology is both necessary and possible.

Notes

Introduction

1. Clarissa A. Leon and Mike Elk, "The Bureau of Labor Statistics Counted Only Eight Strikes in 2020, Payday Report Counted 1,200," *Institute for New Economic Thinking, Perspectives Blog*, July 13, 2021, https://www.ineteconomics.org/perspectives/blog/the-bureau-of-labor-statistics-counted-only-eight-strikes-in-2020-payday-report-counted-1-200.

2. *The Daily*, "Stories from the Great American Labor Shortage," *New York Times*, podcast, August 3, 2021, https://www.nytimes.com/2021/08/03/podcasts/the-daily/coronavirus-hiring-job-vacancies-hospitality-industry.html. While some suggested at the time that we were experiencing a "Great Resignation" in which workers dropped out of the labor market *en masse*, labor market data in early 2022 did not support that interpretation. Paul Krugman, for example, has suggested that the tight labor market was a result of workers moving into higher-paid jobs, increased incidence of self-employment, and reduced immigration during the Trump years. Paul Krugman, "What Ever Happened to the Great Resignation," *New York Times*, Paul Krugman newsletter, April 5, 2022, https://www.nytimes.com/2022/04/05/opinion/great-resignation-employment.html. On recent unionization efforts, see, e.g., Noam Scheiber, "Starbucks Unionization Campaign Pushes on, with at Least 16 Stores Now Organized," *New York Times*, April 8, 2022; Noam Scheiber, "Amazon Workers on Staten Island Vote to Unionize in Landmark Win for Labor," *New York Times*, April 1, 2022.

3. This book borrows from and joins a growing body of scholarship that elucidates the role of data-driven technologies and associated legal regimes in our contemporary political and social order. See generally Julie E. Cohen, *Between Truth and Power: The Legal Constructions of Informational Capitalism* (Oxford: Oxford University Press, 2019); Amy Kapczynski, "The Law of Informational Capitalism," *Yale Law Journal* 129, no. 5 (2020): 1460–1515; Salomé Viljoen, "A Relational Theory for Data Governance," *Yale Law Journal* 131, no. 2 (2022): 573–654; Yochai Benkler, "Power and Productivity: Institutions, Ideology, and Technology in Political Economy," in *A Political Economy of Justice*, ed. Danielle Allen, Yochai Benkler, Leah Downey, Rebecca Henderson, and Josh Simons (Chicago: University of Chicago Press, 2021), 27–60.

4. In the United States, the law of work is divided into three major subfields: "labor law," which covers union organizing and collective bargaining; "employment discrimination," which applies civil rights protections to employment; and "employment law," which includes common law and statutory governance of the individual employment relationship. Michael Fischl, "Rethinking the Tripartite Division of American Work Law," *Berkeley Journal of Employment & Labor Law* 28, no. 1 (2007): 163–216. For ease of exposition I use "labor law" to refer to all three bodies of law.

5. See Erik Olin Wright, "Working-Class Power, Capitalist-Class Interests, and Class Compromise," *American Journal of Sociology* 105, no. 4 (January 2000): 958, 962 (discussing workers' "associational power," as contrasted with their "structural power," or the power that workers may have, individually or collectively, by virtue of their skills or location in a tight labor market).

6. See Neil M. Richards and Jonathan King, "Big Data Ethics," *Wake Forest Law Review* 49, no. 2 (2014): 396 (arguing that privacy should be understood as "encompassing information rules that manage the appropriate flows of information in ethical ways"). See also Julie E. Cohen, "What Privacy Is For," *Harvard Law Review* 126, no. 7 (May 2013): 1906 (arguing that "privacy is shorthand for breathing room to engage in the processes of boundary management that enable and constitute self-development").

7. See the discussion in chapters 1 and 4.

8. While this book focuses on legal changes in the United States, similar but less momentous shifts in workplace governance have occurred in many other nations. See generally Lucio Baccaro and Chris Howell, *Trajectories of Neoliberal Transformation: European Industrial Relations Since the 1970s* (Cambridge: Cambridge University Press, 2017).

9. See the discussion in chapter 2.

10. See Gary Marx, *Windows Into the Soul: Surveillance and Society in an Age of High Technology* (Chicago: University of Chicago Press, 2016), 50–51, table 2.1 (providing a schematic overview of the differences between contemporary and historical forms of surveillance).

11. Marx, *Windows Into the Soul*, 50–51.

12. See the discussion in chapter 3.

13. See the discussion in chapter 3.

14. See the discussion in chapter 5.

15. See the discussion in chapter 4.

16. See the discussions in chapter 3 (on inductive learning generally) and chapter 4 (on the use of inductive learning to hide statutory violations).

17. Lorenzo Franceschi-Bicchierai, "Amazon Is Hiring an Intelligence Analyst to Track 'Labor Organizing Threats,'" *Vice*, September 1, 2020, https://www.vice.com/en/article/qj4aqw/amazon-hiring-intelligence-analyst-to-track-labor-organizing-threats.

18. See Gabriel Winant, *The Next Shift: The Fall of Industry and the Rise of Health Care in Rust Belt America* (Cambridge, MA, Harvard University Press, 2021), 23–24, 262–264 (discussing the latent political and associational power of care workers, a subset of service workers).

19. See the discussion in chapter 6.

20. Morris R. Cohen, "Property and Sovereignty," *Cornell Law Review* 13, no. 8 (December 1927): 8–30; Robert L. Hale, "Coercion and Distribution in a Supposedly Non-Coercive State," *Political Science Quarterly* 38, no. 3 (September 1923): 470–494.

21. Karl E. Klare, "Labor Law as Ideology: Toward a New Historiography of Collective Bargaining Law," *Industrial Relations Law Journal* 4, no. 3 (1980–1981): 450–482; Katherine Van Wezel Stone, "The Post-War Paradigm in American Labor Law," *Yale Law Journal* 90, no. 7 (1981): 1509–1580.

22. Michael Fischl, "Self, Others, and Section 7: Mutualism and Protected Protest Activities under the National Labor Relations Act," *Columbia Law Review* 89, no. 4 (1989): 789–865; Mark Barenberg, "Democracy and Domination in the Law of Workplace Cooperation: From Bureaucratic to Flexible Production," *Columbia Law Review* 94, no. 3 (1994): 753–983; Brishen Rogers, "Passion and Reason in Labor Law," *Harvard Civil Rights–Civil Liberties Law Review* 47, no. 2 (2012): 313–369.

23. All of these bodies of literature are vast. On the tensions between traditional organizing and collective bargaining strategies and movements for racial and gender justice, see, e.g., Marion Crain and Ken Matheny, "Labor's Identity Crisis," *California Law Review* 89, no. 6 (December 2001): 1767–1846; Ahmed A. White, "My Co-Worker, My Enemy: Solidarity, Workplace Control, and the Class Politics of Title VII," *Buffalo Law Review* 63, no.5 (2015): 1061–1140. On the relationship between union organizing and immigrant rights, see, e.g., Jennifer Gordon, *Suburban Sweatshops: The Fight for Immigrant Rights* (Cambridge, MA: Harvard University Press, 2007).

24. Overviews of the emerging literature on law and political economy include Angela Harris and James Varellas, "Law and Political Economy in a Time of Accelerating Crises," *Journal of Law and Political Economy* 1, no. 1 (2020): 1–27 (the introduction to the first issue of the new *Journal of Law and Political Economy*); and Jedediah Britton-Purdy, David Singh Grewal, Amy Kapczynski, and K. Sabeel Rahman, "Building a Law-and-Political-Economy Framework: Beyond the Twentieth-Century Synthesis," *Yale Law Journal* 129, no. 6 (2020): 1784–1835.

25. See Harris and Varellas, "Law and Political Economy": 10 (stating that LPE holds that "law is central to the creation and maintenance of structural inequalities in the

state and the market"); Britton-Purdy et al., "Law-and-Political-Economy Framework," 1792–1793, 1818–1823 (discussing the continued relevance of legal realism today).

26. Angela Harris, "Foreword: Racial Capitalism and Law," in *Histories of Racial Capitalism*, eds. Destin Jenkins and Justin Leroy (New York: Columbia University Press, 2021), vii–xx; David Singh Grewal, "The Legal Constitution of Capitalism," in *After Piketty: The Agenda for Economics and Inequality*, eds. Heather Boushey, J. Bradford DeLong, and Marshall Steinbaum (Cambridge, MA: Harvard University Press, 2017), 471–490; David Singh Grewal, "Book Review: The Laws of Capitalism," *Harvard Law Review* 128, no. 2 (2014): 626–668; Cohen, *Between Truth and Power*; and Benkler, "Power and Productivity."

27. Pauline T. Kim and Matthew T. Bodie, "Artificial Intelligence and the Challenges of Workplace Discrimination and Privacy," *ABA Journal of Labor & Employment Law* 35, no. 2 (2021): 289–315; Ifeoma Ajunwa, "Age Discrimination by Platforms," *Berkeley Journal of Employment and Labor Law* 40, no. 1 (2019): 1–27; Solon Barocas and Andrew D. Selbst, "Big Data's Disparate Impact," *California Law Review* 104, no. 3 (June 2016): 671–732; Pauline T. Kim, "Data-Driven Discrimination at Work," *William and Mary Law Review* 58, no. 3 (February 2017): 857–936. See also Simone Browne, "Race and Surveillance," in *Routledge Handbook of Surveillance Studies*, eds. Kirstie Ball, Kevin D. Haggerty, and David Lyon (London: Routledge, 2012), 72–80 (discussing the relationship between contemporary surveillance practices and social processes of racial differentiation).

28. Important exceptions within labor law include Jeffrey M. Hirsch, "Future Work," *University of Illinois Law Review* 2020, no. 3 (2020): 889–958; Valerio De Stefano, "'Negotiating the Algorithm': Automation, Artificial Intelligence and Labour Protection," *Comparative Labor Law and Policy Journal* 41, no. 1 (2019): 15–46; Jeremias Adams-Prassl, "What If Your Boss Was an Algorithm: Economic Incentives, Legal Challenges, and the Rise of Artificial Intelligence at Work," *Comparative Labor Law and Policy Journal* 41, no.1 (2019): 123–146; and Cynthia Estlund, "What Should We Do After Work? Automation and Employment Law," *Yale Law Journal* 128, no. 2 (2018): 254–326. For an influential treatment of how an earlier generation of information technologies affected work, see Katherine Van Wezel Stone, *From Widgets to Digits: Employment Regulation for the Changing Workplace* (Cambridge: Cambridge University Press, 2004).

29. Langdon Winner, "Do Artifacts Have Politics?" *Daedalus* 109, no. 1 (Winter 1980): 121–136; and Sheila Jasanoff, *Designs on Nature: Science and Democracy in Europe and the United States* (Princeton, NJ: Princeton University Press, 2005).

30. Cohen, *Between Truth and Power*; Yochai Benkler, *The Wealth of Networks: How Social Production Transforms Markets and Freedom* (New Haven, CT: Yale University Press, 2006).

31. Benkler, "Power and Productivity"; Cohen, *Between Truth and Power*; Lawrence Lessig, *Code: And Other Laws of Cyberspace* (New York: Basic Books, 1999).

32. Cohen, *Between Truth and Power*; Frank Pasquale, *The Black Box Society: The Secret Algorithms That Control Money and Information* (Cambridge, MA: Harvard University Press, 2016); Danielle Citron and Frank Pasquale, "The Scored Society: Due Process for Automated Predictions," *Washington Law Review* 89, no. 1 (2014): 1–33. See also Daniel Schiller, *Digital Capitalism: Networking the Global Market System* (Cambridge, MA: MIT Press, 1999) (discussing political economy of information in an earlier period).

33. Adam Smith, *The Wealth of Nations* (London: W. Strahan and T. Cadell, 1776; Chicago: University of Chicago Press, 1976), book 1, chapters I–II (on the modern division of labor and technological innovation; first published in 1776); Karl Marx, *Capital, Volume 1: A Critique of Political Economy* (Hamburg: Verlag von Otto Meisner, 1867; New York: Penguin Books, 1990), chapter 15 (on the use of technology to discipline workers); Joseph Schumpeter, *Capitalism, Socialism, and Democracy* (New York: Harper & Brothers, 1942), chapter 7 (discussing "creative destruction"); Immanuel Wallerstein, *World-Systems Analysis: An Introduction* (Durham, NC: Duke University Press, 2004), 24–30 (summarizing the relationship among technological innovation, monopoly rents, and core/periphery divisions in world capitalism).

34. Kathleen Thelen, *Varieties of Liberalization and the New Politics of Social Solidarity* (Cambridge: Cambridge University Press, 2014); Peter A. Hall and David Soskice, "An Introduction to Varieties of Capitalism," in *Varieties of Capitalism: The Institutional Foundations of Comparative Advantage*, eds. Peter A. Hall and David Soskice (Oxford: Oxford University Press, 2001), 1–68; Gøsta Esping-Andersen, *The Three Worlds of Welfare Capitalism* (Princeton, NJ: Princeton University Press, 1990). For a critical account of the "varieties of capitalism" literature exemplified by Hall and Soskice, see Lucio Baccaro and Jonas Pontusson, "Rethinking Comparative Political Economy: The Growth Model Perspective," *Politics & Society* 44, no. 2 (2016): 175–207.

35. Samuel Bowles and Herbert Gintis, "Contested Exchange: New Microfoundations for the Political Economy of Capitalism," *Politics and Society* 18, no. 2 (1990): 165–222 (heterodox economics); Harry Braverman, *Labor and Monopoly Capital* (New York: Monthly Review Press, 1974) (sociology); Katherine Stone, "The Origins of Job Structures in the Steel Industry," *Review of Radical Political Economics* 6, no. 2 (1974): 113–173 (heterodox economics and sociology); David Montgomery, *Workers' Control in America* (New York: Cambridge University Press, 1980) (labor history). Industrial relations scholars have addressed issues of technology and labor relations as well. See, for example, John T. Dunlop, *Industrial Relations Systems* (New York: Henry Holt & Co., 1958).

36. Winner, "Do Artifacts Have Politics?" 124–25. This issue is discussed in more detail in section 1.2 of this book.

37. Alex Rosenblat, *Uberland: How Algorithms Are Rewriting the Rules of Work* (Berkeley: University of California Press, 2018); Mary L. Gray and Siddharth Suri, *Ghost Work: How to Stop Silicon Valley from Building a New Global Underclass* (New York: Houghton

Mifflin, 2019); Virginia Eubanks, *Automating Inequality: How High-Tech Tools Profile, Police, and Punish the Poor* (New York: St. Martin's Press, 2018).

38. The term has been used by others in the past, including *Schumpeter* (blog), "Digital Taylorism," *The Economist* (September 10, 2015).

Chapter 1

1. Total manufacturing employment declined from a peak of around 19.5 million in 1979 to just under 13 million in 2019. Federal Reserve Bank of St. Louis, "All Employees, Manufacturing," accessed December 12, 2021, https://fred.stlouisfed.org/series/MANEMP (data since 1939). Total service employment increased from around 50 million in 1979 to nearly 110 million in 2019. See Federal Reserve Bank of St. Louis, "All Employees, Private Service-Providing," accessed December 12, 2021, https://fred.stlouisfed.org/series/CES0800000001 (data since 1939). On wages among service workers, see section 1.5.

2. See, e.g., Kathleen Thelen, "The American Precariat: U.S. Capitalism in Comparative Perspective," *Perspectives on Politics* 17, no. 1 (2019): 14–15 (noting the high incidence of low-wage work and precarious work in the US compared with other countries). On the recent growth of economic inequality across wealthy economies, see generally Thomas Piketty, *Capital in the Twenty-First Century*, trans. Arthur Goldhammer (Cambridge, MA: Harvard University Press, 2017).

3. See Wolfgang Streeck, "Taking Capitalism Seriously: Toward an Institutionalist Approach to Contemporary Political Economy," *Socio-Economic Review* 9 (2011): 153 (utilizing a similar definition).

4. Yochai Benkler, "Power and Productivity: Institutions, Ideology, and Technology in Political Economy," in *A Political Economy of Justice*, ed. Danielle Allen, Yochai Benkler, Leah Downey, Rebecca Henderson, and Josh Simons (Chicago: University of Chicago Press, forthcoming, 2022), 37.

5. See Julie E. Cohen, "Turning Privacy Inside Out," *Theoretical Inquiries in Law* 20, no. 1 (2019): 17–23 (discussing the notion of technological "affordances" in relationship to legal theories of privacy); Sheila Jasanoff, *States of Knowledge: The Co-Production of Science and Social Order* (New York: Routledge, 2004), 17 ("science and society are co-produced, each underwriting the other's existence").

6. Benkler, "Power and Productivity," 37.

7. Michael L. Wachter, "Neoclassical Labor Economics: Its Implications for Labor and Employment Law," in *Research Handbook on the Economics of Labor and Employment Law*, ed. Cynthia L. Estlund and Michael L. Wachter (Northampton, MA: Edward Elgar Publishing, 2012), 21. See also Aage B. Sørensen, "Foundations of a Rent-Based Class Analysis," in *Approaches to Class Analysis*, ed. Erik Olin Wright

(Cambridge: Cambridge University Press, 2005), 123 (noting the impossibility of class power in the neoclassical model).

8. See David H. Autor and David Dorn, "The Growth of Low-Skill Service Jobs and the Polarization of the US Labor Market," *American Economic Review* 103, no. 5 (August 2013): 1553 ("Technology in the canonical model [of skill-biased technological change] is assumed to take a factor-augmenting form, meaning that it complements either high- or low-skill workers").

9. See generally Autor and Dorn, "Growth of Low-Skill Service Jobs." On a related note, the Autor and Dorn analysis assumes that wages are set by supply and demand for particular skills. Autor and Dorn, "Growth of Low-Skill Service Jobs," 1554, 1557. That assumption disregards the fact that many vulnerable workers are not covered by minimum wage and collective bargaining laws, or are denied rights under those laws through "fissuring" strategies such as subcontracting and franchising, all of which tend to drive down wages. See the discussion in chapters 2 and 5.

10. Benkler, "Power and Productivity," 45. See also Joshua Cohen, "Research Brief: Good Jobs," MIT Task Force on Work of the Future, October 29, 2020, https://workofthefuture.mit.edu/research-post/good-jobs/, 3 (observing that nearly all commentators on the so-called future of work in the 2010s believed that "the path of technology and its implications for human work are more or less fixed" so that "the only genuinely open question is the public policy response.")

11. Daron Acemoglu, "Technical Change, Inequality, and the Labor Market," *Journal of Economic Literature* 40, no. 2 (March 2002): 13, 49–52.

12. See Wachter, "Neoclassical Labor Economics," 24 (arguing that in a neoclassical model, if markets are competitive, then "there is no need for government policy (or for unions) to ensure that wages rise over time with worker productivity . . . Instead, if unions raise wages above competitive levels, the economy will be less productive.").

13. See generally Claudia Golden and Lawrence F. Katz, *The Race between Education and Technology* (Cambridge, MA: Harvard University Press, 2010).

14. See Wachter, "Neoclassical Labor Economics," 24 (suggesting that a tax-and-transfer system rather than labor market regulations should be used to ensure fair distribution and that "industrial policy should be confined to making markets as competitive as possible"). See generally Louis Kaplow and Steven Shavell, "Fairness Versus Welfare: Notes on the Pareto Principle, Preferences, and Distributive Justice," *Journal of Legal Studies* 32, no. 1 (2003): 331–362. See also Yochai Benkler, *A Political Economy of Oligarchy: Winner-Take-All Ideology, Superstar Norms, and the Rise of the 1%* (unpublished manuscript, September 2017): 13–14 (noting how neoclassical approaches to public policy have influenced legal scholarship).

15. Kathleen Thelen, *Varieties of Liberalization and the New Politics of Social Solidarity* (Cambridge: Cambridge University Press, 2014), 11–18. See also Gøsta Esping-Andersen,

The Three Worlds of Welfare Capitalism (Princeton, NJ: Princeton University Press, 1990), 26–29 (outlining differences among welfare states and their effects on distributive outcomes).

16. Peter A. Hall and David Soskice, "An Introduction to Varieties of Capitalism," in *Varieties of Capitalism: The Institutional Foundations of Comparative Advantage*, ed. Peter A. Hall and David Soskice (Oxford: Oxford University Press, 2001), 38–39. Comparative evidence to this effect is presented in this book at various points, including section 1.5.

17. See Thelen, "The American Precariat," 16 (stating that "one of the most robust findings in the literature on comparative political economy is that the strength of the organized labor movement is associated with lower inequality (especially low-end inequality) and more generous social protections") (citing Evelyne Huber and John D. Stephens, *Development and Crisis of the Welfare State: Parties and Politics in Global Markets* [Chicago: University of Chicago Press, 2001]); Jake Rosenfeld, *What Unions No Longer Do* (Cambridge, MA: Harvard University Press, 2014) (showing that the decline of unions in the US has aggravated income inequality and racial inequality).

18. See David Singh Grewal, "Book Review: The Laws of Capitalism," *Harvard Law Review* 128, no. 2 (2014): 665 (criticizing arguments that distribution should be addressed only through the tax-and-transfer system by noting that "it may be naïve to assume that after letting the inequality-producing market run its course there will be any agent left at the end of the process capable of demanding redistribution.").

19. See Robert L. Hale, "Coercion and Distribution in a Supposedly Non-Coercive State," *Political Science Quarterly* 38, no. 3 (September 1923): 471 (explaining, in a classic article, how the law helps to constitute economic relations and to perpetuate economic inequality); Duncan Kennedy, "The Stakes of Law, or Hale and Foucault!" *Legal Studies Forum* 15, no. 4 (1991): 328–341 (drawing on Hale's work to illustrate how legal entitlements affect labor/capital power relations); Simon Deakin, David Gindis, Geoffrey M. Hodgson, Kainan Huang, and Katharina Pistor, "Legal Institutionalism: Capitalism and the Constitutive Role of Law," *Journal of Comparative Economics* 45 (2017): 189, 194–198 (describing the legal constitution of markets, criticizing classical and modern theories of the firm for disregarding the importance of legal incorporation in facilitating production); Julie E. Cohen, *Between Truth and Power: The Legal Constructions of Informational Capitalism* (Oxford: Oxford University Press, 2019), 4 (discussing the contemporary relationship among legal institutions, the development of networked information technologies, and changes in the political economy).

20. Hale, "Coercion and Distribution," 474.

21. The discussions in this section and in section 1.5 draw on Brishen Rogers, "Capitalist Development, Labor Law, and the New Working Class," *Yale Law Journal* 131, no. 6 (2022): 1842–1879.

22. Yochai Benkler has developed a theory of the political economy of work and technology that has influenced my own. Benkler's is more ambitious—though also more complex—as it aims to explain many fields of social action beyond the workplace. See generally Benkler, "Power and Productivity."

23. Walter Korpi, "Power Resources Approach vs. Action and Conflict: On Causal and Intentional Explanations in the Study of Power," *Sociological Theory* 3, no. 2 (1985): 33. See also Walter Korpi, "The Power Resources Model," in *The Welfare State Reader*, 2nd ed., ed. Christopher Pierson and Francis G. Castles (Cambridge, UK: Polity Press, 2006), 76–88 (describing the application of the power resources model to welfare-state development, viewing the structure and generosity of welfare states largely as an effect of working-class political power). While this book borrows the term "power resources," its analysis does not entirely track the analyses of power-resources theorists in the welfare states literature. This book's analysis is also indebted to Kathleen Thelen's argument that cross-class alliances are important to institutional change over time. See Thelen, *Varieties of Liberalization*, 18–24 (discussing the limits of power resources and neo-corporatist theories of political-economic evolution, proposing an alternative theory that takes account of producer group alliances).

24. Chiara Benassi, Lisa Dorigatti, and Elisa Pannini, "Explaining Divergent Bargaining Outcomes for Agency Workers: The Role of Labor Divides and Labour Market Reforms," *European Journal of Industrial Relations* 25, no. 2 (2018): 165 (distinguishing "three broad categories" of worker-side power resources: "structural, associational, and institutional" or legal/regulatory). On the notion of and importance of workers' "associational power," see Erik Olin Wright, "Working-Class Power, Capitalist-Class Interests, and Class Compromise," *American Journal of Sociology* 105, no. 4 (January 2000): 958.

25. See Guy Mundlak, *Organizing Matters: Two Logics of Trade Representation* (Cheltenham, UK: Edward Elgar Publishing), 23 (noting that industrial relations systems in many wealthy nations are based on a recognition that labor's interests and capital's interests diverge, and therefore that policymaking processes should "give voice to the representatives of the class cleavage").

26. Claus Offe and Helmut Wiesenthal, "Two Logics of Collective Action: Theoretical Notes on Social Class and Organizational Form," *Political Power & Social Theory* 1 (1980): 74; Deakin et al., "Legal Institutionalism," 197. See also *Vegelahn v. Guntner*, 167 Mass. 92, 108 (1896) (Holmes, J., dissenting) (noting that modern enterprises enable combinations of capital).

27. Offe and Wiesenthal, "Two Logics," 74–75.

28. Bruce E. Kaufman, "Economic Analysis of Labor Markets and Labor Law: An Institutional/Industrial Relations Perspective," in *Research Handbook on the Economics of Labor and Employment Law*, ed. Cynthia L. Estlund and Michael L. Wachter (Northampton, MA: Edward Elgar Publishing, 2012), 83.

29. See Wolfgang Streeck, *Buying Time: The Delayed Crisis of Democratic Capitalism* (London: Verso, 2014), 80–84 (arguing that modern states must serve both national citizens and global markets). See also Marc Galanter, "Why the 'Haves' Come Out Ahead: Speculations on the Limits of Legal Change," *Law & Society Review* 9, no. 1 (Autumn 1974): 95–160 (arguing that the U.S. legal system systematically favors wealthy interests because they have the capacity to fight for rules as well as outcomes in litigation).

30. Both Joseph Schumpeter and Karl Marx emphasized this point. Joseph Schumpeter, *Capitalism, Socialism and Democracy* (New York: Harper & Brothers, 1942), chapter 7 (discussing the process of "creative destruction" that fuels growth in capitalist economies). Karl Marx, *Capital, Volume 1: A Critique of Political Economy* (Hamburg: Verlag von Otto Meisner, 1867; New York: Penguin Books, 1990), esp. chapter 12, "The Concept of Relative Surplus Value." See also Immanuel Wallerstein, *World-Systems Analysis: An Introduction* (Durham, NC: Duke University Press, 2004), 25–27 (2004) (arguing that the incessant competition that characterizes capitalism makes profitability very difficult, and therefore leads companies to seek monopoly positions); Streeck, "Taking Capitalism Seriously," 139, 151–152, 154–158 (discussing the constant evolution of capitalist economies due to such pressures).

31. See Immanuel Wallerstein, "Braudel on Capitalism, or Everything Upside Down," *Journal of Modern History* 63, no. 2 (1991), 355 (calling these "high-voltage" profits). See also Wallerstein, *World-Systems Analysis*, 25–29 (discussing the importance of IP protections in creating monopoly rents and dividing the world economy into "core" or profitable processes, which typically enjoy IP protection, and "peripheral" or unprofitable processes, which typically do not).

32. Streeck, "Taking Capitalism Seriously," 154–158. In one view, the use of markets to discipline workers and the poor is foundational to capitalism. See John Clegg, "A Theory of Capitalist Slavery," *Journal of Historical Sociology* 33 (2020): 80 (while markets and a division of labor have existed throughout history, capitalist societies "uniquely deny the vast majority of people any direct (non-market-mediated) access to their means of subsistence").

33. Wolfgang Streeck, "Varieties of Varieties: 'VoC' and the Growth Models," *Politics & Society* 44, no. 2 (2016): 246.

34. See generally Alex Rosenblat, *Uberland: How Algorithms Are Rewriting the Rules of Work* (Berkeley: University of California Press, 2018).

35. As argued in section 1.3, efforts like Uber's—which generate product market rents while eliminating job rents—are an important axis of class conflict today. See also Herman M. Schwartz, "Intellectual Property, Technorents, and the Labour Share of Production," *Competition and Change* (October 28, 2020), https://doi.org/10.1177/1024529420968221 (discussing such dynamics).

36. See Richard B. Freeman and James L. Medoff, *What Do Unions Do?* (New York: Basic Books, 1984), 3–25 (discussing the cartel-like characteristics of unions). See also

David Singh Grewal and Jedediah Purdy, "Introduction: Law and Neoliberalism," *Law & Contemporary Problems* 77, no. 4 (2014): 8 (arguing that political contests under neoliberalism involve the question of who will be subject to market discipline).

37. See generally Karl Polanyi, *The Great Transformation: The Political and Economic Origins of Our Time* (Boston: Beacon Press, 2001).

38. Streeck, "Taking Capitalism Seriously," 162. As discussed in the next section, to say that norms are "solidaristic" does not imply that they are politically progressive. Those norms can be radically democratic in orientation, for example, or they can be racist and misogynistic.

39. Streeck, "Taking Capitalism Seriously," 164. See also Grewal and Purdy, "Law and Neoliberalism," 3–4 (discussing the tension between "democratic demands and market imperatives").

40. See Robert Gordon, "Critical Legal Histories," *Stanford Law Review* 36, no. 1 (1984): 120–121 (observing parallels between classical legal thought and classical political economy, and between legal realism and old institutionalist economics).

41. See Christopher Tomlins, "The Presence and Absence of Legal Mind: A Comment on Duncan Kennedy's 'Three Globalizations,'" *Law and Contemporary Problems* 78, no. 1–2 (2015): 10–14 (suggesting that neoliberalism provides the integrating concepts of contemporary legal consciousness); Jedediah Britton-Purdy, David Singh Grewal, Amy Kapczynski, and K. Sabeel Rahman, "Building a Law-and-Political-Economy Framework: Beyond the Twentieth-Century Synthesis," *Yale Law Journal* 129, no. 6 (2020): 1789 (suggesting that legal theory since the 1980s has been heavily influenced by neoliberalism).

42. See Peter Swenson, *Capitalists against Markets: The Making of Labor Markets and Welfare States in the United States and Sweden* (Oxford: Oxford University Press, 2002) (arguing that companies and workers have often joined together to pass social legislation); Thelen, *Varieties of Liberalization*, 22–25 (discussing the role of cross-class alliances in the recent evolution of welfare states).

43. Wright, "Working-Class Power," 957.

44. Ellen Meiksins Wood, *Democracy Against Capitalism: Renewing Historical Materialism* (London: Verso, 1995), 76 (emphasis in original).

45. See generally Erik Olin Wright, "Foundations of a Neo-Marxist Class Analysis," in *Approaches to Class Analysis*, ed. Erik Olin Wright (Cambridge: Cambridge University Press, 2005), 4–30.

46. See, for example, Adam Przeworski, "Proletariat into a Class: The Process of Class Formation from Karl Kautsky's 'The Class Struggle' to Recent Controversies," *Politics & Society* 7, no. 4 (December 1977): 358–359 (discussing constant changes in class relations under capitalism).

47. Daniel Bell, *The Coming of Post-Industrial Society* (New York: Basic Books, 1973), 134 (arguing that the US "has become a white collar society" due to technological development), 145–147 (arguing that the major axes of labor market conflict going forward will involve race and gender divisions and social conflicts over the quality of services rather than class per se), 148–154 (arguing that the production workforce has become so skilled and educated that it is no longer a working class).

48. Manuel Castells, "Materials for an Exploratory Theory of the Network Society," *British Journal of Sociology* 51, no. 1 (March 2000): 18. See also Nicholas Garnham, "Information Society Theory as Ideology: A Critique," *Society and Leisure* 21, no. 1 (1998): 102–103 (noting Castells's debt to Bell).

49. Manuel Castells, *The Information Age, Vol. 1: Rise of the Network Society* (Cambridge, MA: Blackwell), 255–302 (discussing changes in work relations in so-called network society).

50. Shoshana Zuboff, *The Age of Surveillance Capitalism: The Fight for a Human Future at the New Frontier of Power* (New York: PublicAffairs, 2019). For lucid criticisms of Zuboff's book, see Amy Kapczynski, "The Law of Informational Capitalism," *Yale Law Journal* 129, no. 5 (2020): 1474 (arguing that Zuboff's account disregards "important problems of private power," including how "digital technology has impacted labor"); Julie E. Cohen, "Review of Zuboff's *The Age of Surveillance Capitalism*: *The Fight for a Human Future at the New Frontier of Power*," *Surveillance & Society* 17, nos. 1–2 (2019): 240–245 (arguing that Zuboff largely disregards the role of law in structuring the practices of surveillance capitalism).

51. See generally E. P. Thompson, *The Making of the English Working Class* (New York: Penguin Books, 1963). For a different account of the role of culture in class formation see generally Pierre Bourdieu, *Distinction: A Social Critique of the Judgement of Taste*, trans. Richard Nice (London: Routledge Classics, 1984).

52. Benjamin I. Sachs, "Enabling Employee Choice: A Structural Approach to the Rules of Union Organizing," *Harvard Law Review* 123 (2010): 684–685.

53. See Kate Bronfenbrenner and Dorian Warren, "The Empirical Case for Streamlining the NLRB Certification Process: The Role of Date of Unfair Labor Practice Occurrence," Institute for Social and Economic Research and Policy Working Paper Series (June 2011), https://digitalcommons.ilr.cornell.edu/workingpapers/159 (reviewing anti-union campaign tactics and their efficacy).

54. Offe and Wiesenthal, "Two Logics," 78–79 (emphasis in original). This form of organizing requires fairly "strong ties" in Mark Granovetter's schema as measured by the degree of trust and emotional intimacy among workers. Mark S. Granovetter, "The Strength of Weak Ties," *American Journal of Sociology* 78, no. 6 (1973): 1360–1380.

55. Offe and Wiesenthal, "Two Logics," 78–79; Rick Fantasia, *Cultures of Solidarity: Consciousness, Action, and Contemporary American Workers* (Berkeley: University of

California Press, 1989). See also Mundlak, *Organizing Matters*, 31 (arguing that enterprise bargaining helps constitute workers' identities).

56. See generally Sørensen, "Rent-Based Class Analysis."

57. Sørensen, "Rent-Based Class Analysis," 125–127.

58. Sørensen, "Rent-Based Class Analysis," 151.

59. On skills and occupational licensing, see Sørensen, "Rent-Based Class Analysis," 133.

60. See the discussions in chapters 3–5.

61. See generally C. L. R. James, *The Black Jacobins: Toussaint L'Ouverture and the San Domingo Revolution*, 2nd rev. ed. (New York: Vintage Books, 1989); Cedric J. Robinson, *Black Marxism: The Making of the Black Radical Tradition* (London: Zed Press, 1983; Chapel Hill: University of North Carolina Press, 2000).

62. Within legal scholarship, canonical works include Frances E. Olsen, "The Family and the Market: A Study of Ideology and Legal Reform," *Harvard Law Review* 96, no. 7 (1983): 1497–1578 (arguing that dominant understandings of the market and the family as separate spheres devalue women's economic contributions and reinforce the subordination of women); and Katharine Silbaugh, "Turning Labor into Love: Housework and the Law," *Northwestern Law Review* 91, no. 1 (1996): 1–86 (arguing that the dominant understanding of household labor as an act of love obscures its central importance to our economy). On the intersection of race and gender in employment discrimination doctrine, see generally Kimberlé Crenshaw, "Demarginalizing the Intersection of Race and Sex: A Black Feminist Critique of Antidiscrimination Doctrine, Feminist Theory and Antiracist Politics," *University of Chicago Legal Forum* 1989 (1989): 139–167.

63. Dorothy Sue Cobble, *The Other Women's Movement: Workplace Justice and Social Rights in Modern America* (Princeton, NJ: Princeton University Press, 2003); Eileen Boris and Jennifer Klein, *Caring for America: Home Health Workers in the Shadow of the Welfare State* (Oxford: Oxford University Press, 2012).

64. 29 U.S.C. 152(3) (2018).

65. Title VII of that act, which prohibits employment discrimination, has been amended several times since 1964. The current text begins at 29 U.S.C. 2000e (2018).

66. See generally Gabriel Winant, *The Next Shift: The Fall of Industry and the Rise of Health Care in Rust Belt America* (Cambridge, MA: Harvard University Press, 2021).

67. Destin Jenkins and Justin Leroy, "Introduction: The Old History of Capitalism," in *Histories of Racial Capitalism*, ed. Destin Jenkins and Justin Leroy (New York: Columbia University Press, 2021), 3.

68. On the history of foreclosure, see K-Sue Park, "Race, Innovation, and Financial Growth: The Example of Foreclosure," in *Histories of Racial Capitalism*, ed. Destin Jenkins and Justin Leroy (New York: Columbia University Press, 2021), 27–47.

69. Jenkins and Leroy, "The Old History of Capitalism," 3.

70. Winant, *The Next Shift*, 157.

71. See Ruth Milkman, "Immigrant Organizing and the New Labor Movement in Los Angeles," *Critical Sociology* 26, no. 1–2 (2000): 66 (discussing the role of "shared experience of migration" in recent immigrant worker organizing); James Green and Chris Tilly, "Service Unionism: Directions for Organizing," *Labor Law Journal* 38, no. 8 (1987): 492 (discussing the relationship between "Black pride" and civil rights consciousness and worker organizing among health-care workers, as well as similar efforts among farm workers).

72. See David H. Autor, "Polanyi's Paradox and the Shape of Employment Growth," in *Re-Evaluating Labor Market Dynamics* (Kansas City, MO: Federal Reserve Bank of Kansas City, 2015), 163–164 (discussing complementarities between technology and human capital in midskilled health-care jobs).

73. Germany is the canonical case. See Hall and Soskice, "Introduction to Varieties of Capitalism," 24–27 (discussing various elements of the German industrial relations model, including high investments in skills).

74. My distinction between power-enhancing and productivity-augmenting technologies draws upon Benkler, "Power and Productivity"; Samuel Bowles, "Social Institutions and Technical Change," in *Technological and Social Factors in Long Term Fluctuations*, ed. Massimo Di Matteo, Richard M. Goodwin, and Alessandro Vercelli (New York: Springer-Verlag 1986), 67–88; and Peter Skott and Frederick Guy, "A Model of Power-Biased Technological Change," *Economics Letters* 95, no. 1 (2007): 124–131.

75. See Bowles, "Social Institutions and Technical Change," 78 (using the term "homogenize" rather than "deskill"), 70 (arguing that employers may favor inefficient technologies when doing so helps them contain workers' power and capture a higher share of profits).

76. Bowles, "Social Institutions and Technical Change," 78. Bowles's focus on problems of labor discipline overlaps with some mainstream analyses, including Armen A. Alchian and Harold Demsetz, "Production, Information Costs, and Economic Organization," *American Economic Review* 62, no. 5 (December 1972): 777–795.

77. Samuel Bowles, "The Production Process in a Competitive Economy: Walrasian, Neo-Hobbesian, and Marxian Models," *American Economic Review* 75, no. 1 (March 1985): 31–32.

78. Langdon Winner, "Do Artifacts Have Politics?" *Daedalus* 109 (Winter 1980): 125. See also Benkler, "Power and Productivity," 38 (discussing this history).

79. See Stephen A. Marglin, "What Do Bosses Do? The Origins and Functions of Hierarchy in Capitalist Production," *Review of Radical Political Economics* 6, no. 2 (1974): 70–72, 86. See also E. P. Thompson, "Time, Work-Discipline, and Industrial Capitalism," *Past and Present* 38, no. 1 (1967): 56–97 (contrasting peasants' understanding of time prior to industrialization with the regimentation of time in schools and factories following industrialization).

80. Frederick Winslow Taylor, *The Principles of Scientific Management* (New York: Harper Bros., 1913). See also Harry Braverman, *Labor and Monopoly Capital* (New York: Monthly Review Press, 1974), 76–83 (arguing that Taylor sought to reorganize machine tool production for the purpose of disempowering workers). The sociologist Craig R. Littler has argued that the importance of Taylorism lay less in the erosion of craft skills and more in industrialists' elimination of the internal contracting system that dominated at the time, so that Taylorism lead to direct employment relationships between company and workers and centralized managerial control of the labor process. Craig Littler, "Understanding Taylorism," *British Journal of Sociology* 29, no. 2 (1978): 185–202.

81. Taylor, *Scientific Management*, 63.

82. Karen Levy, "The Contexts of Control: Information, Power, and Truck-Driving Work," *The Information Society* 31, no. 2 (2015): 161.

83. See David Montgomery, *Workers' Control in America* (New York: Cambridge University Press, 1980), 13 (discussing the ethical code of nineteenth-century craft workers, which led them to refuse to work while being watched), 115 (discussing workers' refusal to work while being monitored by industrial engineers in the early twentieth century).

84. James R. Beniger, *The Control Revolution: Technological and Economic Origins of the Information Society* (Cambridge, MA: Harvard University Press, 1989).

85. See Gary Marx, *Windows into the Soul: Surveillance and Society in an Age of High Technology* (Chicago: University of Chicago Press, 2016), 50–51, table 2.1 (summarizing contemporary surveillance efforts and how they differ from historical forms of surveillance); Marion Fourcade and Jeffrey Gordon, "Learning Like a State: Statecraft in the Digital Age," *Journal of Law and Political Economy* 1, no. 1 (2020): 79 (describing new forms of governance and power today as universal, comprehensive, indefinite in temporality, and circular or mimetic).

86. This is a variant on the argument that the law tends to lag technology. See Gary E. Marchant, "The Growing Gap Between Emerging Technologies and the Law," in *The Growing Gap Between Emerging Technologies and Legal-Ethical Oversight: The Pacing Problem*, ed. Gary E. Marchant, Braden R. Allenby, and Joseph R. Herkert (New York: Springer, 2011), 23 (arguing that the law lags technology both because legal regulations "are based on static rather than a dynamic view of society and technology" and because legal institutions take time to revise).

87. Mireille Hildebrandt, *Smart Technologies and the End(s) of Law: Novel Entanglements of Law and Technology* (Cheltenham, UK: Edward Elgar Publishing, 2016), 12 (discussed in Kapczynski, "The Law of Informational Capitalism," 1471).

88. See Cohen, *Between Truth and Power*, 76 (discussing this "emergent limbic media system"), 77 (arguing that "the result is an emergent form of collective consciousness that is primed for precognitive activation and manipulation at scale").

89. See generally Paul Pierson, *Politics in Time* (Princeton, NJ: Princeton University Press 2004) (discussing the long-term evolution of political-economic institutions).

90. The analysis in this section is indebted to Gabriel Winant's recent work, which emphasizes that neoliberalism's politics and institutions evolved from the postwar order, carrying forward many of the tensions and social divisions of the postwar period. Winant, *The Next Shift*, 18. See also Gabriel Winant, "Anomalies and Continuities: Positivism and Historicism on Inequality," *Journal of the Gilded Age and Progressive Era* 19, no. 2 (2020): 286 (suggesting that the politics of neoliberalism can be understood only in "the historical time of capitalism, from primitive accumulation to industrial maturity to overcapacity")

91. Industrial pluralism and its relationship to law are discussed in detail in chapter 2.

92. On the New Deal order, see generally Steve Fraser and Gary Gerstle, eds., *The Rise and Fall of the New Deal Order, 1930–1980* (Princeton, NJ: Princeton University Press, 1989); Gary Gerstle, Nelson Lichtenstein, and Alice O'Connor, eds., *Beyond the New Deal Order: U.S. Politics from the Great Depression to the Great Recession* (Philadelphia: University of Pennsylvania Press, 2019).

93. 29 U.S.C. § 151 (2018).

94. See Erik Olin Wright, *Envisioning Real Utopias* (London: Verso, 2010), 337 (arguing that "advances in bottom-up social empowerment within a capitalist society will be most stable and defendable when such social empowerment also helps solve certain real problems faced by capitalists and other elites").

95. Michael Wachter, "The Striking Success of the National Labor Relations Act," in *Research Handbook on the Economics of Labor and Employment Law*, ed. Cynthia L. Estlund and Michael Wachter (Northampton, MA: Edward Elgar Publishing, 2012), 427–462.

96. This is the essence of the Rehn-Meidner model, which informed Swedish economic policy for decades. Lennart Erixon, "Progressive Supply-Side Economics: An Explanation and Update of the Rehn-Meidner Model," *Cambridge Journal of Economics* 42 (May 2018): 653–697.

97. Freeman and Medoff, *What Do Unions Do?*, 7–9.

98. Wallerstein, *World-Systems Analysis*, 55–59.

99. Grewal, "The Laws of Capitalism," 631. See also David Singh Grewal, "The Legal Constitution of Capitalism," in *After Piketty: The Agenda for Economics and Inequality*, ed. Heather Boushey, J. Bradford DeLong, and Marshall Steinbaum (Cambridge, MA: Harvard University Press, 2017), 489–490 (noting that the postwar era was a time of relative labor scarcity, which bolstered workers' capacity to demand higher wages).

100. See Nelson Lichtenstein, *State of the Union: A Century of American Labor* (Princeton, NJ: Princeton University Press, 2002): 98 (arguing that "the very idea of . . . a harmonious accord is a suspect reinterpretation of the postwar industrial era."). See also the discussion in chapter 2.

101. See Joel Rogers, "Divide and Conquer: Further 'Reflections on the Distinctive Character of American Labor Laws,'" *Wisconsin Law Review* 1990 (1990): 103–107 (summarizing data showing that worker organization after 1947 was largely limited to the geographic areas and industrial sectors that had organized before that time).

102. Sean Farhang and Ira Katznelson, "The Southern Imposition: Congress and Labor in the New Deal and Fair Deal," *Studies in American Political Development* 19, no. 1 (Spring 2005): 7.

103. The causes of stagflation and subsequent deindustrialization are still debated. For an overview of the 1970s as a period of crisis that led companies and investors to pursue various institutional reforms, see generally Streeck, *Buying Time*, 20–34.

104. On the transnational business counteroffensive against the postwar regime during this time, see generally Streeck, *Buying Time*, 24–31.

105. See Financial Services Modernization Act of 1999, 113 Stat. 1338 (1999) (repealing Glass-Steagall Act, which forbade investment and commercial banking within the same enterprise). See also Greta Krippner, "The Financialization of the American Economy," *Socio-Economic Review* 3, no. 2 (2005): 173–208 (financialization explains why "profit-making occurs increasingly through financial channels rather than through trade and commodity production").

106. Christoph Lakner and Branko Milanovic, "Global Income Distribution: From the Fall of the Berlin Wall to the Great Recession," *World Bank Economic Review* 30, no. 2 (2016): 203–232.

107. See Autor, "Polanyi's Paradox," 131–133 (discussing technological change and anxieties over automation in 1960s); Rick Wartzman, "The First Time America Freaked Out Over Automation," *Politico* (May 30, 2017) (discussing automation fears in 1950s and 1960s, caused by incorporation of new technologies into factories and other workplaces).

108. Federal Reserve Bank of St. Louis, "All Employees, Manufacturing/All Employees, Nonfarm," accessed December 12, 2021, https://fred.stlouisfed.org/graph/?g=cAYh (data since 1940).

109. Federal Reserve Bank of St. Louis, "All Employees, Private Service-Providing."

110. See Bell, *Post-Industrial Society*, 129–142 (collecting and analyzing data on growth of services in the 1950s and 1960s).

111. See Federal Reserve Bank of St. Louis, "Labor Force Participation Rate—Women," accessed December 12, 2021, https://fred.stlouisfed.org/series/LNS11300002 (showing an increase from around 32 percent in 1948 to more than 51 percent in 1980, then peaking around 60 percent in 2001).

112. See Federal Reserve Bank of St. Louis, "All Employees, Manufacturing/All Employees, Nonfarm" (showing a drop in manufacturing jobs from 22.7 percent of total employment in 1979 to 18.4 percent in 1983, followed by a continued decline to around 10 percent by 2010).

113. See Autor, "Polanyi's Paradox," 140 (discussing the adoption of industrial robotics in the 1980s).

114. National Academies of Sciences, Engineering, and Medicine, *Information Technology and the U.S. Workforce: Where Are We and Where Do We Go from Here?* (Washington, DC: National Academies Press, 2017), 66; Laura Tyson and Michael Spence, "Exploring the Effects of Technology on Income and Wealth Inequality," in *After Piketty: The Agenda for Economics and Inequality*, ed. Heather Boushey, J. Bradford DeLong, and Marshall Steinbaum (Cambridge, MA: Harvard University Press, 2017), 187.

115. Winant, *The Next Shift*, 3.

116. Gøsta Esping-Andersen, *Social Foundations of Postindustrial Economies* (Oxford: Oxford University Press 1999), 24–26; Torben Iversen, "The Dynamics of Welfare State Expansion: Trade Openness, De-Industrialization, and Partisan Politics," in *The New Politics of the Welfare State*, ed. Paul Pierson (Oxford: Oxford University Press, 1995), 47; Paul Pierson, "Post-industrial Pressures on the Mature Welfare States," in *The New Politics of the Welfare State*, ed. Paul Pierson (Oxford: Oxford University Press, 2001), 83–87.

117. William J. Baumol, "Macroeconomics of Unbalanced Growth: The Anatomy of Urban Crisis," *American Economic Review* 57, no. 3 (1967): 415–426. The phrase "cost disease" does not appear in Baumol's 1967 article but came into wide usage later. E.g., William J. Baumol, with contributions by Monte Malach, Ariel Palbos-Méndez, and Lilian Gomory Wu, *The Cost Disease: Why Computers Get Cheaper and Health Care Doesn't* (New Haven, CT: Yale University Press, 2012). See also Torben Iversen and Anne Wren, "Equality, Employment and Budgetary Restraint: The Trilemma of the Service Economy," *World Politics* 50 (July 1998): 507–546 (arguing that service economies are subject to a "trilemma," in which they can achieve no more than two of three goals: wage equality, low unemployment, and modest public spending); Anne Wren, Máté Fodor, and Sotiria Theodoropoulou, "The Trilemma Revisited: Institutions, Inequality, and Employment Creation in an Era of ICT-Intensive Service Expansion," in *The Political Economy of the Service Transition*, ed. Anne Wren (Oxford: Oxford University Press, 2013), 108–146 (arguing that states

may be able to mitigate the trilemma by encouraging growth in high-value, tradable services like finance, insurance, advertising, and law, and then using the large profits in those sectors to fund social programs).

118. Thelen, *Varieties of Liberalization*, 14.

119. 29 U.S.C. 2101–2109 (2018).

120. Thelen, *Varieties of Liberalization*, 14–15 (on "embedded flexibilization" in Denmark).

121. See Hall and Soskice, "Introduction to Varieties of Capitalism," 24–27 (discussing such elements of the German model and their complementarities with systems of worker interest representation).

122. Thelen, *Varieties of Liberalization*, 30–31 (discussing the emergence of dualism in Germany, where precarious work is common outside the industrial core). See also Tobias Schulze-Cleven, "German Labor Relations in International Perspective: A Model Reconsidered," *German Politics and Society* 35, no. 4 (2017): 46–76 (discussing the German model in greater detail).

123. For overviews of the "new working class" and its particular challenges in the US, see generally Winant, *The Next Shift*; Sarah Jaffe, "The New Working Class," *The New Republic* (February 22, 2018); and Tamara Draut, *Sleeping Giant: How the New Working Class Will Transform America* (New York: Penguin, 2016). In the UK context, see Mike Savage et al., "A New Model of Social Class? Findings from the BBC's Great British Class Survey Experiment," *Sociology* 47, no. 2 (2013): 219–250 (finding that around 19 percent of workers are in the "emergent service sector," and 15 percent are in the "precariat").

124. Occupation-level data given in this paragraph come from the US Department of Labor. Bureau of Labor Statistics, Occupational Employment Statistics, accessed November 25, 2021, https://www.bls.gov/oes/2019/may/oes_nat.htm#35-0000 (data from May 2019).

125. Winant, *The Next Shift*, 5–8.

126. Irene Tung, Yannet Lathrop, and Paul Sonn, *The Growing Movement for $15* (New York: National Employment Law Project, November 2015): 1. Those racial wage gaps also reflect the decline of unions. Jake Rosenfeld and Meredith Kleykamp, "Organized Labor and Racial Wage Inequality in the United States," *American Journal of Sociology* 117, no. 5 (2012): 1460–1502.

Chapter 2

1. The introductory text to this chapter draws from Brishen Rogers, "Capitalist Development, Labor Law, and the New Working Class," *Yale Law Journal* 131, no. 6 (2022): 1842–1879.

2. See generally Felix Frankfurter and Nathan Greene, *The Labor Injunction* (New York: Macmillan, 1930).

3. *Lochner v. New York*, 198 U.S. 45 (1905).

4. *West Coast Hotel Co. v. Parrish*, 300 U.S. 379 (1937) (rejecting a constitutional challenge to state minimum wage law); *NLRB v. Jones & Laughlin Steel Corp.*, 301 U.S. 1 (1937) (rejecting a constitutional challenge to NLRA).

5. *Jones & Laughlin*, 301 U.S. at 45. See also *H.K. Porter & Co., Inc. v. NLRB*, 397 U.S. 99, 108 (1970) (observing that "one of the[] fundamental policies" of the NLRA "is freedom of contract."); Karl E. Klare, "Judicial Deradicalization of the Wagner Act and the Origins of Modern Legal Consciousness, 1937–1941," *Minnesota Law Review* 62, no. 3 (1978): 299–300 (criticizing *Jones & Laughlin* for importing contractualism into the NLRA).

6. Karl E. Klare, "Labor Law as Ideology: Toward a New Historiography of Collective Bargaining Law," *Industrial Relations Law Journal* 4 (1980–1981): 454. See also Christopher Tomlins, *Law, Labor and Ideology in the Early American Republic* (Cambridge: Cambridge University Press, 1993), 32 (identifying a similar conflict between democratically inflected constitutionalism and the common law in the early days of the US).

7. See generally Klare, "Judicial Deradicalization"; Katherine Van Wezel Stone, "The Post-War Paradigm in American Labor Law," *Yale Law Journal* 90, no. 7 (1981): 1509–1580; Karl E. Klare, "The Public/Private Distinction in Labor Law," *University of Pennsylvania Law Review* 130, no. 6 (1982): 1358–1422.

8. Stone, "Post-War Paradigm," 1511.

9. Stone, "Post-War Paradigm," 1515. The canonical cases are the so-called Steelworkers Trilogy of 1960: *United Steelworkers v. American Mfg. Co.*, 363 U.S. 564 (1960); *United Steelworkers v. Warrior & Gulf Navigation Co.*, 363 U.S. 574 (1960); and *United Steelworkers v. Enterprise Wheel & Car Corp.*, 363 U.S. 593 (1960).

10. See Archibald Cox, "Labor Law Preemption Revisited," *Harvard Law Review* 85, no. 7 (1972): 1352 (asserting that "two fundamental ideas lie at the core of the national labor policy: (1) freedom of employee self-organization; and (2) the voluntary private adjustment of conflicts of interest over wages, hours, and other conditions of employment through the negotiation and administration of collective bargaining agreements").

11. Alan Hyde and Mona Ressaissi, "Unions without Borders: Recent Developments in the Theory, Practice and Law of Transnational Unionism," *Canadian Labour and Employment Law Journal* 14, no. 1 (2008): 91–92.

12. Stone, "Post-War Paradigm," 1511.

13. Ruth Dukes, "Constitutionalizing Employment Relations: Sinzheimer, Kahn-Freund, and the Role of Labour Law," *Journal of Law & Society* 35, No. 3 (September 2008): 342–344.

14. Stone, "Post-War Paradigm," 1566–1573.

15. Stone, "Post-War Paradigm," 1571–1572.

16. *American Mfg. Co.*, 363 U.S., at 568.

17. See Eric Tucker, "Labor's Many Constitutions (and Capital's Too)," *Comparative Labor Law & Policy Journal* 33, no. 3 (2012): 358 (contrasting "thin" and "thick" forms of industrial democracy).

18. Such issues came up frequently in postwar labor cases, with courts often ratifying employers' anti-union efforts. See, e.g., *NLRB v. Adkins Transfer Co.*, 226 F.2d 324 (6th Cir. 1955) (no violation of NLRA for employer to close a division to avoid paying union-scale wages); *Textile Workers Union v. Darlington Mfg. Co.*, 380 U.S. 263 (1965) (no violation of NLRA where employer shut down entire business due to anti-union animus). In other cases, courts limited companies' rights to resist unionization. See, e.g., *Fibreboard Paper Products Corp. v. NLRB*, 379 U.S. 203 (1964) (employer must bargain with union over decision to subcontract work within a unionized bargaining unit); *NLRB v. Gissel Packing Co.*, 395 U.S. 575 (1969) (unfair labor practice for employer to threaten to close plant if workers unionize). The facts of *Gissel* nevertheless show that some employers fought bitterly against unionization well after the New Deal. *Gissel*, 395 U.S. at 579–586 (summarizing several employers' unlawful responses to several union campaigns, which included interrogation and termination of union supporters and racist appeals).

19. Stone, "Post-War Paradigm," 1511.

20. The discussion in this chapter uses "neoliberalism" to signify an approach to political-economic governance. See Joshua Cohen and Joel Rogers, "Secondary Associations and Democratic Governance," in *Associations and Democracy*, ed. Erik Olin Wright (New York: Verso, 1995), 12–14, 12n10 (outlining the neoliberal view of the state as evidenced in, for example, Friedrich A. Hayek, *The Constitution of Liberty* (Chicago: University of Chicago Press, 1960)). A related literature uses "neoliberalism" to signify a political rationality or moral theory that encourages individuals to understand themselves as entrepreneurs. On the latter, see Wendy Brown, *Undoing the Demos: Neoliberalism's Stealth Revolution* (Princeton, NJ: Princeton University Press, 2015) (outlining this conception of neoliberalism). Michel Foucault's influential history of neoliberalism has influenced both of these literatures. See Michel Foucault, *The Birth of Biopolitics: Lectures at the Collège de France, 1978–79*, ed. Michel Senellart, trans. Graham Burchell (London: Palgrave Macmillan, 2008), 101–129 (discussing German ordo-liberalism), 185–214 (discussing American neoliberalism).

21. Wolfgang Streeck, *Buying Time: The Delayed Crisis of Democratic Capitalism* (New York: Verso, 2014), 26–31 (outlining the transition to neoliberalism in advanced market economies in the 1970s).

22. Cass Sunstein, "Lochner's Legacy," *Columbia Law Review* 87 (1987): 874.

23. David Singh Grewal and Jedediah Purdy, "Introduction: Law and Neoliberalism," *Law & Contemporary Problems* 77, no. 4 (2014): 5. See also Jedediah Britton-Purdy, David Singh Grewal, Amy Kapczynski, and K. Sabeel Rahman, "Building a Law-and-Political-Economy Framework: Beyond the Twentieth-Century Synthesis," *Yale Law Journal* 129, no. 6 (2020): 1794–1818 (summarizing high-level developments in legal theory during the late twentieth century that were indebted to neoliberalism); Christopher Tomlins, "The Presence and Absence of Legal Mind: A Comment on Duncan Kennedy's 'Three Globalizations,'" *Law and Contemporary Problems* 78, no. 1–2 (2015): 9–17 (suggesting that neoliberalism provides the integrating concepts of contemporary legal consciousness).

24. Grewal and Purdy, "Introduction: Law and Neoliberalism," 5–6; Britton-Purdy et al., "Law-and-Political-Economy Framework," 1810; Foucault, *Birth of Biopolitics*, 131 (suggesting that neoliberalism involves "dissociating the market economy from the political principle of laissez-faire.").

25. Britton-Purdy et al., "Law-and-Political-Economy Framework," 1790.

26. See Quinn Slobodian, *Globalists: The End of Empire and the Birth of Neoliberalism* (Cambridge, MA: Harvard University Press, 2018), 13 (using the term "encasement" to describe the common neoliberal strategy of protecting property rights against democratic infringement).

27. Lina M. Khan, "Amazon's Antitrust Paradox," *Yale Law Journal* 126, no. 3 (2017): 720–721.

28. Henry Hansmann and Reinier Kraakman, "The End of History for Corporate Law," *Georgetown Law Journal* 89, no. 2 (2001): 439–468. See also Michael C. Jensen and William H. Meckling, "Theory of the Firm: Managerial Behavior, Agency Costs and Ownership Structure," *Journal of Financial Economics*, 3, no. 4 (1976): 305–360 (providing economic rationale for shareholder primacy).

29. See the discussion in section 2.3.

30. Grewal and Purdy, "Law and Neoliberalism," 13.

31. Britton-Purdy et al., "Law-and-Political-Economy Framework," 1806–1809.

32. *San Antonio Indep. Sch. Dist. V. Rodriguez*, 411 U.S. 1 (1973) (holding that poverty is not a suspect class in education context); *Lindsey v. Normet*, 405 U.S. 56 (1972) (rejecting the claim for a constitutional right to decent housing). See also *Washington v. Davis*, 426 U.S. 229 (1976) (holding that statutes that have a disparate impact on the basis of race are not invalid under the Fourteenth Amendment unless they were adopted with the intent to discriminate); Britton-Purdy et al., "Law-and-Political-Economy Framework," 1808–1809 (discussing these developments).

33. Noah D. Zatz, "Welfare to What?" *Hastings Law Journal* 57, no. 6 (2006): 1131–1188.

34. Regarding minimum wages, see Daniel Shaviro, "The Minimum Wage, the Earned Income Tax Credit, and Optimal Subsidy Policy," *University of Chicago Law Review* 64, no. 2 (1997): 405–481. Regarding collective bargaining, see Richard Epstein, "A Common Law for Labor Relations: A Critique of the New Deal Labor Legislation," *Yale Law Journal* 92, no. 8 (1983): 1357–1408; Richard A. Posner, "Some Economics of Labor Law," *University of Chicago Law Review* 51, no. 4 (1984): 988–1011.

35. Brishen Rogers, "Justice at Work: Minimum Wage Laws and Social Equality," *Texas Law Review* 92, no. 6 (2014): 1554–1559; Yochai Benkler, *A Political Economy of Oligarchy: Winner-Take-All Ideology, Superstar Norms, and the Rise of the 1%* (unpublished manuscript, September 2017): 10–14, PDF.

36. See Brishen Rogers, "Three Concepts of Workplace Freedom of Association," *Berkeley Journal of Employment & Labor Law* 37, no. 2 (2016): 199–205 (tracing influence of neoliberalism on doctrine surrounding union/member relationships).

37. A major turning point was *Wards Cove Packing Co. v. Atonio*, 490 U.S. 642 (1989). While that case was overturned in substantial part by Congress by passing the 1991 Civil Rights Act, disparate impact doctrine has become far less important as a device for ensuring labor market equality. See Michael Selmi, "Was the Disparate Impact Theory a Mistake?" *UCLA Law Review* 53, no. 3 (2006): 734–749 (summarizing evidence that disparate impact cases are rarely brought anymore).

38. This basic logic was clear in the 1970s. See Alan David Freeman, "Legitimizing Racial Discrimination through Antidiscrimination Law: A Critical Review of Supreme Court Doctrine," *Minnesota Law Review* 62, no. 6 (1978): 1049–1119 (discussing the "perpetrator perspective" that dominates anti-discrimination doctrine).

39. Ahmed A. White, "My Co-Worker, My Enemy: Solidarity, Workplace Control, and the Class Politics of Title VII," *Buffalo Law Review* 63, no.5 (2015): 1111–1118.

40. See Kriston McIntosh, Emily Moss, Ryan Nunn, and Jay Shambaugh, "Examining the Black-White Wealth Gap," Washington, DC: Brookings Institution, February 27, 2020, https://www.brookings.edu/blog/up-front/2020/02/27/examining-the-black-white-wealth-gap/ (collating data regarding the Black-White wealth gap).

41. Katherine Van Wezel Stone, "The Legacy of Industrial Pluralism: The Tension between Individual Employment Rights and the New Deal Collective Bargaining System," *University of Chicago Law Review* 59, no. 2 (Spring 1992): 575–644; Reuel E. Schiller, "From Group Rights to Individual Liberties: Post-War Labor Law, Liberalism, and the Waning of Union Strength," *Berkeley Journal of Employment & Labor Law* 20, no.1 (1999): 1–73. The two regimes are not hermetically sealed off from one another, and workers have often used individual legal entitlements to advance their collective interests. Michael Fischl, "Rethinking the Tripartite Division of American Work Law," *Berkeley Journal of Employment & Labor Law* 28, no. 1 (2007): 163–216; Benjamin I. Sachs, "Employment Law as Labor Law," *Cardozo Law Review* 29, no. 6 (2008): 2685–2748.

42. This discussion draws on Rogers, "Capitalist Development."

43. For a detailed treatment of the causes and consequences of deunionization in the US, see Thomas A. Kochan, Harry C. Katz, and Robert B. McKersie, *The Transformation of American Industrial Relations*, 2nd ed. (Ithaca, NY: Cornell University Press, 1993).

44. *Elk Lumber Co.*, 91 NLRB 333 (1950) (slow-down strikes); *NLRB v. Fansteel Metallurgical Corp.*, 306 U.S. 240 (1939) (sit-down strikes); and *United Auto Workers v. Wisconsin Board*, 336 U.S. 245 (1949) (upholding state law banning intermittent strikes). See also Craig Becker, "Better than a Strike: Protecting New Forms of Collective Work Stoppages under the National Labor Relations Act," *University of Chicago Law Review* 61, no. 2 (1994): 351–421 (providing overview and critique of this body of doctrine). Mass picketing, which was a crucial tactic in New Deal–era organizing efforts, is also illegal in most cases. See generally Ahmed A. White, "Workers Unarmed: The Campaign against Mass Picketing and the Dilemma of Liberal Labor Rights," *Harvard Civil Rights-Civil Liberties Law Review* 49, no. 1 (2014): 59–123.

45. *NLRB v. Mackay Radio & Telegraph Co.*, 304 U.S. 333 (1938).

46. John B. Logan, "Labor's 'Last Stand' in National Politics? The Campaign for Striker Replacement Legislation, 1990–1994," *Advances in Industrial and Labor Relations* 13 (2004): 192–193 (noting increased use of permanent replacements in 1980s).

47. 29 U.S.C. 158(b)(4) (2018). Kate Andrias and Brishen Rogers, *Rebuilding Worker Voice in Today's Economy* (New York: Roosevelt Institute, 2018), 12 (discussing Taft-Hartley revisions). Workers have broader rights to engage in secondary activity when they appeal to consumers rather than workers. See *NLRB v. Fruit & Vegetable Packers, Loc. 760*, 377 U.S. 58 (1964) (peaceful secondary picketing urging consumers not to purchase struck produce at grocery store is not prohibited by NLRA); *Edward J. DeBartolo Corp. v. Florida Gulf Coast Building & Constr. Trades Council*, 485 U.S. 568 (1988) (peaceful leafletting urging consumer boycott of secondary target is not prohibited by NLRA).

48. See Kate Andrias, "The New Labor Law," *Yale Law Journal* 126, no. 2 (2016): 30–32 (summarizing franchising strategies and their effects on workers' rights to organize). See also David Weil, *The Fissured Workplace: Why Work Became So Bad for So Many and What Can Be Done to Improve It* (Cambridge, MA: Harvard University Press, 2014) (noting how large corporations have increasingly shed their role as direct employers by outsourcing work to smaller companies).

49. 29 U.S.C. 158(c) (2018) (protecting employers' rights to express their views on unionization). See generally *Gissel*, 395 U.S., at 575, 618–620 (1969) (discussing how employers can exploit such speech rights to threaten and coerce workers).

50. 29 U.S.C. 159(b) (2018). See also Robert A. Gorman and Matthew W. Finkin, *Basic Text on Labor Law: Unionization and Collective Bargaining*, 2nd ed. (St. Paul, MN:

Thomson West 2004), 76–84, 103–104 (discussing emphasis on single-employer, localized bargaining in the US). While multiemployer bargaining has been common at certain times in our history, it "is and always has been consensual in nature," in the sense that both union and employer have the right to refuse to engage in multiemployer bargaining. *Kroger Co.*, 148 NLRB 569, 575 (1964) (with members Leedom and Jenkins dissenting). For comparative evidence on multiemployer bargaining in the US system and various European systems, see Harry C. Katz, "The Decentralization of Collective Bargaining: A Literature Review and Comparative Analysis," *Industrial & Labor Relations Review* 47, no. 1 (October 1993): 3–22. Chapter 6 discusses recent reform proposals to encourage multiemployer and sectoral bargaining.

51. See 29 U.S.C. § 158(a)(5) (2018) (unfair labor practice for an employer to refuse to bargain collectively with a certified union); 29 U.S.C. § 159(a) (2018) (union "designated or selected" by the majority of workers in an appropriate bargaining unit becomes their exclusive representative); *Int'l Ladies' Garment Workers' Union v. NLRB*, 366 U.S. 731 (1961) (holding that voluntary recognition is lawful, but only if a majority of employees in fact support the union).

52. Unions and companies can, however, negotiate clauses in collective bargaining agreements establishing preferential ground rules for organizing new worksites. *Kroger Co.*, 219 NLRB 388 (1975).

53. Andrias and Rogers, *Rebuilding Worker Voice*, 26–29; David Madland, *The Future of Worker Voice and Power* (Washington, DC: Center for American Progress, 2016).

54. German workers, for example, have a guaranteed voice at the enterprise level through works councils with consultative rights around various issues. Matthew Dimick, "Productive Unionism," *University of California Irvine Law Review* 4, no. 2 (2014): 688n49. See generally Joel Rogers and Wolfgang Streeck, eds., *Works Councils: Consultation, Representation, and Cooperation in Industrial Relations* (Chicago: University of Chicago Press, 1995). Workers in Europe also have more of a guaranteed voice in policymaking through "social dialogue" processes. Lucio Baccaro and Marco Simoni, "Policy Concentration in Europe: Understanding Government Choice," *Comparative Political Studies* 41, no. 10 (2007): 1323–1348.

55. See Jelle Visser and Daniele Checchi, "Inequality and the Labor Market: Unions," in *Oxford Handbook of Economic Inequality*, eds. Wiemer Salverda, Brian Nolan, and Timothy M. Smeeding (New York: Oxford University Press, 2011), 230–256 (arguing that unions' power, coverage, and level of bargaining coordination in particular nations correlates with economic equality in those nations); Kathleen Thelen, "The American Precariat: U.S. Capitalism in Comparative Perspective," *Perspectives on Politics* 17, no. 1 (2019): 14–15 (discussing the close relationship between workers' associational power and welfare state generosity).

56. See Andrias, "The New Labor Law," 19–20, 46–47 (discussing this and other models and the difficulty of replicating them today); Nelson Lichtenstein, *The Most*

Dangerous Man in Detroit: Walter Reuther and the Fate of American Labor (New York: Basic Books, 1995): 271–298 (describing pattern bargaining).

57. Civil Rights Act of 1964, Title VII, Pub. L. No. 88-352 (1964), codified as amended at 42 U.S.C. § 2000e *et seq.* (2018); Occupational Safety and Health Act of 1970, Pub. L. 91–596 (1970), codified at 29 U.S.C. § 651 *et seq.* (2018); Employee Retirement Income Security Act of 1974, Pub. L. No. 93-406 (1974) codified as amended at 29 U.S.C. § 1001 *et seq.* (2018).

58. See the discussion in section 2.3.

59. Americans with Disabilities Act of 1990, Pub. L. 101–336 (1990), codified at 42 U.S.C. § 12101 *et seq.* (2018).

60. See Economic Policy Institute, "Minimum Wage Tracker" (last checked December 28, 2021) https://www.epi.org/minimum-wage-tracker/ (showing that twenty-eight states and the District of Columbia have changed their minimum wage laws since 2014).

61. Annette Bernhardt, James DeFilippis, and Siobhan McGrath, *Unregulated Work in the Global City: Employment and Labor Law Violations in New York City* (Washington, DC: Brennan Center for Justice, 2007).

62. *Payne v. Western & Atlantic R.R. Co.*, 81 Tenn. 507, 519 (1884). See also Clyde W. Summers, "Employment at Will in the United States: The Divine Right of Employers," *University of Pennsylvania Journal of Labor and Employment Law* 3, no. 1 (2000): 65 (arguing that the doctrine "has been, and still is, a basic premise undergirding American labor law," and that it "gives American labor law much of its distinctive character").

63. Michael L. Wachter, "Neoclassical Labor Economics: Its Implications for Labor and Employment Law," in *Research Handbook on the Economics of Labor and Employment Law*, eds. Cynthia Estlund and Michael L. Wachter (Northampton, MA: Edward Elgar Publishing, 2012), 43.

64. Jay M. Feinman, "The Development of the Employment at Will Rule," *American Journal of Legal History* 20, no. 2 (1976): 125–129. Feinman also explains that the rule appears to have been first articulated in its modern form in Horace Gray Wood, *A Treatise on the Law of Master and Servant: Covering the Relation, Duties and Liabilities of Employers and Employees* (Albany, NY: John D. Parsons, Jr., 1877): 271. Feinman, "Employment at Will Rule," 126.

65. *Adair v. United States*, 208 U.S. 161, 174–175 (1908).

66. See, e.g., *Woolley v. Hoffmann-La Roche, Inc.*, 491 A.2d 1257, 1266–1268 (N.J. 1985).

67. For a lucid review of those exceptions and their importance, see Cynthia Estlund, "Rethinking Autocracy at Work," *Harvard Law Review* 131, no. 3 (2018): 803–805

(reviewing Elizabeth Anderson, *Private Government: How Employers Rule Our Lives (and Why We Don't Talk about It)* (Princeton, NJ: Princeton University Press, 2017).

68. Kate Andrias and Alexander Hertel-Fernandez, *Ending At-Will Employment: A Guide for Just Cause Reform* (New York: Roosevelt Institute, 2021), 4.

69. *Woolley*, 491 A.2d at 1266–1268.

70. *Asmus v. Pacific Bell*, 999 P.2d 71, 76 (Cal. 2000).

71. *Epic Sys. Corp. v. Lewis*, 138 S. Ct. 1612, 1619 (2018).

72. Compare *Epic Sys. Corp. v. Lewis*, 138 S. Ct. at 1633 (Ginsburg, J., dissenting) (writing, in summary of the facts, that to "block" class action claims, the plaintiffs' "employers required them to sign, as a condition of employment, arbitration agreements banning collective judicial and arbitral proceedings of any kind"). See also Samuel R. Bagenstos, "Consent, Coercion, and Employment Law," *Harvard Civil Rights-Civil Liberties Law Review* 55 (2020): 410 (arguing that *Epic Systems* and other Roberts Court labor cases "rest on a principle of employee consent that ignores many of the forces that actually impose limits on an employee's choice").

73. *Soto-Fonalledas v. Ritz-Carlton San Juan Hotel Spa & Casino*, 640 F.3d 471, 475 (1st Cir. 2011).

74. Rogers, "Passion and Reason," 315.

75. *Lechmere, Inc., v. NLRB*, 502 U.S. 527, 540–541 (1992). See also Nathan Newman, "Reengineering Workplace Bargaining: How Big Data Drives Lower Wages and How Reframing Labor Law Can Restore Information Equality in the Workplace," *University of Cincinnati Law Review* 85, no. 3 (2017): 727–728 (noting this aspect of *Lechmere*).

76. *Janus v. AFSCME Council 31*, 138 S. Ct. 2448, 2459–60 (2018).

77. Bagenstos, "Consent, Coercion," 435–438.

78. Bagenstos, "Consent, Coercion," 438. See also Rogers, "Three Concepts," 199–205 (discussing, in similar terms, how neoliberalism has influenced jurisprudence around union agency fees).

79. See generally Weil, *Fissured Workplace*.

80. See generally Bruce Goldstein, Marc Linder, Laurence E. Norton II, and Catherine K. Ruckelshaus, "Enforcing Fair Labor Standards in the Modern American Sweatshop: Rediscovering the Statutory Definition of Employment," *UCLA Law Review* 46, no. 4 (1999): 983–1163.

81. *NLRB v. Hearst Publ'ns*, 322 U.S. 111 (1944) (NLRA); *Rutherford Food Corp. v. McComb*, 331 U.S. 722 (1947) (FLSA); *United States v. Silk*, 331 U.S. 704 (1947) (SSA).

82. 29 U.S.C. 152(3) (2018). See also *NLRB v. United Ins. Co. of Am.*, 390 U. S. 254, 256 (1968) (observing that congressional reaction to *Hearst* "was adverse and

Congress passed an amendment ... [t]he obvious purpose of [which] was to have the ... courts apply general agency principles in distinguishing between employees and independent contractors under the [NLRA]").

83. *Nationwide Mut. Ins. Co. v. Darden*, 503 U.S. 318, 324–29 (1992) (common law agency test applies under NLRA, SSA, and the Employment Retirement Income Social Security Act of 1974); 326 (FLSA applies a broader test derived from child labor statutes). See also Restatement (Second) of Agency § 220(2) (Am. Law Inst. 1958) (listing factors that should be used to determine whether a principal legally employs an agent).

84. Noah D. Zatz, "Beyond Misclassification: Tackling the Independent Contractor Problem without Redefining Employment," *ABA Journal of Labor & Employment Law* 26, no. 2 (Winter 2011): 282–283. See also *Sec'y of Labor v. Lauritzen*, 835 F.2d 1529, 1544 (7th Cir. 1987) (Easterbrook, J., concurring) ("The reasons for blocking vicarious liability at a particular point have nothing to do with the functions of the FLSA").

85. See *Lancaster Symphony Orchestra*, 357 NLRB 1761, 1763 (2011) (listing ten factors that the NLRB uses to determine whether an employment relationship exists, but noting that "the same set of factors that was decisive in one case may be unpersuasive when balanced against a different set of opposing factors in another case").

86. Weil, *Fissured Workplace*, 7 (drawing this metaphor).

87. 29 U.S.C. 158(b)(4) (2018).

88. Zatz, "Beyond Misclassification," 288–290. Companies must bargain with unionized workers over decisions to contract out, even though they face no such restrictions in nonunion settings. *Fibreboard*, 379 U.S. at 210. See also *Healthcare Emps. Union, Local 399 v. NLRB*, 463 F.3d 909 (9th Cir. 2006) (unfair labor practice to subcontract work in order to prevent workers from voting in upcoming union election).

89. See Zatz, "Beyond Misclassification," 288–290.

90. Lichtenstein, *Most Dangerous Man in Detroit*, 220–247.

91. Lichtenstein, *Most Dangerous Man in Detroit*, 280–281, quoting Daniel Bell, "The Treaty of Detroit," *Fortune* (July 1950): 53.

92. *Fibreboard*, 379 U.S. at 223 (Stewart, J., concurring).

93. *First Nat'l Maint. Corp. v. NLRB*, 452 U.S. 666, 679 (1981); see also *First Nat'l Maint. Corp. v. NLRB*, 686n22 (holding that whether employers must bargain over decisions to automate work must be decided on a case-by-case basis).

94. See Robert A. Gorman and Matthew W. Finkin, *Labor Law: Analysis and Advocacy* (Huntington, NY: Juris Publishing, 2013): 806 (noting that there are few court or NLRB opinions addressing the duty to bargain over automation decisions).

95. See *First Nat'l Maintenance*, 452 U.S., at 681.

96. See 29 U.S.C. § 158(d) (2018) (specifying that the duty to bargain requires employers and unions to "meet at reasonable times and confer in good faith," but "does not compel either party to agree to a proposal or require the making of a concession").

97. See Melvin Dubovsky, "Legal Theory and Workers' Rights: A Historian's Critique," *Industrial Relations Law Journal* 4, no. 3 (June 1981): 500 (observing that "[m]anagement prerogatives remain a constant area of struggle" since unions have not conceded that management has unilateral authority in that sphere).

98. See *Colgate-Palmolive Co.*, 323 NLRB 515, 515 (1997) (employer must bargain with its employees' union prior to installing hidden surveillance cameras, whose recordings could be used to spot infractions of workplace rules).

99. See *NLRB v. Washington Aluminum Co.*, 370 U.S. 9, 14 (1962) (holding that § 7 of NLRA, 29 U.S.C. § 157 protects workers' rights to engage in collective protest around working conditions, even if those workers had no intention of unionizing).

100. *Legacy Charter*, 2018 WL 3955527 (NLRB. Div. of Judges), 2018 NLRB LEXIS 338 (August 16, 2018).

101. For example, Daniel Solove proposes a taxonomy of privacy law that sorts cases into four categories—information collection, information processing, information dissemination, and invasion into protected spaces—with sixteen subcategories. Daniel Solove, "A Taxonomy of Privacy," *University of Pennsylvania Law Review* 154. no. 3 (2006): 489.

102. See Neil M. Richards and Jonathan King, "Big Data Ethics," *Wake Forest Law Review* (2014): 396 (describing privacy not as centrally concerned with secrecy, but rather as "encompassing information rules that manage the appropriate flows of information in ethical ways"); Julie E. Cohen, "What Privacy Is For," *Harvard Law Review* (May 2013): 1906 ("Privacy is shorthand for breathing room to engage in the processes of boundary management that enable and constitute self-development").

103. See Pauline T. Kim, "Data Mining and the Challenges of Protecting Employee Privacy under U.S. Law," *Comparative Labor Law & Policy Review* 40, no. 3 (2019): 411–416 (gathering cases discussing ways in which modern forms of data analytics enable employers to gather extensive information about workers without risking tort liability).

104. *Restatement (Second) of Torts* § 652B (Am. Law Inst. 1977). See also *Restatement of Employment Law* §§ 7.02–7.06 (Am. Law Inst. 2015) (clarifying that employees have protected privacy interests in their person, physical and electronic locations, and information of a personal nature, and that employers are liable for violations of those interests that would be "highly offensive to a reasonable person").

105. *Koeppel v. Speirs*, 808 N.W.2d 177 (Iowa 2011) (changing room); *Wal-Mart Stores, Inc. v. Lee*, 74 S.W.3d 634 (Ark. 2002) (home); *Sowards v. Norbar, Inc.*, 605 N.E.2d 468 (Ohio Ct. App. 1992) (hotel room).

106. See *O'Bryan v. KTIV Television*, 868 F. Supp. 1146, 1158 (N.D. Iowa 1994) (finding that an employer can search an employee's desk area for work-related documents without violating the employee's reasonable expectations of privacy, and therefore rejecting the employee's claim of intrusion upon seclusion).

107. *Restatement (Second) of Torts* § 652B.

108. Kim, "Data Mining," 415, citing William L. Prosser, "Privacy," *California Law Review* 48, no. 3 (1960): 384. See also Matthew W. Finkin, "Employee Privacy, American Values, and the Law: The Kenneth M. Piper Lecture," *Chicago-Kent Law Review* 72, no. 1 (1996): 256 (observing that once a majority of employers adopt a practice that invades employee privacy, "consent" to the practice "cannot be said to be free").

109. *Vega-Rodriguez v. Puerto Rico Tel. Co.*, 110 F.3d 174, 180 (1st Cir. 1997). See also *Restatement of Employment Law* § 7.06, comment e, illustration 6 (endorsing rule from *Vega-Rodriguez*).

110. *Restatement of Employment Law* § 7.08(c) (protecting employee autonomy interests but permitting employers to take action that infringes on those interests where they have a "reasonable and good-faith belief" that the employee's conduct may harm the business).

111. For notable exceptions, see *Conn. Gen. Stat.* §§31–51q (2005) (creating action for damages where an employer disciplines or discharges an employee for any action that is protected by the First Amendment of the US Constitution); Cal Lab. Code. §§ 1101, 1102 (2005) (protecting employees' rights to participate in political activities).

112. See *Edmundson v. Shearer Lumber Prods.*, 75 P.3d 733 (2003) (rejecting an at-will employee's claim for wrongful termination in violation of public policy where the employer's stated reason for termination was the employee's opposition to one of its political projects). Compare *Novosel v. Nationwide Ins. Co.*, 721 F.2d 894 (3d Cir. 1983) (finding on similar facts that an employee could state a claim for wrongful discharge in violation of public policy given the preeminent importance of political speech under the First Amendment). In subsequent cases, courts have usually declined to follow *Novosel*. Samuel R. Bagenstos, "Employment Law and Social Equality," *Michigan Law Review* 112, no. 2 (2013): 257. See also Matthew W. Finkin, "*Menschenbild*: The Conception of the Employee as a Person in Western Law," *Comparative Labor Law & Policy Journal* 23, no. 2 (2002): 582–584 (comparing US and German law on point, collecting and discussing cases), 578 (noting that under French law, an employer cannot forbid employees from discussing nonwork matters while on the job).

113. Alexander Hertel-Fernandez, *Politics at Work: How Companies Turn Their Workers into Lobbyists* (Oxford: Oxford University Press, 2018).

114. See Matthew W. Finkin, *Privacy in Employment Law*, 5th ed. (Bloomberg Law, 2018): xxxiv, xxxv (observing that in the US, privacy "legislation has been enacted piecemeal" and "most often, issues of privacy remain unspoken to by the law"); Joel R. Reidenberg, "Setting Standards for Fair Information Practice in the U.S. Private Sector," *Iowa Law Review* 80, no. 3 (1995): 506 (noting this "sectoral" development of privacy laws in the US).

115. *HIPAA Privacy Rule*, 45 C.F.R. § 160 (2018); US Equal Employment Opportunity Commission, *Enforcement Guidance on Disability-Related Inquiries and Medical Examinations of Employees under the Americans with Disabilities Act* (July 26, 2000). The Fair Credit Reporting Act also limits employers' rights to gather data about employees and potential employees. 15 U.S.C. § 1681(b) (2018).

116. Biometric Information Privacy Act, 740 Ill. Comp. Stat. 14 (2008); Texas Business and Commercial Code § 503 (2017).

117. For example, a recent wave of laws has forbidden employers to request employees' social media passwords. Marko Mrkonich, Allan King, Rod Fliegel, et al., *The Big Move toward Big Data in Employment* (Littler Mendelson, P.C., August 2015): 14 (showing that twenty-two states passed such laws by 2015).

118. Cal. Consumer Privacy Act of 2018, Cal. A.B. 25 (Cal. 2019) (enacted).

119. Anupam Chander, Margot E. Kaminski, and William McGeveran, "Catalyzing Privacy Law," *Minnesota Law Review* 105, no. 4 (2021): 1755–1756.

120. *GDPR & CCPA: Opt-ins, Consumer Control, and the Impact on Competition and Innovation, Hearing before the U.S. Senate Committee on the Judiciary*, 116th Congress (March 12, 2019) (statement of Michelle Richardson, Director of Privacy and Data for the Center for Democracy and Technology: 5); European GDPR Art. 5(1) (enumerating principles), 6(1)(b–f) (listing lawful reasons for data processing). On the differences between the CCPA and GDPR, see generally Chander et al, "Catalyzing Privacy Law."

121. 18 U.S.C. § 2701 (2018).

122. 18 U.S.C. § 2701(c)(1) (2018).

123. Finkin, *Privacy in Employment*, Ch. 5.III.D.1–2 (discussing state statutes regulating the interception of telephone and electronic communications).

124. Julie E. Cohen, *Between Truth and Power: The Legal Constructions of Informational Capitalism* (New York: Oxford University Press, 2019), 15.

125. William W. Fisher III, *The Growth of Intellectual Property: A History of the Ownership of Ideas in the United States* (self-pub., 1999) (English version), 2, https://cyber.harvard.edu/people/tfisher/iphistory.pdf; James Boyle, "The Second Enclosure Movement and the Construction of the Public Domain," *Law and Contemporary Problems* 66, no. 1–2 (2003): 37.

126. See Cohen, *Between Truth and Power*, 20–24 (tracing developments across a number of IP doctrines). See also Amy Kapczynski, "The Law of Informational Capitalism," *Yale Law Journal* 129, no. 5 (2020): 1512 (discussing "encasement" of IP rights and rights around data flows under international and transnational trade regimes).

127. Catherine Fisk, *Working Knowledge: Employee Innovation and the Rise of Corporate Intellectual Property, 1800–1930* (Chapel Hill: University of North Carolina Press, 2009).

128. Cohen, *Between Truth and Power*, 18.

129. Cohen, *Between Truth and Power*, 91.

130. Lothar Determann, "No One Owns Data," *Hastings Law Journal* 70, no. 1 (2018): 5; Mark A. Lemley, "Private Property," *Stanford Law Review* 52, no. 5 (2000): 1547.

131. *Feist Pub's, Inc. v. Rural Tel. Serv. Co.*, 499 U.S. 340 (1991).

132. *Bilski v. Kappos*, 561 U.S. 593, 611–612 (2010). See also Kapczynski, "Law of Informational Capitalism," 1501 (discussing challenges of protecting algorithms and machine learning processes under existing IP doctrines).

133. Cohen, *Between Truth and Power*, 58.

134. See Kapczynski, "Law of Informational Capitalism," 1508–1510 (discussing the expansion of protections in trade secrets since *Ruckelshaus v Monsanto Co.*, 467 U.S. 986 (1984) (holding that trade secrets entail property rights under the Taking Clause of the Fifth Amendment), including cases such as *Philip Morris, Inc. v. Reilly*, 312 F.3d 24 (1st. Cir. 2002) (striking down Massachusetts law requiring disclosure of cigarette ingredients to state regulators)).

135. See Jamillah Bowman Williams, "Diversity as a Trade Secret," *Georgetown Law Journal* 107, no. 6 (2019): 1702, 1707 (noting and discussing recent claims by companies that hiring algorithms are protected trade secrets).

136. Amy Kapczynski, "The Public History of Trade Secrets," *U.C. Davis L. Rev.* 55, no. 3 (2022): 1367–1443.

137. Julie E. Cohen, "The Biopolitical Public Domain: The Legal Construction of the Surveillance Economy," *Philosophy & Technology* 31, no. 2 (2018): 213.

138. Kapczynski, "Law of Informational Capitalism," 1498. See also Jathan Sadowski, "When Data Is Capital: Datafication, Accumulation, and Extraction," *Big Data & Society* 6, no. 1 (2019): 2 (data is not naturally occurring, but rather "a recorded abstraction of the world created and valorised by people using technology").

139. Such agreements are typically unenforceable against line-level workers. Charles A. Sullivan, "The Puzzling Persistence of Unenforceable Contract Terms," *Ohio State*

Law Journal 70, no. 5 (2009): 1149. Nevertheless, major low-wage employers have increasingly required line-level workers to sign them in recent years. Steven Greenhouse, "Noncompete Clauses Increasingly Pop up in Array of Jobs," *New York Times*, June 8, 2014; Spencer Woodman, "Amazon Makes Even Temporary Warehouse Workers Sign 18-Month Non-Competes," *The Verge*, March 26, 2015, https://www.theverge.com/2015/3/26/8280309/amazon-warehouse-jobs-exclusive-noncompete-contracts.

140. See *Restatement (Second) of Contracts* § 188 (Am. Law. Inst. 1981) (providing a test for enforceability of a covenant not to compete). See also *Hopper v. All Pet Animal Clinic*, 861 P.2d 531, 539–540 (Wyo. 1993) (discussing modern approach to covenants that considers their reasonableness under the circumstances).

141. See *Lucht's Concrete Pumping v. Horner*, 255 P.3d 1058, 1059–60 (Colo. 2011) (holding that continued employment can constitute consideration that binds an employee to a covenant not to compete promulgated by the employer).

142. Orly Lobel, "The New Cognitive Property: Human Capital Law and the Reach of Intellectual Property," *Texas Law Review* 93, no. 4 (2015): 827–833.

143. Lobel, "New Cognitive Property."

144. In important work not finalized as this book went to press, Julia Tomassetti argues that in cases where gig economy workers challenge their misclassification, gig economy companies often argue that they have managerial prerogatives rooted in property rights to surveil and discipline workers who are not their employees. Julia Tomassetti, "Managerial Prerogative, Property Rights, and Labor Control in Employment Status Disputes," *Theoretical Inquiries in Law* 24, no. 1 (forthcoming, 2023).

Chapter 3

1. Nick Statt, "Amazon Says Fully Automated Shipping Warehouses Are at Least a Decade Away," *The Verge*, May 1, 2019, https://www.theverge.com/2019/5/1/18526092/amazon-warehouse-robotics-automation-ai-10-years-away; Amazon warehouse managers, interviews by Frank Levy, May 13, 2019, on file with author.

2. Author tour of Amazon warehouse with Washington Center for Equitable Growth (January 2020); Will Knight, "Inside Amazon's Warehouse, Human-Robot Symbiosis," *MIT Technology Review*, July 7, 2015; Nick Wingfield, "As Amazon Pushes Forward with Robotics, Workers Find New Roles," *New York Times*, September 10, 2017; Brian Callaci, "Digital Scab, Digital Snitch," *Phenomenal World*, May 28, 2020, https://phenomenalworld.org/analysis/digital-scab-digital-snitch.

3. See generally Beth Gutelius and Nik Theodore, *The Future of Warehouse Work: Technological Change in the U.S. Logistics Industry* (Berkeley, CA: UC Berkeley Center

for Labor Research and Education and Working Partnerships USA, October 2019), https://laborcenter.berkeley.edu/pdf/2019/Future-of-Warehouse-Work.pdf.

4. Author tour of Amazon warehouse (January 2020); Evan Ackerman, "Brad Porter, VP of Robotics at Amazon, on Warehouse Automation, Machine Learning, and His First Robot," *IEEE Spectrum*, September 27, 2018, https://spectrum.ieee.org/automaton/robotics/industrial-robots/interview-brad-porter-vp-of-robotics-at-amazon (on use of video cameras).

5. Alana Semuels, "I Delivered Packages for Amazon and It Was a Nightmare," *The Atlantic*, June 28, 2018; Josh Eidelson and Matt Day, "Amazon Work Rules Govern Tweets, Body Odor of Contract Drivers," *Bloomberg*, May 5, 2021, https://www.bloomberg.com/news/articles/2021-05-05/amazon-work-rules-govern-tweets-body-odor-of-contract-drivers.

6. Jeffrey Dastin, "Amazon Hikes Average U.S. Starting Pay to $18, Hires for 125,000 Jobs," *Reuters*, September 14, 2021, https://www.reuters.com/business/exclusive-amazon-hikes-starting-pay-18-an-hour-it-hires-125000-more-logistics-2021-09-14.

7. Noam Scheiber, "Inside an Amazon Warehouse, Robots' Ways Rub off on Humans," *New York Times*, July 3, 2019.

8. Amazon worker, interview by author at Washington Center for Equitable Growth conference on warehouse work, January 2020, Baltimore.

9. A 2021 California statute requires warehouse employers to provide written notice of production quotas to workers. Under the law, workers cannot be required to meet quotas that have not been disclosed or that lead them to miss "meal or rest periods, use of bathroom facilities," or not to comply with workplace safety laws. California Assembly Bill 701 (signed into law September 22, 2021).

10. This term has been used by others in the past, including *The Economist*. Schumpeter (blog), "Digital Taylorism," The Economist (September 10, 2015).

11. Karen Levy, "The Contexts of Control: Information, Power, and Truck-Driving Work," *The Information Society* 31, no. 2 (2015): 161.

12. The term "algorithmic management" is not my own. It seems to have become popular due to a working paper by several Carnegie Mellon researchers. Min Kyung Lee, Daniel Kusbit, Evan Metsky, and Laura Dabbish, "Working with Machines: The Impact of Algorithmic and Data-Driven Management on Human Workers," in *Proceedings of the 33rd Annual ACM Conference on Human Factors in Computing Systems* (April 2015): 1603–1612, https://wtf.tw/ref/lee.pdf.

13. Helpful overviews of these phenomena that have informed this chapter's analysis include Elizabeth Tippett, Charlotte S. Alexander, and Zev J. Eigen, "When Timekeeping Software Undermines Compliance," *Yale Journal of Law & Technology* 19 (2017): 1–76; Nathan Newman, "Reengineering Workplace Bargaining: How Big

Data Drives Lower Wages and How Reframing Labor Law Can Restore Information Equality in the Workplace," *University of Cincinnati Law Review* 85, no. 3 (2017): 693–760; Richard A. Bales and Katherine V.W. Stone, "The Invisible Web at Work: Artificial Intelligence and Electronic Surveillance in the Workplace," *Berkeley Journal of Employment and Labor Law* 41, no. 1 (2020): 1–60; and Jeffrey M. Hirsch, "Future Work," *University of Illinois Law Review* 2020, no. 3 (2020) 889–958.

14. Michael Polanyi, *The Tacit Dimension* (Chicago: University of Chicago Press, 1966), discussed in David H. Autor, "Polanyi's Paradox and the Shape of Employment Growth," in *Re-Evaluating Labor Market Dynamics* (Kansas City, MO: Federal Reserve Bank of Kansas City, 2015), 136.

15. See Frank Pasquale, *New Laws of Robotics: Defending Human Expertise in the Age of AI* (Cambridge, MA: Belknap Press, 2020), 211–213 (reviewing philosophical literature and its relevance to problems in AI development).

16. See Autor, "Polanyi's Paradox," 135–138 (breaking work tasks into "routine," "abstract," and "manual," and arguing that the latter two, though quite difficult to automate using traditional means, may at times be susceptible to automation using machine learning and related technologies).

17. James C. Scott, *Seeing Like a State: How Certain Schemes to Improve the Human Condition Have Failed* (New Haven, CT: Yale University Press, 1998), 87–102 (discussing "authoritarian high modernism"), 309–341 (discussing and distinguishing two forms of knowledge: "techne," which is similar to what this book calls "formal" knowledge, and "metis," which is similar to what this book calls "tacit" knowledge).

18. Scott, *Seeing Like a State*, 6, 256, 310–311.

19. See Pauline T. Kim, "Data-Driven Discrimination at Work," *William and Mary Law Review* 58, no. 3 (February 2017): 879 (describing machine learning as "inductive and atheoretical").

20. Julie E. Cohen, *Between Truth and Power: The Legal Constructions of Informational Capitalism* (New York: Oxford University Press, 2019), 76–89. See also Shoshana Zuboff, *The Age of Surveillance Capitalism: The Fight for a Human Future at the New Frontier of Power* (New York: Public Affairs, 2019) (prominent account of these developments). In my view, as discussed in chapter 1, Zuboff's account is less analytically or normatively compelling than Cohen's.

21. Helen Nissenbaum, "Contextual Integrity Up and Down the Data Food Chain," *Theoretical Inquiries in Law* 20, no. 1 (2019): 238–240. See also Neil M. Richards and Jonathan H. King, "Three Paradoxes of Big Data," *Stanford Law Review* 66 (2013): 42 ("Big data analytics depend on small data inputs, including information about people, places, and things collected by sensors, cell phones, click patterns, and the like" that are "aggregated to produce large datasets which analytic techniques mine for insight"); Neil M. Richards and Jonathan King, "Big Data Ethics," *Wake Forest*

Law Review 49, no. 2 (2014): 394 (The "big" aspect of "big data" is often defined in terms of the "3 Vs": big data analytics help process data that are available in high volume, with a high variety, and are increasingly available or delivered at high velocity). See also Matthew T. Bodie, Miriam A. Cherry, Marcia L. McCormick, and Jintong Tang, "The Law and Policy of People Analytics," *University of Colorado Law Review* 88, no. 4 (2017): 961–1042 (giving an overview of such practices and their intersection with labor laws).

22. See Federal Trade Commission, *Big Data: A Tool for Inclusion or Exclusion?* (January 2016), 1, https://www.ftc.gov/system/files/documents/reports/big-data-tool-inclusion-or-exclusion-understanding-issues/160106big-data-rpt.pdf (noting that "when consumers engage digitally" by shopping, using social media, or using fitness trackers or similar devices, "companies collect information about their choices, experiences, and individual characteristics" which can be used both to discern "market-wide tastes and emerging trends" and "to predict the preferences of specific individuals").

23. Nissenbaum, "Data Food Chain," 240–241. See generally Frank Pasquale, *The Black Box Society: The Secret Algorithms That Control Money and Information* (Cambridge, MA: Harvard University Press, 2016).

24. Pedro Domingos, *The Master Algorithm: How the Quest for the Ultimate Learning Machine Will Remake Our World* (New York: Basic Books, 2015), 5.

25. Domingos, *The Master Algorithm*, 5.

26. See Gary Marcus, "Deep Learning: A Critical Appraisal" (January 2, 2018): 3, https://arxiv.org/abs/1801.00631 ("Deep learning . . . is essentially a statistical technique for classifying patterns, based on sample data, using neural networks with multiple layers"). See also Bodie et al., "People Analytics," 970 (describing data mining as an "automated process of analysis of large databases to find new patterns and relations").

27. See, e.g., Dan Ciresan, Ueli Meier, and Jürgen Schmidhuber, "Multi-Column Deep Neural Networks for Image Classification," *2012 IEEE Conference on Computer Vision and Pattern Recognition* (2012): 3642–3649; Alex Krizhevsky, Ilya Sutskever, and Geoffrey E. Hinton, "ImageNet Classification with Deep Convolutional Neural Networks," *Communications of the Association of Computing Machinery* 60, no. 6 (June 2017): 84–90.

28. Sandipan Dey, "Dogs vs. Cats: Image Classification with Deep Learning Using TensorFlow in Python," *Data Science Central*, August 14, 2017, https://perma.cc/B8RW-AEGW.

29. SAS, "Fraud Detection and Machine Learning: What You Need to Know" (accessed November 17, 2021), https://www.sas.com/en_us/insights/articles/risk-fraud/fraud-detection-machine-learning.html.

Notes to Pages 64–66   197

30. Stanford Machine Learning Group, "MURA: Bone X-Ray Deep Learning Competition," https://stanfordmlgroup.github.io/competitions/mura/ (accessed November 17, 2021).

31. Cade Metz, "AI Is Transforming Google Search. The Rest of the Web Is Next," *Wired*, February 4, 2016; Quoc V. Le and Mike Schuster, "A Neural Network for Machine Translation, at Production Scale," *Google AI Blog*, September 27, 2016, https://ai.googleblog.com/2016/09/a-neural-network-for-machine.html.

32. Google, "AlphaGo," https://deepmind.com/research/alphago (accessed November 18, 2021).

33. Joon Ian Wong and Nikhil Sonnad, "Google's AI Won the Game Go by Defying Millennia of Basic Human Instinct," *Quartz*, March 25, 2016, https://qz.com/639952/googles-ai-won-the-game-go-by-defying-millennia-of-basic-human-instinct.

34. Quoted in George Dvorsky, "Stunning AI Breakthrough Takes Us One Step Closer to the Singularity," *Gizmodo.au*, October 19, 2017, https://www.gizmodo.com.au/2017/10/stunning-ai-breakthrough-takes-us-one-step-closer-to-the-singularity. See also Julie E. Cohen, "Turning Privacy Inside Out," *Theoretical Inquiries in Law* 20, no. 1 (2019): 14 (describing some technologies' abilities to draw out these sorts of inferences as "uncanny" since the machines are clearly not alive and yet act like conscious beings).

35. Kim, "Data-Driven Discrimination at Work," 879. See also Autor, "Polanyi's Paradox," 158–162 (summarizing capabilities and limits of machine learning).

36. Bodie et al., "People Analytics," 970; Nissenbaum, "Data Food Chain," 240–242.

37. Bodie et al., "People Analytics," 971.

38. Salomé Viljoen, "A Relational Theory for Data Governance," *Yale Law Journal* 131, no. 2 (2022): 580. See also Cohen, *Truth and Power*, 67 (describing such processes as "biopolitical in character" in the sense that "they are designed to enable the statistical construction, management of, and trade in populations").

39. See generally, Viljoen, "Democratic Data."

40. Tom Simonite, "These Industrial Robots Get More Adept With Every Task," *Wired*, March 10, 2020. See also Ezra Klein, "Bill Gates: The Energy Breakthrough That Will 'Save Our Planet' Is Less Than 15 Years Away," *Vox*, February 24, 2016, https://www.vox.com/2016/2/24/11100702/bill-gates-energy (quoting Gates predicting that for "pure labor substitution for jobs that are largely physical and visual manipulation—driving, security guard, warehouse work, waiter, maid, that threshold—I don't think you'd get much disagreement that over the next 15 years the robotic equivalents in terms of cost, in terms of reliability, will become a substitute").

41. Sheelah Kolhatkar, "Welcoming Our New Robot Overlords," *New Yorker*, October 23, 2017; Kim Tingley, "Learning to Love Our Robot Co-workers," *New York Times Magazine*, February 23, 2017.

42. Carl Benedikt Frey and Michael A. Osborne, "The Future of Employment: How Susceptible Are Jobs to Computerisation?" *Technological Forecasting & Social Change* 114: 268.

43. Andy Stern with Lee Kravitz, *Raising the Floor: How a Universal Basic Income Can Renew Our Economy and Rebuild the American Dream* (New York; PublicAffairs, 2016), 51–73; Cynthia Estlund, "What Should We Do After Work? Automation and Employment Law," *Yale Law Journal* 128, no. 2 (2018): 254–326.

44. Aaron Bastani, *Fully Automated Luxury Communism: A Manifesto* (New York: Verso, 2020).

45. John Maynard Keynes, *Essays in Persuasion* (New York: Harcourt Brace, 1932), 369.

46. Autor, "Polanyi's Paradox," 131–133. See also the Center for the Study of Democratic Institutions, "The Triple Revolution: Open Memorandum to President Lyndon B. Johnson," April 6, 1963, http://scarc.library.oregonstate.edu/coll/pauling/peace/papers/1964p.7.html (discussing "triple revolution" of cybernation, new weaponry, and global concern for human rights).

47. Nick Gillespie and Ian Keyser, "Puzder on Minimum Wage, Automation, and Withdrawing as Trump's Labor Secretary," *Reason*, September 27, 2017, https://reason.com/video/puzder-trump-labor-minimum-wage. But see Aaron Benanav, *Automation and the Future of Work* (London: Verso, 2020), 2 (noting that European fast food workers already work alongside ordering kiosks and earn higher wages than their American counterparts).

48. Nick Bostrom, *Superintelligence: Paths, Dangers, Strategies* (Oxford: Oxford University Press, 2014), 26–62 (discussing paths to "superintelligence"). See also Erik Brynjolfsson and Andrew McAfee, *The Second Machine Age: Work, Progress, and Prosperity in a Time of Brilliant Technologies* (New York: W.W. Norton & Company, 2014), 39–56; Klaus Schwab, *The Fourth Industrial Revolution* (New York: Crown Business, 2016), 3; Stern (with Kravitz), *Raising the Floor*, 57–60; Domingos, *Master Algorithm*, 43–45 (all discussing the possibility of accelerating technological change due to exponential progress in underlying technologies).

49. Domingos, *Master Algorithm*, 25.

50. Bostrom, *Superintelligence*, 149–153.

51. Despite the prominence of automation fears in public debates, it is challenging to determine the net impact of automation on work. One recent study measured the impact of the introduction of robots on employment levels and wages in local labor markets between 1990 and 2007. In manufacturing, each robot per thousand workers eliminated between three and six jobs within the local labor market and reduced wages by between 0.25 percent and 0.5 percent. Daron Acemoglu and Pascual Restrepo, "Robots and Jobs: Evidence from U.S. Labor Markets," *Journal of Political*

Economy 128, no. 6 (2020): 2188–2244. But see Lawrence Mishel and Josh Bivens, "The Zombie Robot Apocalypse Argument Lurches On," *Economic Policy Institute*, May 24, 2017, https://www.epi.org/publication/the-zombie-robot-argument-lurches-on-there-is-no-evidence-that-automation-leads-to-joblessness-or-inequality (arguing that Acemoglu and Restrepo found forms of automation other than industrial robotics had neutral, or even positive, effects on employment, and their paper had not adequately accounted for job creation within other labor markets during the same period).

52. Martha Gimbel (@marthagimbel), Twitter, August 27, 2020, 11:19 p.m., https://twitter.com/marthagimbel/status/1299184706693599233?s=20.

53. Productivity growth averaged 2.8 percent annually from 1945 to 1970 and 2.2 percent annually during the 1990s dot-com boom but fell to around 1.4 percent annually from 2007 to 2019. US Bureau of Labor Statistics, "Labor Productivity and Costs," https://www.bls.gov/lpc/prodybar.htm (accessed November 19, 2021). See also Jason Furman et al., "Artificial Intelligence, Automation, and the Economy," *Executive Office of the President* (December 20, 2016): 9–10 (noting the slowdown in labor productivity growth generally and in total factor productivity growth, which measures the portion of productivity growth attributable to technological change); Robert Solow, "We'd Better Watch Out," *New York Times Book Review*, July 12, 1987 (noting that the incorporation of computers into production was not apparent in productivity data).

54. US Bureau of Labor Statistics, "Labor Productivity and Costs" (productivity growth in manufacturing around 0.4 percent annually from 2007 to 2019). Levels of "occupational churn," or the net creation of jobs in growing occupations and the loss of jobs in declining occupations, were also low in the 2000s and 2010s. Robert D. Atkinson and John Wu, "False Alarmism: Technological Disruption and the U.S. Labor Market, 1850–2015," *Information Technology & Innovation Foundation* (May 8, 2017): 18.

55. See US Bureau of Labor Statistics, "Labor Force Statistics from the Current Population Survey," https://data.bls.gov/timeseries/LNS14000000 (accessed November 19, 2021) (showing the unemployment rate falling under 4 percent in May 2018).

56. "A Supply Chain Consultant Evaluation of Kiva Systems," *MWPVL International Inc.*, https://www.mwpvl.com/html/kiva_systems.html (accessed November 19, 2021).

57. See Steve LeVine, "Artificial Intelligence Pioneer Says We Need to Start Over," *Axios*, September 15, 2017, https://www.axios.com/artificial-intelligence-pioneer-says-we-need-to-start-over-1513305524-f619efbd-9db0-4947-a9b2-7a4c310a28fe.html (the programmer who developed "back-propagation" method that is at the heart of machine learning now believes that it is a dead end). See also Gary Marcus and Ernest Davis, *Rebooting AI: Building Artificial Intelligence We Can Trust* (New York: Penguin Random House, 2019) (elaborating on the argument that machine learning is not a path to artificial general intelligence). Marcus and Davis nevertheless predict

that once artificial general intelligence is developed using tools other than machine learning (which are not yet available), it will displace a substantial number of workers. *Rebooting AI*, 203–206.

58. Jason Pontin, "Greedy, Brittle, Opaque, and Shallow: The Downsides to Deep Learning," *Wired*, February 2, 2018.

59. See generally, Inioluwa Deborah Raji, Emily M. Bender, Amandalynne Paulada, et al., "AI and the Everything in the Whole Wide World Benchmark" (November 26, 2021), https://arxiv.org/pdf/2111.15366.pdf.

60. Pontin, "Greedy, Brittle." These challenges are compounded by the fact that machine learning is often inscrutable to programmers since programs draw inferences from large data sets that are not apparent to humans. As a result, it can be difficult for programmers to reverse-engineer them and replicate their success.

61. See Aharon Azulay and Yair Weiss, "Why Do Deep Convolutional Networks Generalize So Poorly to Small Image Transformations?" *Journal of Machine Learning Research* 20 (2019): 1–25 (describing hacks that fooled image recognition algorithms by altering one pixel—a change that a human would not even notice).

62. Gary Marcus and Ernest Davis, "GPT-3, Bloviator: OpenAI's Language Generator Has No Idea What It's Talking About," *MIT Technology Review*, August 22, 2020.

63. Kevin Lacker, "Giving GPT-3 a Turing Test," *Kevin Lacker's Blog*, July 6, 2020, https://lacker.io/ai/2020/07/06/giving-gpt-3-a-turing-test.html.

64. Andrew J. Hawkins, "GM Will Make an Autonomous Car without Steering Wheel or Pedals by 2019," *The Verge*, January 12, 2018, https://www.theverge.com/2018/1/12/16880978/gm-autonomous-car-2019-detroit-auto-show-2018; Russell Brandom, "Self-Driving Cars Are Headed toward an AI Roadblock," *The Verge*, July 3, 2018, https://www.theverge.com/2018/7/3/17530232/self-driving-ai-winter-full-autonomy-waymo-tesla-uber (noting Tesla and Google's predictions).

65. Steven Greenhouse, "Autonomous Vehicles Could Cost America 5 Million Jobs. What Should We Do about It?," *Los Angeles Times*, September 22, 2016.

66. Neal E. Boudette, "Despite High Hopes, Self-Driving Cars Are 'Way in the Future,'" *New York Times*, July 17, 2019.

67. Filip Piekniewski, "AI Winter Is Well on Its Way," *Piekniewski's Blog*, May 28, 2018, https://blog.piekniewski.info/2018/05/28/ai-winter-is-well-on-its-way.

68. Cade Metz and Neal E. Boudette, "Inside Tesla: How Elon Musk Pushed an Unflinching Vision for Self-Driving Cars," *New York Times*, December 6, 2021.

69. See Will Knight, "A Radar for Industrial Robots May Guide Collaboration with Humans," *MIT Technology Review*, September 20, 2017 (discussing this problem and current research efforts to overcome it).

70. See Amir Efrati, "Waymo's Big Ambitions Slowed by Tech Trouble," *The Information*, August 28, 2018, https://perma.cc/57CN-VNHR (autonomous vehicles tested in Phoenix were often unable to turn left or stopped suddenly, irritating other drivers). See also James M. Anderson, Nidhi Kalra, Karlyn D. Stanley, et al., *Autonomous Vehicle Technology: A Guide for Policymakers* (Santa Monica, CA: Rand Corporation, 2016), 68–70 (noting the risk that designing alerts into autonomous vehicle systems may reduce safety by lulling drivers into complacency).

71. The videos are available on Boston Dynamics YouTube Channel, https://www.youtube.com/user/BostonDynamics (accessed November 21, 2021).

72. Cade Metz, "These Robots Run, Dance and Flip. But Are They a Business?" *New York Times*, September 22, 2018; Martin Robbins, "How Real Is That Atlas Robot Video?" *The Guardian*, February 25, 2016, https://www.theguardian.com/science/the-lay-scientist/2016/feb/25/how-real-is-that-atlas-robot-boston-dynamics-video.

73. See Dana Hull, John Lippert, and Sarah Gardner, "The Future of Tesla Hinges on This Gigantic Tent," *Bloomberg*, June 25, 2018, https://www.bloomberg.com/news/articles/2018-06-25/the-future-of-tesla-hinges-on-this-gigantic-tent (discussing Elon Musk's plan to build an "alien dreadnought" factory for Tesla's Model 3, which would run at superhuman speeds, and the plan's failure due to engineering challenges).

74. Wayne Ma, "What Apple Learned from Automation: Humans Are Better," *The Information*, June 4, 2020, https://www.theinformation.com/articles/what-apple-learned-from-automation-humans-are-better.

75. Ma, "What Apple Learned." See also Sarah Nassauer, "Walmart Scraps Plan to Have Robots Scan Shelves," *Wall Street Journal*, November 2, 2020 (discussing Walmart's abandonment of large-scale plan to deploy shelf-scanning robots to determine inventory levels).

76. See Zeynep Ton, *The Good Jobs Strategy: How the Smartest Companies Invest in Employees to Lower Costs and Boost Profits* (Boston: Houghton Mifflin Harcourt, 2014), 35–54 (discussing costs of "going cheap" in retail labor strategies, including misplaced inventory).

77. Pasquale, *The New Laws of Robotics*; Daron Acemoglu and Pascual Restrepo, "The Wrong Kind of AI? Artificial Intelligence and the Future of Labour Demand," *Cambridge Journal of Regions, Economic, and Society* 13, no. 1 (March 2020): 25–35.

78. Peter A. Hall and David Soskice, "An Introduction to Varieties of Capitalism," in *Varieties of Capitalism: The Institutional Foundations of Comparative Advantage*, eds. Peter A. Hall and David Soskice (Oxford: Oxford University Press, 2001), 24–27.

79. Peggy Hollinger, "Meet the Co-Bots: Humans and Robots Together on the Factory Floor," *Financial Times*, May 5, 2016; Wolfgang Dauth, Sebastian Findeisen, Jens

Südekum, and Nicole Woessner, "The Rise of Robots in the German Labour Market," *VoxEU*, September 19, 2017, https://voxeu.org/article/rise-robots-german-labour-market; Yochai Benkler, "The Role of Technology in Political Economy: Part 3," *LPE Project*, July 27, 2018 (discussing the work of Hollinger and Dauth et al.), https://lpeproject.org/blog/the-role-of-technology-in-political-economy-part-3. But see Steve Crowe, "Inside the Rethink Robotics Shutdown," *The Robot Report*, November 13, 2018, at https://www.therobotreport.com/rethink-robotics-shutdown (reporting that a leading co-bot company shut down due to low sales; one challenge was keeping co-bots safe for humans to work with, while also engineering them to be strong and accurate enough).

80. Simon Jäger, Benjamin Schoefer, and Jörg Heining, "Labor in the Boardroom," *Quarterly Journal of Economics* 136, no. 2 (2021): 669–725. The authors did *not* find that the stricter form of codetermination correlated with higher wages.

81. For an overview and assessment of worker surveillance products now on the market, see Wilneida Negrón, *Little Tech Is Coming for Workers: A Framework for Reclaiming and Building Worker Power* (New York: Coworker.org: 2021), https://home.coworker.org/wp-content/uploads/2021/11/Little-Tech-Is-Coming-for-Workers.pdf.

82. Matthew W. Finkin, Rudiger Krause, and Hisashi Takeuchi-Okuno, "Employee Autonomy, Privacy, and Dignity under Technological Oversight," in *Comparative Labor Law*, eds. Matthew F. Finkin and Guy Mundlak (Cheltenham, UK: Edward Elgar, 2015): 154–155; Pauline T. Kim, "Data Mining and the Challenges of Protecting Employee Privacy Under U.S. Law," *Comparative Labor Law & Policy Review* 40, no. 3 (2019): 407.

83. See Laura Tyson and Michael Spence, "Exploring the Effects of Technology on Income and Wealth Inequality," in *After Piketty: The Agenda for Economics and Inequality*, eds. Heather Boushey, J. Bradford DeLong, and Marshall Steinbaum (Cambridge, MA: Harvard University Press, 2017), 182 (arguing that one effect of these developments is "disintermediation: a reduction in the vertical layers of middle managers engaged in supervision and an increase in the efficiency and quality of management oversight"); see also id. at 183 (noting that there are no guarantees that resulting efficiency or productivity gains will be shared with workers).

84. See generally Gutelius and Theodore, *The Future of Warehouse Work*. See also Edward P. Lazear, Kathryn L. Shaw, and Christopher Stanton, "Making Do with Less: Working Harder during Recessions," *Journal of Labor Economics* 34, no. S1 (2016): 333–360 (finding empirical evidence that intensified supervision led to greater worker effort, and most of the increase in studied industries came from greater effort rather than task substitution).

85. See generally Alex Rosenblat and Luke Stark, "Algorithmic Labor and Information Asymmetries: A Case Study of Uber's Drivers," *International Journal of Communication* 10 (2016): 3758–3784. See also Esther Kaplan, "The Spy Who Fired Me," *Harper's Magazine*, March 2015, https://harpers.org/archive/2015/03/the-spy-who-fired-me

(noting that a large wholesaler "was able to cut payroll expenses by 25 percent while increasing sales by 36 percent" by implementing an algorithmic tasking system).

86. Judd Cramer and Alan B. Krueger, "Disruptive Change in the Taxi Business: The Case of Uber," *American Economic Review* 106, no. 5 (May 2016): 177–182 (finding that Uber drivers spend a significantly higher fraction of their time and drive a substantially higher share of miles with a passenger in their car than do taxi drivers).

87. Rosenblat and Stark, "Algorithmic Labor and Information Asymmetries," 3758; Alex Rosenblat, *Uberland: How Algorithms Are Rewriting the Rules of Work* (Berkeley: University of California Press, 2018), 91–93.

88. Alex Rosenblat, "What Motivates Gig Economy Workers," *Harvard Business Review*, November 17, 2016, https://hbr.org/2016/11/what-motivates-gig-economy-workers (reporting that a small number of full-time drivers provide the majority of Uber's trips, while a significant number of drivers log on only occasionally).

89. See generally Ryan Calo and Alex Rosenblat, "The Taking Economy: Uber, Information, and Power," *Columbia Law Review* 117, no. 6 (2017): 1660–1668 (detailing these and other efforts).

90. Calo and Rosenblat, "The Taking Economy," 1660–1668.

91. Spencer Soper, "Amazon Drivers Are Hanging Smartphones in Trees to Get More Work," *Bloomberg*, September 1, 2020, https://www.bloomberg.com/news/articles/2020-09-01/amazon-drivers-are-hanging-smartphones-in-trees-to-get-more-work.

92. Jodi Kantor, "Starbucks to Revise Policies to End Irregular Schedules for Its 130,000 Baristas," *New York Times*, August 15, 2014.

93. Kronos, "Hannaford Supermarkets: Hannaford Uses Kronos Optimized Scheduling and Navigator to Streamline Workforce Management," Kronos.com (accessed November 21, 2021), https://www.kronos.com/customers/hannaford-supermarkets.

94. Peter Szekely, "Not So Fast: U.S. Restaurant Workers Seek Ban on Surprise Scheduling," *Reuters*, July 17, 2017, https://www.reuters.com/article/us-usa-fastfood-schedules/not-so-fast-u-s-restaurant-workers-seek-ban-on-surprise-scheduling-idUSKBN1A20VC.

95. Amazon worker, interview by author.

96. Kantor, "Starbucks to Revise Policies."

97. Kantor, "Starbucks to Revise Policies."

98. 29 U.S.C. § 207 (2018).

99. Julia Wolfe, Janelle Jones, and David Cooper, "'Fair Workweek' Laws Help More than 1.8 Million Workers," *Economic Policy Institute*, July 19, 2018, https://www.epi.org/publication/fair-workweek-laws-help-more-than-1-8-million-workers.

100. Tippett et al., "When Timekeeping Software Undermines Compliance." For an illustrative recent wage and hour case and judgment, see *Braun v. Wal-Mart Stores*, 630 Pa. 292 (Pa. 2014) (upholding jury verdict for almost $200 million in back wages and liquidated damages due to the company's failure to pay workers for break times, and other forms of wage theft).

101. See Kirstie Ball, "Workplace Surveillance: An Overview," *Labor History* 51, no. 1 (February 2010): 87–106 (discussing workplace surveillance, both historically and today).

102. Harry Braverman, *Labor and Monopoly Capital* (New York: Monthly Review Press, 1974), 256–258.

103. See generally Levy, "Contexts of Control."

104. Kaplan, "The Spy Who Fired Me." See also *Planet Money*, "The Future of Work Looks Like a UPS Truck," May 2, 2014, podcast, https://www.npr.org/sections/money/2014/05/02/308640135/episode-536-the-future-of-work-looks-like-a-ups-truck (discussing speedups and increased rate of injuries at UPS).

105. Alexandra Mateescu, *Electronic Visit Verification: The Weight of Surveillance and the Fracturing of Care* (New York: Data & Society, 2021), https://datasociety.net/wp-content/uploads/2021/11/EVV_REPORT_11162021.pdf.

106. Danielle Abril and Drew Harwell, "Keystroke Tracking, Screenshots, and Facial Recognition: The Boss May Be Watching after the Pandemic Ends," *Washington Post*, September 24, 2021. See also Communication Workers of America, "CWA Issue Brief: Protections against Abusive Monitoring," February 2014, https://cwa-union.org/sites/default/files/protections-against-abusive-monitoring_cwa-issue-brief.pdf (describing contract language around automated surveillance negotiated by call center workers and others).

107. Colin Lecher, "How Amazon Automatically Tracks and Fires Warehouse Workers for 'Productivity,'" *The Verge*, April 25, 2019, https://www.theverge.com/2019/4/25/18516004/amazon-warehouse-fulfillment-centers-productivity-firing-terminations. See also Callaci, "Digital Scab" (observing that "Amazon's strategy for increasing output in the pandemic seems to be getting its human employees to work harder").

108. Lecher, "How Amazon Tracks and Fires."

109. Lecher, "How Amazon Tracks and Fires."

110. Lecher, "How Amazon Tracks and Fires."

111. Knight, "A Radar for Industrial Robots."

112. For example, Amazon has patented a wristband that tracks workers' movements through warehouses and may vibrate to communicate to workers that they

are grabbing the wrong item. Ceylan Yeginsu, "If Workers Slack Off, the Wristband Will Know. (And Amazon Has a Patent for It)," *New York Times*, February 1, 2018.

113. See Carl Shapiro and Joseph E. Stiglitz, "Equilibrium Unemployment as a Worker Discipline Device," *American Economic Review* 74, no. 3 (June 1984): 433–444 (efficiency wages increase equilibrium unemployment, raising costs to workers of job loss). See also Janet L. Yellen, "Efficiency Wage Models of Unemployment," *American Economic Review* 74, no. 2 (May 1984): 203 (arguing that efficiency wages may be a means of selecting for high-performing workers); George A. Akerlof, "Labor Contracts as Partial Gift Exchange," *Quarterly Journal of Economics* 97, no. 4 (November 1982): 543–569 (arguing that employers may pay efficiency wages in response to norms of fair treatment within the firm or workplace).

114. See Yellen, "Efficiency Wage Models of Unemployment," 201 (arguing that efficiency wages may also be less important "in the secondary sector, where the wage-productivity relationship is weak or nonexistent").

115. Chen Liang, Yili Hong, and Bin Gu, "Does Monitoring Lead to a 'Warm' Start in Online Platforms?" (working paper, August 31, 2016): https://papers.ssrn.com/sol3/papers.cfm?abstract_id=2838045.

116. See Robert Gibbons, "Piece-Rate Incentive Schemes," *Journal of Labor Economics* 5, no. 4 (October 1987): 416 (without the capacity to collectively restrict output, workers cannot hold employers to any promises around pace of work, including pay under piece-rate schemes).

117. See Rosenblat, *Uberland*, 133–37.

118. Transport for London, *The Knowledge of London: An Introduction to Learning the Knowledge of London and the Examination Process* (March 2014), http://content.tfl.gov.uk/introduction-to-knowledge-booklet-04-19.pdf.

119. Ton, *Good Jobs Strategy*, 37–54.

120. Regarding practices in the retail sector, see Bartholomew Clark Watson, *Nations of Retailers: The Comparative Political Economy of Retail Trade* (PhD diss., University of California Berkeley, 2014), https://escholarship.org/uc/item/18z1138t (comparing retailers' integration of information and communications in the US, Denmark, and Germany, finding that Denmark and Germany pursued fewer labor discipline strategies). But see Maarten Hermans and Miet Lamberts, "Digitalization in the Belgian Retail Sector: Tensions, Discourses, and Trade Union Strategy," April 25, 2019 (on file with author) (demonstrating changes in Belgian retail sector that parallel US changes despite substantially different industrial relations systems). Regarding practices in call centers, see Virginia Doellgast, "Collective Voice under Decentralized Bargaining: A Comparative Study of Work Reorganization in U.S. and German Call Centres," *British Journal of Industrial Relations* 48, no. 2 (June 2010): 375 (arguing that US call centers use "a narrow division of labour, tight discipline and individual

incentives" along with managerial efforts to homogenize jobs, while German centers utilize "high-involvement employment systems with broad skills and worker discretion").

121. Thomas Black, "Highly Paid Union Workers Give UPS a Surprise Win in Delivery Wars," *Bloomberg*, November 4, 2021, https://www.bloomberg.com/news/articles/2021-11-04/labor-shortage-ups-union-drivers-give-delivery-service-edge-over-fedex-fdx.

Chapter 4

1. See generally Georgios Paris Loizides, *Deconstructing Fordism: Legacies of the Ford Sociological Department* (PhD. diss., Western Michigan University, 2004), https://scholarworks.wmich.edu/dissertations/1122; Henry Ford Museum of American Innovation, "Popular Research Topics: Ford Motor Company Sociological Department & English School," https://www.thehenryford.org/collections-and-research/digital-resources/popular-topics/sociological-department (accessed November 23, 2021).

2. Henry Ford Museum, "Sociological Department & English School."

3. Henry Ford Museum, "Sociological Department & English School."

4. Loizides, *Deconstructing Fordism*, 145 (detectives), 156 (monitoring outside political activities), 139 (Ford sought to convince workers that their "interests were or should be aligned with the interests of the company and its management," which "of course kept the unions outside the equation").

5. Daniel Solove, "Introduction: Privacy Self-Management and the Consent Dilemma," *Harvard Law Review* 126, no. 7 (2013): 1883. As Julie Cohen notes, that model is indebted to liberal political theory in its view that individual agents are autonomous and in its focus on individual choice as the basis for political legitimacy. Julie E. Cohen, "What Privacy Is For," *Harvard Law Review* 126, no. 7 (May 2013): 1907.

6. Neil M. Richards and Jonathan H. King, "Big Data Ethics," *Wake Forest Law Review* (2014): 412.

7. See, e.g., Richards and King, "Big Data Ethics," 413 (noting these practical difficulties).

8. Solove, "Privacy Self-Management," 1880.

9. Pauline T. Kim, "Data Mining and the Challenges of Protecting Employee Privacy Under U.S. Law," *Comparative Labor Law & Policy Review* 40, no. 3 (2019): 407 (emphasis in original). A company called Identified claimed as long ago as 2014 to have social media data on half a billion individuals. Nathan Newman, "Reengineering Workplace Bargaining: How Big Data Drives Lower Wages and How Reframing Labor Law Can Restore Information Equality in the Workplace," *University of Cincinnati Law Review* 85, no. 3 (2017): 713.

10. Helen Nissenbaum, "Contextual Integrity Up and Down the Data Food Chain," *Theoretical Inquiries in Law* 20, no. 1 (2019): 240–241. See generally Frank Pasquale, *The Black Box Society: The Secret Algorithms That Control Money and Information* (Cambridge, MA: Harvard University Press, 2016).

11. Pasquale, *Black Box Society*.

12. This hierarchical representation of data draws both from Helen Nissenbaum's and Daniel Solove's work. See Helen Nissenbaum, *Privacy in Context: Technology, Policy, and the Integrity of Social Live* (Stanford, CA: Stanford University Press, 2009), 11; Nissenbaum, "Data Food Chain," 223. Nissenbaum's third stage involves dissemination or publication, but those are not the major use cases with regard to employment. Rather, in the workplace, the major use cases involve decisions to hire, promote, fire, and the like. See also Daniel Solove, *Understanding Privacy* (Cambridge, MA: Harvard University Press, 2008), 103 (breaking information use into four contexts that may trigger privacy concerns: collection, processing, dissemination, and invasion); Matthew T. Bodie, Miriam A. Cherry, Marcia L. McCormick, and Jintong Tang, "The Law and Policy of People Analytics," *University of Colorado Law Review* 88, no. 4 (2017): 969 (steps in people analytics include "data collection, data preparation, data mining, interpretation, and acting upon the discovered knowledge").

13. Nissenbaum, "Data Food Chain," 236.

14. This has long been the case, as welfare scholars have documented. Frances Fox Piven and Richard A. Cloward, *Regulating the Poor: The Functions of Public Welfare* (New York: Pantheon, 1971). See also Virginia Eubanks, *Automating Inequality: How High-Tech Tools Profile, Police, and Punish the Poor* (New York: St. Martin's Press, 2017); Mary Madden, Michele E. Gilman, Karen Levy, and Alice E. Marwick, "Privacy, Poverty and Big Data: A Matrix of Vulnerabilities for Poor Americans," *Washington University Law Review* 95, no. 1 (2017): 53–125.

15. Charles Duhigg, "How Companies Learn Your Secrets," *New York Times*, February 16, 2012, discussed in Nissenbaum, "Data Food Chain," 239.

16. Nissenbaum, "Data Food Chain," 244.

17. See Pauline T. Kim, "Manipulating Opportunity," *Virginia Law Review* 106, no. 4 (2020): 871–874 (discussing growth of and effects of online hiring intermediaries).

18. Kim, "Manipulating Opportunity," 871, n12 (compiling evidence).

19. See, e.g., "Chatbot and Candidate Messaging Software," *Ideal.com*, https://ideal.com/product/recruiting-chatbot (accessed November 24, 2021).

20. See generally Bodie et al., "People Analytics." See also Kim, "Data Mining," 406 (through data analytics companies can "make inferences about worker characteristics and to try to predict future job performance").

21. Josh Bersin, "The Datafication of HR," *Deloitte Review* 14, January 18, 2014, https://www2.deloitte.com/us/en/insights/deloitte-review/issue-14/dr14-datafication-of-hr.html.

22. Bodie et al., "People Analytics," 973. See also Bo Cowgill and Catherine Tucker, "Algorithmic Bias: A Counterfactual Perspective" (working paper, *NSF Trustworthy Algorithms*, Arlington, VA, December 2017): 1 ("In many practical settings, the alternative to a biased algorithm is not an unbiased one, but another decision method such as another algorithm or human discretion" that may itself be more biased).

23. See, e.g., Pauline T. Kim and Matthew T. Bodie, "Artificial Intelligence and the Challenges of Workplace Discrimination and Privacy," *ABA Journal of Labor & Employment Law* 35, no. 2 (2021): 289–315; Ifeoma Ajunwa, "Age Discrimination by Platforms," *Berkeley Journal of Employment and Labor Law* 40, no. 1 (2019): 1–27; Solon Barocas and Andrew D. Selbst, "Big Data's Disparate Impact," *California Law Review* 104, no. 3 (June 2016): 671–732; Pauline T. Kim, "Data-Driven Discrimination at Work," *William and Mary Law Review* 58, no. 3 (February 2017): 857–936.

24. For a helpful summary of past and recent scholarship on the embeddedness of intelligence and its effects on AI, see Frank Pasquale, *New Laws of Robotics* (Cambridge, MA: Belknap, 2020), 211–213. See also Safiya Noble, *Algorithms of Oppression: How Search Engines Reinforce Racism* (New York: NYU Press, 2018).

25. Kim, "Data-Driven Discrimination at Work," 873.

26. Jeffrey Dastin, "Amazon Scraps Secret AI Recruiting Tool That Showed Bias Against Women," *Reuters*, October 9, 2018, https://www.reuters.com/article/us-amazon-com-jobs-automation-insight/amazon-scraps-secret-ai-recruiting-tool-that-showed-bias-against-women-idUSKCN1MK08G.

27. Cody Cook, Rebecca Diamond, Jonathan V. Hall, John A. List, and Paul Oyer, "The Gender Earnings Gap in the Gig Economy: Evidence from over a Million Rideshare Drivers" (working paper, National Bureau of Economic Research, Cambridge, MA, June 2018).

28. Bodie et al., "People Analytics," 993–994.

29. Drew Harwell, "A Face-Scanning Algorithm Increasingly Decides Whether You Deserve the Job," *Washington Post*, November 6, 2019.

30. Harwell, "Face-Scanning Algorithm."

31. See Angela Chen and Karen Hao, "Emotion AI Researchers Say Overblown Claims Give Their Work a Bad Name," *MIT Technology Review*, February 14, 2020 (quoting various researchers).

32. Lisa Feldman Barrett, Ralph Adolphs, Stacy Marsella, Aleix M. Martinez, and Seth D. Pollak, "Emotional Expressions Reconsidered: Challenges to Inferring

Emotion from Human Facial Movements," *Psychological Science in the Public Interest*, 20, no. 1 (2019): 1.

33. See Chen and Hao, "Emotion AI Researchers" (reporting that HireVue declined to comment); Harwell, "Face-Scanning Algorithm" (reporting that the company offered "only the most limited peek into its interview algorithms").

34. *See generally* Barocas and Selbst, "Big Data's Disparate Impact"; Kim, "Data-Driven Discrimination." See also Manish Raghavan, Solon Barocas, Jon Kleinberg, and Karen Levy, "Mitigating Bias in Algorithmic Hiring: Evaluating Claims and Practices" (*ACM Conference on Fairness, Accountability, and Transparency*, January 2020): 9–10. https://arxiv.org/pdf/1906.09208.pdf.

35. Harwell, "Face-Scanning Algorithm." HireVue may also serve as a liability shield, since companies typically have no liability for labor law violations by third parties. Hiring platforms that screen candidates for jobs in ways that violate labor laws may *themselves* be liable since Title VII forbids "employment agencies" from discriminating in hiring processes. 2002e-2(b) (forbidding discrimination by employment agencies); 2000e(c) (defining an "employment agency"). See generally Kim, "Manipulating Opportunity."

36. In the national origin context, see *Fragante v. City & County of Honolulu*, 888 F.2d 591, 596 (9th Cir. 1989) (stating that accent and national origin are "obviously inextricably intertwined," so district courts should conduct "a very searching look" into claims where an adverse employment decision was allegedly based on an applicant's nonnative accent); in the race context, see Equal Employment Opportunity Commission, *Compliance Manual, Section 15: Race and Color Discrimination* (April 19, 2006) (stating that "an employment decision based on a person having a so-called 'Black accent,' or 'sounding White,' violates Title VII if the accent or manner of speech does not materially interfere with the ability to perform job duties").

37. See, e.g., *Karraker v. Rent-A-Center*, 411 F.3d 831 (7th Cir. 2005) (defendant's use of Minnesota Multiphasic Personality Inventory was an unlawful medical exam under Americans with Disabilities Act since it was designed to determine whether individuals were suffering from mental health conditions, including depression and schizophrenia). Discussed in Bodie et al., "People Analytics," 993.

38. As several prominent scholars observed in 2019: "The study of algorithmic bias and fairness in machine learning has quickly matured into a field of study in its own right, delivering a wide range of formal definitions and quantitative metrics." Raghavan et al., "Mitigating Bias," 1.

39. Raghavan et al., "Mitigating Bias," 9. It is conceivable that such efforts could be challenged by majority applicants under antidiscrimination laws on a "reverse discrimination" theory, but a company that designs an algorithm to mitigate or eliminate bias faces a very low risk of liability. See Pauline T. Kim, "Auditing Algorithms

for Discrimination," *University of Pennsylvania Law Review Online* 166, no. 1 (2017): 197–202 (arguing that current law does not prohibit companies from taking potential bias into account when seeking to design those systems in ways that do not discriminate).

40. Equal Employment Opportunity Commission, "EEOC Launches Initiative on Artificial Intelligence and Algorithmic Fairness," October 28, 2021, https://www.eeoc.gov/newsroom/eeoc-launches-initiative-artificial-intelligence-and-algorithmic-fairness. See also the discussion in chapter 5.

41. See, e.g., Samuel R. Bagenstos, "The Structural Turn and the Limits of Antidiscrimination Law," *California Law Review* 94, no. 1: 40–45 (discussing the challenges of addressing background distributions of wealth, opportunities, and power through antidiscrimination laws, in large part because judges view those laws as primarily prohibiting wrongful employer conduct rather than seeking to eliminate pervasive status disparities).

42. This heuristic of concentric circles of privacy borrows from Michael D. Birnhack, "A Quest for a Theory of Privacy," *Jurimetrics* 51, no. 4 (Summer 2011): 455 (review of Nissenbaum, *Privacy in Context*).

43. See, e.g., Cohen, "What Privacy Is For," 1911 (privacy protections "creat[e] spaces for the play and the work of self-making").

44. Ari Ezra Waldman, "Safe Social Spaces," *Washington University Law Review* 96, no. 6 (2019): 1541.

45. See generally Kate Andrias, "Union Rights for All: Toward Sectoral Bargaining in the United States," in *Cambridge Handbook of Labor Law for the Twenty-First Century*, eds. Richard Bales and Charlotte Garden (Cambridge: Cambridge University Press, 2019), 56–63 (discussing how enterprise bargaining encourages employer opposition to unionization).

46. See Benjamin I. Sachs, "Enabling Employee Choice: A Structural Approach to the Rules of Union Organizing," *Harvard Law Review* 123, no. 3 (2010): 684–685 (summarizing empirical evidence on incidence of retaliatory terminations and their effect on union campaigns).

47. In a recent case arising out of organizing efforts at McDonald's, for example, an administrative law judge wrote that "the evidentiary issues raised by McDonald's and the Franchisee Respondents have simply been extraordinary," including questioning the authenticity of documents that the company itself had produced under subpoena and refusing to hold pretrial conference calls unless the calls were transcribed. National Labor Relations Board, *McDonald's USA*, Nos. 02-CA-093893 et al., Order Denying Motions to Approve Settlement Agreements (July 17, 2018), 11. See also Noam Scheiber, "Judge Rejects Settlement over McDonald's Labor Practices," *New York Times*, July 17, 2018.

48. *Phelps Dodge Corp. v. NLRB*, 313 U.S. 177 (1941).

49. See Robert A. Gorman, Matthew Finkin, and Timothy P. Glynn, *Cox & Bok's Labor Law*, 16th ed. (New York: Foundation Press, 2016), 81–87 (summarizing current elections process, common criticisms of it, and proposals for reform).

50. See generally Paul Weiler, "Promises to Keep: Securing Workers' Rights to Self-Organization under the NLRA," *Harvard Law Review* 96, no. 8 (1983): 1769–1827; Craig Becker, "Democracy in the Workplace: Union Representation Elections and Federal Labor Law," *Minnesota Law Review* 77, no. 3 (1993): 495–603; Cynthia Estlund, "The Ossification of American Labor Law," *Columbia Law Review* 102, no. 6 (October 2002): 1527–1612; Sachs, "Enabling Employee Choice": 655–728.

51. See generally James J. Brudney, "Card Check and Neutrality: Prospect for Changing Paradigms," *Iowa Law Review* 90, no. 3 (2005): 819–886. See also Brishen Rogers, "Passion and Reason in Labor Law," *Harvard Civil Rights–Civil Liberties Law Review* 47, no. 2 (2012): 348–354 (summarizing contemporary union campaign tactics).

52. *Cemex Construction Materials*, National Labor Relations Board Case Nos. 28-CA-230115 et al., Brief in Support of the General Counsel's Exceptions to the Administrative Law Judge's Decision (April 11, 2022).

53. See generally E. P. Thompson, *The Making of the English Working Class* (New York: Penguin Books, 1963); Guy Mundlak, *Organizing Matters: Two Logics of Trade Representation* (Cheltenham, UK: Edward Elgar Publishing, 2020), 31 (arguing that enterprise bargaining helps to constitute workers' interests and identities).

54. Gordon Lafer, "What's More Democratic than a Secret Ballot? The Case for Majority Sign-up," *Working USA: The Journal of Labor and Society* 11, no. 1 (March 2008): 85.

55. Rick Fantasia, *Cultures of Solidarity: Consciousness, Action, and Contemporary American Workers* (Berkeley: University of California Press, 1989), 110. See also Mundlak, *Two Logics*, 28 (observing that such organizing can "forge a vibrant daily life in which people actively engage in making decisions affecting their lives" in the workplace).

56. *Lechmere, Inc. v. NLRB*, 502 U.S. 527 (1992); *NLRB v. Babcock & Wilcox*, 351 U.S. 105 (1956). See also Cynthia Estlund, "Labor, Property, and Sovereignty After Lechmere," *Stanford Law Review* 46, no. 2 (1994): 308 ("Lechmere essentially recognized an employer's right to exclude others not only for good reasons, but for bad reasons or for no reason at all.").

57. For an overview and discussion of some of the key players, see John Logan, "The Union Avoidance Industry in the United States," *British Journal of Industrial Relations* 44, no. 4 (Dec. 2006): 651–676. See also Nelson Lichtenstein, *The Retail Revolution: How Wal-Mart Created a Brave New World of Business* (New York:

Macmillan, 2019): 187–196 (discussing Walmart's union avoidance efforts, targeted at worksites where unrest seemed to be brewing). When one group of butchers in Canada unionized in 2000, the company stopped employing butchers in stores across its entire North American operations, instead selling only prepackaged meat. Frank Swoboda, "Wal-Mart Ends Meat-Cutting Jobs," *Washington Post*, March 4, 2000.

58. *Peerless Plywood Co.*, 107 NLRB 427 (1953) (holding that such "captive audience" meetings are prohibited only if held within twenty-four hours of an election).

59. Charles Hughes, one prominent anti-union consultant, has argued that "any management that gets a union deserves it," although he insisted that he meant that management can avoid unionization through good employee relations. Logan, "Union Avoidance Industry," 664.

60. Noam Scheiber, "Amazon Workers Who Won a Union Their Way Open Labor Leaders' Eyes," *New York Times*, April 7, 2022.

61. However, an employer often may not grant new benefits to workers during an organizing drive without violating the NLRA. *NLRB v. Exchange Parts*, 375 U.S. 405 (1964).

62. *NLRB v. Gissel Packing Co.*, 395 U.S. 575, 618–619 (1969). The distinction between "threats" and "predictions" has proved difficult to apply in practice. See Robert A. Gorman and Matthew W. Finkin, *Basic Text on Labor Law: Unionization and Collective Bargaining*, 2nd ed. (St. Paul, MN: Thomson West 2004), 177–188.

63. *Republic Aviation Corp. v. NLRB*, 324 U.S. 793, 803 (1945), citing *Peyton Packing Co.*, 49 NLRB 828, 843–844 (1943).

64. *Republic Aviation*, 324 U.S. at 801, citing *Intermediate Report, Republic Aviation*, 51 NLRB 1195.

65. *The Register Guard*, 351 NLRB 1110 (2007); *Purple Communications Inc.*, 361 NLRB 1050 (2014); *Caesar's Entertainment*, 368 NLRB No. 143 (2019).

66. *Caesar's* at 6, also comparing email systems to other property such as "televisions, bulletin boards, copy machines, telephones, or public address systems."

67. *Caesar's* at 10.

68. E.g. *Whole Foods Mkt.*, 363 NLRB No. 87 (2015) at 4; *Rio All-Suites Hotel & Casino*, 362 NLRB No. 190 (2015) at 5.

69. *Whole Foods* at 3.

70. *The Boeing Co.*, 365 NLRB No. 154 (2017) at 5–6.

71. *Design Technology Group*, 359 NLRB No. 96 (2013) (discussion on Facebook about supervisor's harassing, unprofessional behavior, in which workers planned collective

action is protected); *Hispanics United of Buffalo*, 359 NLRB No. 37 (2012) (conversation about coworker's allegedly abusive behavior on Facebook protected).

72. The NLRB's new rules around employer work policies, from *Boeing Co.*, may also create more room for companies to discipline workers for public online speech. See, e.g., *Bemis Company*, 370 NLRB No. 7 (2020) at 2 (finding lawful a social media policy that required employees to be "respectful and professional when using social media tools . . . so as to effectively safeguard the reputation and interests" of the employer and not create an "intimidating, offensive, or hostile work environment").

73. Email to author from Israeli graduate student who is a former union organizer, May 14, 2018.

74. Harold Meyerson, "What Now for Unions?" *The American Prospect*, March 26, 2018.

75. Jodi Kantor and Karen Weise, "How Two Best Friends Beat Amazon," *New York Times*, April 2, 2022 (updated April 14, 2022).

76. See generally, Philip N. Howard and Muzammil M. Hussain, *Democracy's Fourth Wave? Digital Media and the Arab Spring* (Oxford: Oxford University Press, 2013).

77. Andrew Chadwick, *Internet Politics: States, Citizens, and New Communication Technologies* (Oxford: Oxford University Press, 2006), 135–136.

78. Alex J. Wood, "Three Lessons the Labour Movement Must Learn from the Fight for 15 at Walmart," Sheffield Political Economy Research Institute, June 8, 2018, http://speri.dept.shef.ac.uk/2018/06/08/three-lessons-the-labour-movement-must-learn-from-the-fight-for-15-at-walmart.

79. See Kate Andrias, "The New Labor Law," *Yale Law Journal* 126, no. 2 (2016): 50 (discussing the use of social media by Fight for 15).

80. See, e.g., Nahed Eltantawy and Julie B. Wiest, "Social Media in the Egyptian Revolution: Reconsidering Resource Mobilization Theory," *International Journal of Communication* 5 (2011): 1208 ("internet-based communication technologies provide an important additional resource for social movements implemented by 'resource poor' actors, offering a means for mass communication that may have previously been restricted by financial, temporal, or spatial constraints") (citing Donatella Della Porta and Lorenzo Mosca, "Global-net for Global Movements? A Network of Networks for a Movement of Movements," *Journal of Public Policy* 25, no. 1 (2005): 165–190.

81. Fight for $15, Facebook, https://www.facebook.com/Fightfor15; Fight for $15 (@fightfor15), Twitter, https://twitter.com/fightfor15.

82. The Chicago teachers, for example, demanded not just raises and benefits, but also a robust set of welfare and other rights for their students and their families:

racial equity in school funding, resources for homeless students, nurses in every school, and sanctuary schools for immigrant students. Sarah Jaffe, "The Chicago Teachers Strike Was a Lesson in 21st-Century Organizing," *The Nation*, November 16, 2019.

83. See Jamillah Bowman Williams, Naomi Mezey, and Lisa O. Singh, "#BlackLivesMatter: Getting from Contemporary Social Movements to Structural Change," *California Law Review Online* 12 (2021) (presenting a theoretical model of how movements can use social media to move supporters into offline action). But see Zeynep Tufekci, *Twitter and Tear Gas: The Power and Fragility of Networked Protest* (New Haven, CT: Yale University Press, 2017) (suggesting that the capabilities of online organizing may distract movement leaders from the less-glamorous work of building stable institutions).

84. Andrew J. Hawkins, "Uber and Lyft Had an Edge in the Prop 22 Fight: Their Apps," *The Verge*, November 4, 2020, https://www.theverge.com/2020/11/4/21549760/uber-lyft-prop-22-win-vote-app-message-notifications.

85. Mark Barenberg, "Democracy and Domination in the Law of Workplace Cooperation: From Bureaucratic to Flexible Production," *Columbia Law Review* 94, no. 3 (1994): 941. The analogy is to threads in fabric: the "warp" run lengthwise and the "woof" crosswise.

86. 29 U.S.C. §158(a)(3) (2018).

87. *Struksnes Constr. Co.*, 165 NLRB 1062 (1967) (employer commits an unfair labor practice by polling employees regarding union support unless: the employer does so to assess a union's claim that it has majority support, that purpose is communicated to the workers, workers are given assurances against reprisals, the poll is performed via secret ballot, and the employer does not engage in other unfair labor practices). See the discussion of this topic in Newman, "Reengineering Workplace Bargaining," 738–739.

88. Newman, "Reengineering Workplace Bargaining," 709–714.

89. *Great Lakes Chem. Corp.*, 298 NLRB 615, 621 (1990) (considering and rejecting the claim that a commonly used personality test "revealed a person's union sympathies"). See also Sarah Kessler, "Companies Are Using Employee Survey Data to Predict—and Squash—Union Organizing," *OneZero*, July 30, 2020 (quoting former NLRB Chair Wilma Liebman, and the head of data analytics at the law firm Littler Mendelson, Zev Eigen, to the effect that personality tests cannot discern union sympathies), https://onezero.medium.com/companies-are-using-employee-survey-data-to-predict-and-squash-union-organizing-a7e28a8c2158.

90. Newman, "Reengineering Workplace Bargaining," 709–713.

91. Barbara Ehrenreich, *Nickel and Dimed: On (Not) Getting by in America* (New York: Macmillan, 2011), 123–124, cited and discussed in Newman, "Reengineering Workplace Bargaining," 709.

92. Ehrenreich, *Nickel and Dimed*, 123–124, cited in Newman, "Reengineering Workplace Bargaining," 709.

93. Gregory M. Saltzman, "Job Applicant Screening by a Japanese Transplant: A Union-Avoidance Tactic," *Industrial & Labor Relations Review* 49, no. 1 (October 1995): 88–104, discussed in Newman, "Reengineering Workplace Bargaining," 712–713. For a good summary of past literature finding that companies could use screening and hiring mechanisms to deter unionization, see Nicole Kreisberg and Nathan Wilmers, "Blacklist or Short List: Do Employers Discriminate against Union Supporter Job Applicants?" *ILR Review* 75, no. 4 (August 2022): 945–948.

94. Saltzman, "Job Applicant Screening," 88.

95. *McDonald's USA*, Charging Parties' Post-Hearing Brief in Opposition to Proposed Settlement Agreements at 15–16 (April 27, 2018).

96. See the discussion in section 2.3 in chapter 2.

97. Paul Mozur, "In Hong Kong Protests, Faces Become Weapons," *New York Times*, July 26, 2019. Similarly, a recorded video interview would give HireVue and other platforms a decent scan of not only an applicant's face, but also of their voice, another possible means of identification.

98. Kreisberg and Wilmers, "Blacklist or Short List," 943.

99. Lichtenstein, *Retail Revolution*, 186.

100. Ryan Gallagher, "Google Accused of Creating Spy Tool to Squelch Worker Dissent," *Bloomberg*, October 23, 2019, https://www.bloomberg.com/news/articles/2019-10-23/google-accused-of-creating-spy-tool-to-squelch-worker-dissent.

101. Noam Scheiber and Daisuke Wakabayashi, "Google Hires Firm Known for Anti-Union Efforts," *New York Times*, November 20, 2019.

102. Lauren Kaori Gurley and Janus Rose, "Amazon Employee Warns Internal Groups They're Being Monitored for Labor Organizing," *VICE*, September 24, 2020, https://www.vice.com/en/article/m7jz7b/amazon-employee-warns-internal-groups-theyre-being-monitored-for-labor-organizing.

103. Lee Fang, "Facebook Pitched New Tool Allowing Employers to Suppress Words Like 'Unionize' in Workplace Chat Product," *The Intercept*, June 11, 2020, https://theintercept.com/2020/06/11/facebook-workplace-unionize.

104. Kessler, "Employee Survey Data."

105. Lorenzo Franceschi-Bicchierai, "Amazon Is Hiring an Intelligence Analyst to Track 'Labor Organizing Threats,'" *VICE*, September 1, 2020, https://www.vice.com/en/article/qj4aqw/amazon-hiring-intelligence-analyst-to-track-labor-organizing-threats.

106. *Consol. Edison Co. v. NLRB*, 305 U.S. 197, 215 (1938).

107. *Kenworth Truck Co.*, 327 NLRB 497, 501 (1999), discussed in Charlotte Garden, "Labor Organizing in the Age of Surveillance," *St. Louis University Law Review* 63, no. 1 (2018): 61.

108. 29 U.S.C. 158(a)(1) (2018). As Charlotte Garden explains in a summary of the subsequent case law, examples of such "overly intrusive" surveillance include "watching employees with binoculars, watching union activity on a daily basis and for hours at a time, posting guards in previously unguarded areas, [and] photographing or videotaping employees and monitoring their phone calls in response to union activity." Garden, "Labor Organizing," 61–62.

109. Salvador Rodriguez, "Facebook Adds More Guidelines for Internal Employee Speech, Banning Political Images in Profile Pics," *CNBC*, September 24, 2020, https://www.cnbc.com/2020/09/24/facebook-wont-let-employees-use-political-profile-photos-internally.html.

110. Garden, "Labor Organizing," 55.

111. See Garden, "Labor Organizing," 62 (discussing *The Broadway*, 267 NLRB 385, 400 (1983) (after a union drive began, the employer was permitted to expand a "good-night policy," in which senior management stood at the door while workers left to ensure that all packages were sealed and prevent theft, since that policy was in place before the drive and the workers "had become fully familiar" with it).

112. During the Trump administration, two members of the NLRB signaled a willingness to revisit the longstanding rule that management surveillance of union activity can be unlawful even when the workers do not know of the surveillance. *National Captioning Institute*, 368 NLRB No. 105 (2019), n17.

113. Protecting the Right to Organize Act of 2019, H.R. 2474, 116th Cong. (2019). For expert testimony regarding discussion of the act's provisions, see US Congress, House Committee on Education and Labor, Subcommittee on Health, Employment, Labor and Pensions, *Hearing on the Protecting the Right to Organize Act: Deterring Unfair Labor Practices*, May 8, 2019, 116th Congress (testimony of Mark Gaston Pearce, NLRB's former Chairman, and AFL-CIO President Richard L. Trumka); US Congress, House Committee on Education and Labor, Subcommittee on Health, Employment, Labor and Pensions, *Hearing on Protecting the Right to Organize Act: Modernizing America's Labor Laws*, July 25, 2019, 116th Congress (testimony of Richard F. Griffin, Jr., former NLRB Board member and general counsel, and Charlotte Garden, professor of labor and constitutional law at Seattle University School of Law).

114. Nissenbaum, "Data Food Chain," 245.

115. See generally Salomé Viljoen, "A Relational Theory for Data Governance," *Yale Law Journal* 131, no. 2 (2022): 573–654.

Chapter 5

1. *NLRB v. Hearst Publ'ns*, 322 U.S. 111 (1944).

2. *O'Connor v. Uber Tech.*, 82 F. Supp. 3d 1133 (N.D. Cal. 2015) (denying defendant Uber's motion for summary judgment on the issue of employment status in a case arising under California law), final settlement approved by *O'Connor v. Uber Tech.*, 2019 WL 439401 (N.D. Cal, Sept. 13, 2019); *Cotter v. Lyft*, 60 F. Supp. 3d 1067 (N.D. Cal. 2015) (denying defendant Lyft's motion for summary judgment in parallel case), final settlement approved by *Cotter v. Lyft*, 193 F. Supp. 3d 1030 (N.D. Cal. 2016).

3. *Hearst*, 322 U.S. at 117, 120.

4. *Hearst*, 322 U.S. at 120.

5. *Cotter*, 60 F. Supp. 3d at 1081; *O'Connor*, 82 F. Supp. 3d at 1149–1153.

6. *Hearst*, 322 U.S. at 134–135.

7. *Hearst*, 322 U.S. at 117–119.

8. *Hearst*, 322 U.S. at 119.

9. *O'Connor*, 82 F. Supp. 3d at 1149–1153.

10. *Alexander v. FedEx Ground Package Sys.*, 765 F.3d 981, 985 (9th Cir. 2014).

11. *O'Connor*, 82 F. Supp. 3d at 1151.

12. *O'Connor*, 82 F. Supp. 3d at 1149.

13. *O'Connor*, 82 F. Supp. 3d at 1151–1152 quoting Michel Foucault, *Discipline and Punish: The Birth of the Prison*, trans. Alan Sheridan (New York: Pantheon Books, 1979).

14. Alex Rosenblat, *Uberland: How Algorithms Are Rewriting the Rules of Work* (Berkeley: University of California Press, 2018), 139 (discussing Uber's use of its app to monitor drivers' braking and acceleration); Alex Rosenblat and Luke Stark, "Algorithmic Labor and Information Asymmetries: A Case Study of Uber's Drivers," *International Journal of Communication* 10 (2016): 3765 (discussing Uber's monitoring of drivers' routes).

15. See generally David Weil, *The Fissured Workplace: Why Work Became So Bad for So Many and What Can Be Done to Improve It* (Cambridge, MA: Harvard University Press, 2014).

16. See, for example, 29 U.S.C. 152 (2–3) (2018) (defining "employer" and "employee" under the NLRA); 29 U.S.C. 203 (2018) (same, under the FLSA). See generally Catherine Ruckelshaus, Rebecca Smith, Sarah Leberstein, and Eunice Cho, *Who's the Boss: Restoring Accountability for Labor Standards in Outsourced Work* (New York: National Employment Law Project, 2014).

17. See Ruckelshaus et al., *Who's the Boss*, 27–29 (discussing how employee misclassification undermines funding for state unemployment insurance and worker compensation systems).

18. Weil, *Fissured Workplace*, 43–60.

19. Weil, *Fissured Workplace*, 61 (fissuring depends on low costs "of gathering information and undertaking monitoring in light of developments in the digital world").

20. Ruckelshaus et al., *Who's the Boss*, 7.

21. Ruckelshaus et al., *Who's the Boss*, 7, 15–17. See *Yellow Cab Cooperative v. Workers' Comp. Appeals Bd.*, 226 Cal.App.3d 1288 (1991) (finding that cab companies misclassified drivers as independent contractors for purposes of California workers compensation act); *Alexander*, 765 F.3d 981 (finding that FedEx misclassified drivers under California laws regarding wages, hours, and work-related expenses).

22. See Weil, *Fissured Workplace*, 99–121 (discussing history of and recent growth in subcontracting).

23. See Ruckelshaus et al., *Who's the Boss*, 8. For an unusually lucid analysis of subcontracting in agriculture, see *Reyes v. Remington Hybrid Seed Co.*, 495 F.3d 403 (7th Cir. 2005).

24. See Weil, *Fissured Workplace*, 122–158 (discussing franchising and its effects).

25. Weil, *Fissured Workplace*, 131.

26. Samuel Berlinski, "Wages and Contracting Out: Does the Law of One Price Hold?" *British Journal of Industrial Relations* 46, no. 1 (2008): 59–75 (finding wage disparities between in-house and subcontracted janitors and security guards); Rosemary Batt and Hiroatsu Nohara, "How Institutions and Business Strategies Affect Wages: A Cross-National Study of Call Centers," *Industrial & Labor Relations Review* 62, no. 4 (2009): 533–552 (finding wage disparities between in-house and subcontracted call centers).

27. Weil, *Fissured Workplace*, 43–60.

28. Weil, *Fissured Workplace*, 81–85.

29. For a history of legal battles around employee status at the turn of the twentieth century and how those battles influenced the definition of employment under the FLSA, see Bruce Goldstein, Marc Linder, Laurence E. Norton II, and Catherine K. Ruckelshaus, "Enforcing Fair Labor Standards in the Modern American Sweatshop: Rediscovering the Statutory Definition of Employment," *UCLA Law Review* 46, no. 4 (1999): 983–1163.

30. *Hearst*, 322 U.S. at 121.

31. Restatement (First) of Agency § 220 (1933), cited in *Hearst*, 322 U.S. at 120. See also Restatement (Second) of Agency § 220(2) (American Law Institute, 1958)

(updating test for employment, listing factors that should be used to determine whether a relationship constitutes employment).

32. *Hearst*, 322 U.S. at 120.

33. *Hearst*, 322 U.S. at 121.

34. Jennifer Middleton, "Contingent Workers in a Changing Economy: Endure, Adapt, or Organize?" *NYU Review of Law & Social Change* 22, no. 3 (1997): 568–569 (cited in *Dynamex Operations W. v. Superior Ct.*, 416 P.3d 1, 34 (Cal. 2018)).

35. *Hearst*, 322 U.S. at 129.

36. *Hearst*, 322 U.S. at 127–128.

37. Courts and agencies have not always avoided the term "working class." See *Briggs Mfg. Co.*, 75 NLRB 569, 570 (1947) (stating that the statutory term "employee" is "broad enough to include members of the working class generally"). *Briggs* did not involve the employee/independent contractor distinction, but rather the question of whether a worker who has been terminated during a labor dispute can still be an employee of his or her former employer under the NLRA.

38. *Rutherford Food Corp. v. McComb*, 331 U.S. 722 (1947).

39. Labor Management Relations Act of 1947, Pub. L. 80–101 (1947), relevant provision now codified at 29 U.S.C. 152(3) (providing that the term "'employee' . . . shall not include . . . any individual having the status of an independent contractor").

40. *NLRB v. United Ins. Co. of Am.*, 390 U.S. 254, 256 (1968) (observing that the "obvious purpose" of that provision was "to have the Board and the courts apply general agency principles in distinguishing between employees and independent contractors" under the NLRA).

41. *Nationwide Mut. Ins. Co. v. Darden*, 503 U.S. 318, 324–29 (1992) (common law agency test applies under NLRA, Social Security Act, and ERISA).

42. *Rutherford*, 331 U.S. at 727; *Darden*, 503 U.S. at 326.

43. *Cotter*, 60 F. Supp. 3d at 1075–1076; *O'Connor*, 82 F. Supp. 3d at 1138–1140 (both summarizing the test from *S.G. Borello & Sons v. Department of Industrial Relations*, 769 P.2d 399 (Cal. 1989)).

44. *Cotter*, 60 F. Supp. 3d at 1075 (internal quotations and citations omitted).

45. Noah D. Zatz, "Beyond Misclassification: Tackling the Independent Contractor Problem without Redefining Employment," *ABA Journal of Labor & Employment Law* 26, no. 2 (Winter 2011): 282–283.

46. *FedEx Home Delivery v. NLRB* (*FedEx I*), 563 F.3d 492, 497 (D.C. Cir. 2009) (quoting *North American Van Lines v. NLRB*, 869 F.2d 596, 599 (D.C. Cir. 1989)).

47. *FedEx I*, 563 F.3d at 502 (quoting *North American Van Lines*, 869 F.2d at 599).

48. *FedEx I*, 563 F.3d at 497.

49. Zatz, "Beyond Misclassification," 282–283.

50. Joseph Schumpeter, *Capitalism, Socialism and Democracy* (New York: Harper Brothers, 1942).

51. *SuperShuttle DFW and Amalgamated Transit Union Loc.* 1338, Case 16-RC-010963 (NLRB, January 25, 2019) at 5.

52. NLRB, Joint Employer Status Under the National Labor Relations Act, Final Rule, 29 C.F.R. Part 103, 85 Fed. Reg. No. 38 (February 26, 2020), 11184 (providing that one entity is the joint employer of another entity's employees "only if the two share or codetermine the employees' essential terms and conditions of employment," and that "share or codetermine" signifies that the putative joint employer exercises "substantial direct and immediate control over one or more essential terms or conditions of their employment"). The NLRB announced in early 2022 that it was planning another round of rulemaking to determine the standard for joint employment. NLRB, Semiannual Regulatory Agenda, 87 Fed. Reg. No. 20 (January 31, 2022), 5376.

53. NLRB, Joint Employer Status, 11235–11236.

54. See Plumbers Loc. 447 (Malbaff Landscape Constr.), 172 NLRB 128, 129 (1968) (finding no 8(a)(3) violation in this situation).

55. The NLRB pushed back on this practice in the Obama years, armed with a broader standard for joint employment. See *CNN America & Team Video Services*, 361 NLRB No. 47 (September 15, 2014) (finding that CNN violated the NLRA by replacing a unionized subcontractor where the network jointly employed that subcontractor's workers). See also Nathan Newman, "Reengineering Workplace Bargaining: How Big Data Drives Lower Wages and How Reframing Labor Law Can Restore Information Equality in the Workplace," *University of Cincinnati Law Review* 85, no. 3 (2017): 747–749 (discussing these developments).

56. See, for example, *Preferred Bldg. Services*, 366 NLRB No. 159 (August 28, 2018) (holding that certain picketing by subcontracted workers against a user firm was unprotected under the NLRA).

57. This is essentially because vertical tie-ups between the two are permissible. Brian Callaci, "Vertical Power and the Creation of a Fissured Workplace: The Case of Franchising" (PhD diss., University of Massachusetts at Amherst, 2019), 4–13, https://scholarworks.umass.edu/dissertations_2/1696; Sanjukta Paul, "Fissuring and the Firm Exemption," *Law & Contemporary Problems* 82, no. 3 (2019): 68–72.

58. See *Reyes v. Remington Hybrid Seed Co.*, 495 F.3d 403, 409 (7th Cir. 2005) (noting that user firms may have incentives to hire judgment-proof contractors and escape

FLSA liability unless employment is defined broadly enough to capture subcontracted workers).

59. Erik Brynjolfsson and Kristina McElheran, "Data in Action: Data-Driven Decision Making in U.S. Manufacturing," U.S. Census Bureau, Center for Economic Studies, Paper No. CES-WP-16-06 (January 2016): 5, citing R. E. Bohn, "From Art to Science in Manufacturing: The Evolution of Technological Knowledge," *Foundations and Trends in Technology, Information, and Operations Management* 1, no. 2 (2005): 1–82.

60. See National Academies of Sciences, Engineering, and Medicine, *Information Technology and the U.S. Workforce: Where Are We and Where Do We Go from Here?* (Washington, DC: National Academies Press, 2017), 66 (noting that "computer-mediated communications" have made it far easier for companies to outsource and offshore various aspects of production); Weil, *Fissured Workplace*, 63 (companies can use new technologies to "carefully scrutinize performance" by suppliers).

61. Stephen A. Marglin, "What Do Bosses Do? The Origins and Functions of Hierarchy in Capitalist Production," *Review of Radical Political Economics* 6, no. 2 (1974): 91–92.

62. See Mark Anner, Jennifer Bair, and Jeremy Blasi, "Learning from the Past: The Relevance of Twentieth-Century New York Jobbers' Agreements for Twenty-First-Century Global Supply Chains," in *Achieving Workers' Rights in the Global Economy*, ed. Richard P. Appelbaum and Nelson Lichtenstein (Ithaca, NY: ILR Press, 2016), 239–258 (describing "sweating system" and how union "jobbers agreements" stabilized prices and practices).

63. See Nelson Lichtenstein, *The Retail Revolution: How Wal-Mart Created a Brave New World of Business* (New York: Macmillan, 2019), 46–69 (discussing Walmart's logistics system, its technological innovations, and its role in the company's growth). See also Weil, *Fissured Workplace*, 64–72 (discussing companies' monitoring strategies in retail and fast food).

64. Erik Brynjolfsson, Lorin Hitt, and Shinkyu Yang, "Intangible Assets: Computers and Organizational Capital," *Brookings Papers on Economic Activity* (2002): 146.

65. Lichtenstein, *Retail Revolution*, 120, 121–125 (discussing Walmart's wage-setting and employee discipline strategies for its own workers), 174–196 (discussing Walmart's union avoidance strategies at its stores).

66. See Bartholomew Clark Watson, *Nations of Retailers: The Comparative Political Economy of Retail Trade* (PhD diss., University of California Berkeley, 2014), https://escholarship.org/uc/item/18z1138t (arguing that Walmart's business model in the US involved "dominating relationships with suppliers and workers," in contrast with a more collaborative "relational contracting" model that emerged among retailers in Denmark and Germany).

67. Lichtenstein, *Retail Revolution*, 64. In contrast, auto manufacturers often collaborate with suppliers on design and work closely with them on their internal processes in a strategy that several authors term "learning by monitoring." Susan Helper, John Paul MacDuffie, and Charles Sabel, "Pragmatic Collaborations: Advancing Knowledge while Controlling Opportunism," *Industrial and Corporate Change* 9, no. 3 (2000): 443–488.

68. Nathan Wilmers, "Wage Stagnation and Buyer Power: How Buyer-Supplier Relations Affect U.S. Workers' Wages, 1978 to 2014," *American Sociological Review* 83, no. 2 (2018): 216.

69. Josh Eidelson and Matt Day, "Amazon Work Rules Govern Tweets, Body Odor of Contract Drivers," *Bloomberg*, May 5, 2021, https://www.bloomberg.com/news/articles/2021-05-05/amazon-work-rules-govern-tweets-body-odor-of-contract-drivers.

70. See generally Weil, *Fissured Workplace*, 123–132; Callaci, *The Creation of a Fissured Workplace*; Paul, "Fissuring and the Firm Exemption."

71. Charging Parties' Post-Hearing Brief in Opposition to Proposed Settlement Agreements at 17–18, *McDonald's USA*, National Labor Relations Board Cases 02-CA-093893 and 04-CA-125567 (April 27, 2018).

72. Charging Parties' Post-Hearing Brief, *McDonald's USA*, 20 (citing McDonald's regulations providing that "[g]uests should wait no more than 90 seconds from your greeting to the completion of their order" and that their "total experience time should not exceed 3 minutes, 30 seconds").

73. *Browning-Ferris Industries of California*, NLRB Case 32-RC-109684, Amicus Brief of the General Counsel, (June 26, 2014), 15.

74. Weil, *Fissured Workplace*, 146.

75. Nell Walker, "How Marriott Has Achieved the Mammoth Task of Streamlining Its Worldwide Supply Chain," *Supply Chain*, June 3, 2020, https://supplychaindigital.com/company/how-marriott-has-achieved-mammoth-task-streamlining-its-worldwide-supply-chain.

76. Weil, *Fissured Workplace*, 145–46.

77. See Annie Lowrey, "The Rise of the Zombie Small Business," *The Atlantic*, September 4, 2018 (discussing similar business structures in chicken farming).

78. Gabriel Winant, *The Next Shift: The Fall of Industry and the Rise of Health Care in Rust Belt America* (Cambridge, MA: Harvard University Press, 2021), 1.

79. E. Tammy Kim, "The Gig Economy Is Coming for Your Job," *New York Times*, January 10, 2020.

80. See, e.g., *SuperShuttle DFW* (holding that drivers for SuperShuttle, a service that carries passengers to and from airports, were independent contractors); National

Labor Relations Board, Office of the General Counsel, Advice Memorandum, *Uber Technologies, Inc.*, No. 13-CA-163062 et al. (April 16, 2019) (applying *SuperShuttle* to conclude that Uber drivers are independent contractors). See also *Bexar County Performing Arts Center Foundation*, 368 NLRB No. 46 (2019) (holding that unionized musicians whose employer rented space from a performing arts center had very limited rights to enter the center's property for organizational purposes), *enf't denied*, Local 23, *Am. Fed. Musicians v. NLRB*, no. 20–1010 (D.C. Cir., Aug 31, 2021) (finding the NLRB ruling arbitrary).

81. See, e.g., *Lowman v. Unemployment Compensation Bd. of Rev.*, 235 A.3d 278 (Pa. 2020) (holding that Uber drivers are employees for the purposes of unemployment compensation under Pennsylvania law); Karla Adam, "Britain's Supreme Court Rules Uber Drivers Are 'Workers' Entitled to Minimum Wage and Paid Vacation," *Washington Post*, February 19, 2021; Ed Taylor, "Uber Drivers Are Employees, Brazil Court Rules," *BNA Bloomberg*, April 17, 2017.

82. European Commission, *Proposal for a Directive of the European Parliament and of the Council on Improving Working Conditions in Platform Work*, COM(2021) 762 final (December 9, 2021), proposed Article 4.

83. See *Dynamex Operations W. v. Super. Ct. of L.A.*, 416 P.3d 1, 7 (Cal. 2018) (adopting the ABC test for the purposes of state wage orders); California Assembly Bill 5 (2019) (applying the ABC test to all employment status questions under California law; California Proposition 22 (2020) (successful ballot initiative sponsored by gig-economy companies exempting them from Assembly Bill 5). In August 2021 a state judge held Proposition 22 unconstitutional, *Castellanos v. State*, 2021 Cal. Super. LEXIS 7285 (Aug. 20, 2021). The gig-economy companies then appealed. *Castellanos et al. v. State of California et al.*, Calif. App, 1st App. Dist., Div. 4, Case No. A163655 (filed Sept. 21, 2021). The appeal was pending when this book went to press.

84. Protecting the Right to Organize Act of 2019, H.R. 2474, 116th Cong. (2019).

85. Small companies that are treated as contractors by larger firms raise more complicated issues, but they too should perhaps be permitted to coordinate to set prices and minimum terms—at least when confronting a large company that has substantially more market power and operational capacity. See generally Paul, "Fissuring and the Firm Exemption."

86. Noam Scheiber, "Uber and Lyft Ramp up Legislative Efforts to Shield Business Model," *New York Times*, June 9, 2021.

87. Brian Callaci, "Uber and Lyft Are Thinking about a Franchise Model. That Won't Fix the Gig Economy's Problems," *Slate*, August 24, 2020, https://slate.com/technology/2020/08/uber-lyft-franchise-model.html.

88. "Delivery Services: FedEx Will Pay $27 Million to Settle Lawsuit over Classification of Drivers," *Daily Labor Report (BNA)*, No. 236, December 9, 2008.

89. See, e.g., California Labor Code § 218.7 (2018) (providing that construction contractors are liable for unpaid wages owed to employees of their subcontractors).

90. The NLRB is forbidden by statute from employing individuals to engage in "economic analysis." 29 U.S.C. 154 (2018).

91. Wilmers, "Wage Stagnation and Buyer Power," 216.

92. Kate Andrias and Brishen Rogers, *Rebuilding Worker Voice in Today's Economy* (New York: Roosevelt Institute, 2018), 16–20.

93. In New York City, for example, Uber and Lyft became larger than the entire taxi sector in 2017 and continued to gain market share steadily until the pandemic. Nicu Calcea, "Uber and Lyft Are Cutting Even Further into the Taxi Market during the Pandemic," Citymonitor.ai, August 21, 2020, https://citymonitor.ai/transport/uber-lyft-rides-during-coronavirus-pandemic-taxi-data-5232.

94. David Autor, David Dorn, Lawrence F. Katz, Christina Patterson, and John Van Reenen, "The Fall of the Labor Share and the Rise of Superstar Firms," *Quarterly Journal of Economics* 135, no. 2 (2020): 645–709; Gustavo Grullon, Yelena Larkin, and Roni Michaely, "Are US Industries Becoming More Concentrated?," *Review of Finance* 23, no. 4 (2019): 697–743; Lina Khan and Sandeep Vaheesan, "Market Power and Inequality: The Antitrust Counterrevolution and Its Discontents," *Harvard Law & Policy Review* 11, no. 1 (2017): 246–260. But see Kevin Rinz, "Labor Market Concentration, Earnings Inequality, and Earnings Mobility," U.S. Census Bureau, September 2018, https://www.census.gov/library/working-papers/2018/adrm/carra-wp-2018-10.html (arguing that local industrial concentration has declined since the 1980s and that national concentration dropped in the early 1980s before rising in the 1990s).

95. Immanuel Wallerstein, *World-Systems Analysis: An Introduction* (Durham, NC: Duke University Press, 2004), 26.

96. See generally Lina M. Khan, "Amazon's Antitrust Paradox," *Yale Law Journal* 126, no. 3 (2017): 710–805. See also K. Sabeel Rahman, "Curbing the New Corporate Power," *Boston Review*, May 4, 2015; Ganesh Sitaraman, "Regulating Tech Platforms: A Blueprint for Reform," *Great Democracy Initiative*, May 1, 2018; Jonathan Tepper, "The Conservative Case for Antitrust," *The American Conservative*, January 28, 2019.

97. Accessible summaries of this doctrinal evolution and its effects include Khan, "Amazon's Antitrust Paradox," 717–722, and Jedediah Britton-Purdy, David Singh Grewal, Amy Kapczynski, and K. Sabeel Rahman, "Building a Law-and-Political-Economy Framework: Beyond the Twentieth-Century Synthesis," *Yale Law Journal* 129, no. 6 (2020): 1801–1802.

98. See Amy Kapczynski, "The Law of Informational Capitalism," *Yale Law Journal* 129, no. 5 (2020): 1476–1477 (discussing the dominance of Facebook and Google in their markets, observing that "information-intensive markets may incline toward

concentration" because "the informational sector is highly scaleable," enabling companies with "small advantages" to "capture larger shares of the market").

99. On Walmart's growth, see generally Lichtenstein, *Retail Revolution*; on Amazon's growth, see generally Khan, "Amazon's Antitrust Paradox."

100. See Winant, *The Next Shift*, 242–252 (tracing the consolidation of health care in Pittsburgh).

101. Representative works include Autor et al., "The Fall of the Labor Share"; José Azar, Ioana Marinescu, and Marshall Steinbaum, "Labor Market Concentration," *Journal of Human Resources* 57, no S (April 2022): S167-S199; Efraim Benmelech, Nittai Bergman, and Hyunseob Kim, "Strong Employers and Weak Employees: How Does Employer Concentration Affect Wages?," *Journal of Human Resources* 57, no S (April 2022): S200-S250. On the role of law in fostering market concentration, see Suresh Naidu, Eric A. Posner, and Glen Weyl, "Antitrust Remedies for Labor Market Power," *Harvard Law Review* 132, no. 2 (2018): 536–601; Callaci, "Vertical Power," 4–13; Paul, "Fissuring and the Firm Exemption," 68–72; Hiba Hafiz, "Labor Antitrust's Paradox," *University of Chicago Law Review* 87, no. 2 (2019): 381–412.

102. See Sydnee Caldwell and Suresh Naidu, "Wage and Employment Implications of U.S. Labor Market Monopsony and Possible Policy Solutions," in *Vision 2020: Evidence for a Stronger Economy* (Washington, DC: Washington Center for Equitable Growth, 2020), 33–43 (summarizing economic models of monopsony and evidence regarding monopsony power in US labor markets).

103. Elena Prager and Matt Schmitt, "Employer Consolidation and Wages: Evidence from Hospitals," *American Economic Review* 11, no. 2 (February 2021): 397–427.

104. Rachel Abrams, "7 Fast-Food Chains to End 'No Poach' Deals That Lock Down Low-Wage Workers," *New York Times*, July 12, 2018.

105. Prager and Schmitt, "Employer Consolidation and Wages." See also Benmelech et al., "Strong Employers and Weak Employees" (positing that unionization mitigates the effects of industrial concentration on wages).

106. See Nicholas Bloom, Fatih Guvenen, Benjamin S. Smith, Jae Song, and Till von Wachter, "The Disappearing Large-Firm Wage Premium," *AEA Papers and Proceedings* 108 (2018): 317–322 (presenting historical evidence of this phenomenon and its recent decline).

107. See generally Robert Solow, *The Labor Market as a Social Institution* (New York: Blackwell Publishers, 1990). While the large-firm premium has declined in recent years, many large companies have raised wages substantially in the wake of COVID. Michael Sasso, "McDonald's, Amazon Accelerate Push toward Higher Minimum Wage," *Bloomberg*, May 14, 2021. There are no guarantees that they will continue to do so to keep pace with inflation.

108. Bloom et al., "Disappearing Large-Firm Wage Premium."

109. See generally Julie E. Cohen, *Between Truth and Power: The Legal Constructions of Informational Capitalism* (New York: Oxford University Press, 2019), 15–47.

110. Cohen, *Truth and Power*, 37–46; Rahman, "Taming the New Corporate Power." See also generally Nick Srnicek, *Platform Capitalism* (Cambridge, UK: Polity Press, 2017).

111. Each site does, however, employ many content moderators who spend all day reviewing posts that others have flagged for child pornography, depictions of violence, or racist content. Many suffer serious emotional harm from the job. Sandra E. Garcia, "Ex-Content Moderator Sues Facebook, Saying Violent Images Caused Her PTSD," *New York Times*, September 25, 2018. Moreover, microprocessors depend on mining the rare-earth metals necessary for their manufacture, and the affordability of computers and new electronic devices depends on cheap electronics manufacturing—especially in China, where workers have no formal freedoms of speech or association and may face arrest and prosecution for seeking to organize independent unions. On labor practices in China, see Mary E. Gallagher, "China's Workers Movement and the End of the Rapid-Growth Era," *Daedalus: Journal of the American Academy of Arts & Sciences* 143, no. 2 (2014): 81–96.

112. See Khan, "Amazon's Antitrust Paradox," 780–783 (summarizing how Amazon gained market share by exploiting its access to consumer and vendor data); 748–754 (summarizing how Amazon gained market share by foregoing profits for a time).

113. See Khan, "Amazon's Antitrust Paradox," 774–777 (discussing Amazon's competition with delivery services such as UPS, which it and its competitors both utilize); 780–782 (discussing Amazon's exploitation of buyer and seller data to undercut vendors who sell on Amazon Marketplace).

114. Wallerstein, *World-Systems Analysis*, 54.

115. Kapczynski, "Law of Informational Capitalism," 1489. See also Cohen, *Truth and Power*, 42; Khan, "Amazon's Antitrust Paradox," 172 (both noting the tendency toward monopoly among platforms).

116. See Rosenblat, *Uberland*, 114, 129–132 (analyzing how Uber's algorithms may mislead drivers regarding the possibility of surge pricing). See also the discussion in chapter 3 of this book.

117. See generally Cohen, *Truth and Power*, 86–89.

118. Kapczynski, "Law of Informational Capitalism," 1489–1490.

119. Some platforms have implemented appeals processes for such decisions, which give them some indicia of legality. See generally Kate Klonick, "The Facebook Oversight Board: Creating an Independent Institution to Adjudicate Online Free Expression," *Yale Law Journal* 129, no. 8 (2020): 2418–2499.

120. On these and other challenges of regulating platforms, see generally Cohen, *Truth and Power*, 170–201.

121. Friedrich Hayek, "The Use of Knowledge in Society," *American Economic Review* 35, no. 4 (1945): 519.

122. Frank Pasquale, "Tech Platforms and the Knowledge Problem," *American Affairs* 2, no. 2 (Summer 2018): https://americanaffairsjournal.org/2018/05/tech-platforms-and-the-knowledge-problem/.

123. Rebecca A. Johnson and Tanina Rostain, "Tool for Surveillance or Spotlight on Inequality? Big Data and the Law," *Annual Review of Law and Social Science* 16 (2020): 453.

124. Brishen Rogers, "The Social Costs of Uber," *University of Chicago Law Review Dialogue* 82, no. 1 (2016): 89–90, 99–100.

125. Rogers, "The Social Costs of Uber," 96.

126. Brishen Rogers, "Fissuring, Data-Driven Governance, and Platform Economy Labor Standards," in *Cambridge Handbook of the Law of the Sharing Economy*, ed. Nestor M. Davidson, Michele Finck, and John J. Infranca (Cambridge: Cambridge University Press, 2018), 311–314.

127. Rogers, "Platform Economy Labor Standards," 311–312.

128. See, e.g., New York Attorney General, "Gristedes to Pay $3.2 Million in Back Wages and Fees in Deliverymen Case," December 17, 2003, https://ag.ny.gov/press-release/2003/gristedes-pay-325-million-back-wages-and-fees-deliverymen-case.

129. See generally Susan Sturm, "Second-Generation Employment Discrimination: A Structural Approach," *Columbia Law Review* 101, no. 3 (2001): 458–568; Cynthia Estlund, *Regoverning the Workplace: From Self-Regulation to Co-Regulation* (New Haven, CT: Yale University Press, 2010), 75–104.

130. *Faragher v. City of Boca Raton*, 118 S. Ct. 2275, 2293 (1998) (suggesting that a small employer may not need a written sexual harassment policy to avoid vicarious liability for a supervisor's hostile work environment harassment, but that a large employer almost surely would).

131. Noam Scheiber and Julie Creswell, "Sexual Harassment Cases Show the Ineffectiveness of Going to H.R.," *New York Times*, December 12, 2017.

132. Chen Liang, Yili Hong, and Bin Gu, "Does Monitoring Lead to a 'Warm' Start in Online Platforms?" August 31, 2016, https://papers.ssrn.com/sol3/papers.cfm?abstract_id=2838045.

133. *NLRB v. Catherine McAuley Health Ctr.*, 885 F.2d 341 (6th Cir. 1989).

Chapter 6

1. See Wolfgang Streeck, *Buying Time: The Delayed Crisis of Democratic Capitalism* (New York: Verso, 2014), 96 (arguing that under neoliberalism, capitalism is "emptied of democracy").

2. Erik Olin Wright, "Taking the Social in Socialism Seriously," *Socio-Economic Review* 10, no. 2 (2012): 387. See also Axel Honneth, *The Idea of Socialism: Towards a Renewal*, trans. Joseph Ganahl (Cambridge, UK: Polity Press, 2017), 88–89 (arguing that today, the socialist ideal requires democracy in all spheres of social action, including politics, economy, and civil society).

3. Ruth Dukes and Wolfgang Streeck, "Labor Constitutions and Occupational Communities: Social Norms and Legal Norms at Work," *Journal of Law & Society* 47, no. 4 (2020): 612–638; Ruth Dukes and Wolfgang Streeck, *Democracy at Work: Contract, Status and Post-Industrial Justice* (Cambridge, UK: Polity Press, forthcoming). For a complementary recent account of the role of labor law in delegating norm-authorship away from formal state institutions, see Guy Mundlak, *Organizing Matters: Two Logics of Trade Representation* (Cheltenham, UK: Edward Elgar Publishing, 2020), 27–28.

4. All of these issues are discussed in prior chapters of this book. In addition, on fissuring, see David Weil, *The Fissured Workplace: Why Work Became So Bad for So Many and What Can Be Done to Improve It* (Cambridge, MA: Harvard University Press). On management's capacity to resist unionization, see Paul Weiler, "Promises to Keep: Securing Workers' Rights to Self-Organization under the NLRA," *Harvard Law Review* 96, no. 8 (1983): 1769–1827; Craig Becker, "Democracy in the Workplace: Union Representation Elections and Federal Labor Law," *Minnesota Law Review* 77, no. 3 (1993): 495–603; and Benjamin I. Sachs, "Enabling Employee Choice: A Structural Approach to the Rules of Union Organizing," *Harvard Law Review* 123, no. 3 (2010): 655–728. On how our labor law restricts the right to strike, see James G. Pope, "How American Workers Lost the Right to Strike, and Other Tales," *Michigan Law Review* 103, no. 3: 518–553.

5. In recent years, scholars who have proposed far-reaching reforms to our labor laws have also emphasized the need to bolster local union representation. See Kate Andrias and Brishen Rogers, *Rebuilding Worker Voice in Today's Economy* (New York: Roosevelt Institute, 2018), 20–23 (proposing reforms to bolster enterprise-based unionization) and 26–33 (proposing more far-reaching reforms that would complement enterprise-based representation); Sharon Block and Benjamin Sachs, *Clean Slate for Worker Power: Building a Just Economy and Democracy* (Cambridge, MA; Harvard Labor and Worklife Program, 2020), 28–31 (proposing a set of reforms to "transform representation rights," explaining how they would interact with and build upon existing NLRA model of enterprise-based unionism).

6. Block and Sachs, *Clean Slate for Worker Power*, 2 ("Democracy at work should be a right, not a fight.").

7. Sachs, "Enabling Employee Choice," 659–660 (discussing the possibility of a union default); Brishen Rogers, "Libertarian Corporatism Is Not an Oxymoron," *Texas Law Review* 94, no. 7 (June 2016): 1642 (considering the possibility of default representation at the sectoral level); Michael M. Oswalt, "Automatic Elections," *University of California Irvine Law Review* 4, no. 2 (2014): 801–856 (proposing automatic union elections at regular intervals).

8. Oswalt, "Automatic Elections"; Andrew Strom, "Why Not Hold Union Representation Elections on a Regular Schedule," *OnLabor.org*, November 1, 2017, https://onlabor.org/why-not-hold-union-representation-elections-on-a-regular-schedule/.

9. Congress could also guarantee workers a voice at the company level via board seats as Senator Elizabeth Warren and others have proposed. Matthew Yglesias, "Elizabeth Warren Has a Plan to Save Capitalism," *Vox.com*, August 15, 2018, https://www.vox.com/2018/8/15/17683022/elizabeth-warren-accountable-capitalism-corporations. See also Isabelle Ferreras, *Firms as Political Entities: Saving Democracy through Economic Bicameralism*, trans. Miranda Richmond Mouillot (Cambridge: Cambridge University Press, 2020) (proposing a system of 50–50 bicameral governance in firms). There are various examples of worker representation on corporate boards in our own history. Ewan McGaughey, "Democracy in America at Work: The History of Labor's Vote in Corporate Governance," *Seattle University Law Review* 42, no. 2 (2019): 697–753.

10. 29 U.S.C. § 158(a)(2) (2018). See also *Electromation, Inc.*, 309 NLRB. 990, 998 (1992) (holding that an employer violated that provision of the NLRA by unilaterally establishing "action committees" of workers and management to address employee complaints).

11. For detailed proposals along these lines, see Block and Sachs, *Clean Slate for Worker Power*, 37–45; Andrias and Rogers, *Rebuilding Worker Voice*, 26–33; Mark Barenberg, *Widening the Scope of Worker Organizing: Legal Reforms to Facilitate Multi-Employer Organizing, Bargaining, and Striking* (New York: Roosevelt Institute, 2015).

12. In Germany, for example, most collective bargaining agreements are sectoral and negotiated at the regional level. In Italy, sectoral agreements typically cover the entire nation, but regional agreements are also permitted. In both countries, additional terms may be negotiated at the company level. "Living and Working in Germany," European Foundation for the Improvement of Living and Working Conditions, August 6, 2021, https://www.eurofound.europa.eu/country/germany; "Living and Working in Italy," European Foundation for the Improvement of Living and Working Conditions, August 9, 2021, https://www.eurofound.europa.eu/country/italy.

13. Jelle Visser and Daniele Checchi, "Inequality and the Labor Market: Unions," in *Oxford Handbook of Economic Inequality*, ed. Wiemer Salverda, Brian Nolan, and Timothy M. Smeeding (New York: Oxford University Press, 2011), 230–256. The overall complex of policies backing social bargaining also helps backstop social democratic

politics generally. See Streeck, *Buying Time*, 111 ("Central to the Keynesian political economy were the corporatist interest associations of labour and capital, together with the negotiating system established between them").

14. On the tensions between social bargaining and worksite bargaining, see Mundlak, *Two Logics*, 9–34, and 27–28.

15. Various labor law scholars have argued that the US legal regime encouraged such "business unionism" by foreclosing broad-based collective action. William E. Forbath, *Law and the Shaping of the American Labor Movement* (Cambridge, MA: Harvard University Press, 1991) (discussing the US labor movement's comparatively narrow political vision, which reflected decades of confrontation with the judiciary); Melvyn Dubofsky, "Book Review: Christopher L. Tomlins, *The State and the Unions: Labor Relations, Law, and the Organized Labor Movement in America, 1880–1960*," *Law and History Review* 4, no. 2 (1986): 472 (discussing the early history of NLRB, which set the stage for Taft-Hartley and more conservative unionism).

16. Kate Andrias, "An American Approach to Social Democracy: The Forgotten Promise of the Fair Labor Standards Act," *Yale Law Journal*, 128, no. 3 (January 2019): 625. Various state Departments of Labor retain the power to establish such committees under state law. Kate Andrias, "The New Labor Law," *Yale Law Journal* 126, no. 2 (2016): 83–86.

17. Andrias, "Forgotten Promise," 686.

18. Andrias and Rogers, "Rebuilding Worker Voice," 30–31; Block and Sachs, *Clean Slate for Worker Power*, 37–43. For an overview and analysis of important administrative law issues that such proposals may raise, see Andrias, "Forgotten Promise," 693–695.

19. See Block and Sachs, *Clean Slate for Worker Power*, 28–45. Congress could also approximate European "extension laws," for example, by requiring that employers in various sectors pay "prevailing wages," as is now often required in construction for public works and publicly funded projects. Block and Sachs, *Clean Slate for Worker Power*, 43–44.

20. Rideshare Drivers United rejected Uber and Lyft's proposal for what the companies termed a "sectoral bargaining" system in California, in part because it lacked a right to strike. Alexia Fernandez Campbell, "California Just Passed a Landmark Law to Regulate Uber and Lyft," *Vox.com*, September 18, 2019, https://www.vox.com/2019/9/11/20850878/california-passes-ab5-bill-uber-lyft.

21. Matthew Dimick, "Labor Law, New Governance, and the Ghent System," *North Carolina Law Review* 90, no. 2 (2012): 319–378 (arguing that the Ghent System enables significant union strength in Denmark and Sweden despite lack of union security devices in those nations).

22. Lucio Baccaro and Marco Simoni, "Policy Concentration in Europe: Understanding Government Choice," *Comparative Political Studies* 41, no. 10 (2007): 1323–1348.

23. "Social Dialogue," European Commission, accessed November 8, 2021, https://ec.europa.eu/social/main.jsp?catId=329&langId=en.

24. European Commission, *Digital Transformation Monitor, Germany: Industrie 4.0* (January 2017), https://ec.europa.eu/growth/tools-databases/dem/monitor/sites/default/files/DTM_Industrie%204.0.pdf.

25. See, e.g., "National Advisory Committee on Occupational Safety & Health," Occupational Safety and Health Administration, accessed November 8, 2021, https://www.osha.gov/dop/nacosh/nacosh.html (committee has two members representing labor).

26. Gary E. Marchant, "The Growing Gap Between Emerging Technologies and the Law," in *The Growing Gap between Emerging Technologies and Legal-Ethical Oversight: The Pacing Problem*, eds. Gary E. Marchant, Braden R. Allenby, and Joseph R. Herkert (New York: Springer, 2011), 19–33; Simon Deakin and Christopher Markou, "The Law-Technology Cycle and the Future of Work," *Giornale di Diritto del Lavoro e di Relazioni Industriali* 158, no. 2 (2018): 445–462.

27. See Astra Taylor, "The Insecurity Machine," *Logic Magazine*, May 4, 2020, https://logicmag.io/security/the-insecurity-machine (adding "de-digitize" to the contemporary movement slogan "decommodify, democratize, de-carbonize").

28. Ben Tarnoff, "From Manchester to Barcelona," *Logic Magazine*, December 7, 2019, https://logicmag.io/nature/from-manchester-to-barcelona. See also Taylor, "The Insecurity Machine."

29. Movement for Black Lives Policy Platform, "End Surveillance," accessed November 8, 2021, https://m4bl.org/policy-platforms/end-surveillance.

30. American Civil Liberties Union, "ACLU Comment on Appeals Court Ruling in No Fly List Challenge," October 21, 2019, https://www.aclu.org/press-releases/aclu-comment-appeals-court-ruling-no-fly-list-challenge.

31. See Julie E. Cohen, *Between Truth and Power: The Legal Constructions of Informational Capitalism* (New York: Oxford University Press, 2019), 90–93 (discussing this phenomenon and its ideological and legal roots).

32. Michael D. Birnhack, "A Quest for a Theory of Privacy," *Jurimetrics* 51, no. 4 (2011): 451 (noting that once technologies become "socially locked," they are difficult to displace or regulate).

33. See also American Law Institute, *Restatement of Employment Law*, 2nd ed. (St. Paul, MN: American Law Institute Publishers, 2015): §§ 7.02–7.05 (clarifying that employees have protected privacy interests in their person, physical and electronic locations, and information of a personal nature); and § 7.06 (employers are only liable for intrusions into those interests where that intrusion would be "highly offensive to a reasonable person").

34. Julie E. Cohen, "Turning Privacy inside Out," *Theoretical Inquiries in Law* 20, no. 1 (2019): 9.

35. See Pauline T. Kim, "Collective and Individual Approaches to Protecting Employee Privacy: The Experience with Workplace Drug Testing," *Louisiana Law Review* 66, no. 4 (2006): 1009–1034 (overview and critique of early drug testing laws).

36. Genetic Information Non-Discrimination Act, Pub.L. 110–233, 122 Stat. 881 (2008).

37. Marko Mrkonich, Allan King, Rod Fliegel, *The Big Move toward Big Data in Employment* (Littler Mendelson, P.C., August 2015): 14.

38. 18 U.S.C. § 2701 *et seq.* (2018). See also the discussion of this topic in chapter 2.

39. Annette Bernhardt, Lisa Kresge, and Reem Suleiman, *Data and Algorithms at Work: The Case for Worker Technology Rights* (Berkeley: University of California Berkeley Labor Center, November 2021): 22.

40. Bernhardt et al., *Data and Algorithms at Work*, 22, 23.

41. See the discussion of this topic in chapter 4.

42. Ira S. Rubinstein, "Regulating Privacy by Design," *Berkeley Technology Law Journal* 26, no. 3 (2011): 1408–1456.

43. Langdon Winner, *Autonomous Technology: Technics-out-of-Control as a Theme in Political Thought* (Cambridge, MA: MIT Press, 1977): 98–99. See also James Bessen, *Learning by Doing: The Real Connection between Innovation, Wages, and Wealth* (New Haven, CT: Yale University Press, 2015) (discussing the need to ensure that workers have adequate education and skills training to effectively incorporate new technologies).

44. Cynthia Estlund, *Working Together: How Workplace Bonds Strengthen a Diverse Democracy* (New York: Oxford University Press, 2003).

45. See the discussion of this topic in section 2.2 in chapter 2.

46. See Block and Sachs, *Clean Slate for Worker Power*, 67 (proposing that topics of bargaining be expanded to include "technology with impacts on job quality or employment levels"). See also Bernhardt et al., *Data and Algorithms at Work*, 24 (proposing that unions have the right to bargain around employers' use of data-driven technologies).

47. See Block and Sachs, *Clean Slate for Worker Power*, 33–34, 66 (proposing works councils with consultative rights, including around technology).

48. Dimick, "Ghent System," 330n49. See also European Trade Union Institute, "Workplace Participation: Germany," https://www.worker-participation.eu/National-Industrial-Relations/Countries/Germany/Workplace-Representation (accessed March 30, 2020) (summarizing legal rights of German works councils).

49. Jane McAlevey, "The West Virginia Teachers Strike Shows That Winning Big Requires Creating a Crisis," *The Nation*, March 12, 2018, https://www.thenation.com/article/archive/the-west-virginia-teachers-strike-shows-that-winning-big-requires-creating-a-crisis.

50. Juliana Feliciano Reyes, "Hotel Housekeeping on Demand: Marriott Cleaners Say This App Makes Their Job Harder," *Philadelphia Inquirer*, July 2, 2018. See also Sarah Holder, "Why Marriott Workers Are Striking," *Bloomberg CityLab*, October 19, 2018, https://www.bloomberg.com/news/articles/2018-10-19/marriott-staff-won-t-be-replaced-by-tech-without-a-fight.

51. Samantha Winslow, "Marriott Hotel Strikers Set a New Industry Standard," *Labor Notes*, December 20, 2018, https://labornotes.org/2018/12/marriott-hotel-strikers-set-new-industry-standard.

52. In sectors where technological innovation can substantially enhance productivity, robust bargaining rights may even want to be coupled with policies that *limit* labor costs for very productive firms, as under the Rehn-Meidner model, so that those firms have incentives to reinvest profits in innovation. See Lennart Erixon, "Progressive Supply-Side Economics: An Explanation and Update of the Rehn-Meidner Model," *Cambridge Journal of Economics* 42, no. 3 (2018): 653–697 (summarizing the Rehn-Meidner model). While productivity growth is tepid in most low-wage sectors today, productivity growth is decent in warehouses and advanced industrial policies may enable higher productivity growth in manufacturing and elsewhere.

53. Feliciano Reyes, "Hotel Housekeeping on Demand."

54. See Archon Fung and Erik Olin Wright, "Thinking about Empowered Participatory Governance," in *Deepening Democracy: Institutional Innovations in Empowered Participatory Governance*, eds. Archon Fung and Erik Olin Wright (London: Verso, 2003), 3, 5 (highlighting neighborhood governance councils, participatory budgeting, and other public processes as key areas for reform).

55. Anthony Giddens, *The Nation-State and Violence: Volume Two of a Contemporary Critique of Historical Materialism* (Cambridge, UK: Polity Press, 1985), 309. See also Rebecca A. Johnson and Tanina Rostain, "Tool for Surveillance or Spotlight on Inequality? Big Data and the Law," *Annual Review of Law and Social Science* 16 (2020): 453–472 (discussing various uses of novel data-driven technologies to advance public goals).

56. Anouk Ruhaak, "Data Trusts: What Are They and How Do They Work?," Blog, *The Royal Society for Arts, Manufactures, and Commerce*, June 11, 2020, https://www.thersa.org/blog/2020/06/data-trusts-protection.

57. Salomé Viljoen, "A Relational Theory for Data Governance," *Yale Law Journal* 131, no. 2 (2022): 645–647.

58. European Commission, *Proposal for a Regulation of the European Parliament and of the Council on a Single Market for Digital Services (Digital Services Act) and Amending*

Directive 2000/31/EC, COM (2020) 825 final (December 15, 2020), Article 31. See also Mathis Vermeulen, "The Keys to the Kingdom," *Knight First Amendment Institute at Columbia University*, July 27, 2021, https://knightcolumbia.org/content/the-keys-to-the-kingdom (discussing that proposal).

59. K. Sabeel Rahman, "Curbing the New Corporate Power," *Boston Review*, May 4, 2015, https://bostonreview.net/forum/k-sabeel-rahman-curbing-new-corporate-power.

60. Rahman also argues that more robust antitrust enforcement is part of the solution, so that dominant companies would be subjected to greater market competition or even broken up. Rahman, "Curbing the New Corporate Power."

61. Equal Employment Opportunity Commission, "EEO-1 Data Collection," accessed November 9, 2021, https://www.eeoc.gov/employers/eeo-1-survey.

62. *Excelsior Underwear*, 156 NLRB 111 (1966).

63. April Glaser, "Instacart Workers Are Striking because of the App's User Interface," *Slate*, Nov. 5, 2019, https://slate.com/business/2019/11/instacart-workers-striking-app-user-interface-dark-pattern-design.html; Kate Conger, Vicky Xiuzhong Xu, and Zach Wichter, "Uber Drivers' Day of Strikes Circles the Globe before the Company's I.P.O.," *New York Times*, May 8, 2019.

64. For a related proposal, see Block and Sachs, *Clean Slate for Worker Power*, 53 (recommending that workers be permitted to use "the full panoply of employer technology—Slack, Google Docs, online chat, or other means—to be in contact with co-workers during non-work time").

65. The Supreme Court has found such consumer communications important enough to protect them under the First Amendment, even in circumstances where they may have been prohibited by the NLRA as amended. *NLRB v. Fruit and Vegetable Packers and Warehousemen*, 377 U.S. 58, 71–73 (1964).

66. Si Se Puede Women's Cooperative, https://wecandoit.coop (accessed November 9, 2021) (domestic work); Ridefair, https://ridefair.io (accessed November 9, 2021) (taxi and ride share cooperative in Australia). See also Andrew Willis Garcés, "How Uber and Lyft Were Driven from Austin and Replaced with a Worker Cooperative," *Waging Nonviolence*, November 8, 2016, https://wagingnonviolence.org/2016/11/austin-uber-worker-coop (discussing the formation of a similar cooperative in Austin, Texas).

67. Trebor Scholz, "Platform Cooperativism vs. the Sharing Economy," *Medium.com*, December 5, 2014, https://medium.com/@trebors/platform-cooperativism-vs-the-sharing-economy-2ea737f1b5ad; Trebor Scholz and Nathan Schneider, eds., *Ours to Hack and Own: The Rise of Platform Cooperativism, a New Vision for the Future of Work and a Fairer Internet* (New York: OR Books, 2016).

68. Erik Olin Wright, *Envisioning Real Utopias* (London: Verso, 2010), 139.

69. See National Cooperative Business Association, https://ncbaclusa.coop/resources/7-cooperative-principles/ (accessed May 10, 2022) (listing seven principles of cooperative businesses, one of which is "democratic member control").

70. Michelle Camou, "Cities Developing Worker Co-ops: Efforts in Ten Cities," *Imagined Economy Project* (2016), http://imaginedeconomy.org/wp-content/uploads/2016/08/report3_citycoops.pdf (noting how cities have assisted cooperatives through financing and via preferences in procurement efforts).

71. Wright, *Envisioning Real Utopias*, 139–140.

72. See the discussion of this topic in chapter 4. See also Manish Raghavan, Solon Barocas, Jon Kleinberg, and Karen Levy, "Mitigating Bias in Algorithmic Hiring: Evaluating Claims and Practices," Cornell University, December 6, 2019, https://arxiv.org/abs/1906.09208 (providing an overview of the field, including companies' efforts to reduce bias).

73. US Equal Employment Opportunity Commission, "Press Release: EEOC Launches Initiative on Artificial Intelligence and Algorithmic Fairness," October 28, 2021, https://www.eeoc.gov/newsroom/eeoc-launches-initiative-artificial-intelligence-and-algorithmic-fairness.

74. Annette Zimmermann, Elena Di Rosa, and Hochin Kim, "Technology Can't Fix Algorithmic Injustice," *Boston Review*, January 9, 2020, https://bostonreview.net/science-nature-politics/annette-zimmermann-elena-di-rosa-hochan-kim-technology-cant-fix-algorithmic.

75. For a representative contemporary UBI proposal, see Andy Stern with Lee Kravitz, *Raising the Floor: How a Universal Basic Income Can Renew Our Economy and Rebuild the American Dream* (New York; PublicAffairs, 2016) (proposing a UBI of $12,000/year). For earlier UBI proposals, see Philippe Van Parijs, *Real Freedom for All: What (If Anything) Can Justify Capitalism?* (Oxford: Oxford University Press, 1997); Robert J. van der Veen and Philippe Van Parijs, "A Capitalist Road to Communism," *Theory and Society* 15, no. 6 (1986): 635–655.

76. Charles Murray, "A Guaranteed Income for All Americans," *Wall Street Journal*, June 3, 2016 (proposing a UBI that would replace "all other transfer payments and the bureaucracies that oversee them"). Murray's espousal of scientific racism in the past is well known and in my view diminishes the power of his UBI arguments.

77. Chris Weller, "The Inside Story of One Man's Mission to Give Americans Unconditional Free Money," *Business Insider*, June 26, 2016, https://www.businessinsider.com.au/inside-y-combinators-basic-income-project-2016-6.

78. There is another major problem with proposals that would do away with existing benefits: depending on its design, a UBI could easily exacerbate rather than alleviate racialized income gaps. For example, if a UBI were denied to formerly

incarcerated individuals or recent immigrants, that group could then become a permanent underclass of low-paid labor. Brishen Rogers, "Basic Income and the Resilience of Social Democracy," *Comparative Labor Law & Policy Journal* 40, no. 2 (2019): 116–118; Brishen Rogers, "Basic Income in a Just Society," *Boston Review*, May 15, 2017, https://bostonreview.net/forum/brishen-rogers-basic-income-just-society.

79. See Nick Srnicek and Alex Williams, *Inventing the Future: Postcapitalism and a World without Work*, 2nd ed. (London: Verso, 2016), 111 (asserting that "everyone from stock analysts to construction workers to chefs to journalists is vulnerable to being replaced by machines"), 117–123 (advocating for a UBI as a means of both transferring resources from rich to poor and democratizing the political economy).

80. Gøsta Esping-Andersen, *The Three Worlds of Welfare Capitalism* (Princeton, NJ: Princeton University Press, 1990), 37. See also Cynthia Estlund, "Three Big Ideas for a Future of Less Work and a Three-Dimensional Alternative," *Law and Contemporary Problems* 82, no. 3 (2019): 3–4 (arguing that a suite of programs—universal social benefits, expanded investment in care and infrastructure, and mandatory paid leave—would likely be as effective as a UBI and more politically palatable.).

81. Esping-Andersen, *Three Worlds*, 26–27; Frances Fox Piven and Richard A. Cloward, *Regulating the Poor: The Functions of Public Welfare* (New York: Vintage Books, 1972). Corporatist welfare states have been better in this regard, though they also link benefits to contributions, while Scandinavian or "social democratic" welfare states have provided more generous and universal benefits. Esping-Andersen, *Three Worlds*, 27–29.

82. See Wright, *Envisioning Real Utopias*, 219–220 (UBI would raise workers' reservation wage); Stern with Kravitz, *Raising the Floor*, 188 (UBI would be "the ultimate permanent strike fund").

83. *See* Gabriel Winant, *The Next Shift: The Fall of Industry and the Rise of Health Care in Rust Belt America* (Cambridge, MA: Harvard University Press, 2021), 2–4 (discussing the effects of socialization on job quality in a health-care context).

84. Esping-Andersen, *Three Worlds*, 26–28.

85. See Joshua Cohen and Joel Rogers, "My Utopia or Yours," *Politics & Society* 22, no. 4 (1994): 507–521 (making similar argument in the context of proposals for market socialism). See also Cynthia Estlund, "What Should We Do After Work? Automation and Employment Law," *Yale Law Journal* 128, no. 2 (2018): 282n120 (explicitly setting aside the relationship between collective bargaining and automation, but stating plans to return to the issue in future work).

86. While the US hasn't always had an explicit industrial policy, it has long had a tacit industrial policy around military spending, including technological development efforts through the Defense Advanced Research Projects Agency (DARPA). See

Fred L. Block and Matthew R. Keller, *State of Innovation: The U.S. Government's Role in Technology Development* (New York: Routledge, 2011).

87. Dani Rodrik and Charles Sabel, "Building a Good Jobs Economy," in *A Political Economy of Justice*, eds. Danielle Allen, Yochai Benkler, Leah Downey, Rebecca Henderson, and Josh Simons (Chicago: University of Chicago Press, 2022), 61–95 (proposing policies to encourage greater technological diffusion); Frank Pasquale, *New Laws of Robotics: Defending Human Expertise in the Age of AI* (Cambridge, MA: Belknap Press, 2020), 170–198 (discussing the political economy of automation and the possibility of upskilling or increasing the autonomy of nonprofessional jobs); David H. Autor, "Polanyi's Paradox and the Shape of Employment Growth," in *Re-Evaluating Labor Market Dynamics* (Kansas City, MO: Federal Reserve Bank of Kansas City, 2015), 163–164 (calling for policy reforms that would encourage the use of inductive learning technologies to complement semi-professional workers such as phlebotomists); Joshua Cohen, "Research Brief: Good Jobs," MIT Task Force on Work of the Future, October 29, 2020, https://workofthefuture.mit.edu/research-post/good-jobs (proposing similar reforms). On the applicability of such efforts in service workplaces, see Zeynep Ton, *The Good Jobs Strategy: How the Smartest Companies Invest in Employees to Lower Costs and Boost Profits* (Boston: Houghton Mifflin Harcourt, 2014).

88. Varshini Prakash and Guido Girgenti, eds., *Winning the Green New Deal: Why We Must, How We Can* (New York: Simon & Schuster, 2020). See also Movement for Black Lives (M4BL), *2020 Policy Platform*, https://m4bl.org/policy-platforms (accessed November 10, 2021) (proposing interrelated policy reforms to advance economic justice and reshape our political economy).

89. See Kate Aronoff, Alyssa Battistoni, Daniel Aldana Cohen, and Thea Riofrancos, "Strike for Sunshine: To Defeat Fossil Fuel, We Need a Low-Carbon Labor Movement," *The Nation*, November 20, 2019, https://www.thenation.com/article/archive/green-newdeal-labor-movement (observing that "care and education are inherently low-carbon work").

90. For a helpful discussion that links workers' rights to questions of industrial policy and normative theory, see Cohen, "Good Jobs."

91. Jonah Furman and Gabriel Winant, "The John Deere Strike Shows the Tight Labor Market Is Ready to Pop," *The Intercept*, October 17, 2021, https://theintercept.com/2021/10/17/john-deere-strike-labor-market.

92. For a recent discussion of how political parties can use policy levers to demobilize opposing parties, see Alexander Hertel-Fernandez, "Asymmetric Partisan Polarization, Labor Policy, and Cross-State Political Power-Building," *Annals of the American Academy of Political and Social Science* 685, no. 1 (2019): 64–79. See also Paul Pierson, "When Effect Becomes Cause: Policy Feedback and Political Change," *World Politics* 45, no. 4 (July 1993): 595–628.

93. Kathleen Foody and Don Babwin, "Affordable Housing among Chicago Teachers' Demands," Associated Press, October 21, 2019, https://apnews.com/article/chicago-schools-us-news-il-state-wire-strikes-ca-state-wire-7bc567d71d974a8789ffe955df254b02.

Afterword

1. See Julie E. Cohen, "What Privacy Is For," *Harvard Law Review* 126, no. 7 (May 2013): 1922 (noting the influence of "technological sublime" in the US). See also Langdon Winner, *Autonomous Technology: Technics-out-of-Control as a Theme in Political Thought* (Cambridge, MA: MIT Press, 1977).

Selected Bibliography

Acemoglu, Daron. "Technical Change, Inequality, and the Labor Market." *Journal of Economic Literature* 40, no. 2 (March 2002): 7–72.

Acemoglu, Daron, and Pascual Restrepo. "Robots and Jobs: Evidence from U.S. Labor Markets." *Journal of Political Economy* 128, no. 6 (2020): 2188–2244.

Acemoglu, Daron, and Pascual Restrepo. "The Wrong Kind of AI? Artificial Intelligence and the Future of Labour Demand." *Cambridge Journal of Regions, Economy, and Society* 13, no. 1 (March 2020): 25–35.

Adams-Prassl, Jeremias. "What If Your Boss Was an Algorithm: Economic Incentives, Legal Challenges, and the Rise of Artificial Intelligence at Work." *Comparative Labor Law and Policy Journal* 41, no.1 (2019): 123–146.

Ajunwa, Ifeoma. "Age Discrimination by Platforms." *Berkeley Journal of Employment and Labor Law* 40, no. 1 (2019): 1–27.

Akerlof, George A. "Labor Contracts as Partial Gift Exchange." *Quarterly Journal of Economics* 97, no. 4 (November 1982): 543–569.

Alchian, Armen A., and Harold Demsetz. "Production, Information Costs, and Economic Organization." *American Economic Review* 62, no. 5 (December 1972): 777–795.

Anderson, Elizabeth. *Private Government: How Employers Rule Our Lives (and Why We Don't Talk about It)*. Princeton, NJ: Princeton University Press, 2017.

Anderson, James M., Nidhi Kalra, Karlyn D. Stanley, Paul Sorensen, Constantine Samaras, and Tobi A. Oluwatola. *Autonomous Vehicle Technology: A Guide for Policymakers*. Santa Monica, CA: Rand Corporation, 2016.

Andrias, Kate. "An American Approach to Social Democracy: The Forgotten Promise of the Fair Labor Standards Act." *Yale Law Journal* 128, no. 3 (January 2019): 616–709.

Andrias, Kate. "The New Labor Law." *Yale Law Journal* 126, no. 2 (2016): 2–100.

Andrias, Kate. "Union Rights for All: Toward Sectoral Bargaining in the United States." In *Cambridge Handbook of Labor Law for the Twenty-First Century*, edited by Richard Bales and Charlotte Garden, 56–63. Cambridge: Cambridge University Press, 2019.

Andrias, Kate, and Brishen Rogers. *Rebuilding Worker Voice in Today's Economy*. New York: Roosevelt Institute, 2018.

Andrias, Kate, and Alexander Hertel-Fernandez. *Ending At-Will Employment: A Guide for Just Cause Reform*. New York: Roosevelt Institute, 2021.

Anner, Mark, Jennifer Bair, and Jeremy Blasi. "Learning from the Past: The Relevance of Twentieth-Century New York Jobbers' Agreements for Twenty-First-Century Global Supply Chains." In *Achieving Workers' Rights in the Global Economy*, edited by Richard P. Appelbaum and Nelson Lichtenstein, 239–258. Ithaca, NY: ILR Press, 2016.

Atkinson, Robert D., and John Wu. "False Alarmism: Technological Disruption and the U.S. Labor Market, 1850–2015." *Information Technology & Innovation Foundation*. May 8, 2017, https://itif.org/publications/2017/05/08/false-alarmism-technological-disruption-and-us-labor-market-1850-2015.

Autor, David H. "Polanyi's Paradox and the Shape of Employment Growth." In *Re-Evaluating Labor Market Dynamics*, 129–179. Kansas City, MO: Federal Reserve Bank of Kansas City, 2015.

Autor, David H., and David Dorn. "The Growth of Low-Skill Service Jobs and the Polarization of the US Labor Market." *American Economic Review* 103, no. 5 (August 2013): 1553–1597.

Autor, David, David Dorn, Lawrence F. Katz, Christina Patterson, and John Van Reenen. "The Fall of the Labor Share and the Rise of Superstar Firms." *Quarterly Journal of Economics* 135, no. 2 (2020): 645–709.

Azar, José, Ioana Marinescu, and Marshall Steinbaum. "Labor Market Concentration." *Journal of Human Resources* 57, no. S (April 2022): S167–S199.

Azulay, Aharon, and Yair Weiss. "Why Do Deep Convolutional Networks Generalize So Poorly to Small Image Transformations?" *Journal of Machine Learning Research* 20 (2019): 1–25.

Baccaro, Lucio, and Chris Howell. *Trajectories of Neoliberal Transformation: European Industrial Relations Since the 1970s*. Cambridge: Cambridge University Press, 2017.

Baccaro, Lucio, and Jonas Pontusson. "Rethinking Comparative Political Economy: The Growth Model Perspective." *Politics & Society* 44, no. 2 (2016): 175–207.

Baccaro, Lucio, and Marco Simoni. "Policy Concentration in Europe: Understanding Government Choice." *Comparative Political Studies* 41, no. 10 (2007): 1323–1348.

Selected Bibliography

Bagenstos, Samuel R. "Consent, Coercion, and Employment Law." *Harvard Civil Rights–Civil Liberties Law Review* 55 (2020): 225–273.

Bagenstos, Samuel R. "Employment Law and Social Equality." *Michigan Law Review* 112, no. 2 (2013): 225–273.

Bagenstos, Samuel R. "The Structural Turn and the Limits of Antidiscrimination Law." *California Law Review* 94, no. 1 (2006): 40–45.

Bales, Richard A., and Katherine V. W. Stone. "The Invisible Web at Work: Artificial Intelligence and Electronic Surveillance in the Workplace." *Berkeley Journal of Employment and Labor Law* 41, no. 1 (2020): 1–60.

Ball, Kirstie. "Workplace Surveillance: An Overview." *Labor History* 51, no. 1 (February 2010): 87–106.

Barenberg, Mark. "Democracy and Domination in the Law of Workplace Cooperation: From Bureaucratic to Flexible Production." *Columbia Law Review* 94, no. 3 (1994): 753–983.

Barenberg, Mark. *Widening the Scope of Worker Organizing: Legal Reforms to Facilitate Multi-Employer Organizing, Bargaining, and Striking*. New York: Roosevelt Institute, 2015.

Barocas, Solon, and Andrew D. Selbst. "Big Data's Disparate Impact." *California Law Review* 104, no. 3 (June 2016): 671–732.

Barrett, Lisa Feldman, Ralph Adolphs, Stacy Marsella, Aleix M. Martinez, and Seth D. Pollak. "Emotional Expressions Reconsidered: Challenges to Inferring Emotion from Human Facial Movements." *Psychological Science in the Public Interest* 20, no. 1 (2019): 1–68.

Bastani, Aaron. *Fully Automated Luxury Communism: A Manifesto*. New York: Verso, 2020.

Batt, Rosemary, and Hiroatsu Nohara. "How Institutions and Business Strategies Affect Wages: A Cross-National Study of Call Centers." *Industrial & Labor Relations Review* 62, no. 4 (2009): 533–552.

Baumol, William J. "Macroeconomics of Unbalanced Growth: The Anatomy of Urban Crisis." *American Economic Review* 57, no. 3 (1967): 415–426.

Becker, Craig. "Better than a Strike: Protecting New Forms of Collective Work Stoppages under the National Labor Relations Act." *University of Chicago Law Review* 61, no. 2 (1994): 351–421.

Becker, Craig. "Democracy in the Workplace: Union Representation Elections and Federal Labor Law." *Minnesota Law Review* 77, no. 3 (1993): 495–603.

Bell, Daniel. *The Coming of Post-Industrial Society*. New York: Basic Books, 1973.

Bell, Daniel. "The Treaty of Detroit." *Fortune*, July 1950.

Benanav, Aaron. *Automation and the Future of Work*. London: Verso, 2020.

Benassi, Chiara, Lisa Dorigatti, and Elisa Pannini. "Explaining Divergent Bargaining Outcomes for Agency Workers: The Role of Labor Divides and Labour Market Reforms." *European Journal of Industrial Relations* 25, no. 2 (2018): 163–179.

Beniger, James R. *The Control Revolution: Technological and Economic Origins of the Information Society*. Cambridge, MA: Harvard University Press, 1989.

Benkler, Yochai. *A Political Economy of Oligarchy: Winner-Take-All Ideology, Superstar Norms, and the Rise of the 1%*. Unpublished manuscript, September 2017. PDF. http://www.benkler.org/Political%20economy%20of%20oligarchy%2001.pdf.

Benkler, Yochai. "Power and Productivity: Institutions, Ideology, and Technology in Political Economy." In *A Political Economy of Justice*, edited by Danielle Allen, Yochai Benkler, Leah Downey, Rebecca Henderson, and Josh Simons, 27–60. Chicago: University of Chicago Press, 2021.

Benkler, Yochai. "The Role of Technology in Political Economy: Part 3." *LPE Project*, July 27, 2018, https://lpeproject.org/blog/the-role-of-technology-in-political-economy-part-3.

Benkler, Yochai. *The Wealth of Networks: How Social Production Transforms Markets and Freedom*. New Haven, CT: Yale University Press, 2006.

Benmelech, Efraim, Nittai Bergman, and Hyunseob Kim. "Strong Employers and Weak Employees: How Does Employer Concentration Affect Wages?" *Journal of Human Resources* 57, no. S (April 2022): S200–S250

Berlinski, Samuel. "Wages and Contracting Out: Does the Law of One Price Hold?" *British Journal of Industrial Relations* 46, no. 1 (2008): 59–75.

Bernhardt, Annette, James DeFilippis, and Siobhan McGrath. *Unregulated Work in the Global City: Employment and Labor Law Violations in New York City*. Washington, DC: Brennan Center for Justice, 2007.

Bernhardt, Annette, Lisa Kresge, and Reem Suleiman. *Data and Algorithms at Work: The Case for Worker Technology Rights*. Berkeley: University of California Berkeley Labor Center, November 2021.

Bessen, James. *Learning by Doing: The Real Connection between Innovation, Wages, and Wealth*. New Haven, CT: Yale University Press, 2015.

Birnhack, Michael D. "A Quest for a Theory of Privacy." *Jurimetrics* 51, no. 4 (2011): 447–479.

Block, Fred L., and Matthew R. Keller. *State of Innovation: The U.S. Government's Role in Technology Development*. New York: Routledge, 2011.

Block, Sharon, and Benjamin Sachs. *Clean Slate for Worker Power: Building a Just Economy and Democracy*. Cambridge, MA: Harvard Labor and Worklife Program, 2020.

Selected Bibliography

Bloom, Nicholas, Fatih Guvenen, Benjamin S. Smith, Jae Song, and Till von Wachter. "The Disappearing Large-Firm Wage Premium." *AEA Papers and Proceedings* 108 (2018): 317–322.

Bodie, Matthew T., Miriam A. Cherry, Marcia L. McCormick, and Jintong Tang. "The Law and Policy of People Analytics." *University of Colorado Law Review* 88, no. 4 (2017): 961–1042.

Bohn, R.E. "From Art to Science in Manufacturing: The Evolution of Technological Knowledge." *Foundations and Trends in Technology, Information, and Operations Management* 1, no. 2 (2005): 1–82.

Boris, Eileen, and Jennifer Klein. *Caring for America: Home Health Workers in the Shadow of the Welfare State*. Oxford: Oxford University Press, 2012.

Bostrom, Nick. *Superintelligence: Paths, Dangers, Strategies*. Oxford: Oxford University Press, 2014.

Bourdieu, Pierre. *Distinction: A Social Critique of the Judgement of Taste*. Translated by Richard Nice. London: Routledge Classics, 1984.

Bowles, Samuel. "The Production Process in a Competitive Economy: Walrasian, Neo-Hobbesian, and Marxian Models." *American Economic Review* 75, no. 1 (March 1985): 16–36.

Bowles, Samuel. "Social Institutions and Technical Change." In *Technological and Social Factors in Long Term Fluctuations*, edited by Massimo Di Matteo, Richard M. Goodwin, and Alessandro Vercelli, 67–88. New York: Springer-Verlag, 1986.

Bowles, Samuel, and Herbert Gintis. "Contested Exchange: New Microfoundations for the Political Economy of Capitalism." *Politics and Society* 18, no. 2 (1990): 165–222.

Boyle, James. "The Second Enclosure Movement and the Construction of the Public Domain." *Law and Contemporary Problems* 66, no. 1–2 (2003): 33–74.

Braverman, Harry. *Labor and Monopoly Capital*. New York: Monthly Review Press, 1974.

Britton-Purdy, Jedediah, David Singh Grewal, Amy Kapczynski, and K. Sabeel Rahman. "Building a Law-and-Political-Economy Framework: Beyond the Twentieth-Century Synthesis." *Yale Law Journal* 129, no. 6 (2020): 1784–1835.

Bronfenbrenner, Kate, and Dorian Warren. "The Empirical Case for Streamlining the NLRB Certification Process: The Role of Date of Unfair Labor Practice Occurrence." Institute for Social and Economic Research and Policy Working Paper Series (June 2011). https://digitalcommons.ilr.cornell.edu/workingpapers/159.

Brown, Wendy. *Undoing the Demos: Neoliberalism's Stealth Revolution*. Princeton, NJ: Princeton University Press, 2015.

Browne, Simone. "Race and Surveillance." In *Routledge Handbook of Surveillance Studies*, edited by Kirstie Ball, Kevin D. Haggerty, and David Lyon, 72–80. London: Routledge, 2012.

Brudney, James J. "Card Check and Neutrality: Prospect for Changing Paradigms." *Iowa Law Review* 90, no. 3 (2005): 819–886.

Brynjolfsson, Erik, and Andrew McAfee. *The Second Machine Age: Work, Progress, and Prosperity in a Time of Brilliant Technologies*. New York: W. W. Norton & Company, 2014.

Brynjolfsson, Erik, and Kristina McElheran. "Data in Action: Data-Driven Decision Making in U.S. Manufacturing." U.S. Census Bureau, Center for Economic Studies, Paper No. CES-WP-16–06 (January 2016), http://dx.doi.org/10.2139/ssrn.2722502.

Brynjolfsson, Erik, Lorin Hitt, and Shinkyu Yang. "Intangible Assets: Computers and Organizational Capital," *Brookings Papers on Economic Activity* (2002). https://www.brookings.edu/bpea-articles/intangible-assets-computers-and-organizational-capital/.

Caldwell, Sydnee, and Suresh Naidu. "Wage and Employment Implications of U.S. Labor Market Monopsony and Possible Policy Solutions." In *Vision 2020: Evidence for a Stronger Economy*, 33–43. Washington, DC: Washington Center for Equitable Growth, 2020.

Callaci, Brian. "Vertical Power and the Creation of a Fissured Workplace: The Case of Franchising." PhD diss., University of Massachusetts at Amherst, 2019. https://scholarworks.umass.edu/dissertations_2/1696.

Calo, Ryan, and Alex Rosenblat. "The Taking Economy: Uber, Information, and Power." *Columbia Law Review* 117, no. 6 (2017): 1623–1690.

Castells, Manuel. "Materials for an Exploratory Theory of the Network Society." *British Journal of Sociology* 51, no. 1 (March 2000): 5–24.

Castells, Manuel, *The Information Age, Vol. 1: The Rise of the Network Society*, 2nd ed. West Sussex, UK: Wiley & Sons, 2010.

Chadwick, Andrew. *Internet Politics: States, Citizens, and New Communication Technologies*. Oxford: Oxford University Press, 2006.

Chander, Anupam, Margot E. Kaminski, and William McGeveran. "Catalyzing Privacy Law." *Minnesota Law Review* 105, no. 4 (2021): 1746–1762.

Ciresan, Dan, Ueli Meier, and Jürgen Schmidhuber. "Multi-Column Deep Neural Networks for Image Classification." *2012 IEEE Conference on Computer Vision and Pattern Recognition* (2012): 3642–3649.

Citron, Danielle, and Frank Pasquale. "The Scored Society: Due Process for Automated Predictions." *Washington Law Review* 89, no. 1 (2014): 1–33.

Clegg, John. "A Theory of Capitalist Slavery." *Journal of Historical Sociology* 33 (2020): 74–98.

Cobble, Dorothy Sue. *The Other Women's Movement: Workplace Justice and Social Rights in Modern America*. Princeton, NJ: Princeton University Press, 2003.

Cohen, Joshua. "Research Brief: Good Jobs." MIT Task Force on Work of the Future, October 29, 2020, https://workofthefuture.mit.edu/research-post/good-jobs.

Cohen, Joshua, and Joel Rogers. "My Utopia or Yours." *Politics & Society* 22, no. 4 (1994): 507–521.

Cohen, Joshua, and Joel Rogers. "Secondary Associations and Democratic Governance." In *Associations and Democracy*, edited by Erik Olin Wright, 7–100. New York: Verso, 1995.

Cohen, Julie E. *Between Truth and Power: The Legal Constructions of Informational Capitalism*. New York: Oxford University Press, 2019.

Cohen, Julie E. "The Biopolitical Public Domain: The Legal Construction of the Surveillance Economy." *Philosophy & Technology* 31, no. 2 (2018): 213–233.

Cohen, Julie E. "Review of Zuboff's *The Age of Surveillance Capitalism: The Fight for a Human Future at the New Frontier of Power*." *Surveillance & Society* 17, nos. 1–2 (2019): 240–245.

Cohen, Julie E. "Turning Privacy inside Out." *Theoretical Inquiries in Law* 20, no. 1 (2019): 1–31.

Cohen, Julie E. "What Privacy Is For." *Harvard Law Review* 126, no. 7 (May 2013): 1904–1933.

Cohen, Morris R. "Property and Sovereignty." *Cornell Law Review* 13, no. 8 (December 1927): 8–30.

Cook, Cody, Rebecca Diamond, Jonathan V. Hall, John A. List, and Paul Oyer. "The Gender Earnings Gap in the Gig Economy: Evidence from over a Million Rideshare Drivers." Working paper, National Bureau of Economic Research, Cambridge, MA, June 2018.

Cowgill, Bo, and Catherine Tucker. "Algorithmic Bias: A Counterfactual Perspective." Working paper, *NSF Trustworthy Algorithms*, Arlington, VA, December 2017.

Cox, Archibald. "Labor Law Preemption Revisited." *Harvard Law Review* 85, no. 7 (1972): 1337–1377.

Crain, Marion, and Ken Matheny. "Labor's Identity Crisis." *California Law Review* 89, no. 6 (December 2001): 1767–1846.

Cramer, Judd, and Alan B. Krueger. "Disruptive Change in the Taxi Business: The Case of Uber." *American Economic Review* 106, no. 5 (May 2016): 177–182.

Crenshaw, Kimberlé. "Demarginalizing the Intersection of Race and Sex: A Black Feminist Critique of Antidiscrimination Doctrine, Feminist Theory and Antiracist Politics." *University of Chicago Legal Forum* 1989 (1989): 139–167.

Deakin, Simon, and Christopher Markou. "The Law-Technology Cycle and the Future of Work." *Giornale di Diritto del Lavoro e di Relazioni Industriali* 158, no. 2 (2018): 445–462.

Deakin, Simon, David Gindis, Geoffrey M. Hodgson, Kainan Huang, and Katharina Pistor. "Legal Institutionalism: Capitalism and the Constitutive Role of Law." *Journal of Comparative Economics* 45 (February 2017): 188–200.

Della Porta, Donatella, and Lorenzo Mosca. "Global-net for Global Movements? A Network of Networks for a Movement of Movements." *Journal of Public Policy* 25, no. 1 (2005): 165–190.

De Stefano, Valerio. "'Negotiating the Algorithm': Automation, Artificial Intelligence and Labour Protection." *Comparative Labor Law and Policy Journal* 41, no. 1 (2019): 15–46.

Determann, Lothar. "No One Owns Data." *Hastings Law Journal* 70, no. 1 (2018): 1–44.

Dey, Sandipan. "Dogs vs. Cats: Image Classification with Deep Learning Using TensorFlow in Python." *Data Science Central*, August 14, 2017, https://perma.cc/B8RW-AEGW.

Dimick, Matthew. "Labor Law, New Governance, and the Ghent System." *North Carolina Law Review* 90, no. 2 (2012): 319–378.

Dimick, Matthew. "Productive Unionism." *University of California Irvine Law Review* 4, no. 2 (2014): 679–724.

Doellgast, Virginia. "Collective Voice under Decentralized Bargaining: A Comparative Study of Work Reorganization in U.S. and German Call Centres." *British Journal of Industrial Relations* 48, no. 2 (June 2010): 375–399.

Domingos, Pedro. *The Master Algorithm: How the Quest for the Ultimate Learning Machine Will Remake Our World*. New York: Basic Books, 2015.

Dubofsky, Melvyn. "Book Review: Christopher L. Tomlins, *The State and the Unions: Labor Relations, Law, and the Organized Labor Movement in America, 1880–1960*." *Law and History Review* 4, no. 2 (1986): 470–473.

Dubovsky, Melvin. "Legal Theory and Workers' Rights: A Historian's Critique." *Industrial Relations Law Journal* 4, no. 3 (June 1981): 496–502.

Dukes, Ruth. "Constitutionalizing Employment Relations: Sinzheimer, Kahn-Freund, and the Role of Labour Law." *Journal of Law & Society* 35, no. 3 (September 2008): 341–363.

Dukes, Ruth, and Wolfgang Streeck. *Democracy at Work: Contract, Status and Post-Industrial Justice*. Cambridge, UK: Polity Press, forthcoming.

Selected Bibliography

Dukes, Ruth, and Wolfgang Streeck. "Labor Constitutions and Occupational Communities: Social Norms and Legal Norms at Work." *Journal of Law & Society* 47, no. 4 (2020): 612–638.

Dunlop, John T. *Industrial Relations Systems*. New York: Henry Holt & Co., 1958.

Draut, Tamara. *Sleeping Giant: How the New Working Class Will Transform America*. New York: Penguin, 2016.

Ehrenreich, Barbara. *Nickel and Dimed: On (Not) Getting by in America*. New York: Macmillan, 2011.

Eltantawy, Nahed, and Julie B. Wiest. "Social Media in the Egyptian Revolution: Reconsidering Resource Mobilization Theory." *International Journal of Communication* 5 (2011): 1207–1224.

Epstein, Richard. "A Common Law for Labor Relations: A Critique of the New Deal Labor Legislation." *Yale Law Journal* 92, no. 8 (1983): 1357–1408.

Erixon, Lennart. "Progressive Supply-Side Economics: An Explanation and Update of the Rehn-Meidner Model." *Cambridge Journal of Economics* 42 (May 2018): 653–697.

Esping-Andersen, Gøsta. *Social Foundations of Postindustrial Economies*. Oxford: Oxford University Press, 1999.

Esping-Andersen, Gøsta. *The Three Worlds of Welfare Capitalism*. Princeton, NJ: Princeton University Press, 1990.

Estlund, Cynthia. "Labor, Property, and Sovereignty after Lechmere." *Stanford Law Review* 46, no. 2 (1994): 305–359.

Estlund, Cynthia. "The Ossification of American Labor Law." *Columbia Law Review* 102, no. 6 (October 2002): 1527–1612.

Estlund, Cynthia. *Regoverning the Workplace: From Self-Regulation to Co-Regulation*. New Haven, CT: Yale University Press, 2010.

Estlund, Cynthia. "Rethinking Autocracy at Work." *Harvard Law Review* 131, no. 3 (2018): 795–826.

Estlund, Cynthia. "Three Big Ideas for a Future of Less Work and a Three-Dimensional Alternative," *Law and Contemporary Problems* 82, no. 3 (2019): 1–43.

Estlund, Cynthia. "What Should We Do after Work? Automation and Employment Law." *Yale Law Journal* 128, no. 2 (2018): 254–326.

Estlund, Cynthia. *Working Together: How Workplace Bonds Strengthen a Diverse Democracy*. New York: Oxford University Press, 2003.

Estlund, Cynthia, and Michael L. Wachter, eds. *Research Handbook on the Economics of Labor and Employment Law*. Northampton, MA: Edward Elgar Publishing, 2012.

Eubanks, Virginia. *Automating Inequality: How High-Tech Tools Profile, Police, and Punish the Poor*. New York: St. Martin's Press, 2018.

European Commission. *Proposal for a Directive of the European Parliament and of the Council on Improving Working Conditions in Platform Work*. COM(2021) 762 final, December 9, 2021.

European Commission, *Proposal for a Regulation of the European Parliament and of the Council on a Single Market for Digital Services (Digital Services Act) and Amending Directive 2000/31/EC*. COM(2020) 825 final. December 15, 2020.

Fantasia, Rick. *Cultures of Solidarity: Consciousness, Action, and Contemporary American Workers*. Berkeley: University of California Press, 1989.

Farhang, Sean, and Ira Katznelson. "The Southern Imposition: Congress and Labor in the New Deal and Fair Deal." *Studies in American Political Development* 19, no. 1 (Spring 2005): 1–30.

Federal Trade Commission. *Big Data: A Tool for Inclusion or Exclusion?* Report, January 2016, https://www.ftc.gov/system/files/documents/reports/big-data-tool-inclusion-or-exclusion-understanding-issues/160106big-data-rpt.pdf.

Feinman, Jay M. "The Development of the Employment at Will Rule." *American Journal of Legal History* 20, no. 2 (1976): 118–135.

Ferreras, Isabelle. *Firms as Political Entities: Saving Democracy through Economic Bicameralism*. Translated by Miranda Richmond Mouillot. Cambridge: Cambridge University Press, 2020.

Finkin, Matthew W. "Employee Privacy, American Values, and the Law: The Kenneth M. Piper Lecture." *Chicago-Kent Law Review* 72, no. 1 (1996): 221–269.

Finkin, Matthew W. "*Menschenbild*: The Conception of the Employee as a Person in Western Law." *Comparative Labor Law & Policy Journal* 23, no. 2 (2002): 577–637.

Finkin, Matthew W. *Privacy in Employment Law*, 5th ed. Washington, DC: Bloomberg Law, 2018.

Finkin, Matthew W., Rudiger Krause, and Hisashi Takeuchi-Okuno. "Employee Autonomy, Privacy, and Dignity under Technological Oversight." In *Comparative Labor Law*, edited by Matthew F. Finkin and Guy Mundlak, 153–194. Cheltenham, UK: Edward Elgar, 2015.

Fischl, Michael. "Rethinking the Tripartite Division of American Work Law." *Berkeley Journal of Employment & Labor Law* 28, no. 1 (2007): 163–216.

Fischl, Michael. "Self, Others, and Section 7: Mutualism and Protected Protest Activities under the National Labor Relations Act." *Columbia Law Review* 89, no. 4 (1989): 789–865.

Selected Bibliography

Fisher, William W. III. *The Growth of Intellectual Property: A History of the Ownership of Ideas in the United States.* Self-published, 1999, https://cyber.harvard.edu/people/tfisher/iphistory.pdf.

Fisk, Catherine. *Working Knowledge: Employee Innovation and the Rise of Corporate Intellectual Property, 1800–1930.* Chapel Hill: University of North Carolina Press, 2009.

Forbath, William E. *Law and the Shaping of the American Labor Movement.* Cambridge, MA: Harvard University Press, 1991.

Foucault, Michel. *The Birth of Biopolitics: Lectures at the Collège de France, 1978–79.* Edited by Michel Senellart; translated by Graham Burchell. London: Palgrave Macmillan, 2008.

Foucault, Michel. *Discipline and Punish: The Birth of the Prison.* Translated by Alan Sheridan. New York: Pantheon Books, 1979.

Fourcade, Marion, and Jeffrey Gordon. "Learning Like a State: Statecraft in the Digital Age." *Journal of Law and P olitical Economy* 1, no. 1 (2020): 78–108.

Frankfurter, Felix, and Nathan Greene. *The Labor Injunction.* New York: Macmillan, 1930.

Fraser, Steve, and Gary Gerstle, eds. *The Rise and Fall of the New Deal Order, 1930–1980.* Princeton, NJ: Princeton University Press, 1989.

Freeman, Alan David. "Legitimizing Racial Discrimination through Antidiscrimination Law: A Critical Review of Supreme Court Doctrine." *Minnesota Law Review* 62, no. 6 (1978): 1049–1119.

Freeman, Richard B., and James L. Medoff. *What Do Unions Do?* New York: Basic Books, 1984.

Frey, Carl Benedikt, and Michael A. Osborne. "The Future of Employment: How Susceptible Are Jobs to Computerisation?" *Technological Forecasting & Social Change* 114 (2013): 254–280.

Fung, Archon, and Erik Olin Wright. "Thinking about Empowered Participatory Governance." In *Deepening Democracy: Institutional Innovations in Empowered Participatory Governance*, edited by Archon Fung and Erik Olin Wright, 3–44. London: Verso, 2003.

Galanter, Marc. "Why the 'Haves' Come Out Ahead: Speculations on the Limits of Legal Change." *Law & Society Review* 9, no. 1 (Autumn 1974): 95–160.

Gallagher, Mary E. "China's Workers Movement and the End of the Rapid-Growth Era." *Daedalus: Journal of the American Academy of Arts & Sciences* 143, no. 2 (2014): 81–96.

Garden, Charlotte. "Labor Organizing in the Age of Surveillance." *St. Louis University Law Review* 63, no. 1 (2018): 55–68.

Garnham, Nicholas. "Information Society Theory as Ideology: A Critique." *Society and Leisure* 21, no. 1 (1998): 139–152.

Gerstle, Gary, Nelson Lichtenstein, and Alice O'Connor, eds. *Beyond the New Deal Order: U.S. Politics from the Great Depression to the Great Recession.* Philadelphia: University of Pennsylvania Press, 2019.

Gibbons, Robert. "Piece-Rate Incentive Schemes." *Journal of Labor Economics* 5, no. 4 (October 1987): 413–429.

Giddens, Anthony. *The Nation-State and Violence: Volume Two of a Contemporary Critique of Historical Materialism.* Cambridge, UK: Polity Press, 1985.

Golden, Claudia, and Lawrence F. Katz. *The Race between Education and Technology.* Cambridge, MA: Harvard University Press, 2010.

Goldstein, Bruce, Marc Linder, Laurence E. Norton II, and Catherine K. Ruckelshaus. "Enforcing Fair Labor Standards in the Modern American Sweatshop: Rediscovering the Statutory Definition of Employment." *UCLA Law Review* 46, no. 4 (1999): 983–1163.

Gordon, Jennifer. *Suburban Sweatshops: The Fight for Immigrant Rights.* Cambridge, MA: Harvard University Press, 2007.

Gordon, Robert. "Critical Legal Histories." *Stanford Law Review* 36, no. 1 (1984): 57–125.

Gorman, Robert A., and Matthew W. Finkin. *Basic Text on Labor Law: Unionization and Collective Bargaining*, 2nd ed. St. Paul, MN: Thomson West, 2004.

Gorman, Robert A., and Matthew W. Finkin. *Labor Law: Analysis and Advocacy.* Huntington, NY: Juris Publishing, 2013.

Gorman, Robert A., Matthew Finkin, and Timothy P. Glynn. *Cox & Bok's Labor Law.* 16th ed. New York: Foundation Press, 2016.

Granovetter, Mark S. "The Strength of Weak Ties." *American Journal of Sociology* 78, no. 6 (1973): 1360–1380.

Gray, Mary L., and Siddharth Suri. *Ghost Work: How to Stop Silicon Valley from Building a New Global Underclass.* New York: Houghton Mifflin, 2019.

Green, James, and Chris Tilly. "Service Unionism: Directions for Organizing." *Labor Law Journal* 38, no. 8 (1987): 486–495.

Grewal, David Singh. "Book Review: The Laws of Capitalism." *Harvard Law Review* 128, no. 2 (2014): 626–668.

Grewal, David Singh. "The Legal Constitution of Capitalism." In *After Piketty: The Agenda for Economics and Inequality,* edited by Heather Boushey, J. Bradford DeLong, and Marshall Steinbaum, 471–490. Cambridge, MA: Harvard University Press, 2017.

Grewal, David Singh, and Jedediah Purdy. "Introduction: Law and Neoliberalism." *Law & Contemporary Problems* 77, no. 4 (2014): 1–23.

Grullon, Gustavo, Yelena Larkin, and Roni Michaely. "Are US Industries Becoming More Concentrated?" *Review of Finance* 23, no. 4 (2019): 697–743.

Gutelius, Beth, and Nik Theodore. *The Future of Warehouse Work: Technological Change in the U.S. Logistics Industry*. UC Berkeley Center for Labor Research and Education and Working Partnerships USA, October 2019. https://laborcenter.berkeley.edu/pdf/2019/Future-of-Warehouse-Work.pdf.

Hafiz, Hiba. "Labor Antitrust's Paradox." *University of Chicago Law Review* 87, no. 2 (2019): 381–412.

Hale, Robert L. "Coercion and Distribution in a Supposedly Non-Coercive State." *Political Science Quarterly* 38 (September 1923): 470–494.

Hall, Peter A., and David Soskice. "An Introduction to Varieties of Capitalism." In *Varieties of Capitalism: The Institutional Foundations of Comparative Advantage*, edited by Peter A. Hall and David Soskice, 1–70. Oxford: Oxford University Press, 2001.

Hansmann, Henry, and Reinier Kraakman, "The End of History for Corporate Law." *Georgetown Law Journal* 89, no. 2 (2001): 439–468.

Harris, Angela. "Foreword: Racial Capitalism and Law." In *Histories of Racial Capitalism*, edited by Destin Jenkins and Justin Leroy, vii–xx. New York: Columbia University Press, 2021.

Harris, Angela, and James Varellas. "Law and Political Economy in a Time of Accelerating Crises." *Journal of Law and Political Economy* 1, no. 1 (2020): 1–27.

Hayek, Friedrich A. *The Constitution of Liberty*. Chicago: University of Chicago Press, 1960.

Hayek, Friedrich A. "The Use of Knowledge in Society." *American Economic Review* 35, no. 4 (September 1945): 519–530.

Helper, Susan, John Paul MacDuffie, and Charles Sabel. "Pragmatic Collaborations: Advancing Knowledge while Controlling Opportunism." *Industrial and Corporate Change* 9, no. 3 (2000): 443–488.

Hermans, Maarten, and Miet Lamberts. "Digitalization in the Belgian Retail Sector: Tensions, Discourses, and Trade Union Strategy." April 25, 2019, on file with author.

Hertel-Fernandez, Alexander. "Asymmetric Partisan Polarization, Labor Policy, and Cross-State Political Power-Building." *Annals of the American Academy of Political and Social Science* 685, no. 1 (2019): 64–79.

Hertel-Fernandez, Alexander. *Politics at Work: How Companies Turn Their Workers into Lobbyists*. Oxford: Oxford University Press, 2018.

Hildebrandt, Mireille. *Smart Technologies and the End(s) of Law: Novel Entanglements of Law and Technology*. Cheltenham, UK: Edward Elgar Publishing, 2016.

Hirsch, Jeffrey M. "Future Work." *University of Illinois Law Review* 2020, no. 3 (2020): 889–958.

Honneth, Axel. *The Idea of Socialism: Towards a Renewal*. Translated by Joseph Ganahl. Cambridge, UK: Polity Press, 2017.

Howard, Philip N., and Muzammil M. Hussain. *Democracy's Fourth Wave? Digital Media and the Arab Spring*. Oxford: Oxford University Press, 2013.

Huber, Evelyne, and John D. Stephens. *Development and Crisis of the Welfare State: Parties and Politics in Global Markets*. Chicago: University of Chicago Press, 2001.

Hyde, Alan, and Mona Ressaissi. "Unions without Borders: Recent Developments in the Theory, Practice and Law of Transnational Unionism." *Canadian Labour and Employment Law Journal* 14 (2008): 47–102.

Iversen, Torben. "The Dynamics of Welfare State Expansion: Trade Openness, De-Industrialization, and Partisan Politics." In *The New Politics of the Welfare State*, edited by Paul Pierson, 45–79. Oxford: Oxford University Press, 1995.

Iversen, Torben, and Anne Wren. "Equality, Employment and Budgetary Restraint: The Trilemma of the Service Economy." *World Politics* 50 (July 1998): 507–546.

Jaffe, Sarah. "The New Working Class." *The New Republic*, February 22, 2018.

Jäger, Simon, Benjamin Schoefer, and Jörg Heining. "Labor in the Boardroom." *Quarterly Journal of Economics* 136, no. 2 (2021): 669–725.

James, C. L. R. *The Black Jacobins: Toussaint L'Ouverture and the San Domingo Revolution*. 2nd rev. ed. New York: Vintage Books, 1989.

Jasanoff, Sheila. *Designs on Nature: Science and Democracy in Europe and the United States*. Princeton, NJ: Princeton University Press, 2005.

Jasanoff, Sheila. *States of Knowledge: The Co-Production of Science and Social Order*. New York: Routledge, 2004.

Jenkins, Destin, and Justin Leroy. "Introduction: The Old History of Capitalism." In *Histories of Racial Capitalism*, edited by Destin Jenkins and Justin Leroy, 1–26. New York: Columbia University Press, 2021.

Jensen, Michael C., and William H. Meckling. "Theory of the Firm: Managerial Behavior, Agency Costs and Ownership Structure." *Journal of Financial Economics* 3, no. 4 (1976): 305–360.

Johnson, Rebecca A., and Tanina Rostain. "Tool for Surveillance or Spotlight on Inequality? Big Data and the Law." *Annual Review of Law and Social Science* 16 (2020): 453–472.

Kapczynski, Amy. "The Law of Informational Capitalism." *Yale Law Journal* 129, no. 5 (2020): 1460–1515.

Kapczynski, Amy. "The Public History of Trade Secrets." *U.C. Davis L. Rev.* 55, no. 3 (2022): 1367–1443.

Kaplow, Louis, and Steven Shavell. "Fairness Versus Welfare: Notes on the Pareto Principle, Preferences, and Distributive Justice." *Journal of Legal Studies* 32, no. 1 (2003): 331–362.

Katz, Harry C. "The Decentralization of Collective Bargaining: A Literature Review and Comparative Analysis." *Industrial & Labor Relations Review* 47, no. 1 (October 1993): 3–22.

Kaufman, Bruce E. "Economic Analysis of Labor Markets and Labor Law: An Institutional/Industrial Relations Perspective." In *Research Handbook on the Economics of Labor and Employment Law*, edited by Cynthia L. Estlund and Michael L. Wachter, 52–104. Northampton, MA: Edward Elgar Publishing, 2012.

Kennedy, Duncan. "The Stakes of Law, or Hale and Foucault!" *Legal Studies Forum* 15, no. 4 (1991): 327–366.

Keynes, John Maynard. *Essays in Persuasion*. New York: Harcourt Brace, 1932.

Khan, Lina M. "Amazon's Antitrust Paradox." *Yale Law Journal* 126, no. 3 (2017): 710–805.

Khan, Lina, and Sandeep Vaheesan. "Market Power and Inequality: The Antitrust Counterrevolution and Its Discontents." *Harvard Law & Policy Review* 11, no. 1. (2017): 235–294.

Kim, Pauline T. "Auditing Algorithms for Discrimination." *University of Pennsylvania Law Review Online* 166, no. 1 (2017): https://scholarship.law.upenn.edu/penn_law_review_online/vol166/iss1/10.

Kim, Pauline T. "Collective and Individual Approaches to Protecting Employee Privacy: The Experience with Workplace Drug Testing." *Louisiana Law Review* 66, no. 4 (2006): 1009–1034.

Kim, Pauline T. "Data-Driven Discrimination at Work." *William and Mary Law Review* 58, no. 3 (February 2017): 857–936.

Kim, Pauline T. "Data Mining and the Challenges of Protecting Employee Privacy under U.S. Law." *Comparative Labor Law & Policy Review* 40, no. 3 (2019): 405–420.

Kim, Pauline T. "Manipulating Opportunity." *Virginia Law Review* 106, no. 4 (2020): 867–935.

Kim, Pauline T., and Matthew T. Bodie. "Artificial Intelligence and the Challenges of Workplace Discrimination and Privacy." *ABA Journal of Labor & Employment Law* 35, no. 2 (2021): 289–315.

Klare, Karl E. "Judicial Deradicalization of the Wagner Act and the Origins of Modern Legal Consciousness, 1937–1941." *Minnesota Law Review* 62, no. 3 (1978): 265–339.

Klare, Karl E. "Labor Law as Ideology: Toward a New Historiography of Collective Bargaining Law." *Industrial Relations Law Journal* 4 (1980–1981): 450–482.

Klare, Karl E. "The Public/Private Distinction in Labor Law." *University of Pennsylvania Law Review* 130, no. 6 (1982): 1358–1422.

Klonick, Kate. "The Facebook Oversight Board: Creating an Independent Institution to Adjudicate Online Free Expression." *Yale Law Journal* 129, no. 8 (2020): 2418–2499.

Kochan, Thomas A., Harry C. Katz, and Robert B. McKersie. *The Transformation of American Industrial Relations*, 2d ed. Ithaca, NY: Cornell University Press, 1993.

Korpi, Walter. "Power Resources Approach vs. Action and Conflict: On Causal and Intentional Explanations in the Study of Power." *Sociological Theory* 3, no. 2 (1985): 31–45.

Korpi, Walter. "The Power Resources Model." In *The Welfare State Reader*, 2nd ed., edited by Christopher Pierson and Francis G. Castles, 76–88. Cambridge, UK: Polity Press, 2006.

Kreisberg, Nicole, and Nathan Wilmers. "Blacklist or Short List: Do Employers Discriminate against Union Supporter Job Applicants?" *ILR Review* 75, no. 4 (August 2022): 943–973.

Krippner, Greta. "The Financialization of the American Economy." *Socio-Economic Review* 3, no. 2 (2005): 173–208.

Krizhevsky, Alex, Ilya Sutskever, and Geoffrey E. Hinton. "ImageNet Classification with Deep Convolutional Neural Networks." *Communications of the Association of Computing Machinery* 60, no. 6 (June 2017): 84–90.

Lafer, Gordon. "What's More Democratic than a Secret Ballot? The Case for Majority Sign-up." *Working USA: The Journal of Labor and Society* 11, no. 1 (March 2008): 71–98.

Lakner, Christoph, and Branko Milanovic. "Global Income Distribution: From the Fall of the Berlin Wall to the Great Recession." *World Bank Economic Review* 30, no. 2 (2016): 203–232.

Lazear, Edward P., Kathryn L. Shaw, and Christopher Stanton. "Making Do with Less: Working Harder during Recessions." *Journal of Labor Economics* 34, no. S1 (2016): 333–360.

Lee, Min Kyung, Daniel Kusbit, Evan Metsky, and Laura Dabbish. "Working with Machines: The Impact of Algorithmic and Data-Driven Management on Human Workers." In *Proceedings of the 33rd Annual ACM Conference on Human Factors in Computing Systems* (April 2015): 1603–1612, https://wtf.tw/ref/lee.pdf.

Selected Bibliography

Lemley, Mark A. "Private Property." *Stanford Law Review* 52, no. 5 (2000): 1545–1557.

Lessig, Lawrence. *Code: And Other Laws of Cyberspace*. New York: Basic Books, 1999.

Levy, Karen. "The Contexts of Control: Information, Power, and Truck-Driving Work." *The Information Society* 31, no. 2 (2015): 160–174.

Liang, Chen, Yili Hong, and Bin Gu. "Does Monitoring Lead to a 'Warm' Start in Online Platforms?" Working paper, August 31, 2016. https://papers.ssrn.com/sol3/papers.cfm?abstract_id=2838045.

Lichtenstein, Nelson. *The Most Dangerous Man in Detroit: Walter Reuther and the Fate of American Labor*. New York: Basic Books, 1995.

Lichtenstein, Nelson. *The Retail Revolution: How Wal-Mart Created a Brave New World of Business*. New York: Macmillan, 2019.

Lichtenstein, Nelson. *State of the Union: A Century of American Labor*. Princeton, NJ: Princeton University Press, 2002.

Littler, Craig R. "Understanding Taylorism." *British Journal of Sociology* 29, no. 2 (1978): 185–202.

Lobel, Orly. "The New Cognitive Property: Human Capital Law and the Reach of Intellectual Property." *Texas Law Review* 93, no. 4 (2015): 789–851.

Logan, John. "The Union Avoidance Industry in the United States." *British Journal of Industrial Relations* 44, no. 4 (December 2006): 651–676.

Loizides, Georgios Paris. "Deconstructing Fordism: Legacies of the Ford Sociological Department." PhD. diss., Western Michigan University, 2004. https://scholarworks.wmich.edu/dissertations/1122.

Madden, Mary, Michele E. Gilman, Karen Levy, and Alice E. Marwick. "Privacy, Poverty and Big Data: A Matrix of Vulnerabilities for Poor Americans." *Washington University Law Review* 95, no. 1 (2017): 53–125.

Madland, David. *The Future of Worker Voice and Power*. Washington, DC: Center for American Progress, 2016.

Marchant, Gary E. "The Growing Gap between Emerging Technologies and the Law." In *The Growing Gap Between Emerging Technologies and Legal-Ethical Oversight: The Pacing Problem*, edited by Gary E. Marchant, Braden R. Allenby, and Joseph R. Herkert, 19–34. New York: Springer, 2011.

Marcus, Gary. "Deep Learning: A Critical Appraisal." January 2, 2018, https://arxiv.org/abs/1801.00631.

Marcus, Gary, and Ernest Davis. *Rebooting AI: Building Artificial Intelligence We Can Trust*. New York: Penguin Random House, 2019.

Marglin, Stephen A. "What Do Bosses Do? The Origins and Functions of Hierarchy in Capitalist Production." *Review of Radical Political Economics* 6, no. 2 (1974): 60–112.

Marx, Gary. *Windows into the Soul: Surveillance and Society in an Age of High Technology*. Chicago: University of Chicago Press, 2016.

Marx, Karl. *Capital, Volume 1: A Critique of Political Economy*. Hamburg: Verlag von Otto Meisner, 1867; New York: Penguin Books, 1990.

Mateescu, Alexandra. *Electronic Visit Verification: The Weight of Surveillance and the Fracturing of Care*. New York: Data & Society, 2021.

McGaughey, Ewan. "Democracy in America at Work: The History of Labor's Vote in Corporate Governance." *Seattle University Law Review* 42, no. 2 (2019): 697–753.

McIntosh, Kriston, Emily Moss, Ryan Nunn, and Jay Shambaugh. "Examining the Black-White Wealth Gap." Washington, DC: Brookings Institution, February 27, 2020, https://www.brookings.edu/blog/up-front/2020/02/27/examining-the-black-white-wealth-gap.

Middleton, Jennifer. "Contingent Workers in a Changing Economy: Endure, Adapt, or Organize?" *N.Y.U. Review of Law & Social Change* 22, no. 3 (1997): 557–622.

Milkman, Ruth. "Immigrant Organizing and the New Labor Movement in Los Angeles." *Critical Sociology* 26, no. 1–2 (2000): 59–81.

Montgomery, David. *Workers' Control in America*. New York: Cambridge University Press, 1980.

Mrkonich, Marko, Allan King, Rod Fliegel, et al. *The Big Move toward Big Data in Employment*. Littler Mendelson, P.C., August 2015.

Mundlak, Guy. *Organizing Matters: Two Logics of Trade Representation*. Cheltenham, UK: Edward Elgar Publishing, 2020.

Naidu, Suresh, Eric A. Posner, and Glen Weyl. "Antitrust Remedies for Labor Market Power." *Harvard Law Review* 132, no. 2 (2018): 536–601.

National Academies of Sciences, Engineering, and Medicine. *Information Technology and the U.S. Workforce: Where Are We and Where Do We Go from Here?* Washington, DC: National Academies Press, 2017.

Negrón, Wilneida. *Little Tech Is Coming for Workers: A Framework for Reclaiming and Building Worker Power*. New York: Coworker.org: 2021.

Newman, Nathan. "Reengineering Workplace Bargaining: How Big Data Drives Lower Wages and How Reframing Labor Law Can Restore Information Equality in the Workplace." *University of Cincinnati Law Review* 85, no. 3 (2017): 693–760.

Nissenbaum, Helen. "Contextual Integrity Up and Down the Data Food Chain." *Theoretical Inquiries in Law* 20, no. 1 (2019): 221–256.

Selected Bibliography

Nissenbaum, Helen. *Privacy in Context: Technology, Policy, and the Integrity of Social Live.* Stanford, CA: Stanford University Press, 2009.

Noble, Safiya. *Algorithms of Oppression: How Search Engines Reinforce Racism.* New York: NYU Press, 2018.

Offe, Claus, and Helmut Wiesenthal. "Two Logics of Collective Action: Theoretical Notes on Social Class and Organizational Form." *Political Power & Social Theory* 1 (1980): 67–115.

Olsen, Frances E. "The Family and the Market: A Study of Ideology and Legal Reform." *Harvard Law Review* 96, no. 7 (1983): 1497–1578.

Oswalt, Michael M. "Automatic Elections." *University of California Irvine Law Review* 4, no. 2 (2014): 801–56.

Park, K-Sue. "Race, Innovation, and Financial Growth: The Example of Foreclosure." In *Histories of Racial Capitalism*, edited by Destin Jenkins and Justin Leroy, 27–47. New York: Columbia University Press, 2021.

Pasquale, Frank. *The Black Box Society: The Secret Algorithms That Control Money and Information.* Cambridge, MA: Harvard University Press, 2016.

Pasquale, Frank. *New Laws of Robotics.* Cambridge, MA: Belknap Press, 2020.

Pasquale, Frank. "Tech Platforms and the Knowledge Problem." *American Affairs* 2, no. 2 (Summer 2018), https://americanaffairsjournal.org/2018/05/tech-platforms-and-the-knowledge-problem.

Paul, Sanjukta. "Antitrust as Allocator of Coordination Rights." *UCLA Law Review* 67, no. 2 (2020): 378–431.

Paul, Sanjukta. "Fissuring and the Firm Exemption." *Law & Contemporary Problems* 82, no. 3 (2019): 65–87.

Pierson, Paul. *Politics in Time.* Princeton, NJ: Princeton University Press 2004.

Pierson, Paul. "Post-industrial Pressures on the Mature Welfare States." In *The New Politics of the Welfare State*, edited by Paul Pierson, 80–106. Oxford: Oxford University Press, 2001.

Pierson, Paul. "When Effect Becomes Cause: Policy Feedback and Political Change." *World Politics* 45, no. 4 (July 1993): 595–628.

Piketty, Thomas. *Capital in the Twenty-First Century.* Translated by Arthur Goldhammer. Cambridge, MA: Harvard University Press, 2017.

Piven, Frances Fox, and Richard A. Cloward. *Regulating the Poor: The Functions of Public Welfare.* New York: Pantheon, 1971.

Polanyi, Karl. *The Great Transformation: The Political and Economic Origins of Our Time.* Boston: Beacon Press, 2001.

Polanyi, Michael. *The Tacit Dimension*. Chicago: University of Chicago Press, 1966.

Pontin, Jason. "Greedy, Brittle, Opaque, and Shallow: The Downsides to Deep Learning." *Wired*, February 2, 2018.

Pope, James G. "How American Workers Lost the Right to Strike, and Other Tales," *Michigan Law Review* 103, no. 3: 518–553.

Posner, Richard A. "Some Economics of Labor Law." *University of Chicago Law Review* 51, no. 4 (1984): 988–1011.

Prager, Elena, and Matt Schmitt. "Employer Consolidation and Wages: Evidence from Hospitals." *American Economic Review* 11, no. 2 (February 2021): 397–427.

Prakash, Varshini, and Guido Girgenti, eds. *Winning the Green New Deal: Why We Must, How We Can*. New York: Simon & Schuster, 2020.

Prosser, William L. "Privacy." *California Law Review* 48, no. 3 (1960): 383–423.

Przeworski, Adam. "Proletariat into a Class: The Process of Class Formation from Karl Kautsky's 'The Class Struggle' to Recent Controversies." *Politics & Society* 7, no. 4 (December 1977): 343–401.

Raghavan, Manish, Solon Barocas, Jon Kleinberg, and Karen Levy. "Mitigating Bias in Algorithmic Hiring: Evaluating Claims and Practices." *ACM Conference on Fairness, Accountability, and Transparency* (January 2020): https://arxiv.org/pdf/1906.09208.pdf.

Rahman, K. Sabeel. "Curbing the New Corporate Power," *Boston Review*, May 4, 2015.

Raji, Inioluwa Deborah, Emily M. Bender, Amandalynne Paullada, Emily Denton, and Alex Hanna, "AI and the Everything in the Whole Wide World Benchmark," (November 26, 2021), https://arxiv.org/pdf/2111.15366.pdf.

Reidenberg, Joel R. "Setting Standards for Fair Information Practice in the U.S. Private Sector." *Iowa Law Review* 80, no. 3 (1995): 497–552.

Richards, Neil M., and Jonathan H. King. "Big Data Ethics." *Wake Forest Law Review* 49, no. 2 (2014): 393–432.

Richards, Neil M., and Jonathan H. King. "Three Paradoxes of Big Data." *Stanford Law Review* 66 (2013): 41–46.

Rinz, Kevin. "Labor Market Concentration, Earnings Inequality, and Earnings Mobility." U.S. Census Bureau, September 2018, https://www.census.gov/library/working-papers/2018/adrm/carra-wp-2018-10.html.

Robinson, Cedric J. *Black Marxism: The Making of the Black Radical Tradition*. London: Zed Press, 1983; Chapel Hill: University of North Carolina Press, 2000.

Selected Bibliography

Rodrik, Dani, and Charles Sabel. "Building a Good Jobs Economy." In *A Political Economy of Justice*, edited by Danielle Allen, Yochai Benkler, Leah Downey, Rebecca Henderson, and Josh Simons, 61–95. Chicago: University of Chicago Press, 2022.

Rogers, Brishen. "Basic Income in a Just Society." *Boston Review*, May 15, 2017, https://bostonreview.net/forum/brishen-rogers-basic-income-just-society.

Rogers, Brishen. "Basic Income and the Resilience of Social Democracy." *Comparative Labor Law & Policy Journal* 40, no. 2 (2019): 199–223.

Rogers, Brishen. "Fissuring, Data-Driven Governance, and Platform Economy Labor Standards." In *Cambridge Handbook of the Law of the Sharing Economy*, edited by Nestor M. Davidson, Michele Finck, and John J. Infranca, 304–315. Cambridge: Cambridge University Press, 2018.

Rogers, Brishen. "Justice at Work: Minimum Wage Laws and Social Equality." *Texas Law Review* 92, no. 6 (2014): 1543–1598.

Rogers, Brishen. "Libertarian Corporatism is Not an Oxymoron." *Texas Law Review* 94, no. 7 (June 2016): 1623–1646.

Rogers, Brishen. "Capitalist Development, Labor Law, and the New Working Class." *Yale Law Journal* 131, no. 6 (2022): 1842–1879.

Rogers, Brishen. "Passion and Reason in Labor Law." *Harvard Civil Rights–Civil Liberties Law Review* 47 (2012): 313–369.

Rogers, Brishen. "The Social Costs of Uber." *University of Chicago Law Review Dialogue* 82, no. 1 (2016): 85–102.

Rogers, Brishen. "Three Concepts of Workplace Freedom of Association." *Berkeley Journal of Employment & Labor Law* 37, no. 2 (2016): 177–222.

Rogers, Joel. "Divide and Conquer: Further 'Reflections on the Distinctive Character of American Labor Laws.'" *Wisconsin Law Review* 1990 (1990): 1–147.

Rogers, Joel, and Wolfgang Streeck, eds. *Works Councils: Consultation, Representation, and Cooperation in Industrial Relations*. Chicago: University of Chicago Press, 1995.

Rosenblat, Alex. *Uberland: How Algorithms Are Rewriting the Rules of Work*. Berkeley: University of California Press, 2018.

Rosenblat, Alex. "What Motivates Gig Economy Workers." *Harvard Business Review*, November 17, 2016, https://hbr.org/2016/11/what-motivates-gig-economy-workers.

Rosenblat, Alex, and Luke Stark. "Algorithmic Labor and Information Asymmetries: A Case Study of Uber's Drivers." *International Journal of Communication* 10 (2016): 3758–3784.

Rosenfeld, Jake. *What Unions No Longer Do*. Cambridge, MA: Harvard University Press, 2014.

Rosenfeld, Jake, and Meredith Kleykamp. "Organized Labor and Racial Wage Inequality in the United States." *American Journal of Sociology* 117, no. 5 (2012): 1460–1502.

Rubinstein, Ira S. "Regulating Privacy by Design." *Berkeley Technology Law Journal* 26, no. 3 (2011): 1408–1456.

Ruckelshaus, Catherine, Rebecca Smith, Sarah Leberstein, and Eunice Cho. *Who's the Boss: Restoring Accountability for Labor Standards in Outsourced Work*. New York: National Employment Law Project, 2014.

Sachs, Benjamin I. "Employment Law as Labor Law." *Cardozo Law Review* 29, no. 6 (2008): 2685–2748.

Sachs, Benjamin I. "Enabling Employee Choice: A Structural Approach to the Rules of Union Organizing." *Harvard Law Review* 123, no. 3 (2010): 655–728.

Sadowski, Jathan. "When Data Is Capital: Datafication, Accumulation, and Extraction." *Big Data & Society* 6, no. 1 (2019): https://doi.org/10.1177/2053951718820549.

Saltzman, Gregory M. "Job Applicant Screening by a Japanese Transplant: A Union-Avoidance Tactic." *Industrial & Labor Relations Review* 49, no. 1 (October 1995): 88–104.

Savage, Mike, Fiona Devine, Nial Cunningham, et al. "A New Model of Social Class? Findings from the BBC's Great British Class Survey Experiment." *Sociology* 47, no. 2 (2013): 219–250.

Schiller, Daniel. *Digital Capitalism: Networking the Global Market System*. Cambridge, MA: MIT Press, 1999.

Schiller, Reuel E. "From Group Rights to Individual Liberties: Post-War Labor Law, Liberalism, and the Waning of Union Strength." *Berkeley Journal of Employment & Labor Law* 20, no.1 (1999): 1–73.

Scholz, Trebor, and Nathan Schneider, eds. *Ours to Hack and Own: The Rise of Platform Cooperativism, a New Vision for the Future of Work and a Fairer Internet*. New York: OR Books, 2016.

Schulze-Cleven, Tobias. "German Labor Relations in International Perspective: A Model Reconsidered." *German Politics and Society* 35, no. 4 (2017): 46–76.

Schumpeter, Joseph. *Capitalism, Socialism and Democracy*. New York: Harper Brothers, 1942.

Schwab, Klaus. *The Fourth Industrial Revolution*. New York: Crown Business, 2016.

Schwartz, Herman M. "Intellectual Property, Technorents, and the Labour Share of Production." *Competition and Change* (October 28, 2020), https://doi.org/10.1177/1024529420968221.

Scott, James C. *Seeing Like a State: How Certain Schemes to Improve the Human Condition Have Failed*. New Haven, CT: Yale University Press, 1998.

Selected Bibliography

Selmi, Michael. "Was the Disparate Impact Theory a Mistake?" *UCLA Law Review* 53, no. 3 (2006): 701–782.

Shapiro, Carl, and Joseph E. Stiglitz. "Equilibrium Unemployment as a Worker Discipline Device." *American Economic Review* 74, no. 3 (June 1984): 433–444.

Shaviro, Daniel. "The Minimum Wage, the Earned Income Tax Credit, and Optimal Subsidy Policy." *University of Chicago Law Review* 64, no. 2 (1997): 405–481.

Silbaugh, Katharine. "Turning Labor into Love: Housework and the Law." *Northwestern Law Review* 91, no. 1 (1996): 1–86.

Sitaraman, Ganesh. *Regulating Tech Platforms: A Blueprint for Reform*. New York: Roosevelt Institute, 2018.

Skott, Peter, and Frederick Guy. "A Model of Power-Biased Technological Change." *Economics Letters* 95, no. 1 (2007): 124–131.

Slobodian, Quinn. *Globalists: The End of Empire and the Birth of Neoliberalism*. Cambridge, MA: Harvard University Press, 2018.

Smith, Adam. *The Wealth of Nations*. New York: Random House, 1937.

Solove, Daniel J. "Introduction: Privacy Self-Management and the Consent Dilemma." *Harvard Law Review* 126, no. 7 (2013): 1880–1903.

Solove, Daniel J. "A Taxonomy of Privacy." *University of Pennsylvania Law Review* 154. no. 3 (2006): 477–564.

Solove, Daniel J. *Understanding Privacy*. Cambridge, MA: Harvard University Press, 2008.

Solow, Robert. *The Labor Market as a Social Institution*. New York: Blackwell Publishers, 1990.

Solow, Robert. "We'd Better Watch Out." *New York Times Book Review*, July 12, 1987.

Sørensen, Aage B. "Foundations of a Rent-Based Class Analysis." In *Approaches to Class Analysis*, edited by Erik Olin Wright, 119–151. Cambridge: Cambridge University Press, 2005.

Srnicek, Nick. *Platform Capitalism*. Cambridge, UK: Polity Press, 2017.

Srnicek, Nick, and Alex Williams. *Inventing the Future: Postcapitalism and a World without Work*. 2nd ed. London: Verso, 2016.

Stern, Andy, with Lee Kravitz. *Raising the Floor: How a Universal Basic Income Can Renew Our Economy and Rebuild the American Dream*. New York: PublicAffairs, 2016.

Stone, Katherine. "The Origins of Job Structures in the Steel Industry." *Review of Radical Political Economics* 6, no. 2 (1974): 113–173.

Stone, Katherine Van Wezel. *From Widgets to Digits: Employment Regulation for the Changing Workplace*. Cambridge: Cambridge University Press, 2004.

Stone, Katherine Van Wezel. "The Legacy of Industrial Pluralism: The Tension between Individual Employment Rights and the New Deal Collective Bargaining System." *University of Chicago Law Review* 59, no. 2 (Spring 1992): 575–644.

Stone, Katherine Van Wezel. "The Post-War Paradigm in American Labor Law." *Yale Law Journal* 90, no. 7 (1981): 1509–1580.

Streeck, Wolfgang. *Buying Time: The Delayed Crisis of Democratic Capitalism*. New York: Verso, 2014.

Streeck, Wolfgang. "Taking Capitalism Seriously: Toward an Institutionalist Approach to Contemporary Political Economy." *Socio-Economic Review* 9 (2011): 137–167.

Streeck, Wolfgang. "Varieties of Varieties: 'VoC' and the Growth Models." *Politics & Society* 44, no. 2 (2016): 243–247.

Sturm, Susan. "Second-Generation Employment Discrimination: A Structural Approach." *Columbia Law Review* 101, no. 3 (2001): 458–568.

Sullivan, Charles A. "The Puzzling Persistence of Unenforceable Contract Terms." *Ohio State Law Journal* 70, no. 5 (2009): 1127–1177.

Summers, Clyde W. "Employment at Will in the United States: The Divine Right of Employers." *University of Pennsylvania Journal of Labor and Employment Law* 3, no. 1 (2000): 65–86.

Sunstein, Cass. "Lochner's Legacy." *Columbia Law Review* 87 (1987): 873–919.

Swenson, Peter. *Capitalists against Markets: The Making of Labor Markets and Welfare States in the United States and Sweden*. Oxford: Oxford University Press, 2002.

Tarnoff, Ben. "From Manchester to Barcelona." *Logic Magazine*, December 7, 2019, https://logicmag.io/nature/from-manchester-to-barcelona.

Taylor, Astra. "The Insecurity Machine." *Logic Magazine*, May 4, 2020, https://logicmag.io/security/the-insecurity-machine.

Taylor, Frederick Winslow. *The Principles of Scientific Management*. New York: Harper and Brothers, 1911.

Thelen, Kathleen. "The American Precariat: U.S. Capitalism in Comparative Perspective." *Perspectives on Politics* 17, no. 1 (2019): 5–27.

Thelen, Kathleen. *Varieties of Liberalization and the New Politics of Social Solidarity*. Cambridge: Cambridge University Press, 2014.

Thompson, E. P. *The Making of the English Working Class*. New York: Penguin Books, 1963.

Thompson, E. P. "Time, Work-Discipline, and Industrial Capitalism." *Past and Present* 38, no. 1 (1967): 56–97.

Tippett, Elizabeth, Charlotte S. Alexander, and Zev J. Eigen. "When Timekeeping Software Undermines Compliance." *Yale Journal of Law & Technology* 19 (2017): 1–76.

Tomassetti, Julia. "Managerial Prerogative, Property Rights, and Labor Control in Employment Status Disputes." *Theoretical Inquiries in Law* 24, no. 1 (forthcoming, 2023).

Tomlins, Christopher. *Law, Labor and Ideology in the Early American Republic*. Cambridge: Cambridge University Press, 1993.

Tomlins, Christopher. "The Presence and Absence of Legal Mind: A Comment on Duncan Kennedy's 'Three Globalizations.'" *Law and Contemporary Problems* 78, no. 1–2 (2015): 1–17.

Ton, Zeynep. *The Good Jobs Strategy: How the Smartest Companies Invest in Employees to Lower Costs and Boost Profits*. Boston: Houghton Mifflin Harcourt, 2014.

Tucker, Eric. "Labor's Many Constitutions (and Capital's Too)." *Comparative Labor Law & Policy Journal* 33, no. 3 (2012): 355–377.

Tufekci, Zeynep. *Twitter and Tear Gas: The Power and Fragility of Networked Protest*. New Haven, CT: Yale University Press, 2017.

Tung, Irene, Yannet Lathrop, and Paul Sonn. *The Growing Movement for $15*. New York: National Employment Law Project. November 2015.

Tyson, Laura, and Michael Spence. "Exploring the Effects of Technology on Income and Wealth Inequality." In *After Piketty: The Agenda for Economics and Inequality*, edited by Heather Boushey, J. Bradford DeLong, and Marshall Steinbaum, 170–208. Cambridge, MA: Harvard University Press, 2017.

U.S. Equal Employment Opportunity Commission. *Enforcement Guidance on Disability-Related Inquiries and Medical Examinations of Employees under the Americans with Disabilities Act* (July 26, 2000).

Van Parijs, Philippe. *Real Freedom for All: What (If Anything) Can Justify Capitalism?* Oxford: Oxford University Press, 1997.

Van der Veen, Robert J., and Philippe Van Parijs. "A Capitalist Road to Communism." *Theory and Society* 15, no. 6 (1986): 635–655.

Vermeulen, Mathis. "The Keys to the Kingdom." *Knight First Amendment Institute at Columbia University*, July 27, 2021, https://knightcolumbia.org/content/the-keys-to-the-kingdom.

Viljoen, Salomé. "A Relational Theory for Data Governance," *Yale Law Journal* 131, no. 2 (2022): 573–654.

Visser, Jelle, and Daniele Checchi. "Inequality and the Labor Market: Unions." In *Oxford Handbook of Economic Inequality*, edited by Wiemer Salverda, Brian Nolan, and Timothy M. Smeeding, 230–256. Oxford: Oxford University Press, 2011.

Wachter, Michael L. "Neoclassical Labor Economics: Its Implications for Labor and Employment Law." In *Research Handbook on the Economics of Labor and Employment Law*, edited by Cynthia L. Estlund and Michael L. Wachter, 20–51. Northampton, MA: Edward Elgar Publishing, 2012.

Wachter, Michael. "The Striking Success of the National Labor Relations Act." In *Research Handbook on the Economics of Labor and Employment Law*, edited by Cynthia L. Estlund and Michael Wachter, 427–462. Northampton, MA: Edward Elgar Publishing, 2012.

Waldman, Ari Ezra. "Safe Social Spaces." *Washington University Law Review* 96, no. 6 (2019): 987–1018.

Wallerstein, Immanuel. "Braudel on Capitalism, or Everything Upside Down." *Journal of Modern History* 63, no. 2 (1991): 354–361.

Wallerstein, Immanuel. *World-Systems Analysis: An Introduction*. Durham, NC: Duke University Press, 2004.

Watson, Bartholomew Clark. *Nations of Retailers: The Comparative Political Economy of Retail Trade*. PhD diss., University of California Berkeley, 2014. https://escholarship.org/uc/item/18z1138t.

Weil, David. *The Fissured Workplace: Why Work Became So Bad for So Many and What Can Be Done to Improve It*. Cambridge, MA: Harvard University Press, 2014.

Weiler, Paul. "Promises to Keep: Securing Workers' Rights to Self-Organization under the NLRA." *Harvard Law Review* 96, no. 8 (1983): 1769–1827.

White, Ahmed A. "Workers Unarmed: The Campaign against Mass Picketing and the Dilemma of Liberal Labor Rights." *Harvard Civil Rights–Civil Liberties Law Review* 49, no. 1 (2014): 59–123.

White, Ahmed A. "My Co-worker, My Enemy: Solidarity, Workplace Control, and the Class Politics of Title VII." *Buffalo Law Review* 63, no. 5 (2015): 1061–1140.

Williams, Jamillah Bowman. "Diversity as a Trade Secret." *Georgetown Law Journal* 107, no. 6 (2019): 1685–1731.

Williams, Jamillah Bowman, Naomi Mezey, and Lisa O. Singh. "#BlackLivesMatter: Getting from Contemporary Social Movements to Structural Change," *California Law Review Online* 12 (2021): https://www.californialawreview.org/blacklivesmatter-getting-from-contemporary-social-movements-to-structural-change.

Wilmers, Nathan. "Wage Stagnation and Buyer Power: How Buyer-Supplier Relations Affect U.S. Workers' Wages, 1978 to 2014." *American Sociological Review* 83, no. 2 (2018): 213–242.

Winant, Gabriel. "Anomalies and Continuities: Positivism and Historicism on Inequality." *Journal of the Gilded Age and Progressive Era* 19, no. 2 (2020): 285–295.

Selected Bibliography

Winant, Gabriel. *The Next Shift: The Fall of Industry and the Rise of Health Care in Rust Belt America*. Cambridge, MA: Harvard University Press, 2021.

Winner, Langdon. *Autonomous Technology: Technics-out-of-Control as a Theme in Political Thought*. Cambridge, MA: MIT Press, 1977.

Winner, Langdon. "Do Artifacts Have Politics?" *Daedalus* 109 (Winter 1980): 121–136.

Wood, Ellen Meiksins. *Democracy Against Capitalism: Renewing Historical Materialism*. London: Verso, 1995.

Wood, Horace Gray. *A Treatise on the Law of Master and Servant: Covering the Relation, Duties and Liabilities of Employers and Employees*. Albany, NY: John D. Parsons Jr., 1877.

Wren, Anne, Máté Fodor, and Sotiria Theodoropoulou. "The Trilemma Revisited: Institutions, Inequality, and Employment Creation in an Era of ICT-Intensive Service Expansion." In *The Political Economy of the Service Transition*, edited by Anne Wren, 108–146. Oxford: Oxford University Press, 2013.

Wright, Erik Olin. *Envisioning Real Utopias*. London: Verso, 2010.

Wright, Erik Olin. "Foundations of a Neo-Marxist Class Analysis." In *Approaches to Class Analysis*, edited by Erik Olin Wright, 4–30. Cambridge: Cambridge University Press, 2005.

Wright, Erik Olin. "Taking the Social in Socialism Seriously." *Socio-Economic Review* 10, no. 2 (2012): 386–402.

Wright, Erik Olin. "Working-Class Power, Capitalist-Class Interests, and Class Compromise." *American Journal of Sociology* 105, no. 4 (January 2000): 957–1002.

Yellen, Janet L. "Efficiency Wage Models of Unemployment." *American Economic Review* 74, no. 2 (May 1984): 200–2005.

Zatz, Noah D. "Beyond Misclassification: Tackling the Independent Contractor Problem without Redefining Employment." *ABA Journal of Labor & Employment Law* 26, no. 2 (Winter 2011): 279–294.

Zatz, Noah D. "Welfare to What?" *Hastings Law Journal* 57, no. 6 (2006): 1131–1188.

Zimmermann, Annette, Elena Di Rosa, and Hochin Kim. "Technology Can't Fix Algorithmic Injustice." *Boston Review*. January 9, 2020, https://bostonreview.net/science-nature-politics/annette-zimmermann-elena-di-rosa-hochan-kim-technology-cant-fix-algorithmic.

Zuboff, Shoshana. *The Age of Surveillance Capitalism: The Fight for a Human Future at the New Frontier of Power*. New York: Public Affairs, 2019.

Index

2021 American Rescue Plan, 152

ABC test for employment, 119, 223n83
Adair v. United States, 45–46
Algorithmic management, 9, 61, 73–74, 83, 150, 194n12
 and collective bargaining rights, 118, 146
 and gender pay gap, 86
 and hiring, 85, 87–88, 97–98
 and lower wages, 77
 and scheduling, 75–76
 and workers' knowledge, 59, 78
Alphabet, 65. *See also* Google
Amazon, 107, 111, 120
 and $15 starting wage, 58
 Amazon Flex, 71, 116
 Amazon Marketplace vendors, 124–125, 128–129, 226nn112–113
 and platform economy, 121, 124–125, 128, 147, 158
 and robotics, 57, 59, 64, 68, 73
 scheduling practices, 75–76
 Staten Island Warehouse, 2–3, 25, 59, 91
 "taxing" transactions, 124
 tracking workers, 57, 77, 100, 132, 204n112
 and union organizing, 6, 59, 132–133, 135, 137, 145, 154
Amazon Labor Union (ALU), 91, 94–95, 132

Americans with Disabilities Act, 87, 209n37
Antidiscrimination law, 8, 84, 147, 183n38, 209n39, 210n41
Antitrust law, 39, 107, 115, 121, 123, 128, 234n60
Apple, 71
Arbitration, 38, 46, 187n72
Artificial intelligence (AI), 5, 11, 13, 150, 157–158
 discerning patterns in data, 27, 60
 and hiring discrimination, 86–88
 and machine learning, 63, 69, 199n57
 panic about, 65–67
 shaped by labor market shifts, 7, 131, 146–147
 use in Amazon warehouses, 57, 59. *See also* Automation; Robotics
Associational power, 9, 16–17, 19–20, 162n5, 163n18, 169n24, 185n55. *See also* Collective action; Collective bargaining; Unionization
 and fissuring, 49, 107, 110
 labor law reforms in support of, 7, 102, 135, 139, 141, 145–146, 153, 157
 limited by labor regimes, 42, 45, 95, 113, 152
 suppressed by companies, 2–3, 6, 13, 22, 32, 56, 78, 80
 and workers' privacy, 4, 11, 51, 88

Automation, 5, 15, 69, 86, 118, 195n16, 196n26. *See also* Artificial intelligence (AI); Robotics
  fear of, 65–67, 151, 158, 177n107, 198n51
  impact on workers, 71–72, 131, 145, 157, 237n87
  and Kiva robots, 57–58, 68, 71
  and labor law, 188nn93–94
  of productivity monitoring, 2, 59, 77, 127, 204n106
  and Taylorism, 11, 59–62, 73, 80, 82
Autonomous cars, 69–70, 201n70

Barenberg, Mark, 96
Baumol, William, 31, 178n117
Bell, Daniel, 21–22
Benkler, Yochai, 167n14, 169n22, 174n74
"Big data," 55, 126, 195n21
Black Freedom movement, 24
Black Lives Matter movement, 140
Black Radical scholars, 23
Black workers, 24, 32, 40–41, 86–87, 174n71
Boeing Co., 93, 213n72
Boston Dynamics, 70
Bread and Roses strike (1912), 81

Caesar's Entertainment, 92–93, 212n66
California, 71, 105, 113, 120, 218n21, 230n20
  Assembly Bill 701, 194n9
  Consumer Privacy Act (CCPA), 53, 191n120
  Proposition 22, 95, 119, 223n83
Capitalism, 115, 155, 165nn33–34, 176n90
  capitalist development, 8–10, 17–21
  class fissures in, 23, 29
  disciplining workers, 170n32
  functions of institutions within, 14
  and the Great Depression, 37
  race in, 24
  and social empowerment, 176n94
  "surveillance capitalism," 22, 172n50
  in tension with democracy, 13, 18–20, 170n30, 228n1
Care, investments in, 11, 236n80
Care work, 24, 41, 76, 153, 163n18, 173n62. *See also* Health-care workers
  childcare, 1, 20, 133, 149–152, 154
Castells, Manuel, 22, 172n49
Civil Rights Act of 1964 (Title VII), 24, 41, 44, 173n65, 209nn35–36
Class, 1, 9, 43, 219n37, 235n78
  co-evolution with technological development, 4–5, 13–15, 26, 28, 92, 128, 131
  conflicts, 17, 20–22, 27, 170n35
  cross-class alliances, 169n23, 171n42
  and discrimination, 40–41, 84, 87, 142, 151, 182n32
  and identity, 3, 6–8, 23–25, 90, 112, 270n35
  and mobilization, 102, 137, 140, 151–154
  new working class, 29–33, 35–36, 56, 80, 135, 172n47
  role in the book, 14, 157
  and surveillance, 26–27, 74, 88, 120, 142
Climate crisis, 154, 158
Cohen, Julie, 168n19, 172n50, 176n88, 189n102, 197n34, 206n5
  on bio-politics, 55, 197n38
  on privacy, 162n6, 189n102, 210n43
Collective action, 24, 47, 90, 143–144. *See also* Associational power; Collective bargaining; Unionization
  companies' prevention of, 5, 93, 96
  companies' use of, 18
  and labor laws, 36, 45, 134, 152, 230n15
  and workers' privacy, 4, 52, 102
  workers' capacity for, 8, 14, 17, 77–78

Index

Collective bargaining, 4, 15, 30, 95, 122, 128, 162n4, 232n46. *See also* Associational power; Collective action; Unionization
  and algorithmic management, 77, 146, 148
  and automation, 132, 140, 143–146, 148, 233n52, 236n85, 237n87
  and contractualization, 45–47
  and control of information flows, 91
  and digital Taylorism, 60
  enterprise bargaining, 89, 172n55, 210n45, 211n53
  in Europe, 31, 79, 229n12
  and fissuring, 167n9
  and the NLRA, 24, 28–29, 42–43, 48, 113, 135–136
  pattern bargaining, 43–44
  proposed reforms to facilitate, 11, 135, 139, 143–145, 150–151, 154, 232n46
  and racial and gender justice, 163n23
  relationship to the FLSA, 138
  and sectoral bargaining, 137–138, 146, 148, 153, 184n50, 229–230n13, 230n14, 230n20
  and shifts in labor law, 37–38, 40–42, 132–133, 180n10, 181n18, 185nn51–52
  and UAW-GM contract, 50
Comparative political economy, 9, 15–16
Contractors, independent, 79, 106, 220n55, 223n85, 224n89
  and data-driven fissuring, 108–111, 115–120, 138
  employee/contractor distinction, 47–49, 127, 187n82, 219n37, 219nn39–40, 221n58, 223n80
  and entrepreneurialism, 111–114
  misclassification, 3, 119, 188n88, 193n144, 218n17, 218n21
  and surveillance, 58, 132

Contractualization of employment, 45–47
Copyright Act, 54
COVID-19 pandemic, 1, 72, 139, 152, 157, 226
  and joblessness, 68
  and labor shortages, 79
  and transition to service economy, 7, 32, 59, 135, 204n107, 224n93
  and use of monitoring technologies, 2, 77, 158
  worker activism during, 2, 99, 154
Craft workers, 26–27, 32, 49, 62, 175n83

"Data food chain," 84–85, 103, 142
Dedigitization, 140–143, 150, 231n27
Defend Trade Secrets Act, 55
Defense Advanced Research Projects Agency (DARPA), 236n86
Deindustrialization, 16, 30–31, 35, 41, 46, 50, 56, 177n103
Deloitte, 85
Denmark, 31, 205n120, 221n66, 230n21
Deunionization, 15, 44, 122–123, 184n43
Digital Services Act (in European Union), 147
"Digital Taylorism," 11
Disparate impact doctrine, 182n32, 183n37
DoorDash, 2, 75, 123, 126

Economic sociology, 15–16
Ehrenreich, Barbara
  Nickel and Dimed, 96–97
Employee Retirement Income Security Act of 1974, 44
Employment-at-will doctrine, 45–46, 53, 190n112
"Encasement," 39, 41, 49, 59, 182n26, 192n126

Epic Systems Corporation v. Lewis, 46–47, 187n72
Equal Employment Opportunity Commission, 88, 150
European Commission, 118, 120, 147

Facebook, 66–67, 93–94, 121, 123, 125, 224n98
   content moderators, 226n111
   "Facebook Workspace," 100–101
Facial recognition, 77, 98, 132, 140, 142–143
Fair Labor Standards Act (FLSA), 48, 76, 112–113, 138, 188n83, 218n29, 221n58
Fantasia, Rick, 90–91
Federal Stored Communications Act, 53, 142
FedEx, 71–72, 79, 106, 109, 119, 218n21
Feinman, Jay, 186n64
Fight for $15, 25, 58, 67, 94
Fisk, Catherine, 54
Fissuring, 49, 107–110
   examples of, 115–118
   and labor law, 111–115, 135, 138, 167n9
   potential responses to, 118–120, 128
   and role of surveillance, 126, 145, 147, 218n19
Fordism, 26, 206n4
Ford Motor Company, 43, 206n4
   Sociological Department, 81–83, 96
Foucault, Michel, 107, 181n20, 182n24
Franchisees, 42, 47, 79, 122, 124–125, 133, 148
   and fissuring, 49, 108–111, 114–117, 120, 128, 167n9
Freelancer.com, 78

Garden, Charlotte, 216n108, 216n111
Gender, 20, 42, 82, 90
   and artificial intelligence (AI), 86–87
   as axis of labor market conflict, 172n47
   as axis of subordination, 4, 14, 21, 23–25, 33
   pay gap, 86
   and racial discrimination, 163n23, 173n62
   and universal basic income (UBI), 152
General Data Protection Regulation (GDPR), 53, 191n120
General Motors (GM), 43, 50, 69
Genetic Information Nondiscrimination Act, 141
Germany, 31, 72, 139, 174n73, 205n120, 221n66
   workers' rights in, 144, 179nn121–122, 185n54, 229n12
Gig economy, 2, 31, 68, 74–75, 153
   and union organizing, 135, 149, 158
   and worker classification, 44, 105–111, 118–120, 123–129, 193, 223n83
Glass-Steagall Act, 177n105
Globalization, 16, 29–30, 35, 72
Google, 65–67, 69, 121, 123, 125, 224n98, 234n64
   DeepMind, 64
   employee unrest, 99–100
   Go, 64
Gorsuch, Neil, 46
Granovetter, Mark, 172n54
Great Depression, 4, 37
"Great Resignation," 161n2
Green New Deal, 153
Griffin, Richard, 117

Harassment policy, 127, 227n130
Hayek, Friedrich, 125–126
Health-care costs, 28, 140–141, 144–145, 152, 154
Health-care workers, 149, 152–153, 163, 174n72, 236n83. *See also* Care work
   in-home, 20, 30–31, 71, 76, 121, 133, 150
   and market concentration, 122–123
   nonunionized, 44

Index

and workers' rights movements, 24–25, 174nn71
Health discrimination, 30, 53, 65, 84, 87–88, 209n37
Henry Ford Museum of American Innovation, 81
"High-voltage profits," 18, 20, 56, 170n31
HireVue, 86–87, 209n33, 209n35, 215n97
Hiring practices, 11, 55, 78, 107, 111
  algorithms in, 83, 85–87, 98, 102, 142, 150, 192n135
  to deter unionization, 65, 82, 96–97, 99, 215n93
  discrimination in, 74, 127, 147, 209n35
Homogenization of work, 25–26, 78, 174n75, 205n120

Industrial pluralism, 28, 36–38, 45, 56, 93, 133, 176n91, 183n41
Industry consolidation, 19, 107–108, 121, 123, 126, 128, 138. *See also* Market concentration
Instacart, 2, 75, 123, 126
Intellectual property (IP) rights, 10, 23, 30, 54–55, 153, 192n132
  claimed by Uber, 79
  and "encasement," 39, 41, 49, 59, 182n26, 192n126
  role in monopolies, 123, 128, 170n31
Italy, 229n12

Janus v. AFSCME, 47
Jenkins, Destin, 24
Jim Crow era, 24
Joint employment, 56, 114, 117, 120, 220n52, 220n55
Justice for Janitors, 25

Keynes, John Maynard, 29, 66, 230n13
Kiva, 57–58, 68, 71

Labor Management Relations Act of 1947, 219n39
Labor market, 15, 21, 29, 31, 40, 65, 127
  algorithmic management in, 73
  and associational power, 162n5
  and automation, 198n51
  axes of conflict, 172n47
  and disparate impact doctrine, 183n37
  and the "Great Resignation," 161n2
  hiring platforms in, 85, 98
  and monopsony power, 122, 225n102
  power disparities in, 7, 16, 23, 151–152
  shift to services, 19, 66
  specialized knowledge in, 78
  workers' collective power in, 134
Labor violence, 28–29, 81
Latino/a/x workers, 33, 86, 127
Law and Political Economy (LPE) movement, 8–9, 16, 163nn24–25
Lechmere, Inc., v. NLRB, 47, 211n56
Legal Realism, 8–9, 16, 20, 171n40
Leroy, Justin, 24
Levy, Karen, 76
Lichtenstein, Nelson, 99, 177n100, 221nn62–63, 221n65, 222n67
Line-level workers, 21, 59–60, 110, 192n139. *See also* Care work; Service workers
  and automation, 69
  lack of rights, 6, 42, 73, 107, 144
Littler, Craig, 175n80
Ludlow Massacre (1914), 81
Lyft, 66, 75, 95, 120
  as data-driven platform, 107, 121, 123–124
  regulation of, 113, 118–119, 230n20
  sued by drivers, 105–106, 217n2
  and taxi sector, 126, 224n93

Marcus, Gary, 199n57
Market concentration, 39, 60, 121–122, 224n94, 225n98, 225n101, 225n105. *See also* Industry consolidation

Marriott, 117, 145–146
Marx, Gary, 5, 160n10, 175n85
Marx, Karl, 9, 165n33, 170n30
McCormick, Cyrus, 26
McDonald's, 122, 137, 148, 210n47, 222n72
  franchise business model, 42, 97, 111, 117, 124
Minimum wage, 15, 40, 119, 134, 167n9, 183n34, 186n60
  Fight for $15, 25, 58, 67, 94
Minnesota Multiphasic Personality Inventory, 209n37
Monopoly tendencies, 26, 157, 165n33, 170nn30–31
  among platforms, 8, 123–125, 128–129, 226n115
Monopsony, 122–123, 225n102
Murray, Charles, 151, 235n76
Musk, Elon, 200n73

Napster, 66
National Highway Traffic Safety Administration, 70
National Labor Relations Act (NLRA), 24, 28–29, 35–38, 98, 188n94, 234n65
  and employee/contractor distinction, 48, 111–113, 118, 180n5, 187n82, 188n83, 188n85, 188n88, 219n37, 219nn39–40, 223n80
  and employee surveillance, 51, 92–93, 100–101, 148–149, 189nn98, 212n71, 213n72, 216nn111–112
  and employee surveys, 96, 214n87, 214n89
  and joint employment, 114, 117, 120, 220n52, 220n55
  and picketing, 114, 184n44, 184n47, 220n56
  and union organizing, 42–43, 105, 135–136, 181n18, 189n99, 211n56, 212n58, 212nn61–62, 228n5, 229n10
National Labor Relations Board (NLRB), 29, 38, 92–93, 117, 148–149, 216n112
  and economic analysis, 224n90
  history of, 230n15
  and Protecting the Right to Organize (PRO) Act, 102, 216n114
  and recognition of unions, 43, 89–90, 136, 185n51
National Labor Relations Board v. Hearst Publications, 105–107, 111–113, 115, 187n82
National Labor Relations Board v. Jones & Laughlin Steel, 37
Neoclassical economic theories, 23, 78, 110, 167n12, 167n14
  and class power, 14–16, 18, 21, 166n7
Neoliberalism, 4, 19–20, 133, 170n36, 228n1
  and class mobilization, 153–154
  history of, 28–29, 31, 39–40, 49, 176n90, 181n20
  and intellectual property, 54, 182n26
  and labor law shifts, 41, 60, 79, 157, 171n41, 182nn23–24, 183n36, 187n78
  and "workplace neoliberalism," 28, 35–36, 41, 45, 47, 93, 95
New Deal, 4, 19, 82, 181n18, 184n44
  labor regime of, 8, 23–24, 28–29, 38, 42, 48–50
Nissenbaum, Helen, 84, 142, 207n12
NLRB v. Gissel Packing Co., 181n18
"Nudges," 27–28, 74

Obama, Barack, 92–93, 117, 220n55
Occupational Safety and Health Act of 1970 (OSHA), 44
OpenAI, 69
OUR Walmart, 94
Outsourcing, 30, 38, 110, 115–116, 118, 184n84, 221n60

Index

Pasquale, Frank, 84
Patents, 39, 54, 70, 204n112
Pichai, Sundar, 65
Picketing, 42, 49, 93–95, 114, 149, 184n44, 184n47, 220n56. *See also* Strikes
Polanyi, Karl, 171n37
Polanyi, Michael, 61
"Positive class compromise" model, 20, 25, 162n5
Power resources, 14, 18, 169nn23–24
  definition, 17
Precarious labor, 2, 13, 16, 32, 75, 166n2, 179n122. *See also* Line-level workers; Service workers
Privacy, 8–9, 63, 65, 76, 139, 162n49, 166n5, 189nn101–104, 191n114, 216n108
  of consumers, 144–145
  critical theories of, 88, 102, 210n42
  needed for union organizing, 4, 11, 51–53, 58–61, 88, 102, 141–142
  proposed broader protections, 147, 149, 154–155
  workplace *and* worker protections, 44, 79, 82–84, 89, 93, 190n106, 190n108
  and workplace surveillance, 51–53, 83–84, 99, 101, 103, 136, 141–142, 155
Protecting the Right to Organize Act (PRO Act), 102, 119

Race, 20, 40–41, 82, 90, 182n32, 209n36
  and artificial intelligence (AI), 86–88
  as axis of labor market conflict, 172n47
  as axis of subordination, 1, 8, 14, 21, 23–25, 33
  and gender discrimination, 173n62
  and surveillance, 84
Racism, 24, 86–88, 171n38, 181, 226n111, 235n76
Rahman, K. Sabeel, 147, 234n60
Rehn-Meidner model, 233n52

Rents, 23, 70, 123, 131, 165n33, 170n31, 170n35
Republic Aviation Corp. v. National Labor Relations Board, 92
Reuther, Walter, 50
"Right to work" laws. *See* Taft-Hartley Act of 1947
Robotics, 11, 13, 30, 67, 69–70, 158, 197n40, 198n51. *See also* Artificial intelligence (AI); Automation
  and algorithmic management, 73–74, 77
  and Amazon, 1, 57–59, 64, 68, 71, 145
  co-bots, 72, 201n79
  fear of, 65–66
Rostain, Tanina, 126
Ruckelshaus v Monsanto Co., 192n134
Rutherford Food Corp. v. McComb, 113

Saltzman, Gregory, 97
Schumpeter, Joseph, 9, 170n30
Scott, James C., 62, 195n17
Sears, 99
Service economy, 3, 10, 14, 20, 22, 71, 176n117
  need for workers in, 1, 7, 80, 87, 131, 135, 179n123
  and platform firms, 19, 107, 123
  shift to, 30–32, 35, 41, 56, 109, 123, 151, 157
Service workers, 2, 67, 135, 146, 149, 163n18, 166n1. *See also* Care work; Line-level workers
  demand for, 5–6, 30
  as essential, 7
  in Germany, 31
  off-duty conduct, 11
  women as, 23–24
Silicon Valley, 67, 100, 151
Slack, 92, 100, 234n64
Smith, Adam, 9
Social reproduction, 11, 20, 153

Social Security Act (SSA), 48, 188n83, 219n41
Solove, Daniel, 83, 189n101, 207n12
Sørensen, Aage B., 23
Stagflation, 29, 177n103
Starbucks, 116–117
  scheduling practices, 76
  and union organizing, 2–3, 135, 154
Stewart, Potter, 50
Stone, Katherine, 37
Strikes, 82, 89, 102, 135–136, 138, 152.
  See also picketing
  Bread and Roses, 81
  fast-food workers', 2, 133
  internal dynamics of, 90–91
  Ludlow Massacre, 81
  Marriott workers', 145–146
  and Taft-Hartley Act, 42, 49–50
  West Virginia teachers', 94–95, 144, 154
  "work-to-rule," 62
SuperShuttle, 114, 223n80
Supply and demand, 14–15, 18, 167n9
Supreme Court, 37
Surveillance, 22–23, 30, 49, 63, 72, 172n50
  and algorithmic management, 73–74, 77–78
  and Amazon, 132–133, 158
  and communities of color, 140, 164n27
  for labor standards compliance, 120, 127
  to manage workers, 5–6, 26–27, 107–108, 119, 147, 157, 216n112
  of off-duty conduct, 11, 53, 92, 98, 143, 193n144
  to suppress organizing, 83–84, 88–89, 94, 96, 99–101, 131, 134–136, 189n98
  and Uber, 105–106, 126
  and worker privacy, 51–53, 58–60, 141–142, 155, 216n108
"Surveillance capitalism," 22, 172n50
Surveys, 96, 99–100, 214n87
Sweden, 176n96, 230n21

Taft-Hartley Act of 1947, 29, 42, 48–50, 113, 230n15
Target, 84
Tarnoff, Ben, 140
Tax-and-transfer system, 16, 167n14, 168n18
Taylor, Frederick Winslow, 26, 175n80. *See also* Taylorism
Taylorism, 26, 54, 61–62, 175n80
  digital, 11, 59–60, 73, 78–82, 111, 136–138, 145
Tesla, 69–70, 201n73
Thelen, Kathleen, 31, 168n17, 169n23, 171n42, 179n122, 185n55
Thomas, Clarence, 47
Thompson, E. P., 22
TikTok, 94
Tomassetti, Julia, 193n144
Ton, Zeynep, 79, 201n76
Transportation Security Agency (TSA), 83
"Trilemma," 178n117
Trump, Donald, 92–93, 101, 114, 118, 161n2, 216n112
Twitter, 93–94

UAW-GM contract (1950), 50
Uber, 23, 27, 66, 170n35, 203n86, 203n88, 223n80
  exploiting data, 74–75, 78, 86, 107, 148, 216n13, 226n116
  and intellectual property, 79
  and move toward autonomous cars, 69–70
  "phantom" ride requests, 74–75
  and political pressure, 95
  and profitability, 19, 124
  regulation of, 113, 118–119, 230n20
  sued by drivers, 105–106, 217n2, 223n81
  and taxi sector, 120–121, 126, 128, 224n93

Index

Unionization, 32, 79, 82, 94–95, 188n88, 223n80, 225n105. *See also* Associational power; Collective action
 companies' suppression of, 13, 22, 26, 89–91, 96, 108, 144, 157, 212n59
 and COVID-19 pandemic strike wave, 154
 decline of, 15, 41–44, 46
 and fissuring, 108, 118, 120, 122–123
 and labor law reforms, 38, 132, 134, 136, 228n5
 and NLRA, 105, 114, 135–136, 181n18, 189n99, 216n113, 220n55
 requirements for, 3–4, 102
 retaliation against, 6, 35, 37, 211n57
 screening against, 11, 82, 96–97, 99–101, 103, 215n93
 successes, 2, 25, 28–29, 50–51, 59, 132–133
United Auto Workers (UAW), 43–44, 50
Universal basic income (UBI), 151–152, 235nn75–76, 235–236n78, 236nn79–80, 236n82
University of California Berkeley Labor Center, 142
Unpaid work, 23–24, 105, 224n89
UPS, 79, 204n104, 226n113
"Upskilling," 15, 25, 79, 237n87
US Census Bureau, 115
US Constitution
 Fifth Amendment Taking Clause, 192n134
 First Amendment, 190nn111–112, 234n65
 Fourteenth Amendment, 40, 182n32
US Supreme Court, 100, 105–106, 234n65
 and labor standards, 111–113, 127
 and property rights, 37–38, 40, 45–46, 54, 92
 and union organizing, 47–48, 50, 89, 92

Vendors in *Hearst* case, 48, 105–106, 112, 115
Vendors on Amazon Marketplace, 124–125, 128–129, 226nn112–113
Viljoen, Salomé, 65, 103

Wallerstein, Immanuel, 9, 18, 124
Walmart, 120–121, 127, 137, 201n75
 business model, 116, 221n63, 221nn65–66
 and union avoidance, 94–95, 99, 211n57
Welfare states, 167n15, 169n23, 171n42, 185n55
 limited benefits in, 40, 43, 151
 potential reforms, 134, 147, 151–154, 213n82, 236n81
 and service economy, 16, 30–31
Welfare studies, 9, 169n23, 207n14
WhatsApp, 94
White, Ahmed, 41
White supremacy, 1, 20, 24, 41, 84, 86–88, 127, 209n36
Whole Foods Market, 75, 93, 100
Winant, Gabriel, 176n90
Winner, Langdon, 26
Women workers, 30, 151. *See also* Gender
 as devalued, 1, 23–24, 32, 40–41, 86, 127, 173n62
Wood, Ellen Meiksins, 21–22
Worker Adjustment and Retraining Notification (WARN) Act of 1988, 31
Workers' rights movements, 24–25, 28. *See also* Black Freedom movement; Fight for $15; Justice for Janitors
"Workplace neoliberalism," 28, 35–36, 41, 45, 47, 93, 95
Wright, Erik Olin, 20, 22, 134, 162n5, 176n94
Wrongful termination, 5, 22, 89, 190n112, 210n46

Zuboff, Shoshana, 22